D1616871

Studies of the East Asian Institute, Columbia University

The East Asian Institute is Columbia University's center for research, publication, and teaching on modern East Asia. The Studies of the East Asian Institute were inaugurated in 1962 to bring to a wider public the results of significant new research on modern and contemporary East Asia.

China in My Life

A HISTORIAN'S OWN HISTORY

C. MARTIN WILBUR

Edited by Anita M. O'Brien

An East Gate Book

M.E. Sharpe
Armonk, New York
London, England

An East Gate Book

Copyright © 1996 by M. E. Sharpe, Inc.

Cover photograph courtesy of Public Information Office, Columbia University.

Library of Congress Cataloging-in-Publication Data

Wilbur, C. Martin (Clarence Martin), 1908–
China in my life : a historian's own history / C. Martin Wilbur :
edited by Anita M. O'Brien.
p.   cm.
"An East gate book."
ISBN 1-56324-763-1 (alk. paper)
1. Wilbur, C. Martin (Clarence Martin), d 1908–   .
2. Sinologists—United States—Biography.
I. O'Brien, Anita M.
II. Title.
DS734.9.W55A3   1996
951′.007202—dc20
[B]
95-53181
CIP

Printed in the United States of America

The paper used in this publication meets the minimum requirements of
American National Standard for Information Sciences—
Permanence of Paper for Printed Library Materials,
ANSI Z 39.48-1984.

BM (c)   10   9   8   7   6   5   4   3   2   1

Contents

Preface   vii

Photographs follow page 144

1 Childhood   3

2 High School Years, 1923–1927   11

3 Higher Education, 1927–1932   16

4 Kay and I Start Out, 1932–1936   24

5 Building a Career, 1936–1939   41

6 Starting Our Family, 1939–1942   48

7 War Work, 1943–1945   55

8 Back in China, 1945–1946   61

9 A Transition Time   88

10 First Years at Columbia, 1947–1954   91

11 A Year in Japan and Southeast Asia, 1954–1955   104

12 India   125

13 Thailand and Hong Kong   145

14 Tokyo Again   156

15 Teaching and Scholarship   162

16 A Sabbatical in East Asia, 1961–1962   172

17 Academic, Cultural, and Social Life, 1962–1967   200

18 Hawaii, Europe, and a Wedding, 1967–1968   213

19 The Last Years of Teaching, 1968–1976   220

20 Beginning Retirement, 1976–1979   236

21 Our Trip Back to China, 1980   248

22 More Retirement Years, 1980–1983   271

23 Rich Years, 1984–1986   280

24 Last Years in Pleasantville, 1987–1989   295

25 Our New Life in the Quadrangle   300

Index   309

Preface

I wrote these reminiscences of a happy and interesting life between 1988 and 1992, and added a bit in 1995. I was urged, particularly by Chinese friends and former students at Columbia University, to have them published.

Historians like to know what a book of this sort is based upon. Is it based purely on memory—a rather weak foundation? Or is it more firmly based upon document? I had many documents to help me maintain accuracy. There were letters to my parents and my wife. There were journals I kept on trips abroad. I have quoted often from these sources. In addition, I had pocket engagement books from my years at Columbia, and we kept guest books from 1933 onward. They remind us of the people we knew.

I am indebted to Professor Bernadette Li Yu-ning, my former student and now dear friend, for pressing me to publish and using her influence for a favorable decision. My dear friend, Professor Chang Peng-yuan, proposed to the Institute of Modern History, Academia Sinica, Republic of China in Taiwan that it publish the work, which it was willing to do. These friends also raised a subvention.

I have the greatest obligation to Anita M. O'Brien. She voluntarily edited the work, and reduced its length by half.

Many, many thanks go to those former students who subscribed to a publications fund, all unbeknownst to me: Chang Peng-yuan (the organizer), Chang Yu-fa, Chiang Yung-ching, Li Yu-ning, Li Yun-han, Shen Ta-chuan, and Su Yun-feng. The East Asian Institute of Columbia University, where I taught Chinese history for thirty-seven years, is a sponsor and supporter of this work.

My beloved wife, Kay Edson Wilbur, has shared more than six decades of life with me. My appreciation for her help is unbounded. To her I dedicate this book.

C.M.W. 8/21/95

China in My Life

1

Childhood

My memories begin with Shanghai, China, though I can dimly recall a little of my infancy in Kobe, Japan. Why was I in those places? Because my father, Hollis Adelbert Wilbur, was a secretary of the International Committee of the Young Men's Christian Association and had been selected and urged by John R. Mott to take up temporary service in Japan after seven years as general secretary of the Dayton YMCA. In November 1909, when I was eighteen months old, Dad and Mother took the train trip to the West Coast with two little children, and then the steamer crossing of the Pacific, to begin the three-year assignment in Japan. They would also serve the Y in China and Korea before they retired in 1940 in Pasadena, California.

My sister Elizabeth was born in April 1904. I was born on May 13, 1908, and was a sickly child. I suffered from mastoiditis and howled in pain on the train going west until some kindly lady gave Dad and Mother her roomette, where I could be better cared for and others could get some sleep.

Father was a devout Christian with a desire to serve humankind. He was born on April 19, 1874, and was a product of an upstate New York family. His father, Leonidas Franklin Wilbur, was a rural doctor (M.D. Harvard), and his mother, Caroline Frances Martin, a former schoolteacher. They lived in Honeoye, on one of the smaller Finger Lakes south of Rochester, and had five children. One died in infancy. The uncle for whom I am named died in 1894 of yellow fever in Central America, where he was a missionary, only twenty-five years old.

The Wilbur family upbringing was of Christian morality, New England style. It sure took with Father. After teaching in a one-room school for a year, he went to Ohio Wesleyan University and there fell under the influence of the Christian Student Volunteer Movement. He also fell under the spell of Mary Irene Matte-

3

son, my mother, whom he first saw singing in the choir. That did it! Mother was about two years older than Dad, and a very pretty young woman. The Student Volunteer Movement, with the motto "Win the world for Christ in our generation," brought Dad into his career and ultimately to the Orient. How ambitious and naive that motto sounds a hundred years later! Yet it was an inspiring message to young idealists of the 1890s, and there were many of them in the colleges of America. Although my father was swept into that idealistic movement, he was practical enough not to be taken in by such an ambitious aim. I think he just wanted to live a life of service to his fellow human beings. Work for the YMCA was just such service. Dad was slender, about 5 feet 8 inches tall, with an engaging smile, hazel-colored eyes, and prematurely white hair. We children loved him dearly.

Mother, born on January 19, 1872, grew up in Seville, a small Ohio town south of Cleveland. Her father, Horace E. Matteson, was a merchant who owned a variety store. The seven Matteson children, my uncles and aunts on Mother's side, had a Baptist upbringing, whereas Dad's family was New England Congregationalist. Both families were of British and Scottish stock, going back in America for many generations. Dad and Mother were married on August 28, 1901.

Mother was a devout Christian, too. As a young woman she was quite beautiful, with blue eyes, black hair, rosy cheeks, and a fine figure. She was quite different from Dad in one respect—the aesthetic component was strong in her. She had a fine singing voice, and she loved art. She learned to draw and paint in watercolors and pastels. She also loved to write creatively, living at times in the world of her imagination. She was a devout letter writer, and her letters are vivid and much more interesting than Dad's, which tend to recount events dryly or to pose many questions. Their different styles reflected quite different personalities. Dad had a good sense of humor and liked a joke; Mother had a stronger sense of fun, of enjoyment in doing something out of the ordinary: excursions, study groups, social affairs. Dad, I suppose from conservative religious beliefs, asked Mother to give up dancing. She consented, though she enjoyed dancing. Later Dad became more liberal religiously than Mother. I get some of my temperament from both of them. They inculcated in me their ethical values, although their brands of Christian belief did not stick with me.

My memories of Kobe are vague. We had a Japanese maid who took care of me and my brother Halsey, who was born in January 1912. Our house was on a hill and our yard had a persimmon tree—that much I can visualize. When I learned to talk it was English with my parents and Japanese with the servants. I remember the day that my father returned from America, where he had gone to recover from a serious case of influenza. Our maid took Halsey and me to a park where we awaited his arrival. He was nearly a stranger, but I was thrilled to see him again.

We moved to Shanghai in October 1913, when I was five. My memories of our environment are fairly vivid, because we lived in the same house for eleven years, except for furloughs. I didn't find China strange: it was just the place where we lived. We had Chinese servants—a cook, a houseboy, and an amah, or maid of all work, bound-footed though she was. The cook, Ta-ssu-fu, was head man. He did the marketing and cooked Western food according to Mother's instructions. But on Saturdays at noon we had a Chinese meal, which we children thought was the best meal of the week. The houseboy served table and did some cleaning. Shanghai houseboys were trained in Western table etiquette according to a long tradition. Such training still goes on in Hong Kong. Our amah had charge of the children when their parents were out. She did the washing and mending and other small chores, hobbling about on her tiny bound feet. I don't really know how much I may owe to her, or to the other servants, for training in Chinese good manners—such as refusing to go through a door first, or insisting that "the mat must be straight," a Confucian precept. The servants knew little English, and our family was not much good in Chinese, but somehow we communicated.

We lived in a foreign-style brick house on Dixwell Road off North Szechwan Road in the Hongkew district of the International Settlement of Shanghai. The house was a two-family building, divided down the middle, each half surrounded by its own wall and with its own front and side yards. In the rear were servants' quarters where we kids never went.

Shanghai is about the latitude of Florida, 31 degrees north. It is hot and humid in summer and damp and chilly in winter. Our house was heated with coal-burning stoves with tin pipes that brought heat upstairs to round "drums," which gave a little warmth to the sleeping rooms. We children always got chilblains in the wintertime.

A tragedy in our family was the death on November 13, 1914, of Mother's last child, Rosemary, who was only three weeks old. I do barely remember, being then six years old, that both Mother and Sister were very sick with dysentery. I remember Dad telling me of the death of my baby sister. At our next furlough, Mother had the ashes buried in the family plot in Seville, together with the remains of her second child, Hollis, who died before I was born. She grieved over the death of two children, and loved us who lived all the more.

Dad's work took him away quite a lot, since he was adviser to city YMCAs all over China. It was a turbulent time, and as a youngster I worried about him in dangerous places. Once I took a spike off the wall surrounding our yard and put it in his suitcase as a form of protection. Not much protection, but it showed my concern.

I remember a little about the First World War. I was eleven when it was over. Shanghai being dominated by Great Britain, and the United States joining the war in 1917, meant that we young folks were all on the side of the Allies. We were involved in rolling bandages and doing other jobs that supposedly aided our war effort. I remember most clearly my celebration of the surrender of Bulgaria in September 1918. I built a paper fort with crenelated walls and towers to represent the defeated enemy, and I got some Roman candles which I shot at the fort till it caught on fire and burned to ashes. The actual armistice I remember less clearly, but I did see a victory parade.

My first schooling was at Miss Jewel's School, a private elementary school for foreign kids. A few years thereafter came the Shanghai American School, which had day students and boarding students, mostly children of up-country missionaries. I went through eighth grade in SAS when it was located in the Hongkew section. Later it was moved to the French Concession in fine buildings erected in a campus setting. I was not very good in school, partly because I was rather unhealthy as a child and lost weeks here and there.

At the end of eighth grade there was a little conference in which I learned that I would have to repeat the grade because I hadn't done well enough to go on to high school. Actually, it was a decision taking into account the fact that halfway through the next school year our family would be leaving Shanghai for furlough in America, so I would miss part of a grade. Hence, it seemed better for me to consolidate what I had and to enter high school in America. Still, I "failed eighth grade," and that stigma has haunted me. It accounts for my being a bit older than I should have been in the schools I attended thereafter. Two classmates I fell behind were John P. Davies, Jr., who later became an ace Foreign Service officer, and Margaret Armstrong, who married Tilman Durdin, the noted *New York Times* correspondent on China. Peggy Durdin is a writer of note.

Mother taught us manners—not only table manners, but in particular a code of behavior of gentlemen toward ladies: always carry the bundles, always walk on the street side of a lady, open doors, rise when a lady enters, seat her at table, and much more. I'm still uncomfortable if a lady I'm walking with maneuvers herself onto the street side of the sidewalk, putting me on the inner side. Mother's training of us boys to be "gentlemanly" left me with an awe of women, persons exalted, fragile, and mysterious.

Mother developed a great interest in Chinese culture, particularly in all the arts. She had little money to spend acquiring beautiful Chinese things, but she did buy some porcelains and Peking rugs, which later were divided among the three children. Mother was active in the Literary Department of the American Women's Club of Shanghai. The ladies studied Chinese art seriously, visiting private collections and hearing lectures. Mother was the main editor of a collection of the ladies' essays, *Arts and Crafts of Ancient China*, published in 1921. Her paper is entitled "Notable Local Collections of Chinese Art Objects" and describes collections that the ladies were privileged to visit in Shanghai. Doubtless my interest in Chinese art owes much to her, though as a boy I couldn't have cared less. Also, Mother was an avid genealogist and a proud member of the Daughters of the American Revolution. She could wear seven bars, representing seven ancestors who fought in the revolution. Later, she became "Regent" of the China chapter.

Saturdays were the days of play; Sundays of Sunday school and later of church. The American Community Church, interdenominational but Protestant, met downtown, near Nanking Road, and the Royal Asiatic Society museum was nearby. When I grew old enough to go to Sunday School by myself, I used to visit that museum and gaze with great interest at the stuffed animals, birds, and reptiles native to China. I wonder now whether that interest played a part in my later life.

I had a few good friends among the American kids who lived nearby, but no Chinese friends at that stage of my life that I can remember. What a pity! We were an encapsulated foreign community living in a sea of Chinese. I was a spectator of all those around me, and my hope was to be as American as possible. We read American children's books. Mother read a great deal to us children, probably quality fiction. We boys played American and British games—baseball, soccer, even golf in Hongkew Park, which was "reserved for the use of foreigners." We organized track meets and gave blue, red, and white ribbons to the winners of sprints, high jump, and long-distance runs.

Jack Service was one of my closest friends. By coincidence, about the time of our first grades, our two YMCA families were having furloughs the same year and both lived in East Cleveland. Later, Jack's parents, who worked in far-off Szechwan Province, sent Jack to board at the American School, and our home was sort of his foster home during shorter vacation periods. Other friends during this time when we lived on Dixwell Road were Sid Willis, Jack Gray, and Emma McCloy, the latter two being children of Dad's YMCA colleagues. About a mile away lived several other Y families—the Lyons, "Uncle" Willard and "Aunt" Grace, with their daughter, Jean; the Lockwoods, with Bill, a little older than I, but a lifetime friend; and the Harveys, with Paul, also a bit older than I. He once shot me on the forehead with his BB gun.

As part of my American childhood in China, I joined the local Boy Scouts of America troop. I didn't advance beyond Second Class Scout. The reason, I remember, was that I didn't master the Morse Code. Was my unretentive memory the explanation for that failure?

One picture from my China childhood sticks with me—seeing processions of great wooden wheelbarrows, each pushed by one man. Along each side of the wheel, sitting on running boards, would be three Chinese women, their bound feet outward. They were factory workers being taken from their dormitories to work in spinning mills in the Yangtzepoo district east of us. It was a strange contrast, those huge old wheelbarrows passing a modern foreign house on a modernly paved road. I did not realize until much later the economic exploitation to which those passing women were subjected. Footbinding was almost universal in rural China near Shanghai, where these factory workers had been recruited.

Another thing about China that made a lasting imprint on me was the great care we had to take about the food we ate. We were allowed no uncooked vegetables because Chinese farmers spread night soil on their fields as fertilizer.

That was a sure way to spread disease. Later, in America, I became fond of uncooked vegetables, particularly salads. In China I also contracted a fear of spoiled meat because Mother was always so cautious about that danger. I carry this caution to this day.

The grandest, fondest memories of my childhood are the summer months we spent in Mokan Shan, the mountains south of Shanghai, in Chekiang Province. The only way to get to there was to go by canal boat and then by sedan chair up to the inhabited area. One could take a train to Hangchow and there bargain for a houseboat to take one to the foot of the mountains, or one could leave Shanghai by canal boat and make a two-day picnic of it. I shall describe one trip we made by the latter, more exciting way.

We had to take a lot of stuff along for a family of five, as well as the amah, the cook, and the houseboy—bedding, mosquito nets, clothes, sports gear, school books, and lots of food and cooking utensils, not to forget two kittens. All except the animals we sent ahead in a two-man cart under the charge of our houseboy, who would see it stowed aboard, and then our family set off about noon—Dad, Mother, Sister, the amah, each in one rickshaw, and Halsey and I in the fifth. The cook had gone the day before to hire the houseboat, arrange his rake-off, and see that the craft was properly cleaned up. When we arrived at Soochow Creek near the Garden Bridge, there was our wooden canal boat moored by the embankment with our gear being stowed aboard. The boat was about sixty feet long and ten feet wide, of shallow draft, and with a walking plank along each slightly curved side for poling the boat and fending off other craft. A pair of large eyes painted on the prow was the characteristic Chinese touch. The boat could be propelled by a large oar in the rear that was sculled, or by a single sail when the wind was right, or by punting in shallow water. The cabin was roofed with rattan matting, the crew lived aft, and there was a sitting deck forward. Amah shared quarters with our family in the cabin; the cook and houseboy made do with the crew, a husband and wife and two teenage boys.

Once we were all aboard, the captain shoved off at half past two into the foul-smelling creek just in time to throw his rope to the last boat in a train towed by a sturdy launch. Under the Garden Bridge we went, past the British Consulate, and turned up the Whangpoo River, our launch lugging its chain of boats slowly past the Bund with its Customs House and imposing bank buildings, past sailing junks and warships, past Lunghua Pagoda, and so into more open country west of Shanghai. We were heading for the Grand Canal, which links Hangchow in the south with Peking nearly a thousand miles to the north. It took the rest of the afternoon to reach Kashing, an afternoon of gliding past villages of brick houses with tile or straw roofs, farms of flooded rice fields, kids sitting aback the water buffalo they were tending, fishermen in skiffs with their cormorants lined up ready to plunge for fish as soon as our noisy boat train passed, and everywhere the acrid smell of night soil, a smell we boys were quite used to because of our hikes into the countryside around Shanghai.

Just before Kashing on the Grand Canal we broke from the boat train and anchored for the night, but outside the town to avoid swarms of curious viewers. Our cook prepared a supper of rice and baked beans, and several delicious Chinese dishes with the rapturous smell of soy, sesame seed oil, and ginger. We ate with chopsticks, of course, out of Chinese bowls. Then, after a family sing and prayers, we bedded down for the night under mosquito nets. Night sounds were lovely—lapping waters, the creak of the gently rocking boat, an occasional call of a night bird.

Next morning we skirted Kashing and were soon in the broad Grand Canal, where the crew erected the mast with its great ribbed sail, and we glided noise-lessly southward, again through flat countryside easily visible over the banks that were only a few feet higher than water level. As we approached Hangchow we again tied up for a quiet night, but we were off again before dawn by a lesser canal and river system, westward to a small village near the foot of Mokan Shan. Arriving about nine in the morning, we plunged into bedlam. Seeing our boat approaching, chair-bearers and porters lined the dock shouting their bids to take us up the mountain. We had to get all the baggage unloaded so as to reckon how many porters were needed, and we had to keep a sharp eye lest a suitcase or a pukai (a large covered straw basket) disappear. Finally the cook and Dad had bargained for five sedan chairs, six porters had loaded our stuff on their carrying poles, and our boatmen had been paid off. Away we went across the steaming plain. My brother and I had no intention of being carried up that mountain, but after several miles of brisk hiking on narrow paths through the rice field we were ready for the ride. Mother and Amah, with her bound feet, didn't mind riding in the wicker sedan chairs, fixed between two stout poles lofted on the shoulders of a bearer in front and one behind.

After three miles we reached the mountain and began the climb of about three thousand feet on a winding and shady path through beautiful bamboo groves. Up we went into a mist, and then above it, getting glimpses now and then of the fields way below, a scene very like a Chinese landscape painting. It became cooler as we ascended. In some tricky places where one looked over an abyss, the chair men advised us to get down and walk. Thus, we could cling to the inner edge of the path and not look down the hundreds of feet below. Bamboos began to give way to pines, which meant we were nearly there.

Suddenly we boys recognized the post office, then that we were nearing the community swimming pool, then some houses we knew. Finally our procession of chair men and porters arrived at the house we had rented during several previous summers, the house where once a small landslide roared through the hallway during a heavy typhoon. Here we were for another glorious summer—two months that would stretch on endlessly—until suddenly it would be time to close up the house and return to Shanghai for another year at the American School.

Till then, however, we could look forward to hikes around the mountain trails, swimming and tennis, parties, community entertainment nights, and even some classes in useful skills such as sewing and mending for boys. One thing we young fellows did early was to line up families for whom we would serve as intermediate postmen, taking their mail to the post office and bringing back the letters that awaited them there. We were paid about 20 cents a month per household, and if we had ten such households we could make a couple of dollars a month—real money in those days. Part of the fun was the sociability of meeting the other fellows at the post office. With my earnings I loved to buy a jar of pickles. Ever since, I have had a yen for such stuff.

2

High School Years, 1923–1927

Mother and Sister left Shanghai in January 1923 in order to visit India before Dad and we boys, coming in March, would catch up with them. I remember traveling through Hong Kong, Singapore, and especially Penang, with its beautiful beaches and palm trees. All were part of the British Empire. We stopped in Calcutta, where I had the shock of seeing people with features like our own pulling rickshaws and doing other manual work, which always was the work of Chinese where I had been living. This sort of shock, a thoughtless kind of racial arrogance, was common among us young Westerners who grew up in China.

Mother and Sister joined our ship in Columbo, and we traveled together to Port Said at the north end of the Suez Canal, where they left us again for a tour of Egypt. Dad and we boys went on to Marseilles, and then Dad took us to Geneva where he left us in a pension for about six weeks. We were supposed to learn French in Geneva, but what I remember best is the beautiful lake and the delicious breakfasts we had of hot chocolate, croissants, and jam. We seemed quite free to explore the city. Then Dad took us to Berlin, where we met the great sprinter Charlie Paddock, who was on tour for the Y demonstrating his skill. What a thrill for a fourteen-year-old boy! I also remember going to Prague and seeing a student center managed by the Y, where impoverished students could get a cheap meal of a large pickle and a loaf of bread. In 1923 there was a terrible inflation in postwar Germany and Czechoslovakia.

We then went to Portschak in Austria, a resort where leaders of the International YMCA were to hold a conference. It was a beautiful Alpine setting on a lake. There I met my first love, Peggy Robinson, the daughter of a Y secretary who worked in Estonia. It was a shy romance, entirely proper. We corresponded for at least five years, and in my sophomore year at Oberlin I went to New York to see Peggy. She was a really nice girl. However, by then I had met Kay Edson.

In America, which I scarcely remembered, we made several stops to see relatives on the way to Dayton, where we would live for a year. I entered my first year of high school there and seem to have done all right. It was good to be a full-time American boy. I think I had a paper route, and I know I had a bicycle because I was nearly run over by a car. Dad traveled quite a bit, talking about Y work in China, a fund-raising effort.

We returned to China in the summer of 1924. Except for Beth, who stayed in Ohio for college, we were back in the old house on Dixwell Road, but by then the Shanghai American School was open on its new campus in the French Concession. Halsey and I had to get there by street car. We spent a year in the Hongkew section of Shanghai until the summer of 1925, for I remember that during the troubles of that June our trips to school were disrupted. By "the troubles of June" I mean the aftermath of the May 30 Incident, in which Chinese college students and others demonstrating in the International Settlement against certain proposed regulations—actually they were demonstrating against im- perialism—came into confrontation with the Settlement police. The students were fired upon, some were killed, and many wounded. This naturally caused a great political storm, for most of Shanghai's population was Chinese. In my work I have studied available documents and accounts from both sides and have written about the events in two books. The incident was a landmark in China's nationalistic history, though I did not realize it at the time.

We moved during the summer of 1925 to a new compound with seven houses that the Y built in the French Concession on Route Zayzoong for the families of its foreign secretaries. In the same compound were the Grays—Jack, Maude, and Marion; the Barnetts—Genie May, Robert, DeWitt, and Doak; and other families whose names I don't dredge up. The houses were ample, and there was a fine common lawn and a tennis court, our delight. The Barnett boys, Jack Gray, and my brother Halsey all became fine tennis players there. We lived only a mile from the Shanghai American School, the center of our lives, and the Community Church opposite the school.

SAS had a large dormitory for the boarders (mostly children of missionaries), a good classroom building, and ample playing fields. It was an international school in terms of the student body, but the education prepared students for American colleges. Interestingly, Michael Borodin, who was in Canton assisting and steering the Kuomintang and the Chinese Communist Party in their anti- foreign revolutionary activities, found it convenient to enroll his sons, Fred and Norman Gruzenberg, in the school. Why not? They were born and reared in America until their father and mother, Mike and Fanny, moved back to the new Soviet Russia in 1918. The parents were missionaries, too, for their faith in

Marxism-Leninism. I have spent a lot of research time learning about their work in China, from 1923 to 1927, and entitled one of my books *Missionaries of Revolution*.

The French Concession, where we now lived, was quite different from the Hongkew district. In Hongkew certain streets had exclusively foreign homes, but the alleyways contained row houses for Chinese, and Chinese shops with their flamboyant signs lined the commercial streets. The French Concession had been laid out like a minor French colonial capital, with broad avenues planted with shade trees, houses set back in lawns, and very little intermingling of Chinese commerce and foreign residence. Incidentally, Sun Yat-sen had a home there, though he died in March 1925, before we moved. Our school was on the several-mile-long Avenue Pétain, which led to a cathedral in the distance.

My last three years in SAS were happy ones. I was active in the drama group and participated in several plays. I tried to play football but was rather small. One disappointment was that I was pulled out of practice because I was doing poorly in French. By the time I had made up that deficiency and was allowed to play again, I had forgotten the signals. When put in as quarterback, I was at a loss. Thank heaven, I was quickly taken out again and put in as an end! I also played soccer, and I liked the longer-distance runs in track.

In my senior year I edited The *SAS Nooze*, a weekly. Maude Gray was assistant editor and Sid Willis was business manager. This took much time each week for writing editorials, proofreading, and paste-up. I still have a bound copy of the 1926–27 *Nooze*.

I was not a particularly good student, but was good enough to be accepted at Oberlin College. Apparently my parents made the decision for me to apply to Oberlin, a college that many relatives on Mother's side of the family had attended. How fortunate it was for me that I went there, where I met Kay.

My parents saw to it that I had some religious life. The Community Church had fine services, and there was Christian Endeavor, the clublike organization for young folks. Actually, the missionary atmosphere was so pervasive in SAS that everyone tried to lead a "good" life. I remember, however, that a certain adolescent skepticism began to creep into my thinking even before I left home for college. We had some liberal teachers in the school. I remember particularly Maxwell Stewart and his wife, Peggy, who later were active in the Foreign Policy Association; and Mr. Hanson, who taught English. Probably I absorbed a skeptical attitude from them.

While in high school I came to realize that Dad was more liberal than Mother, who was a conformist and very much a patriot. Dad practiced the "social gospel" and read *The Christian Century*, which Mother considered a radical magazine and did not want in the house. In this controversy my sympathies were more with Dad than with Mother.

SAS gave a course on Chinese civilization, which I found interesting. We got a minimum of instruction in Chinese language; living as completely an American life as possible, I learned to speak very little Chinese, and that only some Shanghai street language. Some kids who lived in rural mission stations did become fluent in a local dialect. I must emphasize, however, that China was our "home," and many China "mish kids" went back there at the first opportunity after college, as I did.

In 1926 Dad was asked to go to Japan to help the Y rehabilitate itself after the great earthquake of 1923. He lived in Tokyo and we missed him a lot, as he sorely missed us. So in the summer we all went to Japan to be with him. We spent two months at Karuizawa, a mountain resort much like our Mokan Shan. There we met kids from the American School in Japan, an institution much like SAS. I met Ed Reischauer, Abby Hoffsomer, Stan Sneed, and the Shively kids. Alice Shively and I had a brief flirtation; nothing lasting, however. My sister Beth came to Japan that summer after three years in Denison College, so our family was all together again.

The year 1927 was a dramatic one in China. Sun Yat-sen's Nationalist Party had been revitalized with Soviet Russian guidance and material assistance, and in mid-1926 it undertook, with its much improved armies, to reunify China through a Northern Expedition, a campaign starting from Canton and heading first for the Wuhan cities on the Yangtze River. By then, of course, Dr. Sun was dead and Chiang Kai-shek was on the rise. The Northern Expedition had such a reputation for radical anti-imperialism, also directed against Christian missionary schools and outlying mission stations, that thousands of British, American, and European missionaries, especially in the Yangtze Valley provinces, were advised by their governments to come to Shanghai for safety. Actually, until the "Nanking Incident" of March 24, 1927, there was very little killing of foreigners by the conquering armies or their agitators. However, foreign missionaries and their institutions certainly were harassed, and many families had to flee. Quite a few American refugee kids entered SAS for the spring term. Mother went to Tokyo to be with Dad, but Halsey and I stayed on in our home, into which Jay and Lucile Oliver had moved from Hangchow, a city in the path of the Northern Expedition. We were their wards for half a year. The Olivers became my most cherished Y "uncle" and "aunt." Dad's colleagues were fine men, their wives lovely people. They made a sort of fraternity and we, their children, formed lasting friendships.

During the summer of 1927 Halsey and I joined Mother and Dad in Japan, again spending most of our time in Karuizawa. I have many pictures of my Japan friends and me, including Sid Willis and Halsey, during our second summer there. Such a bunch of dandies, with our straw hats, suits with razor-sharp creases in the trousers, and some of us sporting canes! We had quite a social time, too, with the American girls at the resort.

In late August I sailed for America on a Japanese vessel, the *Toyo Maru*, with

Edwin O. Reischauer (later U.S. ambassador to Japan), Abby Hoffsomer, some other ASIJ graduates, and Sid Willis, on our way to college. Eddie, Sid, and I were bound for Oberlin. What a lark! I certainly felt a man of the world traveling across the Pacific on my own.

In San Francisco I found Jack Service, who had decided to go to Oberlin instead of the University of California. We rode a train across the country together. Knowing I disliked the name Clarence, Jack proposed that from now on I should be called by my second name, Martin.

3

Higher Education,
1927–1932

I remember riding that train on a September afternoon in 1927 bound for Oberlin, Ohio, and finding some other young folks aboard who had the same destination. I was filled with excitement. Later I wrote a description of our arrival for a freshman English class taught by Mrs. Lampson, and I must have conveyed the feeling, for she kept an eye on me. I believe she recommended me for what was a great privilege—to be invited by Professor Archibald Jelliffe to join an informal writing group that met in his home once or twice a month.

Oberlin is in virtually flat countryside. The town is filled with trees and old-fashioned homes. Jack Service and I lived the first semester in a rooming house on the north side because Jack had a cousin there. We took our meals at the freshman men's dorm. During the second semester we moved with Sid Willis to "The Yacht Club." It was just a private rooming house but was close to Plum Creek, a tiny stream, hence its name.

We freshmen wore beanie caps. Sophomores were our tormenters, but members of the junior class were supposed to be our patrons. A lady in the junior class named Helen Hutson got me as her protégé. She was very nice and I got a mild crush on her. Freshmen sat in the balcony during compulsory chapel, and I used to look down for Helen to catch her eye and her smile.

I don't remember for sure what classes I signed up for after reading the requirements, but I do remember English comp, and I think French. Foreign languages are my woe. I know that during my four years at Oberlin I got a lot of English literature and psychology. Outside activities probably took too much of my time.

I went out for cross-country running. Oberlin had a new track coach, Dan Kinsey, who had been an Olympic hurdler. He was a kind and competent young man. Jack and I learned a lot about distance running from Dan. Jack, of course, was a stellar long-distance runner. We made the freshman team, and I would come puffing in, not the last, either. Cross-country running is not a sport but a torture. The men on the rival teams burst forth from the starting line and quickly disappear onto some back road. There the runners spread out, each according to how hard he can push himself, the head and the tail of the runners getting farther and farther apart. Finally, the leaders enter the stadium and sprint or stagger around the last quarter mile, the spectators applauding and urging them on. Mostly a team race is won near the end by the laggards fighting it out.

I also went out for the *Oberlin Review*, the college newspaper, and became a reporter. One got a chance to make friends through outside activities, and friends are important to me. I already knew two girls from SAS in our class, Mary Barlow, a beautiful blond, and Emma McCloy. Emma became a physical education major, which was her father's special field in the YMCA in China.

We had "migration day" to Cleveland in the autumn when Oberlin played Western Reserve or Case in football. Several busloads of Oberlin folks went to Cleveland to cheer our team, which usually lost. Then we went to some restaurant for supper before the buses took us all back. At the dinner that Ed Reischauer and I went to there were several other freshmen at our table. One was Loomie Laird from Ashtabula, Ohio. He seemed to me very sophisticated—he knew what to do at a restaurant, especially about the mysterious matter of tipping. In my senior year Loomie and I were housemates and he was captain of the football team. One evening he recalled that dinner at the restaurant, telling me how awed he was about Eddie and me, people who had been all over the world, knew about traveling on our own. Of course, I revealed how awed I had been about his sophistication, as I saw it.

During the summer after my freshman year, I worked at the YMCA camp of Columbus, Ohio. The senior secretary, Mr. Pontius, must have been a friend of my father. After I wrote him, he immediately gave me a job as a counselor—pack leader—and the job of putting out a camp newspaper. It was a lovely, healthy summer. I swam, tanned, drank huge amounts of milk, and seem to have been a hit with my eight boys in our tent—or was it a cabin?

The big event of my sophomore year was meeting an enchanting young lady. It was early in December 1928. We met because Helen Hutson got me invited to a dance at Keep Cottage. My hostess, Frances Forbes, traded dances with another girl, and I found myself dancing with Kathryn Edson. I had seen her on the stage in a play of the Oberlin Drama Club. We hit it off wonderfully, and I wanted to date her after that one dance. She was willing, too. Kay was about five foot four, slender, dark hair, brown eyes, classic profile, and with a very nice figure—her legs were well worth looking at a second time. The most enchanting thing was her gaiety. She also was an interesting conversationalist, and we found quite a lot in common. She came from a farm in Indiana that belonged to her aunt and uncle, who had given her a home ever since her parents' divorce. She had lived in Mexico and gone to a select girls' school in Indianapolis. She came to Oberlin as a junior at only nineteen, instead of going to Mount Holyoke, as planned, simply because Oberlin was considerably less expensive. Her father was in financial straights. What good fortune that was for me! I was twenty then.

On my first date with Kay after returning from New York, she wore a red dress. I'm still a sucker for a red dress, as some of my lady friends know. After not many dates, Kay was calling me "angel." What a thrill! At the end of the cross-country season I won an O pin and could buy an O sweater, maroon with a golden O. I asked Kay if she would wear my O pin and my sweater. She tells me it was a huge thrill to wear them. Not many sophomores won their letters at midyear. Jack did, and so did Loomie Laird in football, and Eddie Reischauer in tennis.

My sophomore year was a sort of delirium. Kay Edson became the center of my life. We dated as often as we could. One popular outing was "Rec." On a certain number of evenings a week, couples could go to a basement room in Peters Hall to dance for about an hour after supper. Someone played the piano and we danced to the latest tunes—"Stormy Weather," "Mood Indigo," "Smoke Gets in Your Eyes"—that sort of thing. After "Rec" we were supposed to go to the library or our rooms to study, but that is not so easy when one is in love.

Another sort of romancing after Kay and I knew each other well was to sit on the porch of the Yacht Club and "neck." I believe I had never kissed a girl in earnest. Now we kissed and embraced when safely out of sight. But we were a very proper couple. It was the 1920s. Oberlin was a strict place, and we both had Victorian-type upbringings. To use Old Testament language, I "knew her not" until we were married. But petting! It keeps the glands working.

In June, Kay took me to visit her Aunt Mary Edson and cousin Peter. He was a newspaperman and later became a famous correspondent with a syndicated column from Washington, D.C. I remember that visit because Kay had just bought a red dress, rather short—it was the "flapper" age—and she did a dance on the porch. Kay had studied dancing and was very graceful. The red and the short were very attractive. It was then that I was convinced I wanted to marry Kay.

In the summer after my sophomore year I went again to the Columbus Y camp and had another very healthy two months. When Kay and I saw each other again, she thought I looked wonderful. I had gained ten pounds.

Betwixt dating and outside activities, my studies did not get the attention they should have, but I did enjoy certain courses very much, particularly courses in English literature taught by Charles Wager and Arch Jelliffe—courses in classics in translation, Shakespeare, the nineteenth-century poets and essayists. Also I got a lot from psychology courses taught by Pete Cole. The Oberlin psychology department was firmly "behaviorist." Freud was not honored. Behaviorism strengthened my doubts regarding my Christian upbringing. Mother faulted Oberlin for this, but it may be that since I was maturing somewhat, my iconoclasm would have developed whatever college I went to. I was becoming somewhat literary, writing short stories, essays, and some poetry for the Sunday evening literary circle into which Professor Jelliffe invited me. In my junior year I became involved in a literary monthly that my close friend, Howard Doust, started. He named it *The Olympian*, I suppose because it thundered from on high.

In June 1930 Kay graduated from Oberlin and got a job in Detroit to teach health education, in which she had majored at the advice of her Aunt Ora, who was practical enough in those hard times to have Kay take a job-oriented major. My parents came home for another furlough in late spring. They bought a new Chevrolet for $500, and we all learned to drive.

That summer I went to Madison, Wisconsin, to take three courses in summer session. One was French, which was very hard work. Another was a course on Milton, and the third a course on "The Age of Pope." I worked hard at my courses and became especially fond of the last one, particularly fond of Swift. I lived at a fraternity house and enjoyed many friendships.

Mother and I visited the Fuellings' farm in Indiana in mid-August. I drove Mother there from Chicago. We only stayed for two days, but that was long enough for Mother to become acquainted with "jolly, genial, kindly old Uncle John"—as I wrote of him in a letter to Kay, and to know Aunt Ora, who was to me "a huge inspiration." Aunt Ora was a local Daughter of the American Revolution and Mother was greatly involved as State Regent for China. So Aunt Ora invited all the local DAR ladies to a tea, and Mother's watercolor paintings were put on display. Kay and I spent many of the evening hours in a hammock out in the yard, while Aunt Ora and Mother paced about, hoping for the best, not the worst. We got separate lectures. I am sure that Mother was taken with Aunt Ora and Uncle John, and they admired her. It was a good start. It seems that Kay and I had a serious talk about becoming engaged, with Aunt Ora offering advice. We did agree that we would have to wait at least four years to consider marriage. Actually, I was much concerned as to what kind of work I would be undertaking upon graduation. The Depression had already struck.

Kay knocked on death's door in December 1930. She had gone home from Detroit for her Christmas holidays and had a tooth pulled. Unfortunately she got an infection, Ludwig's Angina, which caused lockjaw. She couldn't talk. Alarmed, Aunt Ora called the family doctor, who performed an operation right in the home. After boiling his instruments he cut up under her chin and drained a lot of pus. Kay did recover, but many people do not survive Ludwig's Angina. Not until long after did I realize how much I owe to Aunt Ora and the doctor for my later happy married life.

During my senior year I moved out of the Yacht Club to the Castle. That was where Jack had moved the previous year, and it was where Eddie Reischauer and Loomie Laird lived. Howard Doust and Fred Ficken also were there. We thought we were pretty hot stuff for we had the captains of the football, tennis, and cross-country teams, the editor of the Oberlin Class Annual in Howard Doust, and me as editor of *The Olympian*. Other dignitaries were Herman Burkhardt and Dudley Reed. Stanley Sneed of Japan was a junior among us. Eddie became a Phi Beta, and Fred Ficken a Rhodes scholar. Fred was brilliant, emotional, and very fond of young women. Howard Doust was intense and ambitious, but had a fine sense of humor. Dudley Reed had polio as a child and walked with a limp. He was the most debonair among us. Herman Burkhardt ("Buck"), son of a minister, posed as an iconoclast. We used to have long talks together over a late snack at the Campus Restaurant.

Even without Kay, I enjoyed my senior year and made lifelong friends. Most of them died much too soon. We graduated and went our various ways into the depths of the Depression. We were a cocky bunch.

I spent a great deal of time as editor of *The Olympian*. We aimed for quality—essays, stories, and poetry. We had three faculty advisers but lamentable problems with the printer. Sometimes I worked till early in the morning giving the copy a final proofing before delivering it to the printer, only to have it appear with typos or lines upside down. I also played soccer and had a few parts in plays put on by the Oberlin Drama Club, most memorably a part of one of the workmen-actors in *A Midsummer Night's Dream*.

During my senior year I took German, which proved to be terribly hard for me. It was a five-hour course, and I could not have given it the time it required, for after the first semester I got a D, and after the second, a D plus. Those were the only disgraceful marks I got at Oberlin, and I got more hours of A in the English courses and in a course in Chinese history and literature, from Professor Danton, who had taught at Tsing-hua University in Peking for ten years. That was a second-semester course; I enjoyed it, and it must have influenced my later decision to go into Chinese studies.

Graduation was a big time. Kay came to it. We fellows fixed up the Castle for parents' inspection, though by then my parents were already in Korea, and the parents of Jack and Eddie were in the Orient, too. Fred's minister father and his mother came. With a flourish, Fred showed them his desk, above which were pictures of two seminude girls he had forgotten to take down.

Jack and I had a wonderful time together for about six weeks taking care of Professor Ward's home. We played tennis, and I did a great deal of reading—recent fiction. At the end of the summer, shortly before the Wards' return, Kay came to visit me on her way back to Detroit, and Beth came to be chaperone. This was to mollify Kay's aunt. Beth brought a man along, one Paul Cressey, who was trying to persuade her to marry him and go to McGill, where he had a teaching job. They had met long before at Mokan Shan, and often in Granville, where Paul's mother lived. They began to date in Chicago as graduate students. It was a most romantic house party, but quite proper.

In my senior year and during that summer I was assailed with doubts about myself. I was still somewhat alienated in America and conscious that my four years had been sheltered ones. There were few things I felt sure about except that I loved Kay dearly and hoped to marry her—someday. She seemed a perfect choice for a lifetime companion—vivacious and beautiful, very well read, knowledgeable about music and art, and just lots of fun. I learned to respect her judgment: she was more down-to-earth than I. Kay gradually revealed how unhappy her childhood had been. Yes, I wanted to marry Kay, but I had only a few dollars to my name. I considered myself a liberal and a pacifist, but I was pessimistic about my future. An article I left for *The Olympian* was entitled "In Defence of Suicide." I didn't have suicidal thoughts for myself; I was showing off my "rationality."

Having graduated, I now must begin a career. I considered becoming a psychiatrist until I learned I would need an M.D. and a Ph.D., requiring seven years, which I could not possibly afford. So I thought of becoming a reporter. I did have some writing ability and a good liberal arts education. I had a few interviews, but it was Depression time and there seemed no chance to get that kind of a job. So I cast about for a graduate school where I might study about China and perhaps someday teach Chinese history. I chose Columbia and was admitted. I arranged to stay at International House, near Columbia. Most important, Dad found the money to cover my first year, some from the fund his Dayton friends set up for the education of his children. He also let me use the money I got for the sale of our car, $225. I marvel that we could have afforded graduate school.

When I reached Columbia and went for an interview with the acting head of the Department of Chinese, I discovered that a requirement for the M.A. degree was three years of Chinese. I could not see beyond one. I got a Chinese student to tutor me in beginning Chinese and signed up for second- and third-year classes taught by C. C. Wang. I worked very hard in my room in I-house every morning learning characters, but obviously I couldn't cover three years in one and do all the other course work. I had some good lecture courses: Professor Peake on China's modern revolution, Dr. Arthur Hummel on Chinese intellectual history, and Langdon Warner in Chinese art. For most of these courses I had to write papers. Professor Carrington Goodrich was in Peking finishing research on his dissertation, and I only met him in 1934.

I had little money, but expenses in New York were not great. My room was $5 a week, and I could eat for less than a dollar a day. I paid my Chinese tutor $6 for three lessons a week. In spite of working like a hermit on my Chinese, I did have a good time in New York. I had many old friend there, and gradually looked them up—for example, Jack Gray and Charles Boynton from the Shanghai American School. Jack was teaching in a fairly posh boys school, and poor Charles was desperately looking for a job because he had a girl in New York and wanted to get married. We found a German restaurant where we could get a completely filling meal for thirty-five cents—no dessert necessary. Paul Harvey was married to Hazel, and they had a small apartment. He was studying and working part-time, while Hazel also had a job. I envied them. John Davies looked me up at International House. He had taken exams for the U.S. Foreign Service and was awaiting results.

I visited Kay in Detroit and then at the farm during the Christmas break. Three months away from her left me unbelievably eager to see her again. Besides, I was going to bring her something Uncle Edgar has gotten for me, two aquamarines, of which she should chose the one to be used in her engagement ring. We just had an ecstatic time together; even though I was supposed to reserve some hours each day to review my Chinese.

I made two resolutions after I came back—work harder and be kinder. Also, I quit smoking. Uncle Edgar had the stone that Kay chose mounted in a simple white gold ring, and he let me pay only $75 for it. After Kay had her ring, we considered ourselves officially engaged. But that only made things worse, since I had no job or prospect, and even her job was in jeopardy because Detroit was in a terrible financial bind, the auto industry simply flat.

Somehow, though I studied most of each day, I did give myself some recreation. I went to several plays, usually paying fifty cents to stand in the back, and also to foreign films. Mother's old Shanghai friend, "Aunt" Mary Gamewell, took me to Carnegie Hall to hear Bach's B-minor Mass, and I swore I must hear more good music. I went to the Riverside Church a few times to hear Dr. Fosdick, a fine preacher. I joined in several excursions and parties with friends, and walked quite a bit on the streets of New York. Also I got a locker at the gym and could swim or run on the indoor track. But I wasn't at all fond of winter. Friends mean a great deal to me, both men and women, and in New York I had almost too many.

At Easter time, Kay came to New York and stayed with her sister Elizabeth for a few days. I could hardly wait till she arrived after an overnight train ride. We saw at least one play, for which I had gotten three tickets, *Mourning Becomes Electra*. I also took her to meet "Aunt" Elizabeth Grimball, who wrote Mother that she liked Kay a lot. A couple of years later that visit paid off. We also climbed four floors to the loft studio of my old Shanghai schoolmate, Horace Day, who had spent his years in New York studying art and was now gaining some recognition. Several of his drawings and paintings were in museums and in touring exhibitions.

Howard and Rosalie Doust had invited us to see them in Boston, so we took a cabin in a night boat from New York. If Elizabeth knew about that I don't think she passed it on to Aunt Ora, our formidable conscience. Howard had bought out a publishing company with a good list of books. How he ever afforded to do that, I cannot imagine. We were with them for the weekend, and Ed Reischauer joined us. He was launched on graduate work in East Asian studies at Harvard. One memorable thing about that Boston visit was that Kay and I went to a Daumier show at the Museum of Fine Arts. I had never heard of Daumier (me a graduate of a school with an excellent fine arts department) and was duly impressed. That exhibition is memorable as the first of so many art exhibits that Kay and I have enjoyed together.

Toward the end of the school year, I had to present seminar papers in several of my courses: papers on the Chinese intellectual renaissance, Tang sculpture, and the Chinese labor movement. Also I was looking for a thesis topic. I finally settled on a study of Chinese village government, which I thought would fit into my new-found interest in anthropology. I first tried to work up a bibliography and found that little had been done on the subject systematically. At the same time, I was trying my best to find some way to get to China with Kay. We were determined to be married in the summer if at all possible. I tried for a Harvard-Yenching Fellowship but was politely turned down. My friend Fletcher Brockman, who had retired from the YMCA and was devoting his time to promoting Chinese studies, was unable to help me; in fact he just discouraged me about the difficulty of the field. Kay tried to get a job as a P.E. teacher at Yenching, and there was some unpromising correspondence. Between preparing seminar papers, oral exams, Chinese language, and hunting for a job, that spring was a most distraught time.

What rescued me from the impossible effort to get an M.A. from Columbia in one year, with three years of Chinese, was a cable from Dad that arrived on June 14: "Pettus offers Martin year tuition room board for library work." This was my break! Dr. Pettus was a former colleague of Dad's and now ran the College of Chinese Studies in Peking. I had been advised by Professor Peake and Dr. Hummel that it was the best place to study Chinese.

My letter to Kay was restrained, for I wanted her to be sure she wished to go with me. I told her it would cost each of us $300 to get to Peking. I have her letter of reply written on June 17. The money scared her. She said she had savings of $200 and about $100 on hand. (I had an emergency savings account of just $300 in Dayton.) She ended her letter thus: "Anyway, darling . . . I'm ready for any kind of ocean voyage with you."

After consulting with her aunt, Kay set the wedding date for July 17, just a month away. Her aunt and uncle certainly knew we would marry sometime. But go off to China? And in the midst of the Depression with very little money?

A great change was coming in our lives. "If you want to know more, read on," as the Chinese storytellers say.

4

Kay and I Start Out,
1932–1936

Preparations at the farm for our midsummer wedding were really fine. Kay and I went with Uncle John to the county clerk's office to get our wedding license—a rather embarrassing business because of kidding. We also called on the minister who was to marry us. He gave us a talk about how you have to work to make a good marriage—like a piece of sculpture with many unwanted chips cut away and discarded. He wasn't very clear about the ceremony. It would be a "mosaic ceremony," he said. "When I pause, that's when you say, 'I do.'"

Kay's doctor gave her enough contraceptives for a year, and when Freddie came he gave me some condoms. Uncle John created a lovely floral arbor in front of the fireplace in the living room where we were to take our vows. The day before the wedding our personal guests arrived and were put up in neighbors' homes. Aunt Ora had a wonderful supper the night before the wedding. It was a gay occasion.

We were to be married at ten o'clock on Sunday morning, July 17. It seems I was not supposed to see Kay until the great moment. Quite a few friends of the Fuellings, as well as some of Kay's local acquaintances, came to see her marry her "Chinese boyfriend." I stood under the arch wearing my white summer suit with Herman Burkhardt, my best man. The simple ceremony began when a composer friend of the Fuellings from Indianapolis sang "Trees Where'er You Walk Crowd into a Shade" and "O Promise Me." Then "Here Comes the Bride" was played on the piano. That was our signal. Kay came down the stairs with her sister Miggs and into the living room. Oh! How beautiful she was in her light blue dress, carrying delphiniums and peach-colored gladiolus. Each of us gave the other a great big smile. The minister gave a lovely service, but Kay wasn't sure when she should respond. He paused three times and three times she said "I will." As Beth wrote my parents, "A promising bride." We have a picture taken of us under that arbor, both looking solemn and very young. She was twenty-three and I, twenty-four.

We didn't start off immediately, but had a day between to get properly packed and to visit with Kay's family. On Tuesday morning Uncle John and Aunt Ora took us to the train station and we rode off to Chicago, where my Uncle Burt and Aunt Anna were taking us in for a night. The temperature that day was 104 and the train ride was about five hours, with no thought of air conditioning in those days. We were covered with sweat and grime when we arrived in Chicago.

Next day we began our three-day trip by train to Seattle, from whence our ship, the *Yokohama Maru*, would sail. It wasn't a grand ship, and there were only four passengers for that late July crossing. We sailed on the great northern route up near the Aleutian Islands. Up there it was cold and misty. The captain let us peer at the islands through his telescope. But most of the trip was sunny. It was a lovely ten-day crossing for us newlyweds, who walked the decks and got much better acquainted.

Everywhere the way had been prepared for us. In Yokohama we were met by a Japanese friend of Father, who showed us around, took us to see the beautiful Meiji Shrine, and then gave us a sukiyaki dinner, which was something new for Kay. She remembers vividly being astonished to see hundred of men on bicycles balancing in one hand trays stacked with bowls of noodles. They were delivering lunch to the folks. Two decades later in Tokyo we became quite used to that sight; in fact, we often got lunch delivered to our house by bicycle riders. We then boarded a train for Shimonoseki and had a beautiful ride past Mt. Fuji. The Japanese countryside was full of interest—the farmers tilling in their fields, the villages with thatch- or tile-roofed houses. Our boat for Pusan, Korea, sailed from Shimonoseki. It was an overnight trip. Arriving in Korea, which was long since a Japanese colony, we took a train for the capital, Seoul. There, in the early evening, Dad met us at the station. At long last, we had arrived at home—our home for the next six weeks.

Mother was still at the seashore, because we had arrived sooner than expected, but she returned a few days later. They lived in a foreign-style house near Seoul's West Gate, which still stood, though without its wall. Dad was in Seoul to help the Korean YMCA, which, like many other Korean institutions, was in difficulty with the Japanese administration. The educated Korean people opposed their colonial masters. Dad, I suppose because of his long Japan acquaintanceship, was to serve as an intermediary.

Dad and Mother wanted to take us to the Diamond Mountains, but Kay contracted a terrible rash and went into the hospital instead. That was an experience! In Severance Hospital, where most of the patients were Korean, it was the custom for the families to bring the food to those recuperating. Korean food is strong on kimche, pickled cabbage and spoiled fish drowned in pepper. It smells to heaven. Still, an American and a Korean doctor took good care of her, and Kay survived.

Kay and Dad hit it off famously. Both loved cake. They would sneak into the kitchen at night and have cake and milk. Mother was doing a lot of watercolor painting at this time. We still own seven of her paintings of the West Gate and street scenes. They recall for us the lovely costumes the Korean women wore: pastel-colored blouses and long, full white skirts. Gentlemen of the old school wore white coats, baggy pants, and black horse-hair hats looking like stove pipes. Some carried long, crooked canes; others might carry foot-long pipes of thin bamboo, with an amber mouthpiece at one end and a small brass bowl at the other, a bowl just big enough for a pinch of fine tobacco that would allow one or two puffs. There was a distinctive sound we remember, the sound of women ironing those handsome linen costumes by beating them with paddles on a flat stone. Seoul had been Korea's capital for centuries, but it was a sleepy provincial city when we knew it in 1932.

We had a date in Peiping—as Peking was officially called—for about September 15, when the College of Chinese Studies, Hua Wen Hsueh-hsiao, would open its fall term. It wasn't too convenient to get to Peking from Seoul, but we found a way. We took a little commercial plane that flew to Dairen, and from there a boat to Tientsin, and then a train to Peking. Off we flew in a single-engine prop plane that only made about 2,000 feet. Below us we saw the thatched roofs of farmhouses with bright red peppers drying on them. Once in Dairen, we went to the Yamato Hotel. Dairen was a Japanese-owned city, and the hotel was of Japanese colonial standard. The next afternoon we boarded a small Japanese steamer. At dinnertime, soup was already being served when we came into the dining room. All the spoons stopped in midair as the diners turned to stare at the two foreigners. It was an overnight boat, and in the morning we pulled into Taiku, Tientsin's harbor. But there was no harbor, just a mud bank against which our little steamer sidled up. On the shore was a crowd of coolies shouting their demand to carry our baggage. I could smell a particularly Chinese smell—the smell of night soil on the fields. To Kay it was a stench.

As soon as the gangplank was thrown to shore that swarm of coolies came howling aboard. Very scary! But we defended our baggage and hired two rickshaws to take us to the train station. Luckily we didn't lose a bag. There must have been a long wait for the train, because we didn't approach Peking till nighttime. But what a thrilling approach that was! The September moon was at the full. We passed along beside the great crenellated city wall, passed the Ha-ta Men gate, and finally drew into Ch'ien Men station. There, to our surprise and pleasure, a tall Chinese man, dressed in a long black gown and with the bottoms of his trousers bound like puttees above his cloth shoes, found us amid the throng of disembarking passengers—probably not too difficult a task, since almost everyone else was Chinese. He presented us a note and then led us to a waiting car that took us through the dark and mysterious streets of that ancient city, down a narrow, walled alley that we soon learned to call a *hu-t'ung*, and then stopped at a large double door painted bright red. When the gate was opened, moonlight bathed a flowering almond tree in a lawned compound. It was an unforgettably romantic moment. This was to be our home for the next two years. We had spent from July 19 to September 15 getting there, with help from a lot of people.

Dr. Pettus was away when we arrived, and it was Mrs. Pettus who made us feel at home and introduced us. The College of Chinese Studies was intended primarily to teach spoken Chinese—with emphasis on the Peking dialect—to missionaries, but its methods were too good, and its living arrangements so convenient, that persons of other interests than converting Chinese to Christianity were glad to study there. Kay and I had two rooms in the dormitory for married folks and single men; the other dorm was for single women—an off-limits place. In our bedroom we had twin beds, the only time in our married life when we didn't use a double bed. The study room had two desks, a rocker, and two straight chairs. It also had a small balcony overlooking the campus. There I memorized Chinese characters early in the mornings when it was warm enough. The bathrooms were not far away. We soon made ourselves cozy in our first home together, bought a rug or two and a table for a fern, and decorated the walls with Mother's watercolors.

My job was to work eighteen hours a week in the library, which was well stocked with books on China as well as scholarly journals. A bibliography of its holdings that I helped to produce is still a good reference tool. Mrs. Marvin Williams, a professional librarian, taught me a lot about absolute accuracy and about following the rules for cataloguing and other aspects of library work. That was a valuable learning experience, and I faithfully filled my eighteen hours a week, mostly doing routine chores the first year. Kay got a job teaching English at the YMCA night school three nights a week until she found a job more in her field, teaching physical education at St. Faith's School for Chinese girls. Our finances were thus: My room, board, and tuition were covered by my job. Dad and Mother sent us $50 (gold—that is, U.S.) a month, which converted to about $225 Mex (a term for Chinese silver currency), and Kay earned 40 or 50 Chinese dollars a month during the first year. This gave us enough to live on.

We learned Chinese by the "direct method." For the first few weeks everyone sat in class together to listen to Chinese being spoken slowly, while the speaker pointed to features of the face and body—nose, eyes, mouth, arms—or introduced pronouns—I, he, they—or acted out verbs. For three weeks we didn't hear a word of English. After classes we had private tutoring, each student in a cell with a Chinese teacher who would go over what we had learned. These old teachers knew no English. Since I had no command of spoken Chinese and we weren't yet learning characters, I did profit very much from studying speech. The most difficult part of speech was to remember—nay, internalize—the tones for each monosyllabic word or combination of words. We only heard them spoken with their proper tones. Kay, with her fabulous memory, did better than I did.

Our first few weeks in Peking we explored that lovely old city. It is laid out about the core of the Imperial Palace with an inner city around it. A south-to-north axis runs straight from Ch'ien Men, the front gate of the city, through the Meridian Gate, through the palaces, and then on to Coal Hill on the north, a length of several miles. The palaces are simply magnificent, with red walls, courtyards large enough to hold thousands of people, vast white marble terraces and balustrades, and audience buildings with dazzlingly golden roofs. The grounds were unkempt when we were there, grass growing between the paving stones. In 1980 we saw the palaces all spic and span with thousands of Chinese tourists leisurely enjoying their magnificent inheritance.

The axis gives the direction to the major streets in the city, laid out in a grid around the palace area. We lived to the east of the palaces on an alley off Tung Ssu Pailou—the Four Eastern Arches. Those arches were our guidepost; everyone knew where they were. East of us was one of the eastern gates of the city wall, which still stood in those days. Near us was a market, Tung An Shih-ch'ang, a most interesting place to visit. Besides the shoppers and lookers, there were performing acrobats and storytellers, beating out the rhythm of their stories on a pair of clickers like castanets. The first time we were in the market, looking at a display of cricket cages—yes, cages for crickets—a Chinese gentleman spoke to us in English: "Interesting sport isn't it?" The sport was to have crickets fight each other, like cockfights!

We walked to Coal Hill, from which one could look southward over the roofs of the palaces and see a chain of lakes to their west. We also went out to the Temple and Altar of Heaven, very unkempt, but architecturally striking. Set in a huge park was the altar, a circular white marble terrace perhaps 100 feet in diameter, surrounded by a balustrade. From there a long avenue led to the Temple of Heaven, a round, blue-roofed structure with the imperial red walls. It was semidark within, and there were surprising acoustical features. When we visited the Confucian Temple it was going to wrack and ruin.

Peking had wonderful sounds, smells, and sights. Near our school a pigeon fancier harnessed his pigeons with whistles under their wings: when the flock took off, harmonic music drifted down from the sky. At night we heard the watchman go by, clicking on his bamboo to let us know he was there and all was right. But at dawn we heard the most awful shrieking—it was trussed-up pigs being carried upside down to the slaughterhouse. Other soon familiar sounds were the calls of tradesmen singing out their wares. In the mornings you could smell the "honey carts" carrying away the night soil to put on the fields. A nicer smell came from street-side cooking, the smell of sesame oil and soy. We loved to see caravans of camels trudging in from the north, mingling with Peking's ancient taxis and rickshaws.

We visited the "dog temple," the patron temple of sick dogs, near the college, and it was like nothing we had ever seen. A tiny, dark building of only one room, it was kept by an old woman who slept there on the *kang* (a brick bed that could be heated in winter). The owner of an ailing dog would come and buy some incense and deposit a little clay dog at the foot of an idol. There were hundreds and hundreds of those little clay dogs, and also a box where one's sick dog could sleep at the foot of the idol. It was filthy enough to pass diseases on to each new occupant. Thus the old woman made her living, selling incense and clay dogs.

In the Language School we found congenial fellow students. Mr. and Mrs. George Lerrigo ("Uncle George and Aunt Nettie") were Y colleagues of Dad and Mother. He had spent a career in Canton, and now near retirement he was trying to learn the official Peking dialect. Though they were as nice to us as could be, Uncle George was a narrow-minded super-Christian. Aunt Nettle was kindly and tactful, and she tried to make up for his social blunders. A couple about our age with whom we soon found much in common were Clyde and Betty Sargent. Clyde was not really cut out to be a missionary; he soon left the field. Then there was Gerry Winfield and Louise, who were preparing to go to Tsinan University in Shantung. He was a plant biologist and later became an important person in the Department of Agriculture. One of our best friends was Charles Stelle. Born in Tungchow a little east of Peking, kicked out of Amherst, probably for drinking (remember, it was Prohibition time), he was tall and athletic and wonderfully bright and interesting, but something of a scamp. Another scamp was Janet Fitch Sewell. Kay thinks she wasn't married when we first knew her, and she certainly was an irrepressible flirt. Yet my early letters mention her husband, Jackie. Janet had been a classmate of mine in SAS. She was an artist and showed her artistic temperament—she would do what she damn pleased. There was quite a storm when she sailed into the men's dorm, supposedly forbidden to the women. We had lots of fun with those younger folks.

We have a picture of Charlie Stelle and me looking at a *New Yorker*. He is a very handsome young man. I show the moustache I grew after we arrived in Peking. An amusing story about this, very Chinese: Charlie showed the photograph to his servant, who said, commiseratingly, "Isn't it too bad, such a young man and his father is dead." Charlie asked him why he thought that. "Because he is wearing a moustache" was the reply. According to Chinese custom, no son would dare wear a beard or moustache if his father were alive!

Several most interesting foreigners lived in Peking, with whom we quickly became acquainted. There was a YMCA group: Robert Gailey, a huge older man, had come to Peking shortly out of Princeton where he had been a football star. He knew Peking as well as a native. He had a dry humor and wouldn't let Sarah Pettus lead him into the Oxford Group, with which she was enamored. His Chinese nickname was Liang-pai Chin (meaning 200 catties, about 240 lbs.). He needed a two-man rickshaw. Bob Gailey had been a friend of General Feng Yu-hsiang and used to go to his camp south of Peking to teach him English even on very cold winter mornings. Feng learned that foreigners like ice cream and saw to it that Bob had it even in the coldest weather. Lennig Sweet and his beautiful wife, Helen, were the most active representatives of Princeton among the Y group. They had a lovely old Chinese home, and probably had private money. His father had been governor of Colorado. They were very cordial to us and the Sargents, inviting us for dinner at their home and then taking us to the Peking Hotel for dancing. Dancing became one of our recreational splurges. Lyman Hoover and his Helen were another Y couple more nearly our age. He and I remained friends for many years.

Dr. Pettus was rumored to be arriving soon, and we heard most unpleasant things about him. So many people had had run-ins with him and spoke bitterly about him that we feared the worst. Arrogant, domineering, and dictatorial were words used to describe him. The Chinese staff feared him. We learned they had a particular signal to tell others he was about to enter a room. Since he had a very large head, particularly a broad forehead, they would make a repeated gesture of the open hand toward the head to warn one another. I was beholden to him for my partial fellowship and wondered what our relations would be. Yet when he did arrive back at the college we had no problem. Not that year! In fact, he renewed the fellowship for the following year.

We made friends with a number of Sinologues in Peking. Most important to us was C. W. Bishop, representing the Smithsonian Institute in China. He was an antiquarian, vastly learned about ancient humans everywhere. Mr. Bishop had organized a group of scholars to meet once a month at the German Hotel for dinner and talk. Others in that group were Owen Lattimore, C. Walter Young, Lucius Porter, and Herrlee Creel, who had arrived about the same time as we did. We became well acquainted with the Creels. He was a cantankerous but learned man, delving into China's past as revealed through archaeology. He wrote a popular but scholarly book, *The Birth of China*, which went through several printings. In our second year Herrlee nearly died of typhus. Later he taught classical Chinese language and philosophy at the University of Chicago. His wife Wilhelmina was a marvelous pianist. Later she went to Hungary to study with Béla Bartok. Both Herrlee and Wilhelmina were geniuses in a way, and their temperaments clashed. So they divorced. It was one of our first acquaintances with divorce among friends of our generation, but certainly not the last. Later John Fairbank came into our ken, and then his bride, Wilma. Most of these scholars were on some fellowship or another and were relatively well off compared to Kay and me. But we held our own. We entertained or were entertained by most of them, and knew them for years afterward—a sort of fraternity.

We made some Chinese friends but unfortunately were unable to keep in touch with them after we returned to the States. Some were very nice to us, taking us to Peking opera or to Chinese meals. We still have a fine painting, probably by a well-known artist of the early seventeenth century, that one of our Chinese friends presented to us when we left for the States.

We joined the Peking Union Church, which doubtless pleased my parents.

Apparently I also joined a YMCA group, for a letter to Dad tells him that I was treasurer of the group, but I have no memory of it. We do remember Mrs. Pettus trying to get us into a prayer circle, mostly of Language School and Y folks. Kay knew nothing about prayer meetings, and they were far from my liking, but after all, we were rather dependent on the Pettuses for my job, and Sarah Pettus was very helpful when we arrived. But she was intent on having the meetings confessional sessions à la Oxford Group procedure—one "shares" problems and all pray over them. We went a couple of times but had no problems to share. Yet we were in a missionary environment, and my parents were missionaries, so we acted as though we were Christians.

Poor Kay contracted dysentery not long after we arrived in Peking. China is her nemesis when it comes to dysentery; she always seems to get it. Fortunately a doctor at the Presbyterian mission was able to cure it, but it took weeks.

An amusing incident occurred when the popular writer Lewis Browne, the author of *This Believing World*, and his wife came to stay a few days at the Language School. At a dinner for them to which we were invited, Uncle George undertook to lecture him on his treatment of Christianity as though it were just one of the religions some people believe in. It was a tirade, and poor Aunt Nettie was most embarrassed, as were we all. Perhaps he forgot that Mr. Browne and his wife were Jewish! They visited some of the temples in Peking and were shocked when they saw what people seemed to believe in. Mr. Browne said he would have to revise his chapter on Taoism, which he had derived entirely from accounts based on the classics!

I also got to meet and hear the great French Sinologue Paul Pelliot. He had been in Peking during the Boxer troubles, and this was thirty-three years later, yet he seemed very young. He lectured on Christianity in China during the Mongol period, when it was quite strong among some of the Mongolian tribes. Owen Lattimore gave a talk to the students of the College of Chinese Studies about his tour of Mongolia—just fascinating. Later he wrote the seminal book *China's Inner Asian Frontier*. I reviewed it for a scholarly journal. I have admired Owen for many years. He had great adversity during the McCarthy period but stood his ground bravely.

That winter we learned to ice skate. It was quite the rage to go to the lakes west of the palace and skate among the Chinese devotees. We first learned when Charlie Stelle invited us to visit his parents in Tung-chow. Mrs. Stelle was a marvelous lady. Since they had extra pairs of skates, we could give it a try. Naturally there was a lot of tumbling about, but it was so much fun that we had skates made, which cost us about $15 Mex a pair, including the attached shoes.

It was time to make applications for fellowships again. I tried Harvard-Yenching once more, and also Columbia for a Cutting traveling fellowship. But no luck at all. Somehow, my record was not good enough at that stage of my studies.

War clouds loomed early in 1933. The Japanese Army pushed westward from conquered Manchuria into Jehol Province. Peking streets had many Chinese soldiers, though in a letter I wrote to my parents it didn't seem they would be effective against the Japanese Army. Japanese planes flew over our city, probably to be threatening. Foreign friends discussed leaving, and our Chinese friends were terribly concerned lest Peking itself be taken, because the Chinese army had not been able to hold Jehol and now Japanese troops were at the passes of the Great Wall. Then the apprehension passed. Japan used a strategy of biting off a chunk of China and then consolidating.

I devoted a lot of time to researching and writing my M.A. thesis for Columbia on Chinese village government. Our library had about all the sources I needed, and I did research in Chinese social science writings. As usual, Kay helped with my terrible spelling problem. Finally, sometime in March, I sent it off to Professor Goodrich, who read and accepted it. So in May 1933 I got that degree. Many years later, the editor of the Hong Kong branch of the *Royal Asiatic Society Journal* asked if he might publish it. Thus, nearly fifty years later, that early effort of mine saw print, with an explanatory preface, you may be sure.

In May 1933 Mother came to visit us and paint Peking scenes, of which members of our family have lovely examples. She gave us a guest book and was the first to sign in it, on May 15. It serves to remind me of friends we entertained in those days, including many Chinese, some no longer clearly remembered. Professor Cyrus Peake and Marie came to Peking in July 1933. He had been my mentor at Columbia, and now I had the chance to become more informally acquainted. Much later, we both worked in Washington during the war; but he stayed on in government and I took his place at Columbia, teaching modern Chinese history. I find that a strange circumstance.

Mother took Kay back to Seoul with her, leaving me for a month of studying Chinese alone. They went by train across Manchuria, now under Japanese control, and down through Korea. At the end of July I also went to Korea to join Kay and to spend the month of August with Dad and Mother. Thus ended our first year in Peking, a memorable time for the newlyweds, deeply in love.

In November I noticed a queer feeling in my abdomen and mentioned it to Dr. Logan Roots, who was at the college with his wife, preparing for missionary medical work. He came from a well-known missionary family in Hankow. He advised me to take it seriously and have a checkup. A doctor at Peking Union Medical College examined me and warned that I had an ulcer. He prescribed a very bland diet and complete bed rest. Mrs. Pettus directed the kitchen to provide me just what the doctor prescribed. I was not supposed to do any studying during my recuperation . After five weeks I could leave my room. Unfortunately, the threat of an ulcer has since hovered over me whenever I have been under protracted tension; I have been operated on twice to close a bleeding ulcer or to reduce my stomach and cut down acidity. But that was much later, after I began to teach.

By Christmas time I was back to normal except for care in my diet, and at

New Years I went on an excursion with Kay and a lot of friends to the Great Wall. By then Kay had a new job tutoring the daughter and daughter-in-law of the wealthy banker Chow Tso-min. One of Dad's Y friends, Jimmy Ch'uan, made the arrangements, and Kay received a good salary of $300 a month. She could bank quite a bit of that, and the Chinese banks paid high interest rates even on checking accounts. She went four or five days a week across the city to Mr. Chow's palatial home to give lessons in English and Western manners to the young ladies, aged nineteen and twenty. She also took them to movies or other outings. Everything went well until the young ladies departed for a vacation and for a couple of months she heard no more of them. Then Jimmy Ch'uan appeared again. The girls demanded Kay back as their teacher; they didn't like the older, but cheaper, woman who had taken her place. Mr. Chow had told the girls he would pay $100 dollars a month for each of them for a teacher. So it was arranged that Kay would start teaching again, but to save face, Kay said she would only teach two, instead of three, hours a day—a very appropriate Chinese compromise. She also continued some teaching at St. Faith's School. We were not flush.

A gentleman named Pai had a daughter, Lily, a bit younger than Kay, who offered to help Kay attend Chinese theater. Kay was fascinated with the posturing and acrobatic swordplay of the military operas, and the Pais took us to several. A Chinese theater is a rather nondescript place, but it has a big stage and a noisy— say earsplitting—orchestra. The audience is noisy too, talking and eating and wiping their faces on hot towels that are flung to them by an attendant. Costumes for Chinese opera are gorgeous, but scenery and props are the barest. The audience knew the plays and people would shout approval at a particularly fine rendition of an aria. Usually the female parts were taken by men, who sang in falsetto. Kay learned some of the plots and even could understand some of the words, which isn't easy because they are spoken in a conventionally artificial way.

Our old friend John Davies arrived in October 1933. He had made it in the U.S. Foreign Service and was now posted in Peking to study Chinese. He had a nice house near the college, so we saw much of him. Jack Service also had passed his Foreign Service exams and was sent as a consular clerk to Kunming, way off in Yunnan Province, as his apprenticeship. One reached Kunming in those days through Hanoi in French Indo-China. A year later Caroline Schulz (Jack's girl in Oberlin) came out to join him and they were married. Dear Cary had many of the same China illnesses that plagued Kay.

We made other new friends. John DeFrancis came to Peking, sort of bumming his way around the world, though he was a poor boy. He liked Peking so much that he just settled down in the Language School. Much later he became a great authority on the Chinese language, and we have been close friends ever since. Edgar Snow and his wife, Peggy, also were friendly. He was teaching journalism at Yenching, and she was a journalist too, competitive with him. I had the odd experience of having this pretty young woman try to "vamp" me in a most obvious way. Or do I flatter myself? Arthur and Edna Coons were at the college with their three-year-old son, and we became warm friends. He was the dean at Pomona College and an economist. He was on the Kemmerer Commission advising the Chinese government on currency reform. George Kates had drifted into the school beginning a new career for himself, since he had made a pile as a historical adviser to movie companies and had tired of it. George was the most assiduous student, always conning his character cards. He left the school because Dr. Pettus wouldn't let him study what he wanted to. George plunged into Peking life and remained immersed for seven years. He collected fine Ming and early Ch'ing furniture and wrote a book on Chinese household furniture, and also one named *The Years That Were Fat*, which vividly recounts details of Peking life. Derk Bodde and Laurence Sickman also arrived in Peking, or perhaps we only became acquainted in our second year. Derk became professor of Chinese at the University of Pennsylvania, and Larry became a curator and then director of the William Rockhill Nelson Gallery in Kansas City, which has one of the finest Chinese collections in America, thanks to him. Much of the postwar development of Chinese studies in America came from the young scholars in Peking during the 1930s, most of whom we knew well.

At the college we also knew a German girl, Karen Lohman, an eager Nazi. It was our first introduction to nazism. Her mother was Jewish and had jumped overboard on the way to China. Another unusual person was Edip Bey (Mr. Edip), a Turkish gentleman studying Chinese for reasons we didn't know.

It may have been in this year that Charlie Stelle fell in love with Margaret, a novice missionary in Japan who came to Peking on a visit. We already were fond of Charlie, and we took a shine to Margaret, too. Later they were married. Also that year we made a trip to Tientsin to visit Paul Harvey and Hazel. We continued that friendship when we returned to New York.

What of my second-year studies? I wanted to read the *Shih chi* by Ssu-ma Ch'ien, the great historian of the early Han period, but Dr. Pettus would not permit it. So I took a special course with Mr. Gailey on reading newspaper editorials, which were written in a somewhat literary style and used an extensive vocabulary. I got up at five each morning to put in two hours of study before breakfast. While I certainly didn't master editorial style, Mr. Gailey told me I was doing well.

Using time in the library, I worked up an extensive bibliography on Chinese metallic mirrors, which date back to Warring States times (ca. 300 B.C.), if not earlier. Such mirrors have been much studied because their decor reflects the styles of the times. I wrote a brief introductory article and sent the bibliography to *The China Journal*, which published it—my first scholarly publication.

With spring some of our friends began to leave. The one I most hated to see go was C. W. Bishop, because I admired him tremendously—he was so learned and yet so unassuming—and he was very encouraging. Later I learned that he had written a letter to Professor Goodrich, giving me good marks. And I owe a lot more to him for his help two years later. I went to the station to see him and Peg when they departed. Charlie Stelle also returned to the States; he wanted to begin summer school, so that in the autumn he could go to graduate school. The Coons also departed.

Dad's sixtieth birthday was to come on April 19, 1934. That is a full cycle as the Chinese count age. It was also the time he should retire from the YMCA, which he would have served for some forty years. Dad loved to write to his friends, and he had a host of correspondents. In February I worked up a letter and got it printed, sending it to all the friends I knew of and to the Y offices in several key cities, asking the readers to write letters to Dad on the occasion of his sixtieth birthday, and to send them care of Mother, the matter to be kept a secret. We hoped Dad would visit us sometime in the spring because he had to go to Manchuria on business and then to Shanghai. I kept imploring him not to pass us by. But up to April 15, at least, I thought he had returned to Korea. Suddenly we received a telegram saying he would arrive shortly before his birthday. That was a time for celebration. Kay and Mrs. Pettus schemed up a lovely party for him at the college, with his Y friends as guests. There were red decorations, of course, and endless noodles and peaches of immortality. It was just great to have him with us for a few days. When he got back to Seoul he had a drawer full of letters to read, and he bound them in a book. Dad did not retire, though he went on retirement pay. He continued to serve in Korea and China for another five years.

Kay gave a solo dance at a women's club garden party held at the German Legation, for which she practiced arduously, and her students in St. Faith's School did European folk dances, a great hit. I made a trip to Miao Feng Shan, the pilgrimage place where women go who want children. It was pilgrimage time. We went together to the Western Hills, with its lovely temples and ancient pine trees, for two weekends, I riding my bicycle and Kay using the rickshaw that regularly took her to classes.

With the end of the term approaching, Kay and I had to decide what next. None of my fellowship hopes came through, as usual. Should we stay on in Peking or return to America? I consulted with Dr. Pettus, who made it clear immediately that I could not expect the work-study arrangement again. Nor would he think of allowing me, merely an M.A. from Columbia, to lecture at his college. (This incensed Professor Peake.) Dr. Pettus was very rude about it. Clearly he didn't want me around. Kay and I tried to continue on civil terms with him, but that interview did it. We decided to go back to the States. If possible, I would go to Columbia and work for a Ph.D. Kay might have to find a job somewhere else. Again we were filled with uncertainty—the common lot of many graduate students.

Shortly before we left, Dr. Pettus called me into his office and tried to make up. We stuck out the term, but about June 20, after a round of entertaining and being entertained, we left by train. Johnny Davies and a few Chinese friends saw us off. Since we departed third class, the Chinese may have "lost face." John's gift was a thermos of cold lemonade. Though the last couple of months had been trying, still we had had a greatly enriching two years, years we remember with nostalgia.

We met the Peakes at Pyong-yang (now the capital of North Korea) to inspect a Han dynasty tomb that had been discovered, and to visit a museum that displayed beautiful ancient Chinese lacquer work and other objects that had been excavated. I had become more and more inclined toward ancient China and archaeology as my special fields.

We had a leisurely time with Mother and Dad. We played a lot of bridge and socialized with their foreign friends. Mother tried to fatten us up, because I had written her from Peking that Kay weighed only 102 lbs. and I, 119. Dad showed me a typewritten manuscript, possibly a doctoral dissertation, written by a Korean. It was a study of the economic condition of Korean farmers under the Japanese administration. The research had been done under the auspices of some mission or the YMCA, but it had not been published because the subject was sensitive—it did not favor Japanese colonial policy! I got permission to use it for a popular article and did some observing myself. After returning to the States I submitted it to *Asia*, which published it under the title "Japan and the Korean Farmer." I was paid $75, the first money I earned that way.

Getting back to the States was our next problem. Researching various steamship lines, we decided upon the *Katsuragi* of the Kokusai line, which was supposed to leave Yokohama on September 1, bound for Los Angeles. We prepared our baggage, including a Korean chest we were taking to Beth, and departed a few days after September 1, because the sailing had been delayed. In Tokyo, Mr. Shiratori again assisted us. On September 9 we sailed from Japan, having paid $75 each for the passage. While we debarked in Los Angeles our heavy baggage went on to New York. The Coons met us at the dock and took us to their home for the weekend. We were very eager to learn about the New Deal and economic prospects. Apparently they were looking up a little.

We crossed the continent by train to Kansas City, riding tourist class, and having most of our meals out of a basket that Edna Coons fixed up for us. We only spent $3 for food. Then to St. Louis and southern Indiana. We arrived at the farm before September 28. I had to hurry on to New York to register for Columbia, so went by overnight bus, leaving my train ticket for Kay to use later. Bill and Betty Payne had asked me to stay with them, which I gladly did while getting registered at Columbia and looking for a place where Kay and I could live. I got a room with kitchen privileges, but after Kay arrived we found an ideal apartment back of the Jewish Theological Seminary, close to Columbia, with sitting room and an in-a-door bed, kitchen, bath, and small study. It had reflected sunshine from the windows across the court, and we had to buy furniture, which we did second hand and at the 5 and 10. The apartment cost $40 a month, and we had the right to leave in June instead of the usual October. Kay could leap out of the bed on her side into the kitchen, and I on my side into the little study. That bed determined our sleeping pattern ever after!

How did we finance ourselves? The Wilbur Corporation—Dad's euphemism for family business affairs—sent us $50 a month for nine months, and Mrs. Beaver of Dayton sent a loan of $500, which covered tuition. (By good fortune, I repaid Mrs. Beaver two years later out of the salary of my first job.) There was an account in a Dayton bank that sent us a check now and then, doubtless on Dad's instructions. And soon Kay had some earnings. We kept careful accounts and found we could live on about $125 a month, including rent. Kay fed us for 90 cents a day, a subway ride was a nickel, and we spent almost nothing on clothes.

This would be my second year of formal study at Columbia, and I wanted to make the most of it. I signed up for both Chinese and Japanese language, which was bold, considering my difficulty with foreign languages. The substantive courses were Japanese history with Mr. Tsunoda, a very lovable man devoted to the cause of understanding between Japan and America; anthropology with the famous professor Franz Boas; and the economic history of the ancient Mediterranean world with Professor W. L. Westermann. Boas had had a stroke; his right cheek was paralyzed. What I remember most of his introductory course in anthropology was his refutation of the prevalent idea that race could be equated with ability, particularly mental ability. He devoted much time to that issue. The course under Professor Westermann dealing with the economy of the ancient Near East, Greece, and Rome was fascinating. He was a specialist on ancient slavery. Through his inspiration I settled upon a study of slavery in China as my dissertation topic.

Miss Elizabeth Grimball offered Kay a job as her assistant at the New York School of the Theater, and it proved to be most interesting work. Kay moved into a new world of aspiring actors and modern dance, seen somewhat from the inside. Miss Grimball was a talented teacher, and some of her pupils won fine reputations. Kay worked five days a week from 10 A.M. to 4 P.M., for which she received $40 a month, just what our rent cost. Toward the end of her work, Kay had the opportunity to join in dance lessons given at the school by Kreutzberg, one of the greats of modern dance, and a wonderful opportunity for Kay. It was such strenuous work that after the first couple of days she was sore in every muscle and could barely creep to the subway to go to her job; in fact, I had to make her go.

In a letter to my parents on October 30, I remarked on the sudden death of one of the great Sinologists and ethnologists, Dr. Berthold Laufer of the Field Museum in Chicago, little dreaming that I would succeed him at the museum two years later, though at a much lower level in the hierarchy.

As always, Kay and I had a congenial social life in such spare time as we had. We entertained her sister, Elizabeth, about once a week, also Bill and Betty Payne, and Howard Rymers and his friend, Anna Marie Johnston. Often Howard would drop in on our little apartment, usually after dinner. We also had "Uncle" Fletcher Brockman and some Chinese friends for dinner; the Peakes, C. C. Wang and his lady companion; and much later, Carrington and Anne Goodrich—whom I did not address by first names at that time, he being chairman of my department! Paul and Hazel Harvey returned to New York, disillusioned with the life of an apprentice banker, and of course we entertained them.

Probably at the instigation of C. W. Bishop and Professor Goodrich, and certainly with their support, I applied to the Social Science Research Council for a fellowship for the year 1935–36, to work in Washington at the Smithsonian to learn about museum work, for I had become more and more inclined toward antiquities and ethnology as my field in things Chinese. In February, not yet knowing the results of my application, I made a brief trip to Washington to see Mr. Bishop, call on Dr. Hummel at the Library of Congress, and view the treasures of the Freer Gallery. I didn't then get to meet Dr. Sterling, with whom Mr. Bishop had made arrangements for me to work-study in the U.S. National Museum. In March, however, I learned that the SSRC would grant me a predoctoral fellowship to carry out the program I had outlined. The stipend was $1,600 for the year. Naturally I accepted. That would be the first year I wouldn't be a burden on Dad or his Dayton friends, or be partially dependent on Kay. What a tremendous satisfaction that was!

During my last semester as a graduate student at Columbia, I took classical Chinese with Dr. J. J. L. Duyvendak, a Dutch Sinologue of renown. Finally I got to read in the *Shih chi* and also in the *Han shu,* important historical texts. Later this study was valuable since it was in those two works that I found the basic materials on slavery that I used in my dissertation. I continued in Professor Westermann's course on the economy of the ancient Mediterranean world, and with Mr. Tsunoda on Japanese history and culture. For anthropology I took a course with Professor Ruth Benedict, a handsome and patrician-looking woman, and a splendid teacher. She lectured on the personality-molding quality of culture, a subject she developed in her famous work *Patterns of Culture.* I dropped Japanese. As an exercise in Chinese I translated an article by Liang Ch'i-ch'ao on Chinese slavery. I did a lot of reading for my courses, and also about my dissertation topic. Oral exams for Ph.D. candidates were coming up, and also language exams. Professor Duyvendak passed me in Chinese, but Professor Goodrich found my French deficient, though I thought I could read effectively. I had to give myself a cram course and did eventually pass. My orals came in May, and my examiners were Duyvendak, Goodrich, and Peake. All the reading I had done in Peking and at Columbia stood me in good stead, for it seems I passed with a high mark. Cyrus Peake confided to Kay that the faculty were pleased.

At the end of May we were free to migrate to Washington. In contact with the few China scholars in Washington, we learned that Earl Swisher was leaving and we could rent his apartment for $50 a month, and buy out his furniture for

$50. We had sold off our stuff in New York, so this was ideal. The apartment was only a few blocks from the Library of Congress, near the Supreme Court and the Folger Shakespeare Library. We had one complete floor in a row house.

We had a delightful year in Washington, the most carefree we had ever had. Our stipend covered our needs quite adequately. We explored that lovely city, which was not nearly so built up as it is now. We made new friends. Kay's great aunt, Nan Wiley, the widow of Dr. Harvey Wiley, lived in the fashionable Northwest section, and we visited her. She was an admirable women, one of the great suffragists of her generation, and president of the American Women's Party, either then or earlier. That party advocated complete legal equality between women and men, with no especially favorable treatment for women in any respect. We enjoyed Aunt Nan. Among the Sinological crowd that worked at the Library of Congress on the dictionary of Ch'ing biography under Dr. Hummel we found George Kennedy, whom I had known from high school days. He had come back after college to teach in SAS. We played many evenings of bridge with the Kennedys. I also met Mr. Fang Chao-ying, who we continued to know when he worked at Columbia on the *Dictionary of Ming Biography*, edited by Dr. Goodrich. He was a modest but erudite scholar, as was his wife, Tu Lien-che.

Mother came to Washington in the autumn and rented an apartment near us so she could keep house for Halsey, who was studying for the Foreign Service exams. Of course we saw them constantly. Our guest book shows many dinners with relatives and friends of hers, as well as our own acquaintances.

I enjoyed my work at the U.S. National Museum and absorbed quite a bit about cataloguing, preservation, and exhibiting ethnological specimens. My mentor in the museum was Dr. Judd, who showed me the ropes. A bachelor, he entertained us at the Cosmos Club, a select organization for scientists and other professionals. We entertained him in our $50-a-month apartment. I had a small office in the museum and could visit backstage, the labs, restoration rooms, and storage collections. Becoming interested in the bronze trigger mechanism of Chinese crossbows of the Han period (200 B.C.–A.D. 200), I did a lot of research on that type of weapon. Studying primitive types used in Southeast Asia, the Chinese mechanism, ballistic instruments of Rome, and the most advanced types used in medieval Europe, I came to the conclusion that for its day, the Han dynasty crossbow must have been the most advanced and powerful hand-held weapon anywhere. I wrote a small monograph, *The History of the Crossbow as Illustrated by Specimens in the U.S. National Museum.* This was published in the annual report of the Smithsonian Institution and is still listed in *Books in Print* as a reprint available from the Smithsonian. I also spent some time in the Orientalia Division of the Library of Congress gathering materials for my dissertation and writing one of the biographical entries for *Eminent Chinese of the Ch'ing Period,* edited by Dr. Hummel.

Kay, I remember, had a rather carefree time after five years of constant work for not much pay. She had the ambition to be a writer of fiction, and she did produce the first draft of a novel. She must have abandoned that story, for it is no more. The ambitions stayed with her. As usual, she did a tremendous lot of reading and made a lovely home for us.

Toward the end of our Washington stay we had to look for jobs. I signed up with the University of Chicago Anthropology Department to go on a dig during the summer to learn something about excavating, and Kay got a job as camp counselor for two months in Maine. My work would cost money while hers would earn some. I left Washington about June 15, stopped in Oberlin where I called upon favorite professors, and then went on to Chicago. Mr. Bishop had advised me to go to the Field Museum to apply for a job. Obviously there was a lot of background work done by my friends unbeknownst to me, because when I saw the director of the Field Museum he asked me, "Well, young man. What's up?" I took that as an invitation and replied that I would like a job at the museum. He took it under advisement. I met Mr. Stanley Field, the president of the museum, and Dr. Paul Martin, the chairman of the Anthropology Department.

Somewhat encouraged, I went down to Brookport in southern Illinois where the University of Chicago dig was located. The instructor and man in charge was Thorne Deuel, and there were about ten other men learning how to excavate. Kay didn't keep the letters I wrote her, but I kept hers, so there is a better record of her summer at Camp Pinecliffe for Girls on Crystal Lake, Harrison, Maine, than of mine in southern Illinois. Her letters show that we wrote each other constantly, for we missed one another "fierce." Her camp was good for her. She gained fifteen pounds, learned to swim better—she had never been good at it—and liked the fellow counselors, though not the spoiled little brats in her bunk. I wasn't having nearly so good a time, for we lived in a hot, probably malarial area, spending most of each day very carefully digging in the site of an old Indian village. I learned, however, how meticulous archaeological work must be to preserve a record of each object's location in relation to every other object and within the site itself. If we found a specimen, say a pot or an arrow, we uncovered it with an awl and a duster. Working in the hot sun was not easy. I probably lost weight, though I got very brown and was in good health. Our main recreation was to go across the Ohio River on Saturday nights to Paducah, Kentucky, where we would have wonderful mint juleps before having a proper dinner. Letters from Kay were my chief enjoyment.

Just after the first of August I learned I could have a job at Field Museum as a curator in the Department of Anthropology at the magnificent salary of $2,700 a year. I wrote Kay, and she was delighted, of course. My future was set if I made good. I was to begin work on September 15, 1936.

5

Building a Career,
1936–1939

Field Museum was one of America's outstanding natural history museums. Housed in a handsome Greek revival building overlooking Lake Michigan, the collections were under the charge of four departments—Geology, Botany, Zoology, and Anthropology. The last was my home, and its chief was Dr. Paul Martin, my direct boss. Paul was a really wonderful colleague, perhaps fifteen years older than I, and a specialist on American archaeology. Shortly after I arrived, Clifford C. Gregg became the new director of the museum, but Stanley Field, the president, was the chief policymaker.

My title was assistant curator of Chinese archaeology and ethnology, and I was in charge of the collections that Dr. Berthold Laufer had built up over many years and two expeditions to China long before. My first job was to become acquainted with the collections, mostly Chinese and Tibetan. No one knew in what condition the stored collections were, and I had to find out. A second major job was to go through Dr. Laufer's huge accumulation of notes to see if there was anything publishable. He followed many topics of historical and ethnographical interest, and his interest in mankind was virtually worldwide. He would store away bits of information derived from his extensive reading, putting the scraps in marked envelopes. When invited to present a paper it seems that he would find a subject on which he had collected a lot of data and proceed from there. I had to search those many topical envelopes to see whether there were any manuscripts that could be easily brought to publication. I found that Dr. Laufer had projected a book or a series of monographs on "The American Plant Migration," that is, the spread of plants native to America to other parts of the world, such as tobacco, maize, beans, or the potato. This "migration" had a great impact on Europe and Asia. I found an almost completed manuscript on the so-called Irish potato, which did not take too much effort to bring to publication. During my first year, I prepared that potato manuscript for printing and it was issued as part of the museum's anthropological series. Loads of other work prevented me from bringing out any other of Dr. Laufer's semi-manuscripts.

Another task, eventually, was to improve and modernize the Chinese and Tibetan exhibits. The collections were shown in two large halls on either side of Field Museum's great entrance hall. On one side were archaeological specimens, mostly pottery and porcelain, but also bronze vessels, weapons, and the like. The other hall was divided between Chinese and Tibetan ethnography: clothing, household objects, and costumes and fierce masks on the Tibetan end. But all this was displayed in an old-fashioned way, with labels that were too small to read. Under Paul Martin's inspiration the American ethnological exhibition halls were being modernized with a new conception. Each exhibition case would present a single idea instead of an assemblage of similar artifacts. The single idea might be methods of cultivation, showing Indian women working in a field with stone hoes and a painted background showing a village scene; or it might be weaving techniques. But always attention must be paid to accuracy, without resort to fancy. Labels would be few and easily readable. I hoped to be able to do some of the same type of exhibits.

In my first winter at the museum, Mr. Gregg introduced me to a lady who wanted to be a volunteer—Edna Mandel, the wife of the head of Mandel's Department Store and a very wealthy person. She was interested in China and wanted to do something constructive; she even began to study Chinese with Herrlee Creel at the university. Edna was a little older than I but regarded me as learned; she wanted very much to help in my work, and she certainly did. We slaved together over the collections in the dusty storeroom, bringing things out into the open and cleaning them, cataloguing those that had not been catalogued, and setting up new cabinets built to store things more efficiently. We discovered a large, red-lacquered, canopied Ningpo bed, almost as big as a small room. Dr. Laufer had never been able to exhibit it. Since we would never have space to show it, I persuaded the director to sell it and let me use the money to acquire more useful objects.

There were other jobs I had to learn. The museum received innumerable letters of inquiry, and I had to answer those in my field. Also visitors would come with Oriental objects and ask to have them identified. That I did to the best of my knowledge, but we were not permitted to set a value on these heirlooms because of the risk of suit against the museum. Such work took up too much time. I was supposed to provide publicity stories, when I could think them up, about aspects of the Oriental collections, and I enjoyed doing that. In addition to brief pieces, I wrote eighteen articles for *Field Museum News* during my time there, of which nine were feature stories, each rather novel. Most of them made Chicago's newspapers, too.

Another museum task was to cultivate people of wealth in the hopes they would support the museum financially, and especially make it possible for me to improve and modernize our collections through purchases. There was no chance of undertaking an expedition to China because of the Sino-Japanese War, but opportunities did come up to buy important archaeological specimens from dealers. If our Chinese collections were judged by art standards, they were quite poor, but we weren't an art museum but a scientific one. Dr. Laufer had organized a "Friends of China," which had a membership of well-to-do persons. One of its purposes certainly was to support his work. I was asked to become the secretary of the Friends of China, which meant I had to work up programs to be given at some person's house, and be sure the invitations went out. I gave a speech myself on what could be learned about Chinese life in the Han period through archaeologically excavated materials. Another time I got two Chinese graduate students at the University of Chicago to speak about being a Chinese student in America. One was Tang Tsou, who later joined the faculty of the University of Chicago, and the other was the girl he married. They each got $25, a big sum for them. Dr. Tsou has remained my friend ever since. But I really was not much good at cultivating wealthy Chicagoans. Mr. Kelley of the Chicago Art Institute was far better connected and more skillful than I at that sort of thing.

One wealthy woman, Mrs. George T. Smith, willed to the museum her very fine collection of Chinese carved jades, and it came during my first year. It must have been worth many hundreds of thousands of dollars. It was so valuable that a special workroom was fixed for me with heavy wire grille over doors and windows and only one key, mine. There I studied the collection and Edna and I planned how it should be exhibited. Mr. Stanley Field took a great interest in the plan. He assigned a special room, and the museum bought a large quantity of golden-colored silk to use as the background to show off the pieces, most of which were from the eighteenth century—elaborately carved incense burners, vases, and the like. I had to study the objects in order to write labels, but it was not a subject I knew much about. Dr. Laufer had written the definitive book on the subject, *Jade*. The exhibition when completed was quite spectacular. We had a crowd-catcher.

An exhibit I put up was directed toward the children who visited the museum in droves. It was a display of two Chinese children, dressed in their blue gowns and carrying schoolbooks. Mrs. Stelle in Tung-chow bought the outfits and the school stuff for a boy and a girl, about twelve years old. We had a sculptor at the museum, an artist on relief from the Depression under the Works Progress Administration, and she modeled the figures. Though a small thing, it was a nice stopping point for the guides to show Chicago schoolchildren.

In July 1937 Japan started a new aggression against China, and this time the Chinese government fought back. The two countries were launched on what became a protracted war. Naturally, Kay and I were all for China in that conflict. The newspaper accounts of Japanese atrocities were terrible.

At the end of my first year I was promoted from assistant curator to curator, and my salary was raised to $3,500. Paul Martin was astonished, and Dr. Lewis somehow learned of it, for he told me bitterly that he had worked for twenty-five years in the museum before he received that much. That was embarrassing, but he should have addressed his complaint to the director, not to me. I knew nothing about anyone else's salary. Toward the end of 1937 I was appointed acting chief of the Department of Anthropology when Paul Martin was away. This was a chore and not likely to endear me to long-time members of the Anthropology Department, but I couldn't decline.

I asked permission to take a trip to visit other museums to gain a greater knowledge of Chinese collections, and in October 1938 the museum sent me on a month-long trip. I went first to Detroit, Buffalo, and Toronto (where the great Royal Ontario Museum had a wonderful collection, somewhat like ours); then to Boston, New York, Philadelphia, Washington, and finally Cleveland. At each place I bought pictures to create a file in my office. I made friends with curators and, of course, saw friends and relatives.

On my trip I saw a few most unusual wooden objects in some museums. In Cleveland, for example, the museum had acquired two tall, strikingly painted and lacquered wooden birds. Such objects came from Changsha in central China and were thought to date from the fourth or third century B.C. Their unusualness was due to the fact that Changsha had been the center of a distinct culture, that of the Ch'u state during the Warring States period. Many tombs were found while new airfields were being constructed there, and beautiful objects from them reached the Shanghai dealer market. A dealer named Bensabott brought to the Field Museum a collection of much dried and wrinkled wooden fragments that allegedly came from one Changsha tomb, and it, too, showed traces of lacquer. He had been told that it was some sort of a grille work found within a coffin. Would the museum like to buy that bunch of fragments? First I sent photographs and a sample to a friend at Harvard who had been in Changsha during the time of active tomb robbing, and who confirmed from a study of the lacquer and adhering earth that our pieces probably did come from Changsha. Whether they were worth acquiring depended upon whether the fragments could be restored to something like their original condition. Of course Field Museum had an expert staff of restoration people, but it was a botanist who suggested boiling the fragments in dilute ascetic acid to expand the cells, and then soaking them in glycerine, which settled all through the wood to prevent the cells from collapsing again. That done, our restorer, Mr. T. Ito, carefully fitted the pieces together, forming a perfect grille-like pattern of intertwining wooden ribbons making a grille 68 inches long and 14 inches wide, and tapering slightly at one end. Clearly, it could have been a sort of inner lid to a coffin, and we labeled it so, dating it probably prior to 200 B.C. We exhibited it by itself, and when I visited the museum many years later it was still being displayed.

To show our new acquisition, we emptied a case of bronzes, one of which was of a bear-headed stand that Dr. Laufer had bought in China in 1910. In cleaning it, our technical man uncovered part of an inscription. I asked him to uncover the entire inscription, and discovered that it had a date in the Chinese manner of dating, by an imperial reign period. I knew how to convert such dates, but in this case there were three possibilities. On the basis of style of the decoration, content of the inscription, and opinion of Chinese antiquarians, I settled on the earliest, that is, February 1, A.D. 228. This was just after the end of the Han dynasty, but artistic styles don't change with change of ruling houses, so Dr. Laufer had been correct in dating the stand as Han. But what was the stand for? The answer was in a photograph of a painting I had bought in Boston, which showed T'ang dynasty ladies pressing silk with a brazier with a long handle and with a stand like ours nearby. I also found in a Chinese antiquarian work a picture of such a brazier with its long handle set in a hole of a stand similar to ours. We reexhibited our stand with pictures and its new date, and I wrote an article about it, as well as one about our Changsha grille, for *Field Museum News*. Both stories made the Chicago newspapers.

One nice thing about my job was that scholars in the China field came to see me at the museum. Langdon Warner of the Fogg Museum, with whom I had studied in Columbia, paid me a visit, and Rev. James M. Menzies from the Royal Ontario Museum came to spend a week as our guest, and then went with me to the museum daily, giving me advice and information. Mr. E. G. Hester had made an extensive collection of Chinese celadons in the Philippines. He wanted to place them somewhere, but we were not in a position to buy them. Still, I was interested in the collection and went with him to Ann Arbor to consult a specialist there. Eventually he gave part of the collection to the museum, and we stored the rest. What ultimately happened to the other celadons I can't say; probably he sold them.

All the time I was working on my dissertation, spending two hours each night that I had free. The museum's library was quite good in Chinese books assembled by Dr. Laufer, containing dynastic histories, a number of good Chinese encyclopedias, and books on antiquities. And the nice librarian could borrow books I needed. They even bought for me a Japanese punctuated edition of the *Shih chi.* (Chinese works are not normally punctuated.) I leafed through that book and the *Ch'ien Han shu* (The history of the Former Han dynasty—206 B.C.–A.D. 25) to find every reference I could to slavery. By now I had narrowed my focus to the Han period. I also read Chinese scholarly articles on slavery, and entries on the subject in Chinese encyclopedias. It was slow going. When it came to translating the unpunctuated Chinese historical works I needed help, and I found a graduate student at the University of Chicago, Charles Hu, to help me. Though he was a geography major, he had had a proper Chinese education. I would make the first try at translating, and then he would correct me. Also I had an extensive correspondence with Professor Homer Dubbs at Oxford. He was translating the *History of the Former Han Dynasty* and had to solve many textual and technical problems. His first volume was a big help to me.

Eventually I had accumulated nearly two hundred references to slavery dating from the Former Han dynasty or shortly before and after. Some were only a few words, others fairly long passages in which the context was an important element. They were scattered, almost random, because references to slavery were quite secondary—the historians were not interested in that institution. I found quite a few laws or edicts that pertained to slavery, but no complete law code. In most of my references, the slave was mentioned in connection with the master, or a beautiful slave girl might be taken into the palace, and hence get mentioned and immortalIzed. In the case of a humorous essay I found in an encyclopedia that dealt with the contract for a slave and specified every job he was to do, I had to compare the texts in seven different collections to try to establish the most likely original, since old texts could easily become corrupt before the invention of printing in China. That dissertation was grinding work. What saved me was that Mr. Gregg, on Paul Martin's recommendation, allowed me, as a sort of sabbatical when I had been a curator for quite a few years, to spend two days of museum time a week at my doctoral studies. Furthermore, I was allowed to use one of the Works Progress Administration typists assigned to work at the museum to type the dissertation when I got around actually to writing it. That was a job in itself—to make some coherence out of the scattered material I had gathered and put it in historical context. Of course, there were several drafts before I really was done, and that only with Kay's help to sharpen my style. She thinks my introductory chapter is quite well written.

We had an active social life during our first years in Chicago. Kay had a maid, Hattie, once a week to clean the apartment, which helped. Friends of Uncle Burt and Aunt Anna, John and Mary Wilson, became friends of ours. He was a noted Egyptologist and head of the University of Chicago's Oriental Institute. That was a lovely connection. We also knew Herrlee Creel at the university and his second wife, Lorraine. We also became acquainted with the professor of Oriental art Dr. Ludwig Bachoffer and his wife. They were refugees from nazism and we became rather close. Then there were Mother's friends, Professor Harley F. MacNair and his wife, the poet Florence Ayscough.

Another group of friends we met through Charlie and Margaret Stelle. Dr. William Tucker was from a North China missionary family. Another China connection was with Norton and Mary Lockhard. Of course, we were very close to Charlie and Margaret Stelle, but they went off to Washington at the end of 1937 where he would work on his dissertation.

Because Chicago was a crossroad, we had numerous friends who saw us when passing through. The most delightful and welcome friends were Fred Ficken, back from Oxford and now teaching mathematics at the University of Tennessee, and Jack and Caroline Service, on first furlough from China in December 1938. Oh, what pleasure! Arthur and Edna Coons, and young Arthur, came to see us, as did Cyrus Peake and Carrington Goodrich—we know, because all are in our guest book. Florette Yen, the daughter of Chow Tso-min whom

Kay had tutored for at least a year in Peking, also came through. She married the son of a distinguished Chinese diplomat, W. W. Yen (Yen Hui-ching). Kay and I went to meet her at the railway station, and the Yens were also met by people from the Chinese Consulate. They took Mr. Yen off to do business but gave a car and chauffeur to Florette and Kay, who showed her the sights, and also took her to a couple of department stores to learn about prices.

As always, Kay read a great deal, borrowing books from the neighborhood library, and also worked on a novel—one of the world's lost works. I read a good deal of anthropology, trying to fit myself better into my position in the museum. One summer I took a quick trip out to Paul Martin's dig to see how he did it. The camp was quite comfortable, and the finds not too exciting. Kay and I went often to the Chicago Art Institute, because we were becoming greatly interested in European art, in fact, art from any part of the world. Also we liked contemporary American artists—this was before postwar abstract Impressionism! In a letter to my parents, I named George Bellows, Thomas Benton, Grant Wood, Edward Hopper, and William Gropper as favorites. I didn't even know about American Impressionists or Mary Cassat. I had a long way to go in my art education, and always felt, and feel, that Kay, with her astounding memory, is way ahead of me.

I was being asked to write reviews for such professional journals as *The American Anthropologist, American Historical Review, Pacific Affairs,* and *American Journal of Folklore.* This made me somewhat known in anthropological circles and better known in the Sinological fraternity.

I feel greatly indebted to Field Museum of Natural History. It gave me a job while it was still Depression time. This gave me real security for the first time since I graduated from Oberlin. Also, the promotion and raise after my first year did a lot for my self-confidence. I had kind bosses and believe I could have stayed on as a curator as long as I wished, though things turned out differently.

At the museum I broadened my intellectual interests, and I had time to deepen my knowledge of Chinese antiquity and ancient artifacts. I started a subject card file to record information on many topics, though when I changed my focus to the history of modern China, I had little use for it.

Museum life is quite different from university life. One is more isolated from persons of common professional interests, and one has to be entirely self-motivating. One arranges his one's own schedule. There is no necessity to meet classes at an appointed hour. Yet the relationships within the Anthropology Department of Field Museum were warm and friendly because of Paul Martin's manner of running things.

It was fine to be in a great city with its variety of cultural attractions, and to have enough money to enjoy music and theater. However, we never have been much to eat out; seems to Kay a great waste of money. We had seven years in Chicago, and we remember those years fondly. We were so young, and we could look forward with high hopes.

6

Starting Our Family,
1939–1942

Kay and I wanted to have children, and she was nearly thirty. But did we dare have them in view of her mother's illness? We consulted Dr. Tucker and asked him to get in touch with the doctors at the hospital in New Jersey for their opinion. The answer was ambiguous: one doctor wrote that it would be perfectly safe for us to have children, but the other was not so sure. Bill Tucker advised us to go ahead, and we decided to early in 1939. We were lucky: Kay almost immediately became pregnant. We found a doctor at the Chicago Lying-in Hospital and signed a contract for prenatal care, delivery, and a bit of postnatal care, all for the sum of $75—unbelievable now!

Things did not go well. In a preliminary examination Kay showed a positive 4 in the Khan test. The doctor told her that she need not let her husband know, to which she replied indignantly that he was the first that should know about it, and of course she told me right away. It all came to nothing. Much, much more serious, Kay contracted coreo-meningitis. The hospital gave her the best possible treatment known at that time, but she had frightful headaches, and the sulfa drugs she took gave her deep depression. I tried my best to bring her out of her gloom, and she has often told me how much my encouragement meant to her. She did recover before Johnny came.

Kay's labor pains began at 7:15 P.M. on Friday, October 13, 1939, just as we were cleaning up the evening dishes. "Oh! Oh!" Kay announced. "I've got to go to the hospital." Quickly she packed her small suitcase, while I nervously called a cab. Chicago Lying-in Hospital was only half a mile off, just across the Midway. As the Yellow Cab sped us to the hospital, we both were fearful. Had Kay's coreo-meningitis harmed the fetus? Now it was squirming and kicking, but had the brain been damaged? Would Kay pull through all right?

We were in the hospital a little before eight—the familiar antiseptic smell, the long gleamingly white halls, the efficient admitting nurse and the blue-frocked aide who wheeled Kay to her room. I had only a few minutes to give her love and encouragement until I was led to the husbands' waiting room. The smell of acrid cigarette smoke, the dog-eared magazines, two other men pretending to read, each with a tray full of half-smoked cigarettes. Not much talking among the three of us, all novices at this particular waiting game.

Ages later, at half past twelve, a kind nurse asked if I was Mr. Wilbur.

"Yes. What's up?"

"Your wife has had a lovely baby boy. Mother and baby are both fine. Your wife is sleeping. Come back tomorrow and you can see your son."

I burst from the hospital onto the Midway. A tremendous weight was gone. I gulped the midnight air and shouted, "It's a boy! A fine baby boy!" There was no one there to hear me nor to see me skip across the Midway. Halfway home I did a little dance and turned a double somersault. Then into the empty apartment and my lonely bed.

We named our son John Hollis, after Uncle John and my dad. John was a very good baby and strikingly beautiful. He had a very large head; in fact, it took some weeks before he was strong enough to lift it. Kay nursed him for several months. During his infancy, we always wore masks as we had seen the nurses do. Johnny got fed by the clock, whether he was hungry or sleepy. Kay was meticulous in keeping a record of John's weight each week and other signs of progress. He transformed our lives!

The war in Europe went very badly for the Allied side during 1940. German armies, after invading Norway, Denmark, and Holland, crashed through the Maginot Line, finished the French, and then forced the British to retreat across the English Channel in the heroic evacuation of Dunkirk. Hitler tried to bomb Britain into submission, but failed. The heroic stories of British airmen in shooting down German planes thrilled us. Then Germany invaded Russia, and seemed at first to be victorious on that front too. America was becoming more and more involved under President Roosevelt's policies, such as Lend-Lease. A group of men living near the University of Chicago, led by Professor Paul Douglas, formed a volunteer force, though it only did drilling in anticipation of the possibility that we might get involved in the war. I joined it. Bob Blake, one of our museum friends, was being trained in counterespionage. When he came to dinner one evening he was being shadowed, and his job was to give his shadow the slip, which he did by leaving from the kitchen into the alley.

My dissertation was working its way to a close. I sent most of my translations to Professor Duyvendak in the spring of 1940 for his approval. He made a number of corrections and offered more felicitous renderings of others. Also I think I sent a draft to Professor Goodrich, but he tended merely to be a copy editor. I read all I could about the Former Han period to give my study its proper setting. My first chapter described China's geography and political and class systems at that time, and the second tried to present a workable and precise definition of slavery, and to test the Chinese terms against that definition: in fact, I tried to make the terms prove themselves in their context. Having gotten those preliminaries out of the way, I proceeded to the subject—slavery, beginning with the way persons became slaves in China during my period. I then tackled the question whether prisoners of war were enslaved, which got me into the question of Han warfare. My conclusion was that enslavement of captives in war was probably not extensive. The next chapter had to do with acquisition of slaves through inheritance and through purchase or gift; and on the other hand, manumission of slaves either by individual owners or by the state, for the government owned many slaves. Then I looked at the status of slaves in law and in custom. Next came the question: how many slaves were there in Han times? No real answer was possible, but the evidence I found led me to conclude that slaves were only a small proportion of the population. I then considered the functions of slaves, both privately owned and those owned by the government, under various categories of employment. In my final, synthesizing chapter, I tried to show whether there was evidence of historical development of the institution of slavery over the 225-year period and speculated upon the reason that slavery in the Han period seemed not to have become a key economic institution as it was in ancient Greece. Part II of the dissertation gave the texts and my translations of some 160 documentary evidences I had used.

Our old Peking friend, Clyde Sargent, came through on his way to western China, where I supposed he was going to teach. He had just defended his Columbia dissertation on Wang Mang (the usurper at the end of the Former Han dynasty), so I was filled with curiosity as to what the exam had been like. He reassured me.

I sent my typed dissertation in several copies to Professor Goodrich, probably in February 1941, in order to defend it before the end of the spring term. I asked him whether I might have Professor Westermann and Dr. Karl Wittfogel on the examining committee, along with any others he would appoint. I got the date from Professor Goodrich for a day in late April, and I took off for the East. I remember only a little about the exam: I was at one end of a long table, and Dr. Goodrich, presiding, was at the other end. Examiners were himself, professors Westermann, Peake, and Jeffrey (Near East), and Wittfogel. Westermann seemed delighted, and Peake and Goodrich could find little to criticize. Wittfogel seemed dissatisfied that I hadn't grasped the totality of the Chinese economy, of which he, a Marxist, seemed to consider himself a master. Professor Jeffrey, whom I had never heard of, asked me why I had such a bad style of writing—a really dirty question. I remember Professor Goodrich's nervous laugh. I thought I had quite a good style, and I could only respond that if the style was so bad it was unconsciously so. I assured the examiners that the book would be edited by a very competent editor at Field Museum, because it was to be published as one of the museum's Anthropological Series. The committee voted to pass the dissertation, suggesting only a few revisions.

I sent Kay a special delivery letter and she wrote: "Your special came this morning at 7:30 and we were pleased as punch, John with the envelope and I with the letter. . . . I telephoned Paul [Martin] and he was tickled pink—'The dear old thing, well, well,' was what he said, and he sounded so pleased."

At that time Columbia had the requirement that dissertations must be published before the degree would be given, a very expensive requirement. Also, one must give seventy-five copies to the university. Fortunately, Columbia would accept a contract from a publisher in lieu of the actual book and grant the degree. When I got back to Chicago, I asked Mr. Gregg to sign such a contract. He did so on June 1, 1941, and I was granted the Ph.D. degree on June 3. That was ten years after my graduation from Oberlin and six years after my doctoral orals.

Converting the dissertation to a book was a long process. I spent several months making necessary revisions, some suggested by my readers, Goodrich, Peake, and C. C. Wang. My preface was dated August 1, 1941. The book was finally published early in 1943. Miss Lillian Ross was the editor of F.M. Press and a good friend of ours. She did a fine job. The Chinese characters were a problem. I got a small grant from the American Council of Learned Societies ($300) through my friend Mortimer Graves, with which I could pay George Kennedy at Yale to set the type for all the translations. We also had a small font of Chinese at the museum, and I learned to insert characters into the printed text and index where needed. Our cartographer drew a fine map of Han China. Only I could make the index. There was a lot of proofreading to do. The book of 490 pages became something of a classic in the field of Chinese history, at least in the West. I asked about having the book copyrighted but was told that, according to the museum's concept, our publications were scientific publications and hence should be open to all. My work was not copyrighted therefore, and much later it was pirated.

By now Johnny was talking, and I must mention an amusing incident between us and Mr. Hu, my Chinese friend who had helped me with translating. He was over one time and heard John address me as "Marty-owl." Mr. Hu was shocked and gave us a lecture. We should never allow a person to address a member of the senior generation by his personal name, and absolutely never do so to one's father. That was a gross confusion and disruption of all propriety! However, we American parents like to be intimate with our children.

Two important events in December 1941 transformed our lives. We were listening to a CBS symphony concert on Sunday afternoon, December 7, when an announcer broke in to say that Japanese planes had bombed Pearl Harbor. This act of war meant that America would fight back with all its resources. And soon we were at war with Germany and Italy as well. America and all Americans were profoundly changed by the war.

The second event I announced in the following telegram on December 18: "Good news. Ann Wilbur joined us shortly before midnight, weight six four, cute figure, lots of hair, fine large voice. Kay enthusiastic. Love. Johnny Martin." We were much more relaxed with Ann than we were at first with Johnny. We didn't wear masks, nor feed her each time on the dot of the hour. Kay wasn't able to nurse Ann, so I got the privilege of feeding her the 2 A.M. bottle.

On December 25, 1941, the Japanese easily overran Hong Kong, where Halsey was. He was interned with many other American and British nationals. We had sent him a Christmas present in November, which came back to us nearly a year later. Luckily, by then he was back in the United States.

I wrote a couple of scholarly articles during 1942; one, together with Professor Goodrich, "Additional Notes on Tea," was published in the *Journal of the American Oriental Society*. My translation of the "Contract for a Slave" by Wang Pao, who lived in Szechwan around 60 B.C., mentioned tea, and Professor Goodrich knew of no earlier reference to this Chinese contribution to world culture. So we wrote it up. The other article was published in the *Journal of Economic History* in May 1943, entitled "Industrial Slavery in China during the Former Han Dynasty (206 B.C.–A.D.25)." As do most young Ph.D.s, I was capitalizing on my dissertation.

My dear friend and patron Carl Whiting Bishop died on June 2, 1942. I wrote an obituary notice that was published in the *Far Eastern Quarterly* in February of the next year. Here I quote two passages: "Endowed with a fabulous memory, C. W. Bishop acquired an encyclopedic knowledge of man's culture. With keen analytic ability, rare powers of generalization, and a happy clarity of expression, he was able to extract from this storehouse the essential facts about man's early history and to present them in ordered and highly engaging fashion." And my conclusion: "C. W. Bishop had countless friends. He was kindly, modest, and witty, and generous almost to a fault. Always eager to help younger scholars, he shared freely the knowledge he had acquired through years of study and travel, aided them with their manuscripts, and helped them to become established in their professional fields. Although all who knew him will miss the stimulation of his mind and the warmth of his friendship, death will not end the humanizing influence he brought to studies in the Far Eastern field."

The museum staff began to shrink as one after another joined up. All younger males had to register for the draft, though I, with two children and aged thirty-three, was not immediately liable. I was sounded out whether I would accept a captaincy in a military unit that guarded prisoners of war, but I declined. I was feeling for a job in a highly classified agency in Washington in which Charlie Stelle worked.

The big event of January 1943 was the publication, finally, of my book on slavery in China during the Western Han period. The date was January 15, and the edition was of only 600 copies. I was much relieved to have that out of the way so I could turn to other museum matters, such as renovating the Chinese exhibits, which I was doing slowly.

One series of displays that I am proud of followed the new way of exhibiting pioneered by Paul Martin—that is, to make an exhibit show a single major idea, but simply and attractively. Edna Mandel and I developed one on China's New Stone Age (ca. 3,500–5,000 years ago). It displayed examples of pottery, polished stone tools, woven cloth, and pictures of domestic animals. All labels were in large print, and each started with a verb (e.g., People . . . Lived in villages, grew crops, made pottery). Millard Rogers was a volunteer and had a part in planning the layout. After the war, he became a curator at the Seattle Museum of Fine Art. We introduced color in the background and off-center balance for the specimens shown. Another exhibit showed the difference between two basic neolithic cultures, the Painted Pottery (Yang Shao) and the Black Pottery cultures. A third case showed ten handsome painted pottery vases that the museum acquired. I wrote a long, somewhat technical article about recent discoveries in China that were illuminating its prehistory. As a curator in a scientific museum, I had to keep up as best I could with such developments. *Field Museum News* published my article in the summer of 1943, after I had gone into war work.

Jack Service passed through Chicago in February 1943 on his way from China to Washington and came to the museum for a few hours between trains. He had most discouraging things to say about China—the low spirit of the people, inflation, danger of new civil war, corruption, etc.—all of which I had read about. Mostly, however, in America we heard of the heroic Chinese resistance. This side was exemplified by the visit of Madame Chiang Kai-shek to Chicago in March. She stayed at the swank Drake Hotel, where a reception was held in her honor. Nearly a thousand Chicago dignitaries (including unimportant me) arrived near to 5:00 P.M., when the reception was scheduled. There was an air of expectation among the guests in the grand ballroom. An orchestra sawed away, and there were piles of sandwiches and little cakes. Madame Chiang swept in at 6:30. She was very beautiful, gracious, and obviously strained, and she left soon after arriving. Next day there was an enormous gathering in Soldiers Field, Chicago's great stadium near the lake. There, amid great hoopla, she spoke to an enthusiastic audience. China was still considered our gallant ally, though things were going sour in intergovernmental relations—the reason for Madame Chiang's American tour.

War put a strain on us all. There were shortages and the beginnings of rationing. Someone gave Kay as a special gift a large can of Maxwell House coffee, and she held a coffee-klatch for our friends as a special treat. Prices were rising. We found we had to watch our pennies carefully now that we were feeding and clothing four. Previously we had paid our income tax in one lump, but now we had to pay quarterly. (This was before the withholding tax system, remember.)

On March 21, I wrote as follows:

> It looks as though the Chicago Wilbur family is due for another upheaval. Last night I received a telegram from the Acting Director of Personnel of the Office of Strategic Services in Washington announcing that my appointment had been confirmed, and asking how soon I could report there for work. After consulting with my Director at the Museum tomorrow, I expect to wire that I can begin April 15. If I do, then this family will have one million things to attend to before then. I dread plunging a family of four into Washington in these days, and from all I hear it is simply frightful to find a place to live. From what I have been told of my probable duties—and they are not details but rather general lines—I believe the work will be very interesting and possibly useful toward the war effort. OSS is definitely a war agency, and for a while, at least, I may have the illusion that I am making a direct contribution through the knowledge and training I have. In this respect the work should be a relief after the backwater atmosphere of the Museum. The salary is enough more than we make here so that Kay and I hope to break even on the extra cost of living in Washington, as well as the moving expense, though it is a gamble. The hours are 48 a week, but I am told that anyone who gets away with as little as that is practically on vacation. So I can give much less time to my family than I am able to now. Kay rebuts by saying that at least I can be with my family, rather than off at sea or some camp, as would be the case in the Army or Navy. But oh! "the battle of Washington!" . . . By next Sunday we should be far advanced into utter confusion.

I left for Washington about the first of April. I didn't realize that this was my farewell to Field Museum and most of my friends there.

Washington was just as bad as reputed in the matter of housing. The war was already twenty-two months underway, and all the services headquartered there, as well as the new wartime agencies, had grown and grown. In the two weeks before I had to report for duty, I searched everywhere for a place for our family to live. Finally I found a house in Cabin John, a small village west of the city on the Potomac, and telegraphed to Kay. We could move in on May 15.

7

War Work, 1943–1945

The Office of Strategic Services was created by William "Wild Bill" Donovan with the approval of President Roosevelt to carry out war work that no other agencies were prepared to do. Its work was secret, and all employees had to undergo a careful security check. It was a compartmentalized organization, with one "Branch" not permitted to know about the work of other branches. There were Secret Operations, Secret Intelligence, Morale Operation, and Research and Analysis, and probably others as well. OSS had some remarkable successes and cost a lot of money.

The Research and Analysis Branch was staffed by scholars, and most were specialists on foreign countries, except the economists, who consider themselves universalists. When I reported for duty, R&A was headed by Professor William L. Langer, a historian from Harvard and the author of a great work on *The Diplomacy of Imperialism*. There were several regional divisions under him, and I was to be in the Far East Division, which included India as well as Japan, China, and Southeast Asia. The head of our division was Carl F. Remer, but he was soon replaced by Charles Fahs, a Japan specialist. Within the division there were sections, and the one I was in was China—Political. Charlie Stelle was head of it, and it was he who had engineered my appointment. At first I worked in the new Library of Congress Annex, and my assignment was to follow political developments in wartime China, on the basis of all the information coming in through State Department reports, news accounts, OSS, and other sources. I had to have a security clearance to see items marked secret. Charlie asked me to read *China's Destiny*, attributed to Chiang Kai-shek, probably ghosted, which was published in Chungking on March 10, 1943, and of which a copy in Chinese had been flown to us. After reading it, I should present written and verbal reports.

Charlie thought it would be a good thing to show the folks that we had some linguistic skills.

Our division of OSS had a remarkable crew of scholars, among the best Asianists in the nation, and there weren't too many of them before the war. There was Norman Brown of Pennsylvania, the great Indianist, and Cora DuBois, an anthropologist who had done her field work in the Dutch Indies. Later she was a professor at Harvard. George McCune was one of the few scholars specializing on Korea. Ken Wells was a former missionary in Thailand with a scholarly bent. Evelyn Colbert worked on Japan and became an authority on Japanese labor problems. Others working on China were Derk Bodde of Penn and Ed Kracke, Jr., of Chicago. John Cady was our Burma specialist, later the author of several books on British rule in Burma and on Southeast Asia. Later I recruited John DeFrancis into R&A. Arthur Hersey, Phil Trezise, and Joe Yager worked on the Japanese economy; all later became well known, Arthur in the Federal Reserve Board, and Phil and Joe in the State Department and both ambassadors, later with Brookings. Three of us became presidents of the Association for Asian Studies—Norman, Cora, and I. Kay and I became lasting friends with many of these scholars and with their wives.

I made my report on *China's Destiny* at an early morning briefing at which generals and top brass of OSS were brought up to date. I didn't enjoy reading that book, so nationalistic and so conservative, but I tried to report it straight. Later I was asked to give briefings several times a week on war developments in eastern Asia, really meaning Japan. Most of my up-to-the-minute information actually came from fine-print details in the *New York Times*, which presumably got much of the information from army or navy dispatches. Our division also got out a weekly digest of intelligence, classified secret, since we used secret materials. Later this bulletin led to a tragedy, which I shall explain at the proper time. When I moved up in responsibility, I hired an editor to help with that intelligence digest, but mostly with strategic intelligence papers we issued. Just to give an example, Derk Bodde did a long study of Japanese penetration into Mongolia and Sinkiang. It later became a book. In fact, a number of our studies have been resurrected and either published, such as Evelyn Colbert's work, or become the basis for other books. The R&A files are now declassified and open in the U.S. National Archives.

The house I had rented in Cabin John, which we occupied in May 1943, was a two-story frame house. We had to buy a washing machine, but the rest of our furniture was shipped from Chicago. You got to our house by street car. We entertained new scholar friends from the OSS, and a Chinese anthropologist whom we had met in Chicago, Fei Hsiao-tung, who is still a lion in his field and now a showpiece in the PRC—after having been badly mistreated during the Cultural Revolution. Professor Fei was much offended at the behavior of American GIs in China. George Cressey, Paul's older brother and the well-known geographer of China, had dinner with us on his way to Chungking.

A terrible thing happened one night. Kay was cooking dinner, and I was giving the kids a bath upstairs. I left the room to get a towel and came back just in time to see Johnny up on the window sill with the screen open, then to see him tumble out. I shouted, "My God, Kay, Johnny's fallen out the window!" Then I rushed downstairs and out through the kitchen. Kay and I found John on the ground with his head quite bloody, but he moved, thank the Lord. He had gashed his forehead on a metal hose connection. We carried him up to a bed and called the police, who came quite promptly. Kay phoned a doctor, and he had an ambulance take John to a hospital. We sat outside the operating room and finally heard the surgeon say, "Now John, you're going to be all right." What a relief!

After that brush with death, from which John still carries the scar on his forehead, we wanted to get out of that house. The memory was too painful, and we didn't like our landlord. An opportunity came to go into Park Fairfax, a new development in Alexandria. We rented a duplex apartment with two bedrooms, bath, living room, and kitchen. The rent was $75 a month. It was ideal for us, and the kids soon found playmates. Since we didn't have a car, and probably couldn't get ration tickets for gas anyway, we had to depend on buses for Washington. Kay and some other ladies started a cooperative nursery school, held in a friendly church, and took turns as teachers. John attended, and then Ann when she got old enough.

We saw Sid Willis in uniform as a major, looking very handsome, and Doak Barnett a young lieutenant in the marines. John Wilson visited us, too, and we saw Johnny Davies. He had parachuted into the Burma jungle as part of an operation behind Japanese lines. Washington was full of our friends, such as Herlee Creel and Eddie Reischauer, both involved in secret work.

Soon the war in Europe turned in our favor. American air power devastated German cities. OSS had a hand in picking targets through the work of R&A, which analyzed the German economy's strategic vulnerability. American arms and other war equipment began to reach Russia in large amounts, and the Russian Army relentlessly drove the Germans out of its western regions. The Normandy landing on June 6, 1944 created the long-awaited second front. But there was a great deal of bitter fighting ahead.

The war in the Pacific was going our way, with the continuing destruction of the Japanese fleet and the systematic sinking of Japanese merchant vessels. We read of the situation in nonoccupied China as reported by such correspondents as Brooks Atkinson, Arch Steele, and Tillman Durdin—accounts of inflation, war weariness and corruption; but also of America's efforts in flying in supplies and training Chinese Nationalist troops for combat. As Japan grew weaker, the Chinese Red Army began to operate behind Japanese lines, and we got reports of their success. I felt we must follow these claims systematically, and I assigned one of the analysts to map where the Communist forces were operating. That mapping became valuable as the war began to turn in favor of the Chinese side and it seemed more and more likely that the country might fall into civil war.

We remember the shock at the death of President Roosevelt on April 12, 1945, and our feeling that Truman could never hold his own with Stalin and Churchill. But he did. The war was coming to an end in Europe, but Japan had still not been defeated. I wanted very much to get sent to China, and I started agitating for that. Charlie Stelle had long since been sent there, as had several others of my old China friends.

Early in May 1945 I was assigned to go to San Francisco to be on hand when the conference to found the United Nations took place. It was a very interesting trip, and I enjoyed San Francisco greatly, though I stayed in a cheap hotel, rooming with another R&A person, Jim Pott. Pete Edson was also in San Francisco, reporting on the creation of the United Nations. The Chinese delegation to the UN conference included Tung Pi-wu, a veteran revolutionary and a Communist, and a couple of his assistants. I saw them and Dr. Wu I-fang and Dr. T. Z. Koo, friends of my parents. I interviewed them all and reported their opinions, but I really don't think my contribution was worth my being sent. My transportation and room were paid for, but I had to pay my other expenses, which was hard on our bank account until I got reimbursed. Kay's letters show her anxiety.

I quote one written shortly before I returned. The family had been invited out to dinner: "It really was providential because I simply was down to the last bite except potatoes and bacon, and as it is I'll be able just to squeeze by until Thursday when surely our check will be in the bank. We're still going to have to watch our Ps and Qs after you get home, for out of $195, I have rent, 75, your check is 40, the rest of the Hecht bill, 45.10, Ann's teeth, 20. Total 180.10. Ten to live on for a week! And you know it takes forever for the Gov to reimburse you. Besides the 6 per diem will not, as I see it cover your expenses 31 x 6 = 186." Actually, I don't think we got on easy street financially until our children were out of college.

I worked very long at the office, for the work seemed important. I didn't have much time for the children, but Saturday afternoons and Sundays I was with my family. Sunday mornings I took the kids for our "early morning walk" so Kay could have a longer sleep. We took trips into Washington to a park or the zoo, or a boat ride on the Potomac to Mt. Vernon. Sunday afternoons we often made popcorn, which the kids adored.

Unfortunately, we neglected our guest book, and the only other entry for Washington shows Jack and Caroline Service and their Virginia and Bob, duly signed on June 24, 1945. Jack had returned in April to report to the State Department; he had spent several months in the Yenan area with the Dixie Mission, sent to investigate the war potential of the Chinese Communists.

About the time of Jack's return, Ken Wells, our Thailand expert at OSS, showed me that the magazine *Amerasia*, edited by Philip Jaffe, had lifted one of his reports in our weekly digest, which was supposed to be secret. I reported this to Bill Langer, my chief, and heard no more until Bill Donovan called me to his office with an obscure warning to be careful, which I didn't at all understand. Then on June 6, 1945, the morning radio announced that Jack Service, Jaffe, and others had been arrested.

At that time, Caroline wasn't yet in Washington. We telegraphed her that we would do everything possible to help Jack. His brother's wife phoned me to ask for help. I found out what jail Jack was in and went there to see if there was anything I could do. I bought Jack a couple of packs of cigarettes, but I was kept in a waiting room and not allowed to see him. After about two hours I was called to report to Bill Langer. When I saw Bill, I explained the long relationship between Jack's father and my father, that we were the closest of friends, and that Jack had named a son partially after me. Bill phoned someone, perhaps a security officer or maybe Bill Donovan, and I remember his saying that you can't just laugh off a lifetime friendship.

Writing only from my side, what had happened was that my report on *Amerasia*'s pirating of Ken Wells's article led OSS operatives to raid the offices of that magazine, where they found many State Department documents as well as other secret materials. After this illegal entry the matter was turned over to the FBI. Among incriminating papers were carbon copies of some of Jack's dispatches from China that he had lent to Jaffe. According to Jack, one of his jobs in China had been to brief the press, and he sometimes allowed American correspondents to see his dispatches as background. He had done the same after coming to Washington, in this case to Philip Jaffe. Thus, my report led to Jack's arrest!

However, Jack was released from that jail and was to appear before a grand jury, which should find whether there was a case against him. Two months later the grand jury voted unanimously not to indict Jack, and the State Department reinstated him. It was during this period that Cary brought the family to Washington, and so to come for dinner with us. I saw a great deal of Jack during his time of troubles, and I think he appreciated it, because some of his other friends tried to steer clear.

I was most eager to be sent to China, where R&A had an outpost. I began my applications early in 1945, but decisions took a long time. Finally I was told that I must go to a center outside Washington to be evaluated. I believe OSS pioneered this system of checking up on people before sending them overseas on dangerous assignments, in order to avoid discovering psychological problem cases in the field. The evaluation was an interesting experience. On arrival, all the men were given identical fatigues to wear, and each was given a nickname by which he was to be known. Thus we were all on a common ground of anonymity. We were given certain group tasks to do, and observers saw how we related to each other, who was quick to solve a problem or to take leadership, and so on. Each also had an individual interview with a psychiatrist after filling out a personal evaluation form. I remember one striking thing the psychiatrist said in reference to what I had written in the form about my father. He described

Dad as "having a compulsion to goodness." That struck me as quite correct. Of course, I never saw the psychiatrist's evaluation. Those were kept secret, and I believe later were destroyed, though of course the personnel office or some higher-ups got to see them. However, I must have passed, if that is the right term.

The processing for my departure went on. I was given money to buy officer's uniforms, though I was to be a "technical representative" with the nominal rank of lieutenant colonel. But departure orders did not come. As I think back upon my desire to go to China, I realize that I could not have understood what a burden it would put on Kay. She was a wonderful supporter and understander of my wish, yet I know her heart sank at the thought of a long separation.

We were given a strange assignment in the Far Eastern Division of R&A. I can only remember the general question approximately: Do we have to do what we are planning to do? As Ed Kracke pointed out, since we didn't know what we were planning to do, it was not easy to answer the questions. But our division was in the habit of writing up appraisals of how well Japan was holding out, and when she might collapse. We were not Order of Battle experts, but everyone seemed to believe that Japan still had strong forces on the main islands and that they would fight tenaciously in defense of the homeland. It was commonly predicted that an invasion would cost at least half a million American lives. My brother, by the way, was in the Fifth Marine Division, which would be part of that assault.

We didn't have to wait long to discover what the plan against Japan was—the dropping of an atomic bomb. The first was dropped on Hiroshima on August 6, 1945, and the second on Nagasaki on the 9th. Japan surrendered on August 14.

Our family was on a one-week vacation when surrender took place. We were at an Episcopal Church retreat in the Virginia hills, with woods all around, and good meals for the kids. Finally I was scheduled to go to China, and still wanted to very much, but I feared that Japan's defeat would end that hope. And sure enough, I received a telegram in our vacation place that my trip was canceled. But I decided to pull such strings as I could to get it back on again. When I got back to Washington, I learned that my trip was on again.

8

Back in China, 1945–1946

On Friday, September 7, 1945, Ed Kracke drove our family to the railway station to see me off. I was starting on a long trip to China. I wrote to Kay almost every other day, and she kept my letters.

On the train to New York, I wrote Kay a love letter, with this closing message: "The biggest thing you must do for me is to keep yourself in health, in youth, and in good cheer, so when I see you again we will pick up precisely where we left off on the happy married life." I did get to phone Kay and the kids twice from New York while waiting to be listed for flight. I was lucky enough to get on a flight on Saturday night, heading for Gander, Newfoundland, and then to Africa.

It was a C–54 transport plane, and all the other passengers were in uniform. It was a very smooth night flight. Sunday we were over the Atlantic bound for Casablanca. Here are a couple of descriptions:

> The high spot was about three minutes flying over one of the Azores where we looked down on closely cultivated farm land in little patterns like a quilt, with arbors and orchards tucked in, and wandering roads lined here and there with houses to make small farm villages. It had the neatness and intensive use of land one associates only with the Old World and Orient.
>
> Casablanca is a city in which a French veneer has been laid over the Arab-Moroccan culture. All buildings are white, all homes are behind low walls, the shop signs and street names are in French, about 5 percent of the population is European, and most of the rest appear to be Arabs. The latter dress in flowing wool robes, formless and uninteresting, and their whole tempo is slow. The town is fairly clean, very provincial in appearance, and traffic of bicycles, cars, charcoal-burning autos, buses, trackless tram cars, carriages, and native carts is very nonchalant about traffic rules. . . . We went on a

conducted tour of the native quarter which was not very pleasant, but interesting. Most of us were basically disgusted, though those who had never been out of the United States were doubtless more impressed than those of us who had.

I remember that after we had seen an exhibition by a nude young woman, we were hooted through the narrow streets by many long-robed and veiled women and children, who tried to pinch our bottoms and in other ways annoy us. What can a bunch of GIs do under such a situation except flee? Although we were held for several days in Casablanca, I didn't want any more of the native quarter. I wrote on September 12:

> Still waiting. The prevailing note of this camp is waiting. Everyone is waiting either to get on a plane for home or to a new station. Even the base itself seems to be waiting for all the transient traffic to end so it can fold up and go home. There are men here from Persia, from China, from Italy and France, or from farther east or south in Africa. They keep pouring in, waiting, and then disappearing. Everyone waits for the metallic sound of the public address system, because the first news of flights and lists of passenger comes out over it—"Attention, attention all eastbound passengers. The following passengers will report at the airport at 1700 hours—at 1700 hours, for flight number zero eight three, zero eight three, eastward. . . . That's all." Click.
>
> Meals in army posts run to heavy food and puddings, with very little salads and soups. They say eating gets progressively poorer eastward. Maybe I'll need those vitamins they gave me at the office. But what I will need more is some of your lovely meals. You may not think they are so wonderful, but Johnny and I always do.

Then on September 13 I wrote, "Just a hasty word of love to you and the kids from Cairo. I'm in and out in an hour. The delta is marvelous. Had a most beautiful ride from Casablanca here, stopping at Tripoli; flying along the Med coast—turquoise and gold—and along the route where 8th Army drove Rommel back from El Alamein. Wonderful." And again:

> I am now in India. The flight from Casablanca to here was marvelous, especially the turquoise sea, the fairyland delta of the Nile, with its patchwork quilt of green fields, brown arterial canals carrying the precious life-blood of water, and the towns and villages, brown clusters of close-crowding houses scattered across the landscape like dice tossed carelessly by some mighty gambler. No space stolen from the green fields, no waste in parks, courtyards, wide streets, no houses straggling out into the fields. In some you see minarets and mosques. You cross the brown, winding Nile with its white-sailed Egyptian boats leaning in the breeze. On the east side you begin to see clumps of date palms, which I hadn't seen on the west; why, I don't know.
>
> After an hour at the Cairo airport we sailed on across a desert as wild as any I have seen in movies or pictures, with great curling sand dunes whose ridges had been piled by the wind into knifelike edges weaving across the scene like the rippled sand of a beach. We flew across the Suez Canal, and on to Pales-

tine, where we circled Bethlehem and Jerusalem, where we saw the enterprise of the modern Jewish state in modern buildings and other things mixed in with old synagogues, mosques, and Christian churches. It was just sundown, with the whole sky bright with color; then darkness as we crossed the Dead Sea, and on across Trans-Jordan, Arabia, Iraq, to Abadan on the Persian Gulf, where we had an hour. It was morning when we came down at Karachi, in a fine modern terminal.

Here I got a cool room, a shave, a bath, a long nap, some drinks at the officers' club, good food, and decided to spend the night so I could fly on to Calcutta across India in the daytime.

On September 17 I wrote from Calcutta, where I was destined to be held up awaiting "hump" passage:

The flight from Karachi to here was a wonderful experience. It is across India from N.W. to S.E. You get a marvelous idea of the kind of country India is if you watch and observe. The morning was across the great Sind desert, which didn't look so much like a desert at this time of year at the end of the rainy season. There were considerable signs of life, though obviously a very hard life. I could deduce a great deal by observing the kind of settlements, the relation between houses and water—they weren't related, which showed the pools were bitter—the nature of fields, or rather, pasturage. About noon we came to Agra. By then the country looked richer but was still not very populous—the villages were widely scattered, and the fields were still quite large. We flew in over the city past the beautiful Taj Mahal—a most marvelous thing from the air; and also past a great Mogul castle of red brick or stone with a double wall, the higher and inner one resting on the shoulder of the outer one. Inside were extensive grounds and a palace. After lunch we flew around the Taj so that we saw it from the river side—its main white building with lovely dome, and the four minarets contrasting against the red platform on which they were built. I wondered if the architect had ever imagined his building would someday be seen from the air. If he believed in angels perhaps he did. Across central India we ran onto the flat, rich, rice-growing plains of the Ganges valley, with green fields stretching to the horizon, and the villages deep in trees dotting the landscape in every direction. We also sailed over mountains fairly well forested, with rice fields terraced up the valleys, but not nearly so expertly and daringly done as in China. As we approached Calcutta the landscape became even more watery and green, and the towns showed a new characteristic: they were universally built around the sides of one or more large rectangular ponds which, with the large trees, were the outstanding feature of each settlement. Calcutta from the air was quite ugly—a sprawling, black city with clouds of coal smoke drifting over from nearby steel works.

I've listened on this trip to more American airmen and soldiers, mostly officers, complaining and bemoaning their lot, than I ever heard in one period of my life. This mood of "bitching" is almost pathologic and is recognized as such by some guys who are determined to have none of it (I've only talked to two such). It's apparently the result of home-sickness, fatigue, and frustration. Many of the men have been here two and a half years and are completely fed up. They all want to go home, and that they can't is the basic gripe, but mostly they "bitch off" about the inefficiency and waste and foolishness of the army. They delight in spilling out long stories as examples. There is no doubt a hell of a lot of truth in their observations, and it all adds up to quite an indictment, but none of them see a broad picture—they see the fragments of a picture which just doesn't make sense. . . . Their basic grievance is being away from home so that for most the return home will solve most of the unhappiness. Anyway, darling, I hope I don't catch the sickness.

Because I seemed to be tied down in Calcutta, which has a horrible climate, I used my time to study Chinese and to write letters to each child and a long one to Kay. This latter was sealed and only to be read in case I should be killed, or after my return when we were together. It is too intimate to reproduce here, but I tried to tell the kids, then under six and under four, what sort of a man their dad had been, what his background was, what his ideals were for them as they grew up. And I told Kay that if I should not come back, and she wanted to marry again— but only to the absolutely right guy for her and the kids—she should go ahead with my full understanding. Why these gloomy thoughts, I'm not quite sure, but maybe because flying the "hump" was thought to be dangerous.

Mails were irregular. Kay got my letters much out of sequence. The letters to each child, mailed at the same time, arrived ten days apart. Knowing that I had written to each, Kay held back Ann's letter till John's arrived. That was perfectly in keeping with her even-handed treatment of the children, and her clear understanding of the psychological situation. A wonderful mother, I'm convinced.

In Calcutta Charlie Stelle found me in the officers' club. He had been waiting for nearly a month for ship passage from Calcutta home! With luck he would be back to the States in another month. "There is a terrific backlog, and army red tape grinds slowly." We didn't have too long to talk because Charlie was sort of AWOL from his camp. But I gathered that he and Margaret were washed up.

Finally I got my clearance to fly over the hump from abominable Calcutta to Kunming. On September 25, 1945, I wrote Kay, ecstatically:

Here I am two days in China. . . . I was called at 6:30 in the morning to fly on the 9 A.M. "Trojan" to Kunming. . . . The flight was quite far south, not really the "hump" at all. If you look at a map you'll see we flew almost straight east from Calcutta across the top of the Bay of Bengal to Lashio in Burma, Szemao in southwest Yunnan, from there across Chihhu Lake, and then straight north to Kunming. The country over which we flew was interesting because we were going across mountain chains and rivers that run north to south. The landscape would change rapidly from cultivated river bottoms to quite wild mountains, with hill tribes' villages in clearings perched high up on the hillsides. When we got over Yunnan we really began to see terraced rice fields such as India or northern Burma knew nothing of. Marvelous! And it shows how the Chinese population has pushed itself just as far as it could go before being turned back by the wilderness of mountains and hostile hill tribes and the alien Burmese.

The rivers we crossed are for the book—the mouths of the Ganges, the Bramaputra, the Chindwin, the Salween, the Shuili, the Mekong, and the Red River—I'm giving this from memory without a map; but believe its substantially correct. Up north where the rivers are really close together and the ranges of mountains high, the "hump" must be a colossal trip.

We arrived in Kunming about 3:30, having gained an hour and a half, so our flying time was five hours. It was a beautiful thing to come in over the large Kunming lake, with its mountains on the west, and spreading out into flatlands of flooded rice fields, with diked canals leading through them, a road on each side, and villages spread along the banks of the canals. When we came down onto the field, there was a crowd of blue-clad coolies pulling a roller just like you've seen in the pictures of building the airfields! Also peasants working their fields with their blue jackets and huge broad-brimmed straw hats. I called OSS from the field and someone promised to come out in a jeep for me, and in half an hour Phil Trezise, of whom I had heard a great deal, and who I knew slightly, was there. I drove back through Kunming drinking in the sights. The streets were packed with Chinese, and what a contrast with Calcutta—the people are energetic, virile, full of good humor and noise and purpose. It isn't just the fortunate climate; the basic difference is cultural. The Chinese are like the people from here up to Manchuria, a race that is struggling to live; there is nothing passive about it. To read the shop signs, to see the familiar sights so very much like those of the streets outside Ch'ien Men in Peking, after ten years, was quite an experience.

After settling down, I persuaded Phil to take a walk with me—it was Sunday afternoon—and out we went where we could really mingle and look the streets over. We found chestnuts being roasted in the broad iron kettle, with the man turning the coal dust and the chestnut over and over with his shovel. It reminded me of walks we took in Peking, and also of Sunday afternoon in Washington and popcorn. We saw boys whipping cotton to make it fluffy for pillows and mattresses, the vendors of fried crullers, wine shops and stalls, restaurants, teahouses, and here and there a "modern" department store. Kunming is surprisingly like Peking on a smaller and more crowded scale. I found, however, I didn't understand much of what was being said around me.

I've been stuck right in the OSS Compound getting oriented, meeting people, and sizing up the problem. Its going to be a mighty stiff problem. I'm to run the Reports and Research section, the guts of the Intelligence Division, i.e., Joe Spencer's R&A plus some of Secret Intelligence, and I came the day after the cables from Washington announcing the abolition of OSS and the transfer to State of R&A Branch, and other cables closing out R&A in China by the end of December, and another countermanding that. We hardly know where we stand. Furthermore, Theater has decided we are not to move our headquarters to Shanghai. There is great bewilderment and poor morale in our people; all the best ones who have been here a year or more are going home or have gone, and the newer ones, though very eager to work, are provided no leadership by Joe, who is passive under the situation and eager to turn everything over to me and go. I'm to provide leadership, drive, and get at least two months of top-notch work out of these people who want to do a job but don't know what it should be. All this was quite a shock, as you can guess, and somewhat disheartening, but it does put me on my mettle.

The staff I was supposed to lead and invigorate numbered thirty-five persons. I was then thirty-seven years old.

A big disappointment upon my arrival in Kunming was not to find any mail from Kay, though I was sure she had written. It was just a case of poor APO. Later many letters came, some written right after my departure.

I thought it wise to go to Chungking to call on the American acting ambassador, because R&A was now to be under the State Department, and I needed to know how to operate in that situation. He had no better idea than I did, so I cabled my policy to Bill Langer: that R&A should (a) stay in China as long as possible, to do quality work in this important period; (b) stay close to the rest of OSS for communications and administrative assistance; and (c) concentrate efforts in four key places—Peking, Shanghai, Kunming (as the OSS base), and Chungking. I envisaged an integral intelligence-research operation to serve R&A in Washington, not one divided up among embassy and consulates in China.

Here is a description that I wrote Kay on September 29, 1945:

> Chungking, which I've only been able to observe superficially, is a very different city from Kunming: there are two wonderful rivers which come together here, with marvelous views up and down their courses between very high banks. The city is sprawled all over the cliffs between them so that everything is cramped in the habitable spots and sparse elsewhere. . . . The streets are even more bustling than those in Kunming, and there is a greater spread between laborers struggling under vast loads, farmer folk, small tradesmen and merchants, well-gowned modern girls—ah, these Chinese girls are lovely!—and wealthy folk in fine cars.

Among the friends I saw in Chungking were George and Agnes Greene, Rosamund Frame, Knight Biggerstaff, and Lyman Hoover, our Y friend from Peking days. I had a long talk with Bill Holland, who headed the work of the Office of War Information in Chungking, to learn of their experience in being brought under the State Department two weeks before. We concluded it made little difference to their work.

I got my first letter from Kay on October 1, three weeks after I had left Washington. That was the fault of the Army Postal Service, not of Kay! Oh joy! Now I was retied to my loved ones. In answer, I told her that I drove my first jeep that day. It had been used by Joe Spencer, who had now departed for Stateside. "I just got in, started it up, and drove it downtown to the compound where we work. Naturally I drove very carefully because traffic moves on the left—when it takes any ordered route! I didn't feel like running over a child or a pig on my first trip."

Generalissimo Chiang Kai-shek pulled a coup against the warlord who controlled Yunnan, and who had sent three of his best divisions into Indo-China, which China was to control down to the 16th parallel until a final decision had been made about the future of that French colony.

I described events to Kay on October 3:

This morning we were awakened by sounds of rifle and mortar fire, rather spo-
radic, but enough to let it be known that some sort of a general upset [was under
way] because it came from many different parts of town. The word was that
"The Revolution" had started. People said that with considerable solemnity
and conviction, but didn't seem to know who was revolting. It was just The
Revolution. The radio gave no information, except to break in about every
fifteen minutes to read an announcement from Major General Ormand confining all American military personnel to their quarters during the period of
emergency . . . and establishing curfew from 8:00 P.M. to 6:00 A.M. Later the
word was that the Generalissimo had deposed General Lung of all his com-
mands and governorship and had the troops here to put it into effect. It was
expected to be about over by nightfall. Lung and his wife are said already to
have been taken into custody. Some of our boys who came in from the country
say there is a big show of military power, artillery banging away or cluttering
the roads, roadblocks in intersections in town.

Next day I wrote:

This morning there was a squad of central government troops patrolling
around our neighborhood, going through the motions of being on the alert,
forbidding all civilian movement, and occasionally doing a bit of show-off by
shooting their rifles. We saw them arrest and tie up two men in civilian clothes
who looked perfectly innocent—but who can say? They knocked their heads
on the ground and were led away. At noon it was announced that resistance
had ended, so after lunch we headed down to HQ to do a little work. The
streets were beginning to come cautiously back to life, but most of the shops
were still boarded up. There was still lots of central government troops scattered along the roads and clustered at all bridges and street corners. Machine
guns were mounted at intersections, but no sandbag emplacements or any
tanks or artillery, which we had been told were out. There was considerable
fighting and casualties, but we didn't see any of it. A little more fighting broke
out in the afternoon, so we came back as a convoy of six jeeps. Things were a
little more tense in the city, but again we saw no sign of any resistance. We
hope tomorrow it will all be over.

Clyde Sargent, our old friend from Peking days, walked into my office on
October 4. He had recently been in Sian. He hoped to continue in China for
some time still, though he had been there already for nearly two years. He was
working for OSS. I wrote: "I guess he doesn't love his family as much as I do
mine. I'd like to see them all again quite soon."

A couple of days later I wrote Kay: "The latest news with us is that in about
ten days we will be moving to Shanghai after all. This is really good news for there
is no doubt that Kunming is a backwater even though it is a lovely place for
climate and mountains. . . . I had a swell cable from Langer today in response to
mine from Chungking, quite approving my general policy. And yet to me there
seems still some uncertainty as to whether the State Department will in fact give

orders or we will be somewhat on our own. Until I hear otherwise, however, I shall go ahead and act independently." I was really set up by the prospect of returning to Shanghai after being away for eighteen years.

I saw Professor Fei Hsiao-t'ung, my anthropologist friend from Chicago and Washington times. He was on the faculty of Lien-ta, the Associated Universities from Peking, which had spent the war years on a common campus in Kunming. Faculty and students had been isolated for several days because of the coup against Lung Yun. Professor Fei took a very serious view of the situation, regarding it as the beginning of civil war in China, and that this use of force would put all other military leaders on their guard against Chiang and make the Communists even more suspicious. He looked on it as a reversion to the "dark ages" of military feudalism. He seemed distraught. In any case, he was fearful for the personal liberty of liberals in Yunnan, whom Lung Yun, for all his corruption, protected.

Phil Sprouse, the American consul in Kunming, invited me to dinner. We had the honor of having Philip Martin Service named for us. The other guests were professors Ch'ien Tuan-sheng and Chang Hsi-jou, political scientist on the Lien-ta faculty, and a few others for a swell homeside meal. I heard more outspoken criticism of the "dictator" than I had yet heard in China.

I was now getting letters from Kay in bunches. In one she expressed apprehension lest I somehow get involved in a career that would make China our home, with the United States as a place to visit. I assured her that I much preferred to have my home in America, with the Orient a place to visit. I also described to Kay some little dramas I witnessed in a walk in the commercial section of Kunming:

> In one section there were a lot of coffin shops, with carpenters busy making those massive wooden coffins of joined timbers. The eye-catcher was one scene—a little coffin shop with a partially completed coffin on sawhorses nearly filling the place. The top, bottom, and ends of the coffin were in place, but one side was out, and there stretched out comfortably was the carpenter sound asleep in the coffin! I watched a farmer about thirty years old, with a son about twelve, both in their clean clothes but their huge, flat, big-toed feet still plastered with mud, as they stood before the counter of a shop that sold ceremonial requisites, and bargained for paper cut-outs and a string of firecrackers. It was for some ceremony and they figured what they would need to do it right. They wanted to buy a pair of dipped tallow candles, but apparently even the smallest seemed too expensive. Finally, they had their selection, a small roll of red cut-outs and posters, and a string and a half of small firecrackers, and the father pulled out of his inside vest pocket a couple of wads of paper currency. He and the son counted out the agreed sum—the shopkeeper had figured it on his abacus—and walked off with their treasures, still hankering for those two candles. I talked with some men in a cigarette shop who had on the counter a flat basket with a pile of grasshoppers which a farmer woman was selling from their store. The grasshoppers had been treated in some fash-

ion and were to eat. I watched farmers selling live chickens, which they weighed head down on their balance scale; and salt being sold in large circular disks or cakes, crude gray-colored salt; and saw huge bags of beans being measured out in truncated-pyramidal shaped measures that took two men to lift. There were seal cutters—an old man and his apprentice carefully chiseling out Chinese seals of wood; and pewter, brass, and tin smiths making tea pots, basins, and other household articles. Really, the sights of a city like this are entrancing.

A few days later I described a trip to the mountains west of Kunming:

I went with two other fellows in my (!) jeep. West Mountain forms one edge of Kunming's lake, and it is quite a large mountain with a cliff that comes down to the blue-green waters. It was a lovely sunny day and the pilgrimage was apparently the bright idea of most of Kunming that had transportation. But it didn't matter, the view from the lake, with the city and the distant mountains to the east, was well worth the twenty-mile bouncy ride and the crowds. The Chinese, naturally, had built a temple on the cliffs with walks carved in the cliff face, some of them even tunneled through the rocks on the edge. Aside from that outing, I've done little beside work at the office and take some stuff home at night.

 . . . Tonight we went out to dinner—the *we* is not imperial, it was Otto Anderson and I—at the home of Dr. Chiang Mon-lin, but given by Professor Ch'ien Tuan-sheng, whom I had met at Hot Springs [at an international conference of the Institute of Pacific Relations, probably in 1944]. . . . The party was for ten people, including Phil Sprouse, a Professor Ch'en, an economist from Nankai [could this have been Professor Franklin Ho, who became my fast friend later on?], a professor of Chinese literature named Yang, I believe, a professor of the law school whose name I don't remember, and Dr. Chang Hsi-jou. The house was quite attractive, with several courts, and it backs up against the home of ex-Governor Lung Yun. The meal was brought in from a restaurant, I think, because it was rather cold, but all the dishes were very tasty, starting with four cold dishes—century duck eggs, bacon, meat rolls stuffed with peanuts and shrimp, and sliced meat loaf. Then came egg and cabbage soup, roast chicken, a fish, and two vegetable dishes, and finally a sweet soup with sweet potatoes. We also drank two bottles of very good yellow wine which Mrs. Chiang fished out of a storeroom. After dinner there was a lot of gossiping about campus personalities and local and national politics, with the usual bitter remarks I've heard quite a bit of among Kunming intellectuals.

When copying the above account from a letter to Kay, I wondered how academics could afford such a fine Chinese party under conditions of postwar inflation. Dr. Chiang Mon-lin, in whose home it was given, later wrote an autobiography, *Tides from the West*, published by Yale University Press in 1947 in cooperation with the China Institute of Pacific Relations, of which Dr. Chiang had been chairman. He had his doctorate from Columbia. With the defeat of the

Nationalists and their flight to Taiwan, Dr. Chiang cast his lot with them. He became chairman of the Joint Commission on Rural Reconstruction (JCRR), which did much to plan the land reform and the improvement of agriculture in Taiwan. When Kay and I were there on sabbatical leave in 1961–62, Dr. Chiang was most cordial and helpful to us.

Dr. Ch'ien Tuan-sheng came to America in 1947 for a year's stay at Harvard, where he had done his graduate work. Living in the home of John and Wilma Fairbank, he wrote an influential book, *The Government and Politics of China*, published in 1950 by Harvard University Press under the auspices of the International Secretariat of the IPR. Bill Holland and John Fairbank arranged this. The preface is dated September 1, 1948. The book is hostile to the Kuomintang and its national government. Professor Ch'ien stayed in China after the Nationalists' defeat, but life turned out to be difficult for him during the "Anti-Rightist Campaign" of 1957–58. Thus my two acquaintances were split apart by "Liberation"— the fate of so many of China's Westernized leaders from 1950 onward. Both men have long since departed this earth.

On October 22, 1945, I wrote Kay that I was now back in Shanghai after eighteen years.

The trip down here was more than half at night so we didn't see much of the eastern part of China from the air. To get here from Kunming we flew first to Chungking and had supper at the airfield. That part of the trip I had been over twice before, but there were new sights because we had cloudless flying weather. . . . The plowed fields outside Kunming were a dusty-rose color, the fields in crops were gray-green or pale yellow, the hillsides were a dark red dotted with green of trees. The pattern showed fields backing up into the valleys and spreading everywhere across the plains, with villages either strung along canals or hugging the edge of the plains. Then as we crossed the range that makes the border of Szechwan we saw a new and probably unusual situation for China—a pattern of settlement in which most people do not live in agricultural villages but in separate, rather large farm houses presumably each in the center of its own land. The houses were substantial, mostly built in a U-shape, sometimes enclosed all around by a wall, but the buildings stand around a court which seems to be the threshing floor. Some were large enough for several families; sometimes there were twin establishments, equally imposing, which may represent homes of brothers. Usually the houses were up on hillsides with the open side looking down on the fields below. These must be the homes of landlords, who possibly have their land worked by hired labor. It was an interesting sight to travel for many miles of the approach to Chungking over this pattern so different from the rest of China.

It was dark when we left Chungking, but there was a full moon so we could make out the general landscape without the details. We flew about direct east, and were supposed to pass over Hankow, though we never saw it. We did cross the Yangtze several times at great intervals: it didn't look so very wide, but we were high above it because the country was very mountainous. Finally we hit a great expanse of water with many mountainous islands. It stretched on and on, and we guessed by our time that it was Lake T'ai. Shortly after we reached the east side we went over a lighted city, and were told it was Soochow, so we knew our guess on the lake was right, and also that we would soon be over Shanghai. . . . Suddenly the blazing lights of Shanghai appeared. We were quite low by now, and we could even see a car or two moving in the streets. . . . We sailed across the city to the Bund, turned down river and saw many craft lying in the stream, including one brightly lighted Red Cross ship and another ablaze like a Christmas tree, which may have been a gambling ship. We proceeded down to the mouth of the Whangpu where it joins the Yangtze at Woosung—I used to go down there on an hour's train ride as a boy for hunting—then wheeled west again and came down on the airfield at 10:30 [local time]. We were soon removed from the plane—we had had it practically to ourselves—30 OSS persons, and were brought by car to the Cathay Mansions for billets.

I was terribly exhilarated to be back in Shanghai, but it took some time to become reoriented. The streets seemed narrow, and what I used to think of as large department stores—"Sincere" and "Wing On"— now seemed only small town marts. Soon after arrival I went to a Chinese antique store and bought some eighteenth-century porcelains, which we still have, and a reddish pot from Kansu, which may have been Neolithic. The receipt shows that I paid CNC $17,100, which came to U.S. $16.28. CNC means Chinese National Currency. The returning National Government had imposed its currency on the formerly occupied areas at a confiscatory rate. I enjoyed that visit to a dealer, and wrote Field Museum asking if they wished to send me some money to buy antiques for them. I could mail things back by Army Post.

Bob Chin appeared in Shanghai. He was American born of Chinese ancestry, and had a Ph.D. in psychology. When he was drafted, OSS snapped him up and he was assigned to R&A when I was head of the political section of the Far East Division, so we were well acquainted. He was soon sent out to China where he did testing work with Chinese commandos and officers of the 5th Army. His observations on Chinese personality structure were fascinating. Bob also had been in contact with the Communist New Fourth Army in the territory north of Shanghai, and with a Tai Li man he knew—Tai Li being the head of Chiang's most important secret service. As I wrote Kay, a curious thing was that, "whereas in America he was rather retiring, here he is an aggressive American boy who tells the Chinese off, deals briskly with rickshaw men or coolies, and shows himself generally as a positive, decisive personality. But he is a smart boy—sees nuances, shrewd on personality, up on the gossip, thoughtful in evaluating reports—all in all a great guy to have working for me. He makes me a little nervous, though, because I wonder if he's pulling me to pieces, I mean analytically in his mind."

In a letter to Kay after I had been in Shanghai for about a week I wrote:

Yesterday I lived in Dad and Mother's world, going in the morning to the Community Church, having lunch with Lyman Hoover in the YMCA apartments, meeting friends of the family. The church service was really lovely, with a choir of twenty-two, of whom half were Chinese. The service was conducted with solemnity, and very smoothly, and about 60 percent of the attendance was Chinese, with the Western group of many nationalities and quite a few service men and women.

Lyman Hoover approached me to ask if I would join the Y and work in China, but I had to decline that proposal because I lacked the Christian faith that should be required for one to dedicate himself to Y work. I greatly respected my father's occupation, and admired him and most of his colleagues, but it couldn't be for me.

Many of the Westerners had been interned during the war and had only recently been liberated. Some could not yet recover their homes. I looked up Mr. Boynton, an old colleague of Dad's, who also had been principal of the American School. His son Charles was a chum of mine, but had died. I was able to bring the Boyntons some stuff from the PX. On another occasion, when a roommate was leaving for the States and didn't want to take back some personal things he had acquired, I grabbed it before the room boy could and took it to Mrs. Boynton: two huge cans of fruit juice, at least twenty bars of soap, shaving cream, razor blades, face powder, toilet paper, some medicines, and various other American things—absolutely new—which were almost impossible to buy on the market, and way beyond the Boyntons' means since they had no U.S. salary.

I also called upon Mr. K. Z. Loh at the Chinese YMCA, by invitation, as I had a letter to him from Dad. As I wrote Dad, he greeted me warmly and sent his love to Uncle Hollis, We had a long talk and a pleasant Chinese tea. Mr. Loh told me how they held off the Japanese attempts to take over the Y by "playing with them"—that is, by stalling and tricking them. They were greatly helped by a Japanese Christian named Matsumoto, and writing this now, I believe he is the person who became head of International House in Japan, and a friend of ours. According to Mr. Loh, they never received money from the principal puppets, Wang Ching-wei and Chou Fu-hai, though both offered to contribute. While they had a somewhat difficult time financially, they made out because they had broad middle-class support. They now had 12,000 members, Mr. Loh told me.

Later, I had the opportunity to meet Mr. Loh's sons, one of whom later came to the University of Chicago for graduate work. He came via Pasadena, where Dad helped him to adjust to American life. Later still, he got a teaching job in New Jersey, and Pichon P. Y. Loh and I became close friends. He is a specialist on Chiang Kai-shek, and I have encouraged him in his scholarship. We have been to conferences together both in Taiwan and the PRC. Such are personal bonds in China.

In the same letter to Dad and Mother I wrote, "Shanghai is a terribly expensive place for the residents. No one should come out from the States with a salary other than in U.S. currency. . . . Meals are not much under stateside prices. Nevertheless, it is exciting to be here, and I wish you could be back."

I was invited to a Chinese dinner given by a General Mao, who had been a "guerrilla leader" near Shanghai, it was said. It was a command affair for OSS officers, and very stiff. Lots of talk of Sino-American friendship and U.S. aid. Then OSS gave a return dinner which I had to attend also. More speeches that you needed a shovel to clean up after. OSS had a relationship with Tai Li's outfit, but it was very hush-hush. Later one learned that it was conducted by a Navy captain, "Mary" Miles, and was primarily an anti-Communist undertaking.

Our status was most uncertain. Supposedly R&A was to be brought into the State Department to be its research arm, but was each field office to be under the local consulate? Or was R&A to be a separate unit doing its own analysis and reporting back to Washington? We were in the dark. I went to see the local consul general, whose name I have forgotten, inviting him come and see our office and learn more of our type of work. He did come by appointment, and it was a farce because all the guys were at their desks looking very self-conscious, and it gave an impression of a lot of army men without much to do. I made a mistake to have the visit so staged.

We had morale problems among the R&A staff in Shanghai. There was a report that staff members in Washington were being hired individually and selectively by the State Department, and that enlisted men were being discharged and hired. This was disastrous to morale, creating a huge drive by each individual to get back to the States and settle his own future. Yet my instructions from Langer were that we continue "for some time to come," and continue being directed from R&A Washington. This made me wonder whether the field was being used as a pawn to help sell R&A as a unit into State, but that the battle was being lost and that our men would be the goats of the play. "I naturally am going to stick here until the issue is settled and every one of our guys is properly attended to or returned to the States," I wrote Kay on November 3. "In the meantime I hope we can plow ahead doing a worthwhile job."

The American Embassy in Chungking became preemptive about part of our work in Chungking. It was out of line for them to do so, according to orders they had received from State Department and we had received from Langer, but the matter was political, that is, we had to live with the State Department, and the Chungking embassy's recommendations might influence State Department's attitude toward R&A work in China. So I reported the whole thing to Langer and cabled Len Meeker in Chungking to play the most friendly game possible, and quoted him cables from Langer which were our orders. "Such is my life. It's left me riled up all day, but naturally it will be all over in a couple of days or a week."

On another Sunday I went to the Community Church and heard a young Chinese minister preach. He was the Rev. K. H. Ting. About three years later he and his wife were in New York, and we entertained them. He was a liberal, and reportedly he supported the cause of the People's Liberation Army. While he was visiting Canada, this got him into trouble with American immigration authorities—actually, the State Department, for Immigration does not act alone on political cases—and he was being denied reentry to the States. His wife appealed to us for help and we did what we could, which certainly was not much. Union Theological had much more clout. Eventually K. H. Ting did return, but the affair didn't enhance his appreciation of the United States. I make this digression because Rev. Ting, under the Chinese People's Republic, was permitted to head the only Protestant Theological Seminary allowed to continue, and became a sort of showpiece for visiting Christians from abroad. He was both a patriot and a man of integrity, and endured the difficult years for Chinese Christians. Now he is highly respected in the West, and presumably in China too, where there is a revival of Christian faith.

That same Sunday, Mrs. James Chuan, wife of the person who had acted as go-between for Kay's job in Peking as teacher to the daughter and daughter-in-law of Chou Tso-min, invited me to lunch. We had a very good but simple Chinese meal, the pièce de résistance being *chiaotzu*. Thus, eleven years after we left Peking, a relationship was reestablished. Interestingly, the Chuan family, Christians, were closely connected to Professor Carrington Goodrich, and at the Goodriches' sixtieth anniversary party, held in Riverdale, several of the Chuan family attended, as they had participated in the wedding in Peking as little girls.

I arranged for Len Meeker, Bob Chin, and me to go to Peking for a think session about the broad trends in China. Len, a lawyer by training, came from Chungking, and the three of us flew to Peking where OSS had a hostel. By a snafu I missed the plane that Len and Bob took and had to come next day. My week in Peking, where Kay and I had honeymooned, was the high point of this China tour. OSS had the use of the Chinese mansion that belonged to a younger son of the great viceroy, Chang Chih-tung, one of the Empress Dowager's last advisers. It was located in the East City, about five alleys north of the former College of Chinese Studies, near the Four Eastern Arches (Tung Ssu Pai-lou). Mme. Chang was the hostess. It was a fine Chinese house of many courts, with red pillars and painted beams, lattices, chrysanthemums and pines growing in jars, long corridors and side houses—a veritable maze but comfortable and charming.

Later, I read that Mrs. Chang was arrested in Shanghai as a collaborator with the Japanese. I bet she had to pay a lot of bribes, and I was sure she had been so nice to the OSS contingent in hopes of American help.

I wrote to Kay,

> Peiping takes a long time to get into, I find, and it requires a sense of repose and leisure in order really to get started. Or perhaps it's just myself and my infernal tendency to withdraw from the outer world and from meeting and

cultivating new people and new opportunities, but rather clinging to my home, my office, my past associates, and not participating very much in the world around me. I wonder if this is the way I seem to other people—people of discernment—or whether my tendency to introspection, self-doubting, etc. simply makes me feel defective on this score. And I wonder if it's possible for one to change himself slowly, or whether the mold is pretty well fixed early in life. . . . I started this off as a hymn to Peiping and here I am brooding about myself. That's so silly. But you know I do feel so very much alone here in China—surrounded as I am by friends—without my precious wife, so that my letters to you are a touch of companionship that I greatly need.

We three men were in Peking for a special purpose: to write a summation of our views of the China situation three months after the end of the war. I don't remember the details of the report, which presumably is in the R&A files in Washington, but it was carefully considered and debated among us. Since it principally concerned relations between the CCP and the KMT, we thought it was suitable to be seen by the president and the secretary of state. It was recommended to General Marshall by three important channels. General Wedemeyer complimented Len Meeker on it.

After our return to Shanghai, I wrote Kay:

We had a very good flight down with a perfectly marvelous view of the city [Peking] from the air. We circled the city and there it all was, a huge oblong, the evenly spaced gates, the glistening yellow roofs in the square of the Forbidden City, the string of lakes to its west with the White Dagoba, Prospect Hill and beyond, the Drum and Bell Towers, the green roofs of PUMC, the Temple of Heaven and the bright white disc of the Altar, the old walls north of the city, perfectly apparent from the air, the fringing northern screen of the purple colored Western Hills, the Grand Canal leading east, and the railways spreading out in all directions from Peiping—all set on a perfectly flat plain simply dotted with tributary towns and villages between Peiping and Tientsin. It was one of the most stirring things I've ever seen. We shall do it together sometime. What a thrill we both will get.

In Shanghai I found quite a situation at the office. A letter had come from Colonel James to our military, which showed a clear discrimination between military in Washington and those in the field, to the disadvantage of the latter. The men were fairly wild and George Greene, who was acting for me, had a hell of a time. He was glad to have me back and quit as of the next day. So I had some morale-building to do, and another cable to send off. Changes in the rules on men in the theater getting sent back to the States put some of them at risk of being snatched for extended work in the regular army, which put them in a funk.

However, in a few days a cable came from Washington, telling us to send our military back by the fastest available transportation. The boys were all delighted, but I had a problem to get the guys cleared and still get their jobs done, and then get them onto the boats. Fortunately, I had two excellent navy lieutenants, who helped with the closedown. After all were gone, we would be only seven civilians. The big question in Washington still was whether Congress would approve a budget by July. I wrote to Kay, "If the office is to continue, I fear I'm stuck for a while, several months at least. But believe me, if I find we are passed around to various consuls to use as their handy-men, I'll ask to be called back for consultation, or resign." As for the military, "keeping them here was damn unhealthy and I'm glad for all concerned that their future has been settled. How they hate army life!" This meant the loss of Bob Chin and some other fine analysts.

It was cold in Shanghai during December, and there was a shortage of heating coal. George Greene, who rejoined the National City Bank, bought a ton of hard coal for U.S. $350.00, and stored it on his balcony, safe from thieves. We wore all the warm clothes we had. It was tough on those missionaries who had returned or stayed on after their liberation from internment. One nice thing: I could get American candy from the Army PX, and could pass it out to families with kids. Such a treat to them and to me!

I had my fill of the U.S. Army. One problem was to protect our enlisted men from being grabbed by other units before they could get shipped home. Here is what I wrote on December 7, 1945.

> Boy, am I fed up with the Army—from observing it, I mean. It's the most undemocratic outfit, with all kinds of incompetency in the officer ranks—which hides behind its rank and prerogatives and has it easy—and ill-treatment of the EM ranks; and there are all kinds of waste and bitching and loafing. I have a low opinion of the competency of the average officer and their average civilian background, and believe that a person even moderately conscientious and efficient, with a fair amount of nerve, ought to be a whirlwind in this outfit.

Shanghai began to bore me, and I was eager to get home. As I wrote two weeks before Christmas,

> Darling, please don't fear that I'm content to be away from my family. This whole trip has been entirely temporary for me. I've at no time felt settled or at ease, never even felt unpacked. And I want to get home very, very much. I want a period with us alone, either at home or on vacation together. I want you and me to try to think out our life from now on, both personal and career, and try to lay out a strategy which will get us what we want out of life, and then bang it through. No one will look out for us. We've got to promote our own happiness.

One problem was that neither of us had much money just then or knew how much we were supposed to get from the Government. By moving to Shanghai I was no longer in a "hardship post," though it was much more expensive than in Kunming. Because R&A was to be moved into the State Department, we apparently fell under a different bureaucracy for fiscal matters, and paychecks were delayed. Then because I was no longer under the wing of the army, I was made to move out of our quarters, and we set up a bachelor system at the home of Norwood Allman. However, I was able to send Kay a money order for $150 shortly before Christmas, and hoped it would get there on time.

Because of uncertainties about our real status under the State Department, I decided to fly to Chungking to consult with the chargé d'affaires, Walter Robertson, and establish as good a rapport with him as possible. For I had learned that the embassy personnel were jealous of our existence and of our independence during the past few months while we were, in theory, under the department. We wrote reports and sent them in without their scrutiny; used our own codes and had our own pouches. Some of the Foreign Service Officers considered the situation "intolerable." It was not a healthy situation.

There were other problems: The army—or at least some local colonels—no longer wanted any responsibility for civilian tech reps, and the other half of OSS wanted no more responsibility for R&A. I delegated certain major tasks: Lincoln Bloomfield to be in charge of getting all outstanding reports cleaned up and sent before our military men left for home; a naval lieutenant, Franklin Schaffner, responsible to get the enlisted men actually to and through Port of Embarkation; and Mr. Hogan to take over all billeting and similar problems. "But all seemingly insoluble problems came to me. They are solved eventually. I was particularly worried about Len Meeker, because I had consented to his going to Kalgan from Peking to study the situation and the intentions of the Communists. After two weeks he failed to come out, so I feared he had been detained by the Reds or arrested by Tai Li's secret police. But he did come out with a valuable report.

I took a lot of satisfaction in a report I had made that showed the intelligence materials we had sent back to R&A Washington in the two and a half months since I had taken over on October 1. We had sent back eighty reports, of which twenty-seven were well-rounded analyses of particular subjects, and also sent fourteen intelligence cables on topics requested by Washington. Our map people had collected and sent back some 6,000 different maps from China, and the book-collecting unit had sent back some 4,000 free China, puppet, and Japanese publications, and had an estimated forty mail sacks of other publications to be processed. Eventually, this printed material went to the Library of Congress.

In Chungking, Robertson was cordial and we had a friendly talk, and I believed that if he had his way, our problems could be worked out all right. "But it is abundantly clear from the attitude of the Foreign Service personnel whom I met at the embassy (Robertson is not one of them) that they are snooty, scornful and resentful. Perhaps I would be, too, if I were in their position, but it's not an atmosphere I would work in, and I'm not asking for a job." Otherwise, my two days in Chungking were agreeable. I met a number of interesting people, and had dinner with Knight Biggerstaff and Camilla, who had Dr. and Mrs. Wu Wen-tsao as the other guests. He is a sociologist on the Yenching faculty, who now worked for his government. Everyone was much concerned about the developing hostility between the government and the Communists. Knight had considerable respect for the recently resigned ambassador, Hurley, and said he really slaved to try to bring about a compromise between the two sides.

Later, I telegraphed to Mr. Robertson at the embassy, advising him of Meeker's trip and suggesting that he have Meeker report to General Marshall when he arrived. This did happen, and Marshall commended Lt. Meeker on his information.

I began to wonder about my next job. The museum didn't attract me after the excitement of the war work and my growing interest in contemporary affairs. I wrote Kay that I doubted that I would want to make Chicago our home, but if I were to live there—God forbid!—that I supposed the University would be all right, except that I wouldn't want to work under Herrlee Creel. Subsequent letters often brought up the question of what we should do next.

I wondered whether, when I got back to Washington, I'd be offered a job in the State Department and at what salary. "I'd like the offer," I told Kay, "so I could use it as a bargaining chip, in shopping for another job," for in my mood as of then, I really didn't want to work in the department. Yet, I was then making $7,175 a year, far more than the museum held out as salary on my return there, which I remember as being $4,200.

On New Year's Eve I sent my last cable to William Langer, the R&A chief, using our own code, attended the wedding of one of our men, a Korean American lieutenant, and after the reception piled Lincoln Bloomfield and Franklin Schaffner (my right and left hands) onto a truck for the airport, because they were flying home. Bob Chin had already sailed, taking along the material for Kay's new fur coat. I urged Kay to try to see them after their return because they were swell guys. Then I picked up our secretary, Ann Goodpasture, to take her to a New Year's Eve party being put on by the Kunming OSS contingent to spend away their bar profits. Ann, too, was bucking to return Stateside.

An interesting thing happened on January 1. Traffic changed from going on the left—the British system—to passing on the right—the American way. Everyone predicted absolute chaos, but somehow, because of lots of advance preparation, it went off smoothly, and ever since then China has had traffic going on the right side of the street, except maybe in rural areas where no pattern exists at all.

A Christmas box from Kay finally reached me, having gone first to Kunming, then to Shanghai but quickly sent to Peking, and then back to where I actually was. The package had a lot of useful things, but the very best was some new pictures of the kids to go with my treasured picture of Kay. Everyone admired the pictures, and I put them on a stand by my bed so I could look at them first thing when I woke up. We still have those lovely pictures of John and Ann, aged six and four, grinning happily and somewhat shyly. Kay wrote that John was doing well at his school, and the teachers were pleased with him. Ann, not yet four when Kay wrote, was beginning to read.

I received a nice letter from the acting chargé of our embassy in Chungking,

Smyth. He seemed impressed with the report I had written on our outpost's activities between October 1 and December 31. He also said some nice things about Len Meeker's visit to Chungking where he reported to General Marshall. I had copies made and sent the original to Langer. The guy who signed it (Knight Biggerstaff may have written it, I speculated) had been quite cool and formal toward me in Chungking, "so I took the honey with some vinegar, Chinese style."

In mid-February, after hearing from Morrison and Fahs, who had been most derelict in not writing me before, I reluctantly agreed to stay till mid-May in order to assist in a transition. As I wrote Kay in a later letter, I am an organization man, just like my dad, with loyalty to a group. That's the way it was with Field Museum, and as it was to be later in my attachment to Columbia's East Asian Institute. But my agreement to stay on another three months meant more isolation and hard work for Kay with the kids. The winter had not been easy.

I acquired a two-room apartment together with another chap, and a cook-boy recommended by the Boynton's cook. To Kay:

> The apartment faces south, and being so high, it has a fine view. The living room looks rather bare because it has no curtains and no pictures, but it has a rug, a sofa and matching easy chair, a dining room table, which we have placed by two big windows so we can look out while eating. There is some other miscellaneous furniture, all of which belongs to someone who left in haste when the war ended. If he is a neutral he will doubtless someday show up and claim it, and then we will be reduced to almost nothing. But he may be a collaborator. Funny feeling to be using stuff of some ghostly owner. . . . Our cook, whom we call Lao K'o, does very well in a small space of the narrow kitchen, which has an electric refrigerator and stove, sink and cupboard, and his chair. There is also a bedroom in which are the ghostly owner's bed and an army cot, two dressers, one of which has a drawer missing—probably used as a box to carry off valuables—and a big chair too disreputable for the living room. Chauncy and I copped it from the hall where some neighbor had pushed it in scornful rejection. There is a bathroom which has an odd phenomenon for this city—hot water! Because the Hamilton House is taken over by the Army we have hot water, made with Navy fuel oil. Thus does the army, navy, and consulate conspire. . . . I sleep in a sleeping bag, so I took the cot, while Chauncy uses the bed, which appears to have been an in-a-door in some previous mutation. The spark of life in our bedroom is the pictures on my dresser of you and the kids. Lovely picture, my joy and consolation.

I did begin to have guests, mostly Chinese acquaintances, but also some of the European friends I had made, and also some of those friends of my parents, who had been so thoughtful in inviting me to their homes. Shanghai became more familiar. I have always found great interest in foreign places and how the folks do things. I wrote Kay:

Yesterday morning I took a walk along the river front, seeing the line of cruisers and destroyers silhouetted in the early morning sun; the junks, tugs, and small sampans respectively sailing, plowing, or scampering about on the brown river; people out on the tide flats hastily picking up small sea creatures for food; coolies unloading firewood and charcoal from junks drawn up on the shore and stacking it onto rubber-tired carts for delivery about the city. It's quite a lively scene, but still has that early-morning calmness and matter-of-factness that's different from the more frantic mid-day bustle that reminds one of ants scrambling wildly over some choice morsel of fallen food. This city is an amazingly crowded and jostling place, and people must queue up in long lines for busses, for eating, and for movies. In fact, each morning when I go to the office there is a long line—a block long—waiting for the telegraph office to open. Even at 7:00 A.M. yesterday the line-up was already there.

One of those vivid scenes that sticks in the memory: I was standing on a bridge over Soochow Creek, and there was a vendor of sugar cane squatting on the sidewalk in the sun, his basket beside him, a rather tall, deep basket with stalks of sugar cane arranged in a sort of inverted cone. Safely tucked in the basket, enjoying the sunshine but protected from tumbling out by the cane stalks, was the man's baby, probably less than a year old, and having a hell of a gay time! Lovely scene. Usually I see at least one bright scene a day.

Field Museum sent me $2,500 to purchase specimens. There was no letter, as the money was sent by cable to the National City Bank. This made me nervous, because I was not allowed to set up a bank account except in Chinese currency and dared not convert the money because Chinese currency was depreciating daily; but I certainly couldn't keep that amount of American currency on hand. I kept U.S. $500 and let the bank hold the rest for me in their vault. George Greene was helpful in this. But what was the propriety, as a State Department employee or as a tech rep in the army, of my purchasing specimens for an American museum and using APO to send them back? "Since it's purely 'philanthropic,' I'm just going to be quiet about it and go ahead." I planned to keep meticulous accounts and receipts, and asked Kay to keep mum about my operations. What I didn't consider was the propriety of buying antiques and shipping them out of China.

My first purchases for the museum were some thirty-five items, mostly bronze weapons, but one Han lacquer bowl, and two early mortuary figurines of wood, painted, and two small Scythian bronzes, one of which I thought would come out quite nicely when cleaned. This took care of the initial $500, and I planned to spend the rest only on high-quality stuff. But prices were climbing constantly because of the fall in the value of Chinese currency. Every dealer really wanted American dollars, which was what I had. Before I left China, I sent three packages of purchases to Kay to forward to the museum.

Practically the last of the R&A civilian group had departed when Ann Goodpasture sailed back to the States in late February. I gave her a letter for Kay, whom she promised to go and see. Now I was practically alone except for several Chinese who gathered information from the Chinese press and journals. Minta Chow translated articles, and I edited her product. In this situation, I thought often of my dad, how he spent long months separated from the family when we were children in Shanghai and he in Japan. How awfully lonely he must have been. And Dad didn't have as many other interests as I did to absorb his spare time. And also I thought of Mother, who, like Kay, had the responsibility of the family to herself. Dad's passion for writing letters was his way of filling the void. I found myself in the same predicament. Some days I wrote two letters to Kay. But due to poor mail service her letters came weeks late, mixed in sequence, and so did mine to her.

An Austrian couple lent me some curtains, and I deduced that they were looking for the security of friends in the very precarious position they were in under the "protection" of the Chinese Foreign Affairs Board, or whoever it was who looked after Austrians and Jews and Koreans in Shanghai. "Really, Chinese official incompetency and graft make me retch! The point I want to make is that when it comes to a pinch you surely need to have friends who will stand behind you and help, and you have to be willing to help your friends when they are in a spot. How profound!"

> At the age of 37, still full of starry-eyed naivete, I begin to comprehend the very great importance of politics in any plans one has, either personal or institutional. How innocently I was raised by two other-worldly parents! So far, such achievements as I've made seem to me to have been through friendly connections, willingness to work a little harder, and a fairly warm disposition; but I'm far from satisfied with achievement. However, I hardly know how to go about playing politics. Would you, Kay?
>
> Do you suppose that during the next half of our lives we could do some really first-class job both professionally and domestically? I mean achieve national importance and recognition in some field, and also have a rich and happy private life? I'd like our second half to be a very satisfying one. But I really don't know exactly what we need to do in either line. Don't think me too grandiose.

After he got back to the States and was once more in R&A, Bob Chin wrote me that there seemed no sign of an effort to send out a replacement. He laid a bet 90 to 10 that there would be no replacement by May, and 50/50 that there wouldn't be one by August. Bob and Ed Kracke were my really honest friends in OSS; others were more interested in looking out for themselves and playing the politics of bureaucratic survival. It was useful to keep an outpost in China.

We had Edmund and Marian Clubb for dinner. He had been consul general in Vladivostok for the past year and a half, and had crossed Russia a couple of times. His estimate of Russia was very interesting: He believed it much less strong than most assume, and that a good show of force on our side would quickly force Russia to retreat. Russia was a great believer in the fait accompli, such as its actions in Manchuria: take what it wants and then discuss later. He believed the looting of Manchuria was all planned long in advance and very carefully executed. He believed Russia did have permanent designs to control Manchuria and integrate its development into that of Soviet Siberia. Russia is unbelievably poor in consumer goods, and the people were very tired of "five-year plans," so that when the current one was announced it was politically necessary to announce great quotas of food, cloth, shoes, and radios to be produced at the same time. He reported that there were between 5 and 15 million penal workers whose forced labor was very inefficient. Russians marveled at the productivity of Japanese prisoners of war by contrast. Russia was barren culturally because of the enforced rigidity of thought. The people from top to bottom were almost neurotically fearful of being accused of improper thoughts. Soviet leaders had an inferiority complex in their foreign relations. Such were some of Edmund's observations.

We continued to know the Clubbs after meeting them a bit earlier in Washington. He was persecuted under the anti-Communist witch hunts (how ironic!), left State for early retirement, and became the author of two important scholarly books, as well as being an adjunct professor at Columbia when I also was teaching there. Edmund died in his mid-eighties.

During my stay I saw several art collections, as well as visiting the antique stores, so my knowledge of Chinese antiquities did increase. For example,

> Yesterday afternoon I went with a friend to see what is reputed to be the best collection of Chinese early jades and bronzes in Shanghai, and it was a marvelous collection, though the owner was a vain little man, and his boasting was rather annoying. He is a Chinese and made heaps of money through speculating and real estate, and probably collects as a form of security. Nevertheless, he does have marvelous pieces, some wonderful Shang jades, beautiful Warring States pieces, and he showed me four or five bronzes which are magnificent. One unbelievable piece was a huge Shang axe at least 14" across the blade, with a great tao-tieh on the blade, with teeth and ears in open-work. It must have weighed 10 lbs., and could have been a very effective guillotine. The design was powerful. He had two bronze vessels worthy of the Freer Gallery. It was a real treat to see these things.

Larry Sickman, whom Kay and I had known in Peking, and who was curator of Asian art at the Kansas City museum, came over from Tokyo to see me "officially," and of course I had him to dinner. His mission was to invite me to take a job in Japan on the commission that was working on the restitution of art and archaeological treasures taken by the Japanese. Naturally, I turned him down: my eyes were firmly fixed on Park Fairfax in Alexandria, Virginia.

I had begun to write letters to various universities inquiring about their plans for developing Far Eastern studies, and telling of my interest in teaching. I also wrote Mortimer Graves in the American Council of Learned Societies, who would certainly know of all development plans, and to Carrington Goodrich.

I received a letter from Jack Service in Tokyo, who disliked his job intensely but hoped he might be in Washington soon. He said there was no sign of any desire to have him in China. "Considering the smear campaign against him here last spring, I suppose it may not be wise to bring him back until a coalition government has been formed. His brother Dick in Tsingtao is being smeared right now by KMT people, who think he is Jack (this came to me through several sources)." I warned Dick privately. He replied, thanking me and saying my tip-off was confirmed just after he received my letter, and that it partly arose from the belief he is Jack. "Nice business!"

Here I should like to quote a few descriptions that I wrote Kay about things I saw in Shanghai:

> Sunday I went for a walk along the Bund, and found a little park at the juncture of Soochow creek and the Huangpoo. It costs 5 CNC to go in, which is 1/4 of a cent in our money. After I was in, I well remembered the park from my childhood, with its rock garden in the middle with marvelously intertwining paths and mysterious nooks. But it's pitifully plain and small now! It's a fine place to watch the native boats come in and out the creek. The tide was ripping out and these boats—small sampans sculled by a single person, often a women, or coal barges, or sailing boats with general cargo, or bamboo rafts—would come storming down the river with the tide and then round the point and struggle to make it into the creek against the tide, with men poling like mad to keep off the point; or they would come sailing up the river [against the tide] on the fairly stiff breeze, and then drop sail and scull furiously so as not to be swept back into the river. Sometimes the boats would almost crash into one another, and then the shouting would be frantic and the boatmen would jam their poles into each other's boats and push with might and main. Very amusing. The kids would love it.
>
> There has been an extraordinary spectacle outside our apartment window and seven stories down, these last few days. Poor people lining up for some magic certificate that allows them to buy flour at 6,000 CNC a bag. There have been hundreds of them down there in the alley, arriving early and waiting all day in the rain. The crowd psychology is amazing—how queues form up apparently spontaneously; how they suddenly dissolve and form up elsewhere; how some cluster of unformed people suddenly rushes for a queue and bursts it apart and wriggles in; then the people in the queue hug each other as tightly as possible (men and women intermixed) in order not to get chiseled apart. Through all this there is a continuous tumult, rising and falling, and generally a congenial baseball park-like atmosphere. The perspective [from seven stories up] made it especially interesting, like a weird camera shot in a movie—everyone seems a dwarf, and the walking and running seems a sort of gliding or darting, since you don't see the legs move. I could hardly tear myself from the window morning and noon.
>
> And all the wharf sights: the cargo junks and lighters side by side along the banks, piled high with crates and boxes and bales of merchandise; with coolies picking their way under huge loads from boat to boat and then along the dock to the street edge, singing their high-pitched wailing chant; the families of

boatmen squatting in the tiny after-cabins eating their food served up by the old grandmother; children, boys, men and girls who all live and work, bathe, sleep, make love, defecate, gossip or dream in those cramped quarters. It's a whole life we can hardly imagine, so conscious of tides and winds, of things which live or float in water, of the automatic rules of boating. Marvelous.

Shanghai street scenes are exciting, too, but there are so many people—so unbelievably many people—hurrying, and crowding aboard things, or lining up for things, or dodging things, or quarreling, or staring, or gathering up or selling things. The streets and sidewalks and alleys and stores and houses all team with people, idle or busy, but mostly quite inefficiently busy doing things by manpower. What a social adjustment this crowding of people involves, what complexity of organizations to keep the whole multitude with its millions of conflicting purposes all in order. . . . I haven't even scratched the surface of Shanghai—me, an old office book-worm—but I have mixed and explored quite a lot.

Tonight riding out to the theater in a rickshaw I marveled at the gregariousness of the Chinese, swarming on the sidewalk after the day's work, gossiping, bathing, kids playing the street, about half the adults cuddling babies, young men and their gals strolling about arm in arm, and everyone seeming very content without any of the pleasures we have to amuse ourselves. In some ways it's still a folk society.

I had to cable home occasionally, and told Kay how we did it in postwar Shanghai:

You go into the cable office and there always is a mob. You hand your cable to someone on the fringes of the crowd which pass it hand over hand to the counter. There it sits on a stack. From time to time clerk number 1 picks up the stack and turns it over so first shall be first and last shall be last. He counts the words and figures out the price on each cable, and passes them on one by one—after putting his "chop" on them—to clerk number 2. He recounts the words and then makes out a receipt in duplicate. Then he passes receipts and cable to clerk number 3, who calls off a name and announces the price. Some soul in the mob digs in for his money, holds it up and it is passed along to clerk number 3, who chops the receipt and attempts to make change. Usually he claims he can't make exact change, but the receipt and change get passed back to the lucky person, who then lunges his way out of the mob to fresh air and triumph. It usually takes an hour, everyone is in pretty good spirits and gets chummy, but it's a damn nuisance.

I flew to Chungking again for consultations, in theory to make suggestions on how the embassy could do a better research job, since the old R&A was now to be integrated into State Department, with outposts directly under the various embassies. I was cordially received this time, was shown how information gathering works—actually just the initiative of individual Foreign Service Officers—and asked to make a recommendation for a research model. After a couple of interesting days, in which I got better acquainted with some of the men, and got to know them "with their hair down" and "bitching," I did make a series of written proposals, which were discussed, but it was clear that this was just advisory, because I didn't intend to be involved in it. Later, I was urged to stay on for another half year to get things started, but firmly declined. Getting to Chungking and back in April took a lot of initiative and wire pulling because Air Transport Command was closing down in China, and the embassy was about to move to Nanking. Planes were heavily booked, but now I was a State Department employee and had a certain priority.

On April 25, 1946, I wrote to Kay on the situation in China:

> Really, China has gotten itself into a hell of a mess—there is a very severe inflation; there is the threat of a severe famine; there is heavy fighting in Manchuria and unless a real compromise can be worked out soon this is sure to spread to North China; there is great lack of respect for the government and widespread criticism of inefficiency, corruption, and stupidity; and there is a feeling of despair widely prevalent and a weak-kneed dependence upon the U.S. to solve for China all manner of problems. I do believe the KMT is very rotten and yet its leaders are utterly determined to maintain their grip on the country, their special position in terms of political and economic control, in defiance of agreement reached in Chungking both with the Commies and the minor parties. The Commies are equally determined, and have the stuff, at least to maintain their control of North China, and also to extend their political power. I charge the KMT right-wing as being more responsible, but the Commies, too, have been very rigid. There is sure to be a long, long period of great disorder in China, but it's not possible for me to predict whether this will develop into a revolution or extensive civil war, or will somehow be held to a simmering and sporadic turmoil. I rather guess the latter, because the KMT is going to discover that it can't really whip the Commies (who certainly can't whip the KMT by direct assault) and won't risk its existence in a real full-scale war against the Commies. But it will take years for the KMT to cleanse and improve itself and develop a positive political program to compete with the Commies, if it really ever can.

Reading my letters to Kay, I note that I had become acquainted with some Chinese Communists in Shanghai. I invited a group of them to dinner, including Chang Han-fu, whom I had met in San Francisco, where he was a secretary to Tung Pi-wu; P'an Tzu-nien, editor of *Hsin Hua jih-pao* (The New China daily); Ch'iao Mu, who was second level, and his wife, Kung Peng, a secretary to Chou En-lai; and Mr. Lu Ting-i, the Communist "minister of publicity." I also invited Han Ming, a Chinese newspaper editor friend, who had become a sort of discussant of current events with me. He was a friend of Jack's, I think, and certainly Jack knew the others in the group I had invited. Five guests came. It was a successful party with rather nonpolitical conversation. Miss Kung Peng (Mrs. Ch'iao Mu) was a rather forthright Yenching graduate of a type of whom we know several. Ch'iao Mu was an intellectual young chap, very alert and broadly informed. P'an Tzu-nien, whom I had had twice to dinner, was a quiet scholarly man. Chang Han-fu was the fifth. I enjoyed giving the party, and invited any and all to look us up if they came to the United States.

Later, they invited me to see an exhibition of wood-block prints done in Yenan at the Lu Hsun Academy. Connie Yuan begged to come along, so I asked if she might see the exhibition too. The younger sister of T. L. Yuan, the eminent librarian, Connie had been very helpful to me in my household buying. The prints were very well executed, some of them outright propaganda, some illustrative of features of Yenan life, and some modifications of Chinese folk art. In these the artist took gaily colored New Year's posters, extracted the superstitious elements (gods of fertility, etc.), and replaced them with simple concepts that the Communists were plugging, such as production campaigns, health campaigns, with simple slogans. They still looked like peasant posters but told a different story. Some of it was very handsome graphic art. The friends then insisted I stay for dinner, which I hadn't understood was part of the invitation, but I did stay. Lu Ting-i was host. We had a good but simple Chinese meal and quite a talk. My Communist Party acquaintances within a few years became rather important persons in China. Remembering how natural it was to meet them in 1946— though I suppose they and I were being shadowed—I am bemused at my change of attitude toward the CCP within a few years. At the time, however, I looked on all sources of information on China as important for my work.

My travel orders to return to America came on May 13, my birthday. I hoped to arrange a quick flight, but I still had quite a bit of work to close out the "shop." I had made a lot of friends in Shanghai and felt I should say farewells. For example, I returned the curtains all properly washed and ironed to my Austrian friends, with soap, cigarettes, smoking tobacco, and candy wrapped inside. I went for the last time to the Community Church, where I saw many of my parents' friends. In one of my last letters to Kay I wrote, "All the Chinese I know are just yearning and aching to come to America. It's sort of a national disease, which just now I, too, am suffering from in an acute form." To them I passed out invitations to visit us in America, too.

I wrote a long letter to John DeFrancis, who I understood would come out to replace me, though we would not overlap in China. I told him all about our Chinese personnel, library and equipment, records and property, and then gave him my opinion of various official Americans he would probably have to work with or under. Then I offered the following advice on manner of operating:

1. Try to see the top of any organization and then work down.
2. Decide what you want to do, get general approval from whoever is your superior, and then go ahead and do it. Everyone is much too busy to supervise or help in detail.
3. A little secretiveness has prestige value among Americans. Among Chinese the word "intelligence" has a bad sound; we stick to "research," and are very open in a generalized way about our work. Almost any answer given promptly will suffice.

After having quoted this, I wrote to John DeFrancis, asking if he remembered any of this. Did he come out to China to replace me? He replied from Honolulu, where he now lives, that he didn't come out to China but resigned from OSS to take up a fellowship. He doesn't even remember a plan for him to replace me. So, in the end, Bob Chin was right. No one came out, and all my sticking it out was futile!

In a very few days I was able to get a flight straight to San Francisco, with a single refueling stop at Johnston Island, as I remember. We landed in America on May 17. My China stay was over. It would be more than twenty-five years before I set foot again on the China mainland.

9

A Transition Time

My last letter to Kay, written on May 18, 1946, was from Pasadena, where I was with Dad. From San Francisco I had talked with Kay and the kids by phone the first moment I got into a hotel room. Mother was already in the East seeing Halsey, who was now back from Japan. "Dad and I are having a fine time without the strain of mutual reforming," I wrote. I really did enjoy that relaxed visit with only us two. In Pasadena I went to see our old Peking friends, Arthur and Edna Coons. Arthur was now president of Occidental College. He had no particular leads for me in respect to a possible job. I also saw George and Evelyn McCune, Korea specialists, who were on their way to Berkeley, where he was to teach at the University of California. They were dear friends from R&A days. Unhappily, George had only a few more years to live. His death was a great loss to our field. We are still in correspondence with Evelyn, who made herself an authority on Korean art.

I arrived in Washington about May 20 and immediately phoned Kay. Then I took a familiar bus to Park Fairfax, where my darling and our two kids met me at the bus stop. I was still in uniform, but the kids were used to seeing soldiers. I wonder if they really remembered me. Still it was a grand reunion. The kids had grown, and my sweetheart was more beautiful than ever. It took only a little time to become reacquainted with Johnny and Ann, such attractive children. Kay had done a splendid job with them during the eight months I was gone. Now it was springtime in Washington. No more colds!

Back at the office I found a very different atmosphere from that when I left. Many colleagues had gone back to their peacetime jobs. The main preoccupation of those remaining was over the question of whether R&A would actually become a permanent part of the State Department. Would everyone be taken in? A bureaucratic struggle was under way, with Congress undecided whether to fund the continuation of the old OSS and other wartime agencies. Our old élan was gone. We were no longer helping to win the war, but just watching for signs of how the wind was blowing. Charlie Stelle, now firmly ensconced, assigned me to be a liaison between the newly named Office of Research and Intelligence and the newly named Central Intelligence Agency, and I may have been on the payroll of CIA though actually working in State—an anomalous situation. I was not keen to work in government under such conditions, and I began a campaign to find a teaching job. But it was a bit late to find one for the autumn of 1946. I pinned my hopes on Carrington Goodrich and Mortimer Graves to let me know if they heard of a teaching position available in my field. I now wanted to work on modern and contemporary China, that is, to teach recent Chinese history.

As an aside, let me say that eventually R&A was firmly integrated into the State Department, not parceled up, and is now called the Bureau of Intelligence and Research. It seems to have had a reputable history, and many of my old pals became Foreign Service officers and even rose to be ambassadors.

Sometime in the spring of 1947 I had a letter from Dr. Gregg Sinclair, president of the University of Hawaii, asking if I would be interested in a professorship there to teach Chinese history. I was. But before he made me a specific offer I had a letter from Professor Goodrich, followed by one from Schuyler Wallace. They offered me a teaching position in the Department of Chinese and a place on the staff of a yet-to-be-created East Asian Institute at Columbia University. What a break! I have often speculated how very different our lives would have been had we gone to Hawaii rather than to Columbia. It turned on a few days between letters.

I found out that my candidacy at Columbia had to be approved by the history department, and that Professor John Krout, head of the department, read my published dissertation and advocated my appointment. Later we became good friends. Probably my old professor W. L. Westermann, who was still teaching ancient history, endorsed me too. We also became friends, as he lived in White Plains and we often met on the train. Appointments require a lot of passing-upon at Columbia. I hadn't realized that the rank of associate professor, which I was offered, meant tenure.

One problem was salary. Columbia offered me $6,000 a year, with the possibility of earning an extra $1,200 for teaching in summer session. My salary at the State Department was $8,000, which was comfortable. However, Kay agreed that we could squeeze our living expenses that much, and I accepted the offer without bargaining. That was a mistake. Living expenses and growing children cost more than that salary could sustain. I was naïve about academic matters and ever so happy to be invited to Columbia. The position was the one that my former professor, Cyrus Peake, had given up.

Now that I had accepted a job at Columbia, which began officially on July 1, 1947 (though I didn't need to report till September), I resigned with polite regrets from Field Museum and notified State that I would terminate as of September 1. I had considerable accumulated leave, so I could use July and August for course preparation, while receiving pay from both institutions. We would need every cent, what with moving costs and the frightening prospect of buying a house.

I wrote Dad in June 1947 about our financial situation. What with uncashed bonds, other savings, money from Field Museum that I had contributed toward my pension, and money the government would pay us when we canceled its pension, we would have about $3,900 to put into a house. If 20 percent were required as a down payment, we could look for something in the $15,000 range, which seemed an enormous amount to us then. As I wrote Dad, I looked forward to teaching and expected to be challenged and stimulated. "It is a credo with me that drastic changes in job, demanding hard work, and a new outlook are important stages for continued intellectual growth and professional advancement."

We were really babes-in-the-woods about house-buying. Carrington Goodrich told us of a house in Riverdale, where he lived, but when we heard that the asking price was $28,000 we didn't bother to look. Over in Leonia, New Jersey, where some Columbia faculty lived, we saw some big old houses that Kay called "wife breakers," so we started looking in the White Plains area. We found a house in Valhalla, north of White Plains, that was nearing completion by a speculative builder. The price was within our means, $15,500. The contractor promised he could have it ready for occupancy by September 15, a date that would let us move in before I started teaching.

We were concerned about schooling for the kids. We were told that our children would go to the Valhalla Elementary School, so we went to see the school. The principal, we were told, was an Oberlin graduate. But we found after we had moved in that we were in a separate school district with a one-room school with all eight grades, presided over by a seventy-year-old teacher. Imagine that in Westchester County, New York, in 1947!

We procured a bunch of books from the government about care and repair of a house, about landscaping and gardening—fascinating details about plumbing, heating, electricity, furnace care, planning closets, painting, the placement of trees and shrubbery, pests, and so forth. Kay and I poured over them with the greatest interest. It was going to be work and fun to convert a raw house and grounds into a comfortable home.

10

First Years at Columbia, 1947–1954

I began teaching in late September 1947, and believe me it was not an easy thing to convert myself, even though I had several months of preparation. I was responsible for two graduate courses. One was on the modern period in East Asia, which I decided to begin at about 1600 and divide into two epochs to correspond to the two semesters. There would be about fifteen two-hour lectures in each semester. The course covered China and Japan, because Hugh Borton, the regular modern Japan professor, was still in the State Department. I assigned readings and required two critical book reviews, one comparing two or more works on the same general topic. Also there were examinations at the end of each semester. I was a conscientious grader.

The other course was a master's-level colloquium and seminar on modern China in which I tried to broaden the students' thinking about the subject of history, that is, to include the culture, social organization, economy, and intellectual currents. In effect, I hoped to steer them away from exclusively political history and relations with the West. We would have assigned readings and discussions, while the students would also define their research topics and spend time doing research for a thesis, or at least an important paper. My reading in anthropology and the sociology of China led me in that direction.

In addition, I was to participate in a bibliographic seminar on China taught by Dr. Goodrich and Mr. C. C. Wang. I didn't enjoy that, though I learned a lot from them. One other responsibility to the department was to participate in dissertation reading and in the defenses. Most of the early students were already "in the pipeline," and they knew a lot more about their special subjects than I did. But I have a critical mind and I do like to see evidence for assertions and theories, so I probably made a contribution.

When I joined the Department of Chinese and Japanese it must have been one of the smallest at Columbia. It included the departmental chairman Dr. Goodrich, Mr. Wang, and Tsunoda *sensei*, as we always spoke of, or to, our venerable Japanese teacher and librarian. These three had been my teachers twelve years before. The eminent Japan cultural historian, Sir George Sansom, was scheduled to join the department as soon as he could free himself from British government postwar service, and Hugh Borton also would rejoin the department sometime. Mr. Ichiro Shirato taught the courses in Japanese language. I tried to study Japanese with him but couldn't combine it with becoming a teacher, for I spent several days each week—even nights into the wee hours—preparing for those two-hour lectures on Mondays at 2:10 P.M. and my colloquium-seminar on Wednesday afternoons.

In 1947 there was relatively little scholarly literature on modern China as compared with the situation twenty years later, when much fine new work had been published. One great asset was *Eminent Chinese of the Ch'ing Period*, edited by Dr. Arthur Hummel, with most of the better contributions done by Fang Chao-ying and his wife, Tu Lien-che. They were dedicated scholars, objective and penetrating. They knew the Chinese sources as few others did. In two volumes, *ECCP* contained several hundred scholarly biographies of important statesmen, rulers, commanders, writers, thinkers, and artists in China from the late Ming into the 1900s. Excellent indexes and cross-references made it possible to read by epoch or by subject. I spent a great deal of time on that work, and it surely raised the level of my lecture course.

The departmental offices were in 307 Low Library. That building in the center of Columbia's campus is now used exclusively for administrative offices, including those of the president, while the three-story rotunda is used for indoor ceremonials. In 1947 the Chinese and Japanese library was housed on the third floor, so our offices were there also. Soon, however, the East Asian Institute was created, and in 1948 I moved into an office in a brownstone on 118th Street. Our parent organization, the School of International Affairs, was nearby, as was the already flourishing Russian Institute. Its director was Geroid T. Robison, an eminent historian of Russia, whom I had known in R&A. The idea of the school and of its institutes was an outgrowth of wartime experiences. A number of universities ran special programs to train officers of the armed forces in foreign languages and to give them a knowledge of the lands in which they might be assigned to fight or govern. Columbia had run a school for naval officers, and that was the germ of the idea for a School of International Affairs. There was another stimulus: the experience of the American government when the war began of needing all manner of experts on foreign countries for positions in strategic studies, intelligence, or propaganda offices, as well as providing information to the armed forces. Leaders of American academia felt a sense of urgency to prepare more persons for careers in foreign matters than had been available when the war began. Now the United States was a world power and was sure to have large responsibilities abroad. Professor Schuyler Wallace dreamed of a School of International Affairs that would have a number of regional institutes; in fact, he wanted to cover the world! The emphasis, however, would be on modern times and the social sciences.

Columbia had several eminent faculty members in the Russian field, and it was also well regarded for its East Asian specialists, though there were not many. We had a long and impressive tradition. Besides those whom I have mentioned in our department, there were Professor Nathaniel Peffer in the Government Department, an expert on modern Chinese politics, and Professor John Orchard on the economic geography of East Asia. After Hugh Borton returned and Sir George Sansom joined the faculty, our strength on the Japan side was enhanced. Because of his eminence, Sir George was to be the director of the East Asian Institute. Other faculty members whom I have mentioned constituted an executive committee, and we spent the year 1948 laying plans, deciding on requirements for the certificate, and getting out publicity to attract graduate students. A lot of good students were returning from the war, strongly interested in the lands in which they had served. The Rockefeller Foundation was helping to finance the school and its first two institutes. Through its help we were able to attract Professor Franklin Ho, a well-regarded economist of Nankai University, to join our economics faculty and be part of the East Asian Institute.

Three elements characterized our thinking about the EAI: we would have a strong language component—three years of Chinese or Japanese—and the institute would be a center of research on modern and contemporary East Asia. Also, we would try to bring to Columbia East Asian specialists who were also social scientists, such as anthropologists, sociologists, or political scientists, who would teach both in the institute and in their departments. That would take time, money, and diplomacy to persuade the departments of this need. The language requirement would be no problem for students who had special training in Japanese or Chinese as part of the war effort, but we would have to provide specialized language courses for the others. This was the beginning at Columbia of the intensive language courses that consumed half of a graduate student's time during the first year, often followed by a summer, too.

Columbia's program to strengthen foreign area studies and give the social sciences a foreign area focus was actually part of a national effort, with such schools as Harvard, the University of Washington, and the University of California at Berkeley in the lead, as well as Columbia. Our main rival, of course, was Harvard. Gradually various other universities took up the challenge, and now foreign area subjects are taught in colleges and universities all over the United States. Graduates with a Ph.D. from these and other major graduate schools provided the specialist faculty for this national development. It was a heady enterprise, about which I will be writing more.

I enjoyed being a member of the faculty at the university where I had done my graduate work. I became reacquainted with Professor Westermann, whose course on the history of the ancient world had led me to take up slavery in China as my dissertation topic. I also became a little acquainted with Ruth Benedict, whose anthropology course had so interested me. She was a beautiful, patrician lady, somewhat austere, it seemed. Her book *Patterns of Culture* is a classic. During the war she used her ability to analyze cultures to study Japanese culture, though from afar, and to show how it affected Japanese behavior. She later published her findings in *The Chrysanthemum and the Sword*. Also, I became acquainted with members of the History Department, in which I had a seat. It was then a very distinguished department.

After my first year of teaching I undertook two courses in summer school, for with a new house we needed the extra money. One was given five days a week, and the other twice a week, for six weeks straight. That was sort of grueling, because I had a two-hour train ride each day. After having given the lecture course, however, I was able to enrich it while resting a bit on my notes. After Hugh Borton returned to our department, I no longer ventured to teach about Japan; that was *his* field.

Since I taught at Columbia for twenty-nine years, there are many students from those early years whom I don't remember, but several stand out. Julie How was one of the earliest students to impress me. Later her career and mine became intertwined. She was a graduate of Vassar and came to Columbia for her M.A. in Chinese history. Her father was a Shanghai man and her mother was Cantonese, so she spoke both dialects as well as Mandarin. She had both a Chinese and a Western education. For her M.A., I suggested that she undertake a study of one of the founders of the Chinese Communist Party, Ch'en Tu-hsiu. In 1949 she completed a fine thesis on "Ch'en Tu-hsiu's Thought." It was never published but is often referred to by others who have written on this important intellectual's career.

On the first day in my second year of the lecture course on the history of modern China, there sat a beautiful young blond lady in the front row. She was a senior at Barnard, nineteen and recently married, and her name was Rhoda Weidenbaum. Later she enrolled in the East Asian Institute and the Department of Chinese and Japanese, and she got her master's under my guidance. She also served for a couple of years as secretary of the institute. Kay and I have continued to be warm friends with Rhoda and her husband, Sherman. I helped Rhoda get her Ph.D. after her three children were grown, though she took it at the University of Connecticut.

I should now return to the other half of my life—wife and family. We acquired a dog and a cat for the children. The dog was a white and black terrier—sort of—whom we named "Spot." He was about half-grown so he adapted to our household readily. The kitten we got was from the vet who looked after Spot. In the car coming back from that visit, Ann made the ecstatic statement that became part of her parents' cherished memories—"Just think, a kitty!"

The kids' school was unsatisfactory: eight grades in one room with an elderly teacher, and half the students coming from a nearby home for boys. The big advantage was that it required few taxes to support, and Mrs. Reynolds was the principal landowner in the school district as well as the sole member of the school board. A very cozy arrangement! Shortly after moving into our home we met another couple who had children in the school, Milton and Gil Walman. Apparently they also had bought their house not knowing the school situation. Kay and I called on the official who supervised small schools in Westchester to protest this antiquated school. He said he could do nothing about it unless the voters in the school district voted to improve the school and raise the taxes to pay for improvements. The first step was to elect a new school board. So Milt and I called on neighbors and sought their votes for us to join Mrs. Reynolds on the board. In the annual meeting of the school district, we surprised Mrs. Reynolds by getting a resolution passed that created a three-member board, and then we got ourselves elected as the two other members. There was little we could do, however. We did arrange to have a part-time art teacher come to offer some enrichment. Mrs. Reynolds turned the tables at the next school district meeting by getting a resolution passed reverting to the old system. Since I had been voted to a two-year term (Milt to one year), I continued as a member with Mrs. Reynolds for another year. By then, Kay and I realized there was no hope of really improving the educational situation, so beginning in September 1949 we started sending John and Ann to the Bedford Road School in Pleasantville, for which we had to pay tuition. That led quite naturally to our move to Pleasantville three years later.

In the autumn of 1948 Kay and I began to think about our children's religious education. We both had religious upbringing, and we wanted John and Ann at least to know about the Christian heritage. So we took them one Sunday to the only Protestant church in Valhalla, a Methodist one. They came out of Sunday School with pamphlets about the life of Jesus that were just too much for us, and we never took them back again. I saw a notice in the White Plains paper for a "Community Church." Since I had gone to an interdenominational church in Shanghai that was also called a "Community Church," we decided to try it. We heard an intelligent sermon by a handsome, white-haired minister named Clifford Vessey. The congregation was not large, perhaps seventy-five people. When the kids got out of Sunday School they were very pleased. It was United Nations Sunday, and each had been asked to pass the basket. So we went back again. Soon we were liking the church, and people were most friendly. One day Cliff Vessey came to call at our home to ask whether we would like to join. I told him frankly that I was an agnostic. Would I be welcome? He assured me that members of the church were free to hold any beliefs they wished to. Also we learned it was a Unitarian church, though we didn't quite know what that meant. Kay was all in favor of joining, so we "signed the book" sometime that autumn and were members for forty years. Our children got a liberal and ethical religious education, while we became acquainted with some wonderful people, among the dearest friends we ever made.

The History Department of the University of California at Berkeley invited me to teach summer school in 1949, and it seemed a wonderful opportunity and excuse to take the kids on a trip west. Professor Woodbridge Bingham, whom I had known in Washington, arranged the invitation. We started off when my regular teaching responsibilities were over. We couldn't very well take our dog, so we left him at an animal shelter. We were able to leave the cat with the people from New York who rented our house for the summer.

In Berkeley we rented the house of a faculty member who was away. It gave us a wonderful view of San Francisco, particularly at night, so sparklingly lit up across the Bay. In the daytime, at about noon, we could see the fog rolling in over San Francisco, cold air sucked in from the Pacific by the heated air in the desert behind Berkeley. We had a great time that summer. Kay put the kids in the university's summer school, an adjunct of the School of Education with a very innovative program.

Kay and I were entertained by some of the History Department faculty, including, of course, the Binghams. I gave one public lecture, I think on modernization in China. Otherwise I used my stuff from Columbia's summer session for the classes I had.

When we returned to Westchester, full of eagerness to recover our Spot before we even got home, we were told by the keeper that Spot, on seeing us start off in the car, had scrambled over a wire fence ten feet high and taken off after us. Of course, he could never catch us. The keeper of the shelter tried several times to find him near our home, and got our neighbors to watch for him, but without success. It was sad news. Obviously, we would have to get another dog.

We resumed our church connection and began to be invited to the homes of some of the friendly members. Also, we began to entertain foreign students. I see in our guest book Ben and Dorothy Wu (Li Ya-shu). Nearly forty years later I had a letter from Dorothy in Peking, who remembered our hospitality. As intellectuals, tainted by the American connection, they had a rough time during China's Cultural Revolution, but they survived and were now teaching once more. Another Chinese couple we entertained was Minta Wang and her husband Ernest. Minta had worked with me in Shanghai in 1946, and they had finally made it to the "promised land," five years later. In the summer we tried to find them jobs, but our effort ended disastrously, due to misunderstandings on both sides. Better not to get too involved in other people's problems, perhaps.

I took the summer of 1950 off from teaching, receiving a grant from the funds of the East Asian Institute to work on research plans. By then the People's Liberation Army had won its civil war, and in October 1949 Mao Tse-tung had proclaimed the establishment of the People's Republic of China, with its capital in Peking. That was a world-significant event. Doing a lot of reading on what was known of the Chinese Communist movement and searching our Chinese library to learn what it could tell, I produced a research prospectus that showed systematically, though in a chronological way, what needed to be studied about that history. Next I commissioned a bibliography of our Chinese holdings on the CCP, and then I arranged for Mr. Shirato to do a bibliography of our Japanese holdings on the subject. The East Asian Institute published both as study aids. They were the first such inventories.

A problem was that I couldn't take out much time for research during the school year. We were now getting lots of graduate students, and they took time. Because our family finances were very tight, I went to Dean Krout to get permission to take another part-time job at Sarah Lawrence College. I remember going into his office to explain that on my salary we just weren't able to make it. He completely understood. "Let's face it," he said, "Columbia just doesn't pay enough." So I accepted a job that took two days a week in Bronxville. My schedule was Monday-Tuesday-Wednesday at Columbia and Thursday-Friday at Sarah Lawrence. I was paid $2,000 an academic year for those two days a week, but that extra $220 a month surely did help with family expenses.

I liked teaching at Sarah Lawrence. It was an innovative college for women, almost all wealthy girls. My teaching was close to tutorial. I had a class once a week but saw the girls individually for discussion of their reading. I ran into some cases of girls who needed or were having therapy, but on the whole they were nice kids, trying hard. One who it seems I inspired was Merle Goldman (her married name). She did her graduate work at Harvard and now is one of the stars of Communist China studies, particularly emphasizing the treatment of intellectuals.

I did the Sarah Lawrence stint for two years, but then had to give it up because my duodenal ulcer, returned. I had to undergo an operation to have a perforation of my insides sewed up. All concerned thought I should not try to do so much. Also, I smoked fairly heavily and had to quit—for a while.

Let me mention one interesting happening that I can't date exactly. One day I was at the East Asian Institute on 118th Street when John D. Rockefeller III came to the office looking for Sir George Sansom, who was away. He told me that he was very concerned by the growing anti-American sentiment in Japan among intellectuals and proposed to do something about it. He would like the institute to take charge of a program to bring influential Japanese intellectuals to the United States for visits, and in reverse to send leading American intellectuals to Japan. He believed this would help to counteract the trend in Japan that he feared, and he would finance the program for five years. I told Mr. Rockefeller that I would immediately inform Sir George. In a little while Columbia organized the program, with Harry Carmen, who had just retired as dean of Columbia College and was very widely connected, as executive secretary. The program was a great success.

A big event happened in 1951. We decided we might as well go and live where the kids were now enjoying school, so we bought land in Pleasantville. Kay discovered a steeply sloping lot facing south, which was the direction we insisted upon since it is so wonderful in the winter. It had lots of large trees and was covered with bushes and vines. Apparently it once had been an apple orchard, but it must have been abandoned long before. The lot cost us only $550 because the village owned it and wanted to get it back on the tax rolls. We had to promise to build within one year. So we had to find an architect. There is a community near Pleasantville called Usonia, where all the houses are modernistic and every plan had to be approved by Frank Lloyd Wright. After viewing houses designed by several architects who lived in Usonia, we decided that the most effective one for us was Aaron Resnick. He had the reputation of sticking within the price that his clients set, if he accepted the commission.

Planning for our new home was thrilling. Aaron Resnick looked over the land, asked us to have a survey that would show the bigger trees and the slope lines so he could place the house advantageously, and then gave us his preliminary drawings. These we studied and discussed with him, and we finally had him go ahead with working drawings and specs so that we could get bids. I believe we had set a price of $18,000 as the highest we could go. This was 1952, when that was not an unreasonable price. He planned a house of two stories, but stretching from east to west, and with lots of big windows facing south to take full advantage of winter sunshine. The kids' rooms would be down below, and our bedroom and the living areas were to be on the second floor to benefit from the higher view.

The lowest bid was well over $20,000, but Aaron was able to cut down here and there, make the halls and stairway a bit narrower, so that a contractor agreed to take it on for $18,200. He promised to begin July 1 and to finish in September. I undertook summer school again, for we had to muster all the money we could, over and above the mortgage we negotiated at less than a 5 percent interest rate.

In 1952 Kay and I were 43 and 44, full of energy. We tackled the painting and staining of our new house, and we tackled our wild grounds, pulling up vines and digging out undergrowth. We put in a front lawn, though the slope was so steep that later I found I must put on spiked shoes to mow it. One Saturday a group of students came out from the East Asian Institute to help with the work. They laid the downstairs floor tiles that day, which was quite a big job. Many times thereafter we entertained students, but never again using them as a workforce.

I was careful in my teaching to keep records on my students, and I have five notebooks with a page for each enrollee in a class or seminar. Those who were merely auditing or who skipped classes often have very little about them, but for those who took the courses for credit, I have a sketch of their personalities as projected on me, and their grades and class rank. I graded exams blind. On required papers, I had the students put their names only on the back and I read and commented on the essays not knowing whom I was addressing. I was particularly careful in my notes on graduate students to say whether I thought they should or should not be encouraged toward the Ph.D. Recently I looked at the first of those notebooks, covering the years from 1947, when I really was a novice teacher, till the end of the 1953–54 academic year. It seems I had about 300 students in those seven years: not a large number, really. One early student was Robert Elegant, who later became a foreign correspondent stationed in Hong Kong and after that turned to fiction, writing racy stories about people involved in historic events in China. His *From a Far Land* was published in the summer of 1987, and he sent me a copy with a complimentary inscription, for it dramatized the period about which I have written several scholarly books.

Many of the M.A. and Institute Certificate students went into government work, business, or foundations. Some of those early students did go on later for the Ph.D., such as Sam Chu, Chun-tu Hsueh, Olga Lang, Jim Morley, and T. K. Tong. All became good friends. I participated in about a dozen doctorates during those early years, but few who were my primary responsibility. This means that I read their dissertations carefully and sat on the defense. Among them were Ted DeBary and Donald Keene, who later joined the department and have become eminent in the field. Dick Irwin, an Oberlin friend who had then been a teacher in Oberlin in Shansi and had already done his graduate course work, was another with whose dissertation I became involved.

With the fall of mainland China to the Communists there were many Chinese intellectuals who managed to get to the United States but were unemployed. Congress voted millions of dollars to assist them with jobs till they could get settled. It was something like the WPA during the Depression. I agreed to take three gentlemen under my wing at Columbia to work on the research project that our institute supported. Julie How was employed by the project, which was designed to find and translate important historical documents of the Kuomintang and the Communist Party. Since she had no teaching responsibilities, she actually supervised the three middle-aged gentlemen in their translations, which were not very literate. I had gone to Stanford to see what the Hoover Institute had that would be interesting, and there I was shown the collection of documents that had been seized in a raid on the Soviet Embassy in Peking in April 1927. These were documents of the Chinese Communist Party, and of the Soviet advisers who worked with the Kuomintang from late 1923 to 1927. The collection was in Chinese, and we had the set in our Columbia library. It was very extensive—several hundred documents in ten Chinese volumes. Just to learn what was included was almost a project in itself. The three assistants came in handy.

I should describe the circumstances of the raid because I have spent many years of research connected with the discovered documents. In 1927 Peking was under control of Chang Tso-lin and his clique based in Manchuria. There was a Kuomintang organization in Peking in which Chinese Communists played a leading role, because at that time the two parties were intertwined. From the point of view of the Peking government the KMT and CCP were subversive, as indeed they were, since they sought to overthrow the government and replace it. Some Peking leaders of the two parties were using buildings within the Soviet Embassy compound as their sanctuary. In view of this, the Chinese Foreign Office asked permission of the diplomatic corps for the Metropolitan Police to enter and arrest the suspects. This was granted, and on April 6, 1927, the raiding party entered the grounds of the Soviet Embassy and arrested a number of members of the two parties, including the cofounder of the CCP, Li Ta-chao. They also seized a lot of Chinese documents, which turned out to be from the Communist Party.

Then another incident occurred. The police saw smoke coming from a building where someone was burning documents. They called a fire department, which put out the blaze, and the police seized many partly burned and unburned documents in Russian, for the burning was being done in the office of the Soviet military attaché. The police carried away several truckloads of documents. The Russian government demanded that everything be returned. Instead, the Peking government organized a translation and publication commission. Only a small part of the papers were ever published in Chinese, and even fewer in Japanese or English. It was those published documents that we investigated. Were they genuine? What did they reveal? These questions arose because the Soviet government claimed that forged documents could be, and were, inserted.

I wrote to General John Magruder, who had been Major Magruder, the American military attaché at the time, and whose office assisted in the arrangement of the documents and the planning of their translation. He assured me of their genuineness. We also submitted photographs in the State Department archives of some thirty of the Russian originals to David Dallin for a judgment. He was Russian and an expert on Soviet foreign affairs. He found only one of them to be very doubtful, perhaps a forgery, and of course we did not use that one, although it was the first document published in English translation. It was a very inflammatory document. Many years later, in November 1986, a researcher in the Peking Academy of Social Sciences, Ms. Hsi Wu-i, told me in Canton that she had interviewed the elderly Chinese head of the Translation Commission, who had told her that document had indeed been forged, but it was the only one forged. Later she sent me a copy of the interview protocol. Miss Hsi knew our book and that we had rejected that document.

Our main way of certifying the documents we wished to use was to judge their accuracy by comparison with other sources and with historically verifiable circumstances. For example, a speech by Chiang Kai-shek, translated into Russian, then back into Chinese by the commission, could also be found in a collection of Chiang's papers. Even errors tended, at times, to substantiate the genuineness when we saw that the translators in Peking were ignorant of details about situations in Canton some years earlier. They often garbled names that came from Cantonese through Russian, then back into Chinese script. Here

Julie's knowledge of Cantonese was invaluable. We could not prove the accuracy of all of the documents we wanted to use, but enough of them stood the tests that we felt confident in our selection.

Julie and I discussed for many hours the historical value as well as the authenticity of the documents that our Chinese collaborators were roughly translating, and we moved naturally into preparing a publication of the most significant of them—as it seemed to us at the time. In the 1950s not much was known in the West about the early history of the collaboration between the KMT and the CCP, nor of the Russian involvement in China, although that involvement was much on the minds of the other powers in the 1920s. For readers to understand the significance of the documents required a lot of historical narrative on our part. I commissioned Julie to try her hand at it, and she wrote most of the explanatory historical narrative. Our several roles were explained in my introduction. I left for Japan in 1954 when the work was nearly complete and picked it up on my return.

I was due a sabbatical in 1953, after six years of teaching, but since that was the year Carrington Goodrich was due to have his sabbatical, he asked me to postpone mine for a year. In 1953 and 1954, Senator Joseph McCarthy resumed his accusations against the State Department and against the army for harboring Communists, as he alleged. They seemed very wild charges, and America became quite tense. In the spring of 1954 the Army-McCarthy hearings were broadcast on television. I remember watching the sensational hearings at the Faculty Club. Little did I realize then that I would also become an indirect victim.

When thinking about my sabbatical, I consulted with Sir George Sansom about whether it would be better to bore in on one particular research topic or try to have a more broadening experience. He recommended that I use the year away to broaden my outlook and knowledge. After considering options and discussing everything with Kay, we decided to try to go to Japan. From there I hoped to travel around the rim of China to observe the influence of the People's Republic on the other peoples of Asia. For Americans, except those of the extreme left, China was a forbidden land so soon after the Korean War. I applied for a Fulbright grant for the Japan part, and to the Ford Foundation's Foreign Area Fellowship program for support of my travels. The Ford Foundation learned that I was in for a Fulbright grant and agreed to cover the outside travel.

Here is where McCarthyism came in. When I applied for a passport, I was turned down! When I inquired why, I was informed of several charges against me: It had been alleged that I had been affiliated (1) with the Committee for a Democratic Far Eastern Policy and (2) with the American League for Peace and Democracy, both of which were cited by the attorney general as Communistic or subversive. (3) It was also alleged that I was a member of the China Aid Council, which had been cited as a Communist front organization. Finally, (4) it was alleged that I had been a book reviewer for the Institute of Pacific Relations's magazines *Pacific Affairs* and *Far Eastern Survey*.

With advice from Jack Service I got a lawyer, Mr. Leo Rosen, a civil liberties specialist. I must say that poor Jack had been abruptly dismissed from the State Department and was now living in Queens with Cary and their daughter, Virginia. He had a job in a company that made steam traps.

I gave Mr. Rosen the facts: that I had never been a member of the first three organizations and that I had written several book reviews, perfectly appropriate work for a professor. Though I did not subscribe to the principle of "guilt by association," I also did not claim the privilege of "innocence by association," but I pointed out a number of high State Department officials who also had written for those journals, including John Foster Dulles, whose speech before the Philippine Institute of Pacific Relations was published in the same issue as one of my reviews. Mr. Rosen had my statement made into a legal affidavit, which began with a categorical disclaimer that I was or ever had been a member of the Communist Party. It was dated July 1, 1954.

I then went to Washington for an interview with the Passport Office to defend myself. I took along a testimonial letter to Mrs. Shipley, the director of the Passport Office, written for me by Kay's cousin, Peter Edson, a nationally syndicated columnist who had great clout. It must have helped! I was courteously treated in Washington and had my hearing before two State Department security officers, or perhaps they were from Mrs. Shipley's Passport Office. After about half an hour, they promised me my passport. Later I learned that the Passport Office was trying, in such procedures, to protect itself from charges by McCarthy. I remember that I got the passport that very afternoon. Mr. Rosen charged me only fifty dollars for his help, which certainly was in consideration for a harassed professor and a friend of Jack's.

Still thinking we were to get a Fulbright grant to go to Japan, and with the backing of the Ford Foundation, we had made plans to depart on August 1. We rented our new house for a year. But then I got the shocking news from the State Department, in a mimeographed form letter, that I had been turned down for a Fulbright fellowship. No reason was given. Under these circumstances, what could we do? Here is where friendships counted. I told Schuyler Wallace and Hugh Borton, acting director of the institute, about the problem. Schuyler told me to phone Cleon Swazie, who ran the Foreign Area Fellowship program at the Ford Foundation. Cleon said he would have to make some inquiries, but he promised to get back to me. In less than a week, the East Asian Institute put up some money and the Ford Foundation some more, so that with my half-salary for the sabbatical we could make it. That was phenomenal! I had been under a lot of tension during the previous two months.

We departed as planned, once more to drive across the country with our kids. We left Pleasantville on July 28, 1954, in a big second-hand Buick. We crossed the continent in less than seven days, clocked 3,020 miles, and our total cost was $305.33. Of this, about $115 was for work on the car before and during the trip, and $190 for travel expenses. Certainly it was a cheap way for four to cross the country, but hard work.

We were with the parents in Pasadena for more than two weeks, because freighters never seem to be on schedule. One day I went to call on Mr. Chang Kia-ngao, a friend of Franklin Ho, who had given me a letter of introduction. Mr. Chang was a retired financier, longtime head of the Bank of China, and an important official under the national government. He was now a professor at Loyola University in Los Angeles. I have notes on our long discussion about conditions in China and the attitudes of overseas Chinese toward the Communist regime. He gave me letters of introduction to his former associates in several of the countries I was to visit.

On the day we were to sail, August 19, we were driven to San Pedro to board our Japanese freighter, the *Nikko Maru*. We had told our children that we wouldn't be going on a very big boat, and apparently they imagined it would be some small and dangerous vessel. When we drove onto the dock and that 10,000-ton freighter loomed gigantic above us, their fears entirely vanished.

11

A Year in Japan and Southeast Asia, 1954–1955

Eight days out on the MS *Nikko Maru* on our way to Japan, I wrote my parents:

> We have found this ship to be a very fine vessel indeed, and the passengers, officers, and crew very good company. The kids are having a wonderful time. Johnny has made friends with one of the junior officers and is giving him English lessons, in exchange for which John gets taken on tours of the ship's more interesting nether regions, and he haunts the bridge. Ann is taking Japanese lessons from Sachiko Mizoguchi, who is a daughter of the owner of the Kokusai Company (managers of the line and several others). She is about 18 and has been in America attending Colby Junior College. She is returning to Tokyo for the rest of her education. Our apprehensions about the kids being bored were baseless; they are having the time of their lives. Ann reported that her first four days aboard were the happiest four days of her life. She, too, found a junior officer patron.

The ship was diverted to Kobe and would then go to Yokohama via Nagoya, so we left her temporarily at Kobe and headed for Kyoto on September 4. On the ride there, memories of Japan rushed through my mind as we passed by tile-roofed villages, tightly planted rice fields, low hills with pine trees and bamboo.

Kyoto was rather tantalizing and frustrating. We only had two days there, and it took a little time to settle in a hotel. We took a four-hour excursion the first afternoon, which took us to a great temple, the detached palace of the Tokugawa shogunate, a Shinto shrine with a beautiful garden, and the Iwasaki mansion, the former home of a millionaire, set in the most lovely imaginable Japanese garden.

The second day we took the street car to Nara. There we went to the temple of the great seated Buddha, cast in bronze in A.D. 749 and of a height of 53 feet. There is a lovely park in Nara, with many tame deer, and also some beautiful old temples. But this visit produced another kind of frustration—the friction between the generations. After a little temple gazing the kids were bored stiff, and they wanted to watch a baseball game. Kay and I wanted to stroll and gaze. This clash can produce quite a bit of heat, and that can spoil an outing. So we did some of both, sightseeing and baseball-watching, and went to a Japanese eating place for lunch of soba—noodles in a strong soup, garnished with bits of fish and vegetables.

In the evening, back in Kyoto, we went for dinner to the home of Jack Meskill and his wife. Jack was working on his doctorate from Columbia and later became a member of the faculty of Barnard College, teaching Chinese history. They lived in a small Japanese house, which gave us a taste of what our living would be. Next day we went by express train to Nagoya to rejoin our boat. Our two-day "shore leave" had been quite a splurge.

The kids were overjoyed to be on board the *Nikko Maru* again and to visit with the friendly officers. In Yokohama, where we arrived on September 7, we were met by John Howes, a graduate student at Columbia. He had arranged for the house we were to live in, a charming Japanese house set in an informal garden with well-pruned azaleas, maples, pines, and bamboos. Before entering we took off our shoes, for this was a real Japanese house. Our part of the house was U-shaped, built around a small inside garden planted with bamboos and pines, but looking outward on two sides into the gardens. The dining and kitchen wing were in Western style, so to speak, with cold running water, a three-burner gas plate, and a small but wonderful refrigerator. This area had a wooden floor and four chairs around a table, so we could sit up some of the time. There was also a bathroom, with an area in which to soap oneself and rinse off thoroughly, after which one got into a large wooden tub, about three feet deep, in which to soak in scalding water. As head of the household I was supposed to go first, but I always had to go last, since I am not good at scalding water. The toilet did not have a flush system; our night soil was taken off once a week by the *benjo* man.

Upstairs there was a small room with a lovely view over the rooftops. It had a wooden floor, allowing a desk and chair. I copped it as my study. The Japanese part of the house was beautiful with its tatami (straw mat) floors, shoji walls (sliding doors of lattice covered with translucent white paper), and a veranda of highly polished wood. In the living room was a very low table, beautifully finished, at which we should kneel when drinking tea. One wall had a two-compartment *tokunoma* (the beauty place) in which to hang a scroll painting, arrange a vase of flowers, and display some treasured ceramic or lacquer piece. (Our enjoyment of this was the reason we had a tokunoma built into our house in Pleasantville nine years later.) The rooms in the Japanese-style section of the house were virtually empty—except for the one low table, no furniture at all; only some scattered cushions to sit or kneel on. Everything else was tucked away in closets behind sliding doors. This traditional Japanese part of the house was spacious and airy. It soothed the soul. We were to sleep on the straw matted floor on futons (thick quilts). That would take some getting used to.

Our rent was 30,000 yen per month, and we would have to pay for our utilities, so the cost came to about $100 a month. The house was in Sakura Shin-machi, meaning "new cherry blossom street," a suburb in Setagaya-ku, on the west side of Tokyo. On clear days we could see Mt. Fuji. The village, for that is what it was, had one main shopping street that led to the Tamagawa streetcar line. The street was lined with Japanese shops—for flowers, groceries, fish, hardware—and a few soba shops and other little restaurants. Delightful! Many people wore kimonos and *geta* (wooden clogs). Most of the houses in the residential section were set behind walls, for it was a fairly prosperous suburb. From one home near us we heard lovely piano music—Bach and Beethoven. We soon learned how much the West had influenced the Japanese in cultural matters.

We learned that Tokyo had four symphony orchestras, Western ballet, many concerts, excellent European and Japanese films, not to speak of the popular American ones that our kids loved to see. We were flabbergasted to visit Maruzen Bookstore and find long shelves of foreign books on all sorts of subjects—literature, art, economics, medicine, science, engineering, psychology, the Western classics, with large sections of German and French books and great collections of paperbacks published abroad.

We got the kids bikes so they could ride to the American School in Japan, where John entered the freshman class and Ann the eighth grade. They settled in, Ann quickly, John with considerable anxiety and suspicion. John explored our area on his bike and became acquainted with some Japanese college boys. Very soon he brought two of them home to lunch unannounced, to Kay's considerable annoyance. The kids made friends at the school, which had an international student body, though it taught according to American standards preparatory to college. Ann signed herself up for all the extra courses she might take—music lessons, Japanese, typing, art—so as not to be bored, for she convinced herself that the texts for her required classes were all ones she had used at Pleasantville in the seventh grade. It wasn't as easy for John to accustom himself to the strange land. He felt uncomfortable because the people stared at him. He was nearly fifteen and rather tall—certainly compared with Japanese young folk.

We had a housekeeper, Kawagiri-san, a Christian and a widow with several sons, the youngest of whom, Koji, just about John's age, lived in our house. Kawagiri-san knew a little English, but the main thing was that she could do the routine shopping and cooking and could help Kay in other ways when I was off on my southern tour. She taught Kay flower arranging and some Japanese and helped her entertain Japanese women. We paid her 12,000 yen per month.

I tried to help Kay become independent in getting around Tokyo so she could visit friends, go to art museums and department stores, and do the necessary banking. Ultimately she did find her way about the city as need be, though the kids were better at it.

In September I was invited by Bill Holland to attend the international IPR Conference in Kyoto, which was a fine opportunity to meet Japanese intellectuals and people from India, Pakistan, Indonesia, the Philippines, Britain, France, Canada, and Australia, as well as other Americans. The meetings lasted most of ten days and were stimulating without too serious fireworks, though Indians were strongly critical of American policy in Asia. I could not detect any pro-Communist sentiments; indeed, one common denominator was the rather hostile attitude toward communism in all the delegations, as concerned their own countries.

During a weekend break I went to Kobe and called at the YMCA, where my father had begun his work in the Far East, and where he had helped to build the first Y building. Dad had given me a letter to the general secretary. I was most cordially received and wrote to Dad afterward, describing the new building and its activities. Several secretaries and retired workers remembered him with affection. I also spent a day with Stirling Takeuchi, who had been a visiting scholar at the East Asian Institute for two years. He was a professor at Kansai Gakuin University.

I made a point to discuss with the Japanese delegates, and with some of the Indians, the attitudes of their publics toward China—that is, Communist China. It was a fine opportunity to become acquainted in a natural way, and to begin exploring my general topic of research—Communist China's influence on other Asian countries. One thing I learned from some of the Japanese delegates was their concern at the "reverse course" instituted by American policy in regard to Japan—that is, to encourage redevelopment of Japanese industry, perhaps even the Zaibatsu, and the creation of Japanese self-defense forces. This was a basic turnaround in reaction to the Korean War in which the United States was dependent upon Japan as a base and a source of supplies and hence developed the conception of Japan as an ally against the Communist block. Some liberal or leftist Japanese feared this as a first step toward reviving militarism. One of the Japanese delegates was Shio Sakanishi, whom we had known in Washington in 1935, working at the Library of Congress. She had been interned for a time during the war but was repatriated and became a widely respected columnist and novelist.

Back in Tokyo I had plenty of contact with young American students who had done graduate work at Columbia, many in the East Asian Institute, including Peter Berton, Paul Langer, Donald Keene, Herschel Webb, Leon Hurwitz, Jack Meskill, Francis Weinberg, and our valiant helper, John Howes. On October 15 we had those studying in Tokyo for dinner at our pleasant house. It was easy to entertain such a group, because we just ordered in a Japanese meal from a nearby restaurant. Each of them later became a professor, except Fran. Among them they have published many books and articles on Japan.

I continued my interviewing of Japanese persons in public life for three more weeks before departing for a journey south. I interviewed four Japanese journalists, three YMCA secretaries, scholars who specialize on China, a few students, members of the U.S. Embassy and the Nationalist Chinese Embassy staffs, and business leaders. I also went to five universities to talk with professors and visited two research institutes, one a pipeline for Chinese Communist publicity, and the other within the Japanese Foreign Ministry. I was frequently entertained, for I had many letters of introduction. As a result, we developed quite a social life.

I sent a report to the Ford Foundation, and to the East Asian Institute also, about my findings after six weeks in Japan. I first told of the types of persons I had interviewed, the institutions I had been to, visits to bookstores, and careful reading of the three English-language newspapers—*Mainichi*, *Asahi*, and *Japan Times*, as well as my discussions at the Institute of Pacific Relations Conference. Here I quote a few passages from that preliminary report.

> Practically everyone with whom I have talked expressed the view that the general Japanese view is favorable toward mainland China and the accomplishments of its Communist regime. This attitude, it is stated, is not based upon detailed information on what has happened in China during the past five years. Rather it springs from a sentimental attitude combined with a persistent press campaign to present the Chinese People's Republic in a favorable light.

Under background factors, I mentioned Japan's historic ties with China, the thousands of Japanese who have lived in China and consequently feel they know the country and people; many have an affectionate regard for them. Business with China held a great attraction: 600 million customers! I reported on the persistent effort of the PRC to project the most positive image through its publications, the work of a pro-Communist Japanese research and publicity organization (which I had visited), and the pro-China slant of three of the four most popular Japanese magazines directed toward educated Japanese.

The attitudes toward Communist China and Soviet Russia were very different, I was told: the one friendly and the other hostile. The friendly attitude was in contrast to a growing anti-American sentiment among intellectuals. Insofar as America was losing prestige, China, its antagonist, seemed to be gaining. The favorable attitude was growing because of three series of events. One was the repatriation of thousands of Japanese civilians and military personnel from China, an event carefully staged to extract the maximum favorable publicity for China. The PRC controlled the selection of those first repatriated; their public reports mostly lauded China. The second series of events was the visits of Japanese delegations to China and their reports as given in the press. These visits, too, were carefully staged: the visitors very well treated and shown only what the government wanted visitors to see. Initial reports were almost universally favorable. An

American student of Japanese communism observed that it would be about as difficult to get an unfavorable report on "People's China" published in Japan as it
would be to get an article lauding the PRC published in the United States. The
third factor was economic. Japanese industry was in decline after the great production expansion during the Korean War, and many believed that increased
trade with China would make up the slack.

China and the USSR had launched a peace offensive, hoping to attract Japan
out of the free-world bloc, and I gave examples of the various initiatives coming
from China. However, the price tag China placed on its peace offer was interpreted
as requiring Japan's abrogation of the U.S.–Japan Security Treaty. There was
little inclination among Japanese leaders for that switch. But the themes of
peaceful coexistence, trade, and Asia for the Asians might have very strong
appeal. What was the significance of these things? Would favorable attitudes, if
they continued, be translated into positive acts such as the establishment of
regular commercial relations and ultimately diplomatic relations between the two
countries? This seemed likely. Would they lead to greater neutralism in Japan, or
even in the direction of Japan's dependency upon China and Russia? Clearly the
Communist states were working toward that goal. An international struggle centered right there. Questions such as these opened the door to many other complex
and interesting issues of fact and interpretation.

My tentative report was dated October 22, 1954. On October 29 I left for
Taiwan. On the plane I wrote in my journal about my impressions of Japan.

Tokyo impresses me by its bustle. Everything is swarming and active, the
streets thronged with many sorts of vehicles—bicycles, carts, motor scooters,
motor bikes, motor tricycles of many sizes, small taxis, cars—small and big—
buses, streetcars. The trains and streetcars and buses are jammed. Department
stores throng with people. But there is also a great deal of wasted time. There
are a great number of small shops, each crowded with goods of all sorts.
Business seems slow. Downtown Tokyo has scores of banks and many new
office buildings, and there are many universities and schools.

Yet there is a small depression in Japan brought on by the government's
deflationary policy. Unemployment figures are growing; business in small
shops seems, on the surface, slow. It is terribly hard for university students to
get jobs; at least their view is very pessimistic.

Politically Japan seems unsettled. The conservative parties are split inter-
nally and cannot seem to coalesce. The two socialist parties have not effected a
reunion. Japanese intellectuals are being fed by their magazines, and are feeding each other, with anti-American propaganda, yet Japan is tightly tied to
America by the Security Treaty, by American bases, by financial and economic ties. Japan is trying hard to find markets all over the world but is having
difficulty in reconciling with the Philippines and Indonesia and being admitted
to GATT and is restrained from trade with mainland China. It is very frustrating for businessmen. Intellectuals seem quite leftist. Propaganda that appears
to an American as definitely Communist-inspired circulates unchallenged (?)

among academic and other intellectuals, at least as one may judge from the magazine world and what I am told. But if intellectuals are leftist, business people and government are conservative. The "general public"—what do I know of it? The articulate segments of the population seem to be spiritually or emotionally quite unsettled. I got this impression strongly at the IPR Conference through statements made by university people, government people, and writers: uncertainty how far back the "reverse course" would take the country in education, in constitutional change, in remilitarization, in centralization, in attempts at thought-control, in increasing the power of a conservative bureaucracy. There was uncertainty about Japan's international position. Dislike for the close ties to the United States, but some fear of Russia; longing to be neutral and free of armaments burden, but also a wish to be independent where power and geography makes independence for Japan unattainable. Fear of the hydrogen bomb—almost pathological fixation on this problem. Dislike of some for communism and violent tactics, but emotional sympathy and intellectual assent for the Communist "peace offensive." The whole range of civil liberties, which intellectuals defend and fear may be snatched away, is supported by Communists (when not yet in power). This throws them and the liberal intellectuals into the same camp on issues of freedom and rights. I did not see any evidence of liberals turning their back upon or opposing any present Communist policies. It would be very hard to draw a line between the Communists and left Socialists so far as I could see, though I never probed deeply into that. . . .

My first impressions of Taiwan are from my journal, written on October 29, 1954, more than eight years after I had left Shanghai in May 1946:

Seems very much a familiar Chinese town. Much more leisurely than Japan. Rather slipshod, easygoing. Lacks the intensity of Tokyo. Certainly not so crowded. It seems a provincial city, which it is. One sees many men in uniform, but they don't seem very military. . . . There are a great many pedicab drivers sleeping or just loitering, waiting to pick up a fare. One wonders— where is the emergency? Is there a sense of mission and drive? Certainly there are no visually evident signs of fear of attack or preparations of civilians for war. Is there a drive toward modernization or toward economic expansion? Or is it just easygoing, happy-go-lucky China?

In Taipei, the capital of the island and its largest city, I stayed at the YMCA where Mr. Arnold, a friend of the family, was the fraternal secretary. It cost me NT $60 per night, the equivalent of U.S. $1.50. Mr. Arnold had arranged several meetings for me, and I also had letters of introduction. Being a Columbia professor was a help in meeting people, for many Chinese had studied at Columbia. The first evening I was a guest for dinner at the home of Ms. Whipple, the American cultural attaché, where I met several friendly Chinese intellectuals, and after that we went to a concert of Chinese music.

A couple of days later I walked over to the amusement district in the western part of the city. What a tremendous bustle! One passed clusters of open-stall restaurants with the rich smell of frying foods, that peculiar pungent smell of the oil used to fry bean curd. Each stall was lighted by a single bulb, having one table or a long bench, then a smoking hot dish of food, and people sitting around with bowls of rice or noodles and some bits of meat. Just a little further on were one- or two-story department stores, or places selling firecrackers for President Chiang's birthday the next day, and barbershops and bookstores. Also tearooms with subdued lights, small tables, and couples eating cakes or drinking coffee. Then the movie theaters. There were four of them, all but one showing American movies. Outside each was a tremendous crowd—probably the people who had bought their tickets and were waiting for the change of shows. Such a gregarious, uninhibited bunch! No Japanese stiffness. Little apparent self-consciousness. Just a lot of men and women, youths, soldiers, children, all having a sociable time. All the while pedicab drivers trilling their bells and shouting to get through, cars honking, and no one seeming to pay much attention to these intrusions.

I interviewed quite a few Americans, including two old friends and the American ambassador, Mr. Rankin. Also I called on the president of National Taiwan University and seven or eight Chinese professors and government officials to whom I had introductions. Dr. Chiang Mon-lin, an old friend and now chief commissioner of the Joint Commission on Rural Reconstruction, arranged a trip for me to see their work in progress. This organization was made up of three Chinese and two American commissioners, agricultural economists, with a small staff of specialists, guiding the development of agriculture in Taiwan after the land reform program. The work of JCRR was a great success story and an example of the best sort of American developmental aid being carried through by the host country. Chinese officials and Americans with whom I talked were all very proud of JCRR. It had roots in Jimmy Yen's rural reconstruction efforts and had been tried in West China during the last years of the war, but without success in inflationary wartime conditions.

In the afternoon I was picked up by three persons from JCRR in a car and taken to the country. They were Dr. S. C. Hsu, director of the Health Division, Mr. Liao Chi-tsing, coordinator of 4-H work, and Mr. Lin Lieh, a land redistribution expert. We drove out into farm country and stopped first at a Farmers Association. I was told that under a recent reorganization only actual farmers, 70 percent or more of whose income came from farming, were members. They elected their board, which hired the manager who directed the staff. Through the association the farmers got fertilizer in exchange for rice. There was a rice mill that charged both farmers and government for milling rice. We saw bins full of rice. Also a savings bank for farmers that paid interest at between 1 percent and 1.9 percent per month. Cloth, farm tools (such as sprayers), and other necessities were sold through the association at lower than retail prices. I was told that there was a network of such associations all over the island, and that in them were the beginnings of grassroots democracy.

We then went to a rural health center. There was a little cement building of standard unit design in which there were a doctor, nurse, lab technician, midwife, and clerk. Several farm women were having their babies looked after. One young woman was dressed in a brilliant red dress and her mouth was well smeared with lipstick. It was an efficient little building, and I was told there were a large number of them throughout the island. They had vaccinated about 85 percent of the children against TB and were moving up to the older age groups. They had stores of modern medicines—sulfa drugs and mycins—which they showed to me. They also had scales, a microscope, sterilizers, and so on. The staff were trained or retrained in refresher courses. Dr. Hsu gave me a torrent of explanation about the development of them—he was a perfect dynamo at age forty-nine, terrifically enthusiastic, and seemed very capable. Anyway, it added up to a network of rural public health stations that were locally requested (by village elders) and locally financed, though medicines, supervision, and training came from JCRR. This network was the basis of efficient rural public health. They also had a program for school health, to be conducted by the teachers. And they were gradually working toward a program of planned parenthood, which had to be approached carefully because of fear of American Catholics, on one hand, and of Chinese Nationalists, on the other. It would be worked in gradually on a foundation of home economics, child care, and the general health program. (In 1977 I was told of the success of the planned parenthood program, and how the population increase had been brought down to about 2 percent per annum.)

We also went to a land-record office, where I was shown the cadastral maps that showed each plot of land, the landownership books, and the record cards of field ownership. I now believe these records were inherited from the Japanese administration, though updated during land redistribution. All these were the basis for the land distribution program, which, I was told, had been entirely carried through. The JCRR had had an important part in it.

We went to a vocational agricultural school with 750 boys of junior and senior high school age. The teacher showed us around the rather grim, sparse dormitories with about 20 boys per room, sleeping on tatami. Their supper was rather sparse, too, it seemed to me. A canister of rice, a little box of dried fish, and some soup. We were told there were to be two vegetables, no sweets, no fruit. There was much about the school and the look of the kids that reminded me of Japan. But the place had no Japanese beauty. Some of the children were playing basketball; a few others were studying in the dim afternoon light of their class rooms. Most of them, I was told, would not go back to farming.

Another person I talked with was Professor Richard Walker of Yale University and later of the University of South Carolina. He was one of the first American scholars to settle down for a year in Taiwan, and he has been committed to the Nationalist cause ever since, as have I. I went to dinner in the little Japanese house that he and his wife had rented. One of the things that Dixie told me was how brave the Chinese academic people were, living on poverty-level salaries, which required them to hold extra teaching positions or to write articles constantly to earn a few more dollars. I found this still to be so seven years later, when Kay and I were in Taiwan as Fulbrighters. However, things improved greatly in a few years. During the Reagan administration Professor Walker was appointed the American ambassador in Seoul, Korea.

I went down to the southern part of the island to visit Kaohsiung, which had been laid out grandly by the Japanese for the capital of their southern empire. Now it was the heavy-industry center of the island. I was shown a shipyard, an aluminum-processing factory, and several others, but it seemed to be rather small-time industry. Ten and twenty years later, when I visited it again, the manufacturing industry in Kaohsiung was really impressive. On the train back north I met Olive Lawton, a missionary in Taiwan who had been a schoolmate of mine in Shanghai. She told me a little about Chia-i, her station of the past two years. She noted that the mainlanders had put down roots, and she didn't know of much antipathy between mainlanders and Taiwanese. She showed real enthusiasm for 4-H work, saying it had given the rural boys a big lift. She mentioned great receptivity to Christianity among mainlanders since the fall of the mainland to the Communists. She didn't confirm from her experience a spirit of superiority and inferiority among the two sections of the population.

I took an excursion to Sun-Moon Lake, a beauty spot in the mountains in the center of the island. The trip down by bus was full of interesting sights of early morning farm and village occupations. A few things I noted:

— how many women work in the fields alone or with the men
— kids—even very young ones—carrying baskets of things on the carrying pole along with their parents
— JCRR threshing machines being used in the fields
— bicycles used to carry freight
— ducks, chickens, geese, and even turkeys in large numbers in the villages and farmyards
— large numbers of children
— not much land wasted in graveyards (one fairly large "arm-chair type" grave had cabbages planted all about it and partly up the sides, but neatly, and not intruding onto the grave itself)
— the meticulous care used in farming (Taiwan is one big vegetable garden)
— the pajama-type clothes of the country folk—for men, pants and jackets in black, blue, grey, and even white; for women, the "house dress" in bright colors, but occasionally a woman in trousers and jacket, sometimes of the North China bright blue
— lots of bamboo and banana groves, and what may have been coconut trees
— lots of people using the side of the paved roads as drying floors for rice, or shrimps, or something white I didn't recognize.

I shouldn't let it appear that I merely traveled about looking at the folks. I was constantly interviewing. One of the most convincing talks was with Kempton Fitch, an old friend who worked for the American Economic Aid Mission and told me in detail of the great care in planning for particular projects, the technical review by the J. G. White Engineering Firm, careful cost accounting, and tight American control over the funds until the project was completed. He was confident that the American taxpayers were not being rooked by graft, as had been the case on the mainland. Kemp was not cynical or critical. He said the government was fortunate to have so many able administrators and technically trained men, enough to govern the province effectively.

Another most interesting talk was with Mr. K. P. Chen, the founder of the Shanghai Commercial and Savings Bank. I had an introduction to him from Julie How, who referred to him as Uncle. Most of our talk was about difficulty in persuading overseas Chinese capital to invest in Taiwan. Several obstacles: So long as the prime consideration of the government was to retake the mainland, then business and development of the island would be treated as secondary. To get overseas Chinese to invest there was difficult under any conditions. What would be the attraction? Could good profit be made and taken out? In Singapore, for example, the overseas Chinese had their familiar institutions—banks, associations, clubs, rubber plantations, tin mines. Their capital had roots. To lift up some and deposit it in Taiwan was like pulling up a tree to transplant it. It takes time to get accustomed to doing that, to be persuaded it is sound and profitable. The businessmen from overseas and the government officials who invited them to come to Taiwan "spoke a different language." The officials did not understand business very well, and many really despised it. If the businessmen asked what guarantee was given that they could take out their profits, the officials said, "You are not patriotic." But that was a different language from that of the merchants. Profits and patriotism are two different languages. Taiwan didn't have the facilities or institutions for business. New private commercial banks, such as Shanghai Commercial and Savings Bank, could not start business there. There was no stock market, and very little local capital, so the institutions of capitalism had not developed. Therefore it wasn't easy for new outside capital to come in. But the central point was that government was concentrated on retaking the mainland. This determined tax policy and many other things vital to business. Mr. Chen was hoping, however, that gradually overseas Chinese would develop more confidence and begin to invest there. He said they absolutely would not invest anything in the mainland at that time. He emphasized that coexistence with communism would not work, and that America must stay strong.

After eleven days in Taiwan, which created a strong interest in the place and its future, I wrote to Kay from Hong Kong:

> I had a fine time in Taiwan, as you might judge from my letters. However, I felt a little inhibited in writing from there because I didn't know about secret

police and opening mail, and perhaps getting people into trouble. . . . I was moderately well impressed by the show there; and I came to the conclusion that the national government can bear to have open-minded persons come there and have a look at what they have been doing for the island with U.S. help. Possibly there is an alternative to the Communist way of development, right there on the island, but nothing startling or spectacular yet. But something may be moving that will bear comparison to what the Communist Chinese leaders are doing with Russian help. The land reform, so far as I could learn, was conducted thoroughly, fairly, and moderately. The landlords were compelled to sell their land above a certain number of acres to the government, but they got something in return. The tillers got the land. And there is no plan to take it away from them again as the Communist collectivization program has it. There aren't many flies in the cities of Taiwan either, but no one has made the hullabaloo about it that the Communists do in Peking.

There is a fine system of rural public health stations, and also farmers associations that I was assured were real farmer-owned and democratically controlled cooperatives. There is considerable evidence of rural prosperity (by Chinese standards): country girls wearing bright new clothes, having their hair curled, and wearing lipstick; lots of bicycles, electric power all over (from the Japanese days, but rehabilitated). The island is very productive, too.

There are many things to be improved. Bureaucracy is much too big, but that is a form of relief for the faithful. The troops one sees all over certainly don't look much like soldiers, but I didn't get to see field forces. Anyway, there are far too many of them unproductive. If a police state exists, it's kept out of sight, and one sees no sign of regimentation or inhibition—but such matters are very difficult to know about if they are kept behind the scenes. I tried to evoke criticism of the regime but got very little, and that only from Americans with whom I got onto a pretty friendly basis. There was criticism but all expressed mildly, as points that needed improving; and there was far more genuine praise and general satisfaction.

All in all, I came away well impressed, but not entirely trusting my judgment. I had a long talk with the *Christian Science Monitor* man for this part of the world, who has been several times to Taiwan over the past six years and had just come back. His observations were similar to mine, and he showed me a write-up he did on a three-day country trip he took with Doak Barnett and one of the commissioners of the JCRR, and the senior engineer of the J. G. White Co., which is the watchdog engineering firm employed by our government to see that our economic aid is effectively used. His detail was much greater than mine, but the direction was the same. . . . Frankly, I felt I wanted to go back and see some more, dig a little deeper. Maybe I will.

Hong Kong was a wonderfully stimulating place. British rule and capitalism—Chinese and Western—had made it incomparably the showcase of colonial rule. Chinese entrepreneurs thrived there. The harbor was breathtakingly beautiful, with high peaks set within blue waters. I stayed with Bob Berton, who was working with Chang Kuo-t'ao on Chang's memoirs. Chang was one of the earliest members of the Chinese Communist Party, and one of its top leaders until 1938, when Mao Tse-tung bested him in a power struggle. I had a couple of talks with him and found him a most engaging and very courteous person. I saw a number of other people, including Allen Whiting and Hank Lieberman, correspondent for the *New York Times*. Hank confirmed my impressions of Taiwan, but Allen was very critical of the regime there, considering it just as authoritarian as the regime on the mainland, using similar brainwashing techniques for prisoners on Green Island, suppressing press freedom, and running a sham parliament.

John Keswick, head of Jardines in Hong Kong, talked with me about trade with the mainland. He was pessimistic, believing that half of China's export commodities were pledged to Soviet Russia, and the rest would be allocated among many competitors. Besides, there was little the West wanted from China. He had talked with a Japanese who had served for twenty years in China and had recently returned from a trip there. He agreed that the China trade would not be large for Japan, though whatever there was would be helpful. Mr. Keswick also told me of several Chinese acquaintances of his who had gone back recently but vowed never to return to China because their treatment was so bad. The impression he gave me was that China was paranoid just then.

Hong Kong is where Julie How spent much of her childhood, and she had given me introductions to several Chinese of note. Here are some reflections on Hong Kong as I saw it briefly in November 1955, a lovely time of the year in South China.

> There are great contrasts of wealth and poverty. It is a modern city with beautiful streets and handsome buildings, especially modern apartment buildings dotting the Peak. But there are terrible slum quarters, with tightly packed buildings five stories high, filled with people, the streets simply swarming. Even worse are the squalid squatter colonies inhabited by refugees from the mainland, with thousands of shacks put together of tin and cardboard with no plan, little sanitation—simply awful places, through which rage terrible fires that render thousands of people homeless. Yet Hong Kong is an efficiently managed place, with plenty of police, good water and public communications, and money to be made by those who have a little capital and skill. There are many separate social worlds in Hong Kong. Certainly the British stand somewhat aloof, but how many strata there are in British society, one doesn't know. There are Chinese businesspeople who mingle with British and American businessmen, and there are Chinese intellectuals—mostly refugees—who engage in writing and scheming, and who touch the few American intellectuals at many points.
>
> It is the great lookout place for China-watching. There must be many strata in the Chinese community, by speech groups, places of origin, and occupation. I couldn't begin to see into that world of shopkeepers, boatmen, peddlers, factory workers, and handicraftsmen, not to mention the thousands and thousands of jobless refugees. Hong Kong must be a very tempting prize with its first-class harbor and berthing facilities, its light industry and skilled workforce. It could be taken fairly easily, as the Japanese took it in late 1941.

I left on November 25 after two interesting weeks, bound for Rangoon.

Burma is a place where I had never been, and an entirely new culture. As the plane descended to the Rangoon airport, I wrote in great excitement:

> Flying across the Gulf of Martaban, first a strip of tide lands, then the rectangular fields of the wonderfully rich delta—the miles and miles of fields amid winding rivers. Water seems absolutely controlling the landscape. Coming down over Rangoon, I saw the first spire of a pagoda. It is a city with its suburbs in the fields.

Dr. John Scott Everton and two others met me at the airport. John was the Ford Foundation representative in Burma and was very helpful in arranging my stay and many introductions. John is just my age, and we continued our acquaintanceship when he brought his family home through Tokyo, and then later, by strange coincidence, he rented a house in Pleasantville directly below ours. The others who met me were Professor John Seabury Thompson, a former student at the Shanghai American School and a former Columbia graduate student (I was on his Ph.D. committee), now on a Ford Foundation grant in Burma; and Eugene Turner, Jr., a YMCA secretary. Gene and his wife, Marjory, invited me to stay with them for a couple of days till I could be put up elsewhere. But as it turned out we got on famously and they insisted that I stay the whole time with them. The foreign community that I met reminded me much of the missionary community in Seoul as Kay and I knew it in the early 1930s.

The first morning there I took a walk to see a new culture. My first impressions were of leisure, no crowding, a restrained gaiety. The men and women both wore long skirts, the women with light-colored bodices, the men with colored shirts. Often both were smoking cigars. Transportation was by bullock carts, buses, jeeps, tri-shaws, and lots of bicycles. Rangoon seemed a confusing city downtown. Wide streets and a few modern buildings—banks, a hotel, government offices. But everything extremely messy and confused. Less order than one would find in a Chinese street! The Chinese bazaar section was indescribably messy and confused, with merchants spreading their wares on the sidewalk, hanging things from roofs—the most disordered street I had ever seen.

The contrast between Rangoon and Hong Kong was startling. In Hong Kong public communication was efficient and up-to-date; in Rangoon, equipment was falling to pieces. In Hong Kong everything was well policed and fairly tidy; in Rangoon, there seemed to be little policing, and everything was in disorder. There was a polyglot appearance to the street crowd. The city gave the impression of a provincial capital or a sprawling state capital. Of course, Burma had been part of the British empire and then had a brief period under Japanese control.

I also walked around the corridors of the municipal office building. It was unbelievable how inefficient and lackadaisical those offices seemed. Many people doing absolutely nothing. A few clerks typing slowly away. Much loitering.

One morning Eugene Turner took me to see the activities of the Sixth World Congress of Buddhists, being held on the outskirts of Rangoon. The conference was scheduled to last two years, and one of its main activities was to prepare an official Pali text of the scriptures. Buddhist priests from Ceylon, Thailand, Cambodia, and Burma as well as observers from northern Buddhist countries were gathered there. A large meeting hall was covered by an artificial mountain so that it was a cave. About 500 priests in saffron robes were working on the text, chanting it; we saw many visitors dressed in bright clothes observing the ceremony while sitting on floor mats in reverential attitude. It was an impressive service.

We visited the peace pagoda erected under sponsorship of Prime Minister U Nu. Inside were several large gilt statues of the Buddha, and in front of each were banks of flowers. It was lovely to see families of Burmese kneel down before the statues with flowers in their hands and pray. Even the little children were learning to pray. One had the feeling that this form of Buddhism is still a vital, personal religion.

Outside we saw Burmese families having their picnics. Again a charming sight, everyone so mild and congenial and sociable. Not in the rather extroverted way of the Chinese, who really are rather boisterous, but in a sort of gentle sociability. I thoroughly enjoyed seeing this center and learning that it was planned to be a center of a revived Buddhism for southern Asia. In fact, there is a political as well as a religious aim in all this, I understood: the aim of strengthening Buddhism against the onslaught of communism. Little was said of that side of the movement, however.

I also visited the cultural exhibition put on by the Chinese government to show the modern arts and crafts of China. It was shown in the city hall, at the entrance to which there were crossed flags of the Republic of Burma and the People's Republic of China. Exhibition cases were filled with fine Chinese porcelains, textiles, lacquer, and wood, stone, and ivory carvings. I went twice and observed mixed crowds of Burmese, Chinese, and Indians, afternoon and evening. It was a very effective show.

One wonderful Sunday evening was spent seeing a Burmese play, presented outdoors in the grounds of the Burma Translation Society. We got there early and were ushered up to seats at the front reserved for special guests. We inspected the orchestra, mostly drums and clarinets with some other instruments. The drums were in sets of graduated pitch that could be tuned, and much time was spent in tuning them up. One drummer sat with twenty-two drums around him, which he beat with his fingers and hands. There were nineteen graduated cymbals in another setup. The clarinets were really beautiful, and the men who played them enjoyed showing their virtuosity. When the whole orchestra was in full voice, with clarinets trilling, drums and cymbals echoing, clappers clapping, and men chanting, it made a fine sound.

The play was a legendary-religious tale about the founding of Ceylon, full of kings, ministers, gods, ogres and ogresses. It was declaimed in a fine style of Burmese, with occasional singing. The costumes were simply gorgeous and gave me the impression they were Cambodian, though perhaps it was just the Hindu influence. Both men and women wore bright-colored costumes covered with jewels, and with towering headdresses. Between scenes of great formality, during which the actors were rather wooden and showed no participation while another actor was declaiming, there would come informal and apparently impromptu acts in which the performer told jokes to the great delight of the audience, occasionally went into a dance, and generally had a fine time. The rapport between audience and performer was close and all enjoyed themselves.

I went to the Shwe Dagon Pagoda one morning. A guide attached himself to me immediately. I climbed a long flight of stairs all under roof, and with stalls on each side where flowers for the Buddha and religious books are sold. Finally we got up to the great platform around the golden spire. The platform was paved with marble and quite clean because each morning volunteer groups washed it down. At the top of each of the four approaches, which were at the four cardinal points, there was an altar to the Buddha. In between, all around the central spire, were innumerable altars in bright red, gold, or white. The effect was of a bewildering variety of beauty and color. The lovely Burmese people in their bright clothes were worshipping most devoutly with flowers in their hands. Monks in yellow robes walked around the platform, which took about five minutes to circle. Apparently, wealthy persons scattered uncut gems as a form of gift to the poor, for we saw several children crawling about to find these gems in the cracks between the marble paving slabs. The spire of the pagoda soared up to the sky. One could see how much Buddhism meant, by observing the great reverence shown by those who were worshipping.

My main purpose in being in Burma was to learn what I could about attitudes toward and influences of the great neighbor to the north, the People's Republic of China. One approach was to visit bookstores and see what literature was being featured. There were several leftist bookstores: one near the Sule Pagoda near the center of town sold exclusively Chinese and Russian propaganda books, a full array from Peking's Foreign Language Press, and works of Mao Tse-tung and Liu Shao-ch'i. The prices for books from China and Russia were very low, but I didn't see many buyers in that store. Educated Burmese all know English. Books in Burmese were fewer. I also saw some open-air stalls selling Chinese Communist literature downtown. The People's Literature Bookshop had a more balanced selection in current affairs and modern history, and even one book by Raja Huthesing, which reported unfavorably on his trip to China, but there also was the full display of Foreign Language Press magazines from China in English. In the back room I saw more than a thousand unopened packages of books lining the walls from floor to ceiling, with a Russian return address.

On the other side there was the Chinthe Bookstore, with a wonderful display

of books published in America, some rather high-priced, and with one shelf
of definitely anti-Communist books, especially anti-Russian. This was a project
of the Asia Foundation (at that time a CIA subsidiary, I believe). It also had a
bookmobile. Several Burmese I met knew exactly what the Chinthe Bookstore
was. During an hour and a half there I saw only a couple of people come in to
browse. The American manager told me that he recently went to customs to get a
shipment of books, only 200 packages, but saw more than 2,000 packages for the
Chinese and Russian embassies.

Miss Virginia Geiger, the American cultural attaché, told me of the program
to translate American books—classics and contemporary fiction, biographies,
and works on American government and society—into Burmese. So far they had
produced 85 works, and they helped the publishers by buying about 1,500 out of
an edition of 4,000. The books that the American embassy bought went to
Burmese reading rooms run by the government, youth centers, and so forth. The
Burmese government approved of this work, yet the government was apprehensive that the United States would gain too much influence. The government
performed a sort of balancing act between the Communist countries and the
Western ones.

The USIS Library was a fine place. It had a large reading room with long
tables and a great variety of current magazines, including technical ones. There
were about thirty readers. There was a well-stocked reference room, a music
room, and a children's room. It was the liveliest book place I visited, and a great
credit to the United States and to American librarianship. "Imagine that sort
of place coming under the axe of Cohn and Shine!" I wrote. They were aides of
Senator Joseph McCarthy who went around the world in the early 1950s inspecting USIS libraries and trying to terrorize the librarians.

By contrast, I saw the "library" of 6,000-student Rangoon University, the
only university in Burma. The library was a two-story building with large, empty
shelf-space. The card catalogue showed a limited supply of books. In the office
of the assistant librarian (the position of librarian was purely honorary) I saw one
desk and the floor piled high with books being catalogued. There was also a
twenty-four-drawer card catalogue for the Special Collection, open only by permission of the Librarian and not known to the students. It contained many recent
books on the Far East, and why it was "special" I couldn't learn. The library was
open from ten to four. The reading room had seats for about 100, and I counted 9
users at 10:30 that Saturday morning. In the stacks I saw books and magazines
piled on the floor. It was disgraceful. In addition, the university's departments
had special libraries, with the books in locked cabinets. We visited the economics library, which was particularly noted. In a one-room library with about
twenty desks and eight or ten bookcases behind glass there were no readers, just
a librarian. With due allowance for Japanese destruction and postwar troubles, if
there were a real will to have a library as an intellectual center, the university
could have created one, I speculated. Apparently the administration didn't care.

As I wrote in my journal, "I would be extremely suspicious of any A.B. degree granted from a university with such an attitude toward books and reading."

Everywhere I went I was cordially received, and I did not detect an anti-American attitude. The Japanese minister told me that if he went around to the top men in government he would not find expressions of anti-Americanism.

Another subject of great interest was the struggle between Peking and Taipei to win and hold the support of the Chinese community in Burma—a struggle going on all over Southeast Asia. The Chinese were the merchant class, though they shared that role with Indians. There were said to be about 100,000 Chinese. The Embassy of the People's Republic of China was very active, I was told. It had a system of economic controls over Chinese by offering bank loans without collateral if there were two guarantors. The conditions were that the recipient must send his children to Communist-controlled schools, fly the PRC flag on specified days, and not hire any anti-Communists in the business. The Chinese Accountants and Bookkeepers Union was completely Communist controlled, I was told, so the embassy could easily learn the internal business condition of larger Chinese businesses. To try to control the Chinese schools, the embassy imported Chinese textbooks and sold them at nominal prices. Of 236 Chinese schools in Burma, only 6 were using non-Communist textbooks by the beginning of 1951. But a countermovement located in Singapore to produce non-Communist books had resulted in an almost even division among the Chinese schools in this war of texts. Of course, the division of loyalty was not clear-cut, for the contest was fierce. The embassy was intensifying its efforts by creating sports clubs, supplying equipment, and sponsoring interscholastic meets. However, in 1953 the Burmese government ordered all embassies to stop sponsoring athletic meets, and forbade the sending of films and other propaganda materials to schools. So the Chinese embassy used the Burma Workers and Peasants party (a Communist front) to distribute for it. The embassy also bought out three Chinese-language newspapers, but the other side also had papers.

The embassy had been unsuccessful in its efforts to gain control over the leadership of the three main Chinese secret societies, so it was infiltrating and trying to gain control from below. Also it helped to create rival organizations of the same name, sometimes causing protest riots. My informant estimated that the score was about even, though the embassy had much more to spend than the anti-Communist Chinese side. An anti-Communist Chinese estimated that as to Chinese middle schools, the score was about even, but in addition there were two Chinese middle schools—one Catholic and one Baptist—that were well attended. Other activities of Peking's embassy that I was told about by some Chinese were a Chinese hospital, an Overseas Chinese Welfare Commission, the bringing in of teachers from the mainland, and the subsidizing of schools. But the real work was covert—various forms of pressure on the Chinese community.

The Burmese government was apprehensive about this struggle, for the Chinese in Burma could become a fifth column. The government decreed that any

Chinese students who went to the mainland for study could not return to Burma.

Another factor that influenced the government's attitude was the presence of Nationalist Chinese troops that had retreated into northern Burma (and also northern Thailand), and who by then were deeply involved in the drug trade. They were an invitation to the People's Republic to send in an army and clean them out. The Burma Army could not protect its northern borders nor do the job of cleaning out the invaders itself.

I had so much enjoyed a trip away from Taipei that I thought it would be great to get out of Rangoon, too. So I arranged for a trip by steamer to a delta town, Maubin. I had as companions two young Karen men who knew some English. At 6:30 that morning we went to the jetty and found our steamer already crowded with people sitting on mats with their baggage around them. However, right up front on the upper deck was a special place that cost three times the regular fare and had very few people; there we found chairs and a table. The tide was low, and a beautifully painted Burmese junk was stranded high above the water line. The colorful Burmese crowd bustled about on the shore, as I wrote just after we took off early in the morning on December 9.

> After a little ways we came into the Twante Canal, which was dug by Turkish prisoners during the First World War. It connects Rangoon River with the creeks and streams of the Irrawaddy delta. We pass along between fields with clusters of houses, not large enough to be called villages. We see cattle grazing, and pass by a small pagoda not very well kept. There have been small canoes, paddled by one or two persons, and larger sailing craft with high pointed prow, brightly painted and with an eye on each side of the bow, as with Chinese junks. But there don't seem to be many people on shore, so near to Rangoon. The houses one sees, or at least those at the small town of Twante, which we passed, are built up on stilts. They are "basha huts" made of bamboo poles and mats for sides. After 22 miles of canal we entered the Irrawaddy, or at least one of its streams, and are steaming up it. It seems about a quarter of a mile wide. One sees banana trees and houses here and there along the shore, but not so very much life. But as we have gone further up the river the shoreline becomes more frequently spread with villages. One sees women bathing and washing clothes, children swimming, laundry spread to dry, boats drawn up to shore. The villages are always under trees and stretched along the water front. The water is very brown but flows quite smartly along. The brown water, green fringe of trees, and the blue sky provide three bands of color.
>
> The Burmese passengers are a mild and peaceable-seeming people. We have a police escort of nine, but most of them are asleep. About half the passengers are sleeping too, at 11 A.M. Others—men and women—are smoking the big local cigars. One way is to smoke with the burning part down in a glass or cup. Why, I don't know, but I've seen a number of people do it. This boat is quite filthy.

We arrived at Maubin, a town of about 20,000, at about 11:30 and stayed there till nearly 4:00, visiting the bazaars, going to an American Baptist mission with its school for about 300 kids, looking in on a rice mill owned by an Indian, and watching laborers carrying bags of rice from a storehouse to the shore. We went into a Chinese tea shop and variety store to have a cup of tea and get out of the sun. The man of the store was wearing Burmese clothes, but his wife was dressed in Chinese pajamas. Though he was from Fukien, we were able to talk a bit in Mandarin. He sent a boy to show me the Chinese school, though it wasn't in session. I met the principal, Mr. Wang. He was a modern young Chinese, a 1946 graduate of Lien-ta, the wartime associated universities in Kunming. In appearance the school was neutral, with pictures only of Sun Yat-sen and Confucius. Neither Chiang nor Mao showed his face there. They got their textbooks from a firm in Singapore. He said it was very hard to maintain a neutral school, and said theirs was one of the few in the delta.

We also walked through the bazaar area, a number of blocks filled with little stalls up off the ground with the proprietors, usually a proprietress, sitting amidst the wares—cloth, pots and pans, fish, vegetables. Here and there a sewing machine in action. Then we found the municipal quarters, a small house with two rooms, one called a library, the other an office. In the first were three people reading newspapers. One case of books, with the donor's name inscribed above, was locked. No books were available to read. I asked in the office why the books were locked up and was told the people had no interest in the library. It seemed more likely that the library took no interest in the people.

Our boat was late, as usual, but we finally got on board. First class was all filled with army personnel, and there was only one seat available. So I rented a mat for our small company and got regular-class tickets. This was a blow struck for democracy, but I'm sure the significance completely escaped my escorts. Back in Rangoon at 8:30, we found a crowd on the dock, waiting for the upriver trip the following morning. The people were going to grab good spots, put down their mats, and go to sleep.

I have records of interviews with eight Burmese, mostly officials, and I talked about conditions in their country with nine others. In the foreign community, I talked with the British ambassador, the American chargé, the Japanese minister, and several members of their staffs who were very well posted on matters of my main interest—China. I talked with members of the overseas Chinese community, two reporters, the editor of an opposition newspaper, the manager of a socialist bookstore and of an anti-Communist bookstore, and three university professors. One matter of inquiry was the direction and rate of progress toward the goals the government had set for itself. The director of education, an extremely intelligent and humane man, held me in a long conversation on the government's effort to bring schooling to all, and schooling that will prepare a citizenry for a democratic welfare society. The director of mass education told me what is done in that line and showed me around the training center. The minister of land nationalization and agricultural cooperation, who had been twice to China to see what was being done there, but not to Taiwan, told me of plans and methods of land reform in Burma. I heard a great deal about ambitious national plans and saw or was told about some solid accomplishments. Several Burmese in private life hinted at police-state methods. I personally experienced a fluorescence of bureaucracy in getting a police permit to stay an extra week.

At the university I talked with several professors and learned something of the radicalism of student leadership. The condition of the library was depressing and made me wonder what kind of leadership Burma would have in twenty years or so when this crop of students moved toward the top.

A few little nice things about Burma: Women smoking big cigars. A boat or a trishaw was likely to have a vase of flowers at the front. People were generally not bashful or self-conscious, but a young girl should not be stared at. The women's costumes were graceful and pretty, but they neither flattered nor exposed any of the female figure. (Chinese girls in Hong Kong made a fine art of showing the beauty of their legs.) The sounds of the lizard on the wall, cherk, cherk, cherk. The all-night theatrical with actors cracking jokes and the audience roaring with laughter.

I had enjoyed my days in Burma and learned a great deal more than I have included here. On the flight to Calcutta on December 11, I wrote a few reflections:

> This little nation could never stand up against the colossus China. The responsible leaders must be fearful of Chinese aggression and leap upon the idea of peaceful coexistence and noninterference in the affairs of other nations. That's exactly what they long for.
>
> Socialism and the welfare state are going to be very difficult, given Burma's circumstances. There aren't very many trained people to run government enterprises. The Burmese aren't experienced in business, anyway. For the government to operate public utilities is quite a problem. The post office is an inefficient mess. The Inland Water Transport Co. is going to seed. Burmese bureaucracy is inefficiency and red tape gone wild. How can ambitious plans be carried out?
>
> In some elements of the welfare state, Burma is making strides. The Mass Education Movement, the expansion of public school education, the Burma Translation Society—these seem to be going ahead vigorously. There are other lines of progress. But I suspect that work that requires precision, large-scale interlocking organization, and standards of mechanical accuracy will not make much headway. Burmese don't seem to care. They are too happy-go-lucky. And they have no tradition nor much personnel for such techniques. After all, it has been a colony, Chinese and Indians dominate commerce, and British business dominates anything large-scale. Buddhism is a real force in Burmese life and accounts in part for the genial personality of the people. I don't understand how it works, but the happy-go-lucky attitude, the acceptance of fate, and the kindliness toward animals are somehow linked. One sees swarms of monks out "begging" for food in the morning (actually offering the laity the opportunity to gain merit by giving them food). There are numerous pagodas, and much wealth has been expended in gilding their bulbs and spires.

12

India

India is tremendous! I had two and a half months there in the best time of the year, mid-winter. The variety and vigor and complexity of Indian culture bowled me over. Its culture is so different from that of China, of which I had a little knowledge, that I simply soaked up impressions of Indian customs and manners, dance, music, architecture, sculpture, and other forms of religious expression. I arrived in Calcutta on December 12 and left Madras on February 26, having visited six major cities, talked with numerous influential Indians, many Americans, and some Europeans, traveled widely by car and train, visited some villages, and learned a great deal about Indian aspirations and shortcomings. Ford Foundation auspices were valuable in gaining me entrée. I became fairly conversant with "public opinion" regarding China and wrote an article on "Mao's 'Paradise' as Seen from India," which was published in *The Reporter* (May 19, 1955). Discovering that remarkable country was one of the great experiences of my life.

The introduction to Calcutta was at dawn as a bus took me from the airport to the Great Eastern Hotel in downtown Calcutta. Hundreds of people were sleeping on the streets like so many corpses stretched out on burlap and covered with shrouds of cloth. Cows roamed the streets, and I wondered which was the more valued, the humans sleeping on the sidewalks or the cows. As I wrote after arriving at my hotel:

A pleasant scene was the sweepers cleaning up refuse and hosing down the streets. One sees all sorts of vehicles—carts, pedicabs, rickshaws, buses, trams, autos. The rickshaw pullers give one a shock. Their costume is so odd, with folds of whitish cotton cloth draped around their hips and legs and a shapeless something wrapped around the head and torso. But most startling is to see

Caucasian-featured, though dark-skinned, people doing this menial work. There but for the grace of God went I.

Through the help of the Ford Foundation, I had been invited to stay with Dr. R. Ahmed in Calcutta. He was the minister of agriculture of West Bengal, and he invited me by letter to stay in his home after I had indicated that I would enjoy being a paying guest in an Indian home. Dr. Ahmed had gone to America many years before and worked his way through the University of Iowa, and then earned a degree in dentistry. Later he founded a dental college in Calcutta but gave it to the state when he began to devote full time to politics. He and Mrs. Ahmed were off in Delhi for a conference when I arrived, but he left a message for me to go out to the house, where his daughter, Zohra, would receive me. I did go out, and Zohra and I got acquainted. She overcame my apprehension about intruding on a Muslim family, and we agreed that I should come back in the late afternoon and take a guest room that had been prepared for me on the ground floor. It would be comfortable, and, she assured me, I would not intrude on the rest of the family. So I moved there. What a break!

There were three daughters living in the household and one son: Leila, a welfare worker in a factory, who was divorced but had two children in the home; my hostess, Zohra, whose husband, an army officer, was on duty in Kashmir; and the youngest, Zuleikha, age 16 and very self-conscious, but a nice kid. The son, Rafey, was mentally "not up to the mark" but was married. His wife seemed halfway between daughter and servant—in short, an Indian daughter-in-law. It was an extended family. Another daughter lived in New Delhi and was said to be a famous artist.

The system of dining in that household mystified me. Only after the senior Ahmeds returned did I eat with some other members of the family. Apparently they ate at various times to suit themselves. Two or three servants cooked and served and did washing and housework, a doorman ran errands, and there was an old fellow who helped in taking care of me. The food, I thought, was rather indifferent, though I didn't try to eat the hot curries. Usually there were about six dishes, such as stew, boiled vegetables, a gravy of stewed beans, rice, chunks of fish, tomatoes and onions, and so on. Good manners prescribed that the hosts fill my plate whether I wanted something or not. I enjoyed the breakfasts best; they were in Western style.

Dr. Ahmed was a fine person, vigorous, frank, and cheerful. His wife seemed much less well developed—in fact, seemed self-conscious and lacking confidence—but friendly. Leila was direct, against any hypocrisy, had a good sense of fun, and was companionable. Zohra was more complex. She knew social graces and how to assume them, but I felt she was not always honest. She seemed to have an anti-American bias, though perhaps unconsciously.

The first evening I was taken out for a concert of folk music in the home of a friend's friend. My escort, Mr. S. A. Masud, had recently returned from an

Indian cultural mission to China. A well-known barrister who taught in the Law College, he was active in the Sino-Indian Friendship Society. The cultural delegation got the royal treatment during a month with visits to Peking, Mukden, Sian, Nanking, Shanghai, Hangchow, and Canton. Things that impressed Mr. Masud were the fact that everyone was at work and working hard, and that there was no real international news in the newspapers and it was impossible to learn what was going on in the world. Chou En-lai had assured the group that in the future there would be an independent judiciary and growth of the legal profession, but for the present this could not be done.

At the University of Calcutta I met several faculty members. Professor D. N. Banerjee, head of the political science department, greeted me warmly and told me a bit about the problem of student unemployment after graduation, a bad situation, due in part to West Bengal's huge refugee population, which makes it difficult to absorb new people into the workforce. For any good job, he said, there would be a thousand applicants, creating a situation of great frustration and most favorable for Communist agitation. We talked a bit about China and Taiwan, and he was amazed to hear of some two million refugees from the mainland in Taiwan. We agreed that we know nothing about attitudes toward the Communist regime among Chinese common people on the mainland. He had some disparaging things to say about Indians who visit China for a few weeks, having their contact entirely through interpreters, and then come back as experts. They speak widely and praise the Communist Chinese regime extravagantly. We also talked about pay of academic people, which he felt was much too low, especially in the lower ranks.

Professor J. P. Niyogi, dean of the Faculty of Arts, a very kindly gentleman near retirement age, confirmed the deplorable job situation for students and placed some of the blame on educators for not having the guts to insist on improving the standards among colleges. They are so dependent upon tuition fees that they have huge classes, and students often don't even know the names of their teachers. He was not convinced that economic conditions were improving enough to help relieve the problem of students, a very fertile ground for communism. Students are the ones who shout slogans and throw the rocks in demonstrations, he said. He showed me the university library for the 1,400 students in the arts. It had about 200,000 volumes, he said, and the fairly large reading room was about half full of readers at about 5 P.M. It was an active, lively place, a great contrast with the library of Rangoon University.

Sri Tripurari Chakravarty taught modern Chinese history at the University of Calcutta, He was a fine-looking man, age fifty-eight, who looked much younger. He told me he was president of the Calcutta Sino-Indian Friendship Association and a vice president of the All-India Association. He had gone to China in September 1951. He was favorably impressed by economic and social development there: no beggars, no flies, the policemen directing traffic wore masks, as did food sellers on station platforms. He was impressed by the sense of dignity of the ordinary person, by the happiness on the faces of people he saw. The country was trying to solve the problems of poverty. Then he recited a passage from Isaiah about making the desert bloom. This is clearly what he thought China was accomplishing. The regime was trying to create conditions of equality among the people. He said he had been able to move about with some freedom in Peking: sometimes able to dismiss his guide. He did mention that counterrevolutionaries were in jail, but then quoted what Chou En-lai had told him of it being a democratic dictatorship, a people's dictatorship over the counterrevolutionaries. Asked whether he thought India would have a revolution like that of China, Professor Chakravarti said, "No. India is too moral, too mature, too peaceful." I asked whether there was a difference between Indian attitudes toward China and toward the Soviet Union. He replied that there was much more friendship for China. There is the long border, the unbroken tradition of friendship and cultural relations.

The theme of an age-old friendship between the two countries was stated often in my talks with Indians. It was clearly a propaganda line that had taken hold. Writing long afterward, one can look back on the shattering of that enthusiasm by the brief war along the Himalayan borders in 1962, when the Chinese forces humiliated the Indian Army.

In contrast to these friendly talks with fellow professors, I had one with a lecturer, S. K. Chaterjee, in which I ran into strongly anti-American sentiment. He was aggressive, opinionated, and uninterested in anything I had to say except to refute it. He chided me on American treatment of Negroes, and when I tried to explain that efforts to change attitudes go slowly, and then used the analogy of India's efforts to change attitudes toward untouchables, he had the nerve to tell me there were no untouchables in India, and that the problem of caste was already solved. My later travels convinced me that was an outright lie. He was very much for Communist China and anti-Chiang Kai-shek. I summed up my account of our talk: "The guy was lucid, sharp, aggressive, and I bet he's a popular prof." For my purpose of studying Indian attitudes toward China, it was a good interview.

My host, Dr. Ahmed, told me about seeing Mr. Nehru on his return from a recent visit to China. He addressed a crowd of a million people in Calcutta's large central park. Mr. Nehru told of reaching Peking and asking his secretary to get him the daily papers. There was only one in English, and in it there was only news about China; no foreign news. When Nehru is in India his secretary lays before him all the papers, fifteen of them, of all shades of opinion. The point Nehru was making, said Dr. Ahmed, was that China was free to have its method and India free to have its method. In all the time the prime minister was in China, no one suggested to him that India should do as China was doing, and no one compared what the two countries were doing. However, Nehru was much impressed when his valet was invited to the state dinner being given for the prime minister. The valet asked Mr. Nehru whether he should go, and Nehru told him certainly he should go, which he did. This made a great impression on Dr. Ahmed as an evidence of democracy in China.

I had the feeling that Dr. Ahmed was torn between the wish to get things done, as China seemed to be doing, and the desire to maintain democratic methods. When I asked where do you draw the line—how much totalitarianism in order to get things done—he readily agreed it is a difficult point. He said I should be aware of one thing, that under no circumstances would India go to war. The Indians were determined and united on that.

Another talk was with Sri S. K. Mukerjee, Speaker of the West Bengal Legislative Assembly, who had recently returned from a seven-week tour of China as a guest of the government in connection with the celebration of the fifth anniversary of establishment of the people's government on October 1, 1949. He was writing a book about China based on his carefully kept journal. He felt their group could not have been deceived through hours and hours of talking all over China, though always with interpreters, and by checking impressions with other Indians who took other trips. He was impressed by the condition of farmers and gave me the horror statistics about their previous landless situation. Still, he thought the standard of living in villages was lower than in India. In cities the department stores were crowded with people and goods. He described his impression in going from Calcutta to Canton, where there were no beggars and everyone was hard at work. (In Hong Kong, by contrast, there were beggars and signs warning against pickpockets.) But in Canton he was struck by the miserable condition of the rickshaw pullers. He was depressed by the fact that in schools everyone was studying Marx and Lenin, and that no other political ideas could be studied—impossibly stultifying. He said the whole nation was being galvanized for the liberation of Taiwan. I told him about Taiwan as I had seen it, asking him how, realistically, it could be liberated, or the problem be settled peacefully.

My talks in Calcutta were a foretaste of what I heard in many other talks elsewhere. An attitude of admiration for the new China, but apprehension about the dictatorship through which things are accomplished. The expression "China and India, friends forever" was very much in use.

One day I took a train to Santineketan, about ninety miles from Calcutta. It was the place where Rabindranath Tagore established a school and a rural improvement program. Also, Carrington and Anne Goodrich had spent the previous year there during a sabbatical, he teaching a course on China, and she studying Buddhism. Everything about the trip was interesting: getting myself to the station early in the morning; being almost automatically picked up by a uniformed man who helped me find the ticket office, some breakfast, and then a seat in second class; watching the crowds at the stations en route. I wrote to Kay:

At Bolpur, the station for Santineketan, I was met by the keeper of the guest house of the school and driven up to the lodgings, and persuaded to spend the night. I got to look around the campus (they hold many classes under the trees), to attend a concert of Indian music put on by the students and faculty, and to call upon several people and learn about the school. Today I was off to see the work of the Srineketan project, which is sort of rural development work. They are trying to improve in all ways the life of their district by means of public health cooperatives, training in such arts and crafts as improved carpentry techniques, hand weaving, pottery, etc.

A doctor who supervises the health work is placed in a group of villages, which organize a health cooperative and whose members each pay annual dues of a few rupees for the doctor's salary. The doctor becomes a focal point for social and other kinds of education, since he is the outsider who gains the real confidence of the villagers. Besides administering curative medicine, the doctor leads in the effort to get better public health—use of latrines, digging of sanitary wells, etc., all simple things, but hard to accomplish among ill-educated people, who are on the edge of poverty constantly.

Nutrition is a difficult problem. The villagers subsist altogether too much on carbohydrates, getting very little animal proteins and vitamin foods. With poor nutrition there is a low level of energy. Village development requires a multifront attack, as the problems are all interrelated.

The teacher of carpentry had been trained in Sweden years ago. His aim is to train carpenters who can work in villages to make improved tools and better woodworking for furniture and housing. He proudly told me he had trained more than a thousand boys, and most of them are in villages all over India. He showed me an exhibition he has prepared to teach the students the properties of various Indian woods, the nature of diseases of wood, and how to cure them. Oddly, the captions were all in English. Probably the instruction is in Bengali. All the tools being used in the carpentry shop were European or American, which obviously the village carpenters could never afford. He seemed a born teacher and was filled with enthusiasm for his work. Long ago he designed a movable latrine; he said they were in use all over India in rural areas.

I saw dyeing of yarn, handloom weaving, leather work, pottery, etc. being done by students who should then teach these crafts in rural area; but how much these skills do get out into the villages is difficult to judge. There is a great effort to promote handicrafts, and in Calcutta there are many outlets for selling handloomed textiles and other handicraft items. But the government, in rather bureaucratic ways, makes it difficult for tourists to send such things out, as I found when I took a package to the post office.

Dr. Ahmed kindly arranged for me to visit the Damodar Valley Project when my stay in Calcutta came to an end. It had been an unusual experience to spend ten days in an Indian home, and I have often thought how interesting it probably is to our Chinese or Japanese guests to spend a few days with us in Pleasantville. One friend even wrote up the experience in his journal and later published it in a Taiwan magazine.

I'll quote my letter to the kids describing the next episode:

Dr. Ahmed arranged for me to be given the VIP tour, and I am a guest of the Damodar Valley Corporation, which is much like our American Tennessee

Valley Authority. I was met when I got off the train last evening by a young Indian lady who is public relations officer at one of the dam sites. She drove me to the dam, had dinner with me, and then came back next morning to show me the sights. I saw a big dam under construction. They were mixing concrete in a huge machine operated by a complicated switchboard in the control tower, which determines exactly how much rock, gravel, sand, cement, and water go in each batch, depending upon what part of the dam it will be used for. In another part of the dam I saw women (who do a lot of the heavy work here and in Burma) carrying rocks on their heads in baskets. Machine power and woman power side by side! The dam is for flood control, hydroelectric power, and irrigation. After this phase of the four dams is completed there will be over a million acres of land irrigated, making it two-crop land instead of one. Also there will be ample electric power for this potentially most important industrial area. There will be no more floods in what used to be a very dangerous region. The total cost of Damodar Valley first phase (the four dams and their hydro-electric plants, one big thermal electric plant, and the irrigation system, and one 80-mile ship canal, which will bring traffic from the sea right to this industrial region) is to be 946 million rupees, or about 201 million dollars.

In the afternoon I was driven about eighty miles to another dam site. We came to a small town where there seemed to be some sort of a celebration, and I asked if we might stop and have a look. We discovered that in half an hour Vinoba Bhave, the follower of Gandhi, who is walking about India asking people to give their land to him to distribute to landless farmers, was to hold a meeting. I was taken in tow by a magnificently bearded Muslim on the local welcoming committee, Mohammad Ibrahim Khan, who spoke beautiful English. He took me to the headquarters where Sri Bhave was resting before going to his meeting. I didn't meet him, but he had my card and knew I was taking his picture as he marched to the meeting surrounded by his followers.

On the train to Benares two ministers from the Shan States of Burma were my traveling companions in a compartment. Both men, it turned out, were hostile to Communist China. They gave examples of the harsh rule in Yunnan across their border. I showed them an item in the paper in which U Nu reported that he was sincerely convinced that China wished to live in peace with Burma. Chinese leaders had told him that they had no connection with the Burmese Communists. My companions laughed, and one said that the article only reported what U Nu said he had been told, not what he believed. They also talked about the KMT troops in Burma, who had degenerated into bandits and opium smugglers. The opium, they said, is grown in China and sent across the border where the KMT troops take it and smuggle it into Thailand, and thence it goes to Singapore or Hong Kong.

After these companions left the train at Gaya, a party came aboard—a Buddhist monk, the Venerable Amritananda of Nepal, who spoke excellent English, and several Japanese Buddhists whom he was guiding to the Buddhist holy places in India, a middle-aged gentleman from Hawaii, a young Nisei from Sacramento who was studying Buddhism, preparing to follow in the footsteps of his father, who was a Buddhist priest, and three young fellows from Tokyo and Keio universities. One was the son of the abbot of an important temple in Tokyo. After we got acquainted, I gave him Kay's address and promised to write her that he would get in touch with her. Later he did, and it led to an interesting development in her life.

On December 27 I left for Lucknow by train. I met an Indian Army doctor named Mehta, who had been up to Tibet to bring out the Indian consul general, who was ill. He told me about evidences of the Chinese Army in Tibet, the hostility of the Tibetans toward them, but the patience and tactfulness of the Chinese in refusing to be insulted. The Tibetans want their Dalai Lama back and hate the Panchan Lama, according to him. My Indian acquaintance reflected sentiment in the Indian Army that giving up an Indian interest in Tibet had been a serious mistake. He spoke of the plateau as a huge natural air base from which China could dominate northern India and much of Asia.

While traveling I tried to notice the literature being sold on railway platforms. There was no Communist stuff in English from Russia or China, and I was told its sale was banned by the government. But one can buy *Blitz*, a pro-communist, hate-America tabloid, flashy, smartly put together, with its sexy side deriving from American movies—pictures of girlie pinups. The advertising was almost entirely of American movies! In Lucknow, I went to several bookstores and found plenty of American paperbacks and general literature in English and very little English-language stuff from China. At a People's Bookstore there was the full range of propaganda literature and magazines from Russia and China, but I didn't see many customers, perhaps two in an hour.

I went to the University of Lucknow, which has some fine buildings of Mogul architecture, contrasting with the Hindu architecture of Benares. There were some lovely buildings in Lucknow, which retained the now somewhat faded grandeur of Oudh, once a northern Indian kingdom. Lucknow was the center of the Mutiny of 1857, and the ruins of the British Residency—where an English battalion put up a prolonged defense against equally determined Indian attackers—are preserved in a lovely park as a monument to both sides.

At the university I met several friendly faculty members and learned something of the rivalries and jealousies within such an institution. As only one example, Dr. Karlash Singh, a young psychologist trained at Harvard, told me he was trying to do a study on attitudes of villagers toward each other and on certain subjects. He feared that if it became known in the university, jealous persons might try to frustrate his work, so he was going ahead with it quietly, not discussing it in the university. Odd. Questions in such a study have to be very specific and not generalized. Ask a man so abstract a question as "What do you think of America?" and he will reply, "What do I think of America?" Because Indian society is authoritarian in structure, everyone is above or below others. Attitudes toward others depend upon whether ego is below the other person, in which case he should be subservient, or above the other, in which case he should act as a superior. As an example, he told me that an American professor will give a talk in India. In the question period someone will dispute some point. The American professor will say, "Yes, there is much in what you say, but perhaps some other factors should be considered," and so on. He will not positively refute the questioner. The audience will take this to show the professor doesn't know his stuff. In public speaking the Americans aren't as elegant as the English; therefore some Indians think they are not as intelligent. There is a fairly widespread idea that not the best American professors come to India, only the mediocre ones, he said. But the influence of American social science is immense in India. No one else is doing anything to speak of. This remark was in response to my observation of the fine collection of social science books I had seen in the University Library. The library was well organized and well patronized by students.

In New Delhi I first stayed in a hotel but later was granted the privilege of staying in a lodge used for members of parliament, but mostly vacant, since parliament was not in session. There, for a very low price, I got a room with bath and three meals a day if I wanted that many. The morning always began with English tea—boiled—and biscuits. Also in New Delhi I had fine contacts through the Ford Foundation office and my recent acquaintance, Mr. Azim Housain, who had been a guest in our home. He was fairly high in the Indian Foreign Office and arranged for me to meet several officials. And on the personal side, I learned that our old Peking friends, Jackie and Janet Sewell, were in New Delhi, he working in the U.S. Information Agency.

The Community Projects Office of the Planning Commission, with which the Ford Foundation worked closely, laid on a trip for me and an Indian gentleman to visit Nikoleri. We drove about eighty miles northward, en route passing places where literally an acre or so of red peppers were spread out to dry or were heaped in great piles. Nikoleri is a town built for refugees, indeed it was torn from the jungle. There were three training centers. One was for village-level workers, the all-purpose young men who go to the villages with some knowledge of agricultural science, machinery, public health, and many other useful things. One village-level worker will have from five to ten villages in his charge. They were high school graduates of village background. They lived in rather spartan quarters, ate on a cement floor, and did a good deal of manual work. We saw some ploughing, others working on the pump of a tube well.

The second sort of training class was for social organizers, who are assigned two to a block of about a hundred villages. They are supposed to be holders of the B.A. degree. Among the class we saw were about fifteen young women. We interrupted their class and were even called upon by the principal to make a speech. The social organizers know about literacy education, arts and crafts, and so on. There is something Gandhian or Tagore-like about their function.

The third group consisted of Community Project organizers, the top administrative people for a block of one hundred villages. They were mostly civil servants, receiving six-weeks' retooling to prepare them with the philosophy of their new kind of work. They were mature men. We were called upon to make a speech to them, too.

After lunch we went out to look at villages. We descended upon the first one in three carloads, for the organizers were with us inspecting a village or two. The villagers were quite up to it and not at all ruffled. Doubtless they had many such descents.

As we arrived, the village school was in session, the kids sitting on the ground in the sun, and their teacher, a man, standing behind a sort of desk. The village was notable for having filled in its lanes and paved them with brick, with drains on either side. Some of the houses had hearths with chimneys, an innovation brought by the project. Without chimneys the smoke just fills the house, curls out under the eaves, and causes near blindness to the women who have to cook indoors during part of the year. It amazed me that so simple a device hadn't long since been perfected by rural India, itself. We saw the improved well, so constructed that drawn water would not trickle back into the well—a great sanitary improvement since the well-side is a place for washing clothes and bathing. We also visited the outcast section of the village and found their courtyard clean and five big roosters strutting around in it. The outcasts had a well of their own, but we were told this was only a matter of convenience and that they could use the other well too, if they wished. I wondered if this were so; perhaps they never had the wish to use the higher-caste well.

The second village was bigger, older, and more prosperous. But the access road was so deplorably bad that it must have been impassable during the monsoon. Road building and surfacing to correct this monsoon-time isolation was going on at a lively pace all over India. We saw a number of such access roads on our drive to Nikoleri. This village had larger houses, their door posts were carved, and there were painted designs about the entry ways. The village roads wound around between high walls of courtyards or houses. We saw some women on their rooftops drying clothing. We also came to the outcast quarters, where the women were much less furtive than were the better-class women, who had to cover their faces when we approached. I was able to take pictures of the outcast women working at the well and pounding grain. We went into two houses and saw how neatly they were kept. One man's house was beautified by a small flower garden and painting of the walls of the courtyard. He had won a prize for this in a house-beautification project. We also saw the scientifically constructed grain storage bin in his house.

At the Panchayet meeting place there was a lively discussion between Mr. Siderani and me on one side and the leader of the Panchayet representing the assembled men on the other. I was asked how my village was run, the size of my taxes, how much wheat could be grown on an acre of land in the United States (I didn't know that), and how large an average farm was. The leader of the Panchayet, who was not the oldest male by any means, was a well-informed, articulate, and cocky villager who hadn't traveled even so far as Delhi, but who read newspapers and had a fair knowledge of what was going on in India and the world. Why only he spoke and everyone else was content to listen, I don't know.

I was asked to write in the village book and found the names of Don Price and John Howard (both of the Ford Foundation office in New York) ahead of mine by a few weeks. I thanked the village for its hospitality and friendship and wished it peace and abundant harvest, which seemed to strike the right note.

I continued interviewing Indian journalists, officials, educators, and others about their attitudes toward China, and have a sheaf of write-ups. I will quote from only one, a talk with India's vice president, Dr. Radakrishnan, held on January 20, 1955.

> We met in his home. When he heard that I had recently been in Taiwan he asked about conditions there, but he really was not interested in my description. He said the Chinese leaders have a very deep distrust of American intentions. They believe we want to overthrow their government, as evidenced by our support of Chiang Kai-shek, who is committed to that end. Their fear is of the same order as our objections to Communist attempts to subvert other governments. We ought to be able to understand such fears. So America should let China know that it has no such intentions. He said the same to people in the State Department, and they admitted America had no intention to overthrow the Chinese government. But they didn't want to say so. Only Chiang and Rhee want war, as only they might get any advantage from it. As Eisenhower told him, "We can only hiss at each other, but we can't bite."
>
> Dr. Radakrishnan emphasized that we have to have some faith in other men; otherwise one's attitude is just rigid. In the long run the people of Russia can't simply be kept down. Since Stalin's death things are easier in Russia and there have been many signs of conciliation toward the West.
>
> But there is the problem of Germany. Stalin told him, when he was ambassador to Russia, that if Germany could be disarmed for twenty or thirty years it was possible to consider the withdrawal from Eastern European states. But America wouldn't consider it, replying that the plan for the European army was set. He also told me that he once proposed to American Ambassador Kirk that both Russia and America should agree not to have any abuse of the other in their press or radio for six months. The reply came back from Acheson, that Stalin can control his press; we cannot. I pointed out that it was impossible for the American government to make the American press desist. He thought our wartime censorship proved we could.

I never published all my findings. Yet interviewing was a great way to learn and gave me an introduction to many people and an insight into Indian opinion and attitudes during that year, 1954–55. All upper-class Indians I met were fluent in English. I also read the English-language press. One thing that interested me was the columns for people seeking matrimony. Families of men and women seeking mates for their children would advertise their qualities, especially their education (I sometimes saw "failed B.A." to indicate level of advancement!), and the texts often emphasized the fact of, or the requirement for, light skin. That was a point of distinction in northern India: the upper classes were fair skinned.

Near the end of my stay in New Delhi I gave a dinner party for some of the people who had been particularly helpful to me. I really had had a wonderful learning experience in New Delhi, and many people made that possible. I could not adequately express my appreciation to them all.

After leaving, I wrote reflectively:

> New Delhi is laid out magnificently as a monumental city—a great capital of a vast realm. The long avenues, the circles where diagonal roads cross, the residencies of princes built in uniform style, the monuments to the various states and to British kings and governors, the India Gate and the stately Secretariat block with the viceroy's palace (now the president's house) standing at the end of a long, broad avenue—all these give a sense of quiet grandeur. And the Indian leadership is keeping up the tradition. The great Republic Day parade was in the tradition of smartness and pride of service which the English rulers here inculcated.
>
> There are many indications that the society of rulers and ruled has not vanished, but this is to be expected. The disparities between persons of station and their servants is marked. The different sections for the spectators at the parade: on the one hand, the scores of thousands who hurried along on foot or in tongas to get an early seat on the grass or standing room behind the ropes, as contrasted to the Westernized hundreds who came in cars with passes for the reserved section with chairs to sit upon. The Gymkanna Club where the well-to-do dine and dance and listen to a concert given on a Sunday afternoon by a regimental band. The abruptness and authoritarian way in which an official bangs a bell to call a bearer and orders him to take a message or perform some other service. I saw it in government offices and in university offices, too, and in the Western Court, where I stayed. New Delhi is far more orderly than Rangoon as a capital city. The offices seem more efficient, the civil service knows what it is doing, there don't seem to be such swarms of hangers-on in every office, though I wasn't in many: three in addition to the Ministry of External Affairs, which I visited twice. Municipal services seem well run, traffic controlled effectively.
>
> There is a purposiveness about the Indians I happened to come in contact with: they are building the future India and are proud of what they are working for. There is no doubt that India has lots and lots of very competent engineers and administrators and other civil servants, a legacy from the Raj.
>
> The educated Indians I met are friendly; they seem to think of themselves as part of the Western world, though doubtless they consider themselves Asians, too. The professors I met, most of whom had studied abroad, or the officials who talked to our orientation seminar and stressed the democratic nature of their programs, who spoke fluently in English as though it were their mother tongue, are sophisticated and cultured people, certainly versed in the Western tradition, and no doubt in their own tradition, too. But I was only in three Indian homes. Indians have been friendly toward me and not offensive

regarding America—e.g., students at the Delhi School of Economics or at St. Stephens College, or casual acquaintances on the train, persons I phoned up and asked to call upon. But I suppose most of them were Western oriented and polite to a professor. I've heard of really stinking experiences that Americans have had with Indians, who were arrogant and insulting. I only had two such experiences, but neither too unpleasant and both in Calcutta.

The editorial comment in *Times of India*, *Hindustan Times*, and *The Statesman* about the current "Formosa Crisis" has been moderate and not unfriendly to America. Yet Indian foreign policy runs cross grain to American in regard to Asia, particularly China. So far as I can tell there is very little public disagreement with Indian policy re China—i.e., trust and friendship. I believe the Indian government would like a good deal more American aid and would like to be more free in determining what it gets and the use of it. At least from what economists like Gadgill and Rao, and persons who lectured us on India's economic needs, have said, as well as Azim Husain's frank discussion of American assistance, I gather there is a good deal of dissatisfaction with things as they are.

I left New Delhi on February 8, headed for Bombay on the west coast, traveling by train. Here's from my notebook:

An Indian official and I had a long and interesting talk. Mr. J. L. Bhargawa was going to his station at Indore, where he is in charge of the National Savings Office, a scheme of the government to provide a savings system for the small man, similar to our postal savings, and thus to mobilize the small capital of the country for the government's development plans. There are about four hundred district branches, he said, and they plan to extend it through post offices and agents to ten thousand. They hope to use village Panchayat heads as agents for the people's savings. He had been posted in Calcutta two years ago and said he used the USIS library a great deal, and that the American woman librarian had helped him greatly, getting him books he wanted to read about American savings methods and letting him borrow books not supposed to circulate. He also mentioned the Village Development Program, which he said had been started by the Ford Foundation. Two pleasant signs of appreciation for American effort. Our long conversation about America and India, about the small influence of Russia and China here, about Nehru's visit to China, and about the strength of the Communist movement, I've recorded in that sheaf of write-ups. He mentioned that 40 percent of India's national budget is spent for the armed services and yet it is reduced in size and tends toward becoming a highly specialized service—with expensive equipment.

In Bombay I got in touch with a former student, Paul Kreisberg, by then a young vice consul. He put me in touch with two Indian gentlemen, who began immediately to introduce us to Bombay. Mr. Gopal S. Pochacher took Paul and me in the afternoon to an Indian home where a ceremony was going on:

There was a reading of the scriptures (Bhagavad-Gita), a sermon, and reciting in honor of some one deceased. The male guests sat on the floor of one room, the female guests in another. There was a group of men at one side who performed part of the ceremony by joining occasionally in a chant, and who were making mudras with their fingers to invoke the deity. The principal reciter sat at the front of the room under a canopy, reciting the Gita by heart. He also spoke in Sanskrit, which our guide said was perfect. He gave a sermon betimes. We were told this erudite person was only 24 years old. The men among whom we sat were in rapt attention and you could see their heads wagging as they listened. When we left we were each given a little packet wrapped in newspaper. In it were Indian sweets, coconut, bits of rock candy, sugar, etc.

Then we went to the home of a wealthy Indian, a very large house in which four brothers live as a joint family. The house had been added to from time to time as the family grew. The object of our visit was to see the paintings of one of the young men of the family, Abhay Khatau. He was at one time incapacitated by a crippling disease which has impeded his speech. He and his beautifully dressed young wife showed us his paintings, which certainly have a strong character, particularly a sensitive line and bold use of color. It was also experimental. However, it was also sentimental and immature, I should say. This was an interesting experience, and the young couple, as well as Mr. Pochacher, began planning things for me to do in Bombay.

I had the chance to interview the leader of the Praja Socialist party, Mr. Ashoka Mehta; a trade union leader, Mr. R. A. Khedgihar; and two newspaper editors, Mr. Karnath and Frank Moraes, and also several people in an anti-Communist front. I also talked with American consular folk, introduced by Paul Kreisberg.

The trade union leader, a Socialist high in their federation, had gone to Peking the previous year as a fraternal delegate to a convention of the Chinese Federation of Trade Unions. He had great admiration for accomplishments in China and thought the conditions of workers had much improved—though he had never been there before. But he was not at all in sympathy with the totalitarian way, with the loss of freedom—as he put it—and he said quite flatly he would rather have India go more slowly and maintain democracy and individual freedom.

Here are my reflections upon leaving Bombay, a great port facing the Arabian Sea:

A beautiful city with many elements of Western modern society such as beautiful apartment buildings fringing the water-front, fine drive ways, efficient public bus and tram systems, lots of electric power so there is an electrified commuting train system and the city lit up at night by a myriad of street lights. There are a large number of cars, modern hotels, and cinema. Most of the men I saw wear Western clothes, mostly white trousers and shirts, and many women are dressed in skirts and blouses, or street dresses (I am told they are either Parsees or Christians, many being Anglo-Indians). There are also many lovely saris. But side by side and intermixed is old India and poverty. For example, the working-class women, either Gujarati or Marathi, dress in short bodice and sari, of which, however, one end is tucked up between the legs making a sort of trousers. These women do a lot of the hard labor, as in construction work, carrying big loads on their heads. There are also many beggars, which jars me. There are densely crowded regions and real slums. And, as in Calcutta, one sees many signs of unemployment. People doing nothing, people doing trifling work or trying to hawk trinkets or gadgets. I saw a woman patiently standing on a street corner holding out two items—I forget what—in hope someone might buy. I could not be quite callous enough not to react unhappily to the evident disparity of wealth and poverty. And I hope India falls to with a will to eradicate this disparity in living standards. There is surely trouble ahead if it doesn't.

I don't think I touched below the surface in Bombay. I was in several homes, some of very wealthy people, others of middle class, and one definitely lower middle class home. Yet everywhere I found great warmth of hospitality for a foreign guest.

I left Bombay on February 18, after having been there only six and a half crowded days. I went on a swanky, air-conditioned train, for it was a twenty-seven-hour trip to Madras, which cost U.S. $27. We arrived at Madras city about 6:30 on Saturday night so I decided to use Sunday for sightseeing. I went down to Mahabalipuram, which is about fifty miles south of Madras, using the rickety bus. Mahabalipuram is said to have been a flourishing port in the seventh and eighth centuries and had some ancient monuments. This was barefoot land. By far the greater number of people even in Madras city went without shoes. It was hot—80 or 90 degrees. In the rice fields I saw women in bright-colored sari wading in the muck, planting seedlings. There were innumerable water buffalo and cattle of all description. I had never seen smaller cows, certainly under four feet high.

During this journey I saw many beggars, also some lepers, and a squatter colony right by the bus station, reminding me of Calcutta. When we had our picnic at the tourist center, we were ringed around with children with hungry eyes. Of course we shared our food, but it was so little for so many.

I got back to the hotel just in time for a bath and to get over to the arts center where there was a dance recital. It wasn't as fiery as the Barahata Natyam can be, though the dancer was nice looking, which helped. Next day I started work in my last city in India, having lined up a couple of editors to see, some university people, a trade union man, and people in the consulate.

On leaving India with deep gratification for the rich experiences I had enjoyed, I mused:

> It may be a superficial observation, but it seems there is one stratum of Indian society which is actively working for modernization, that is participating in and aware of what is transpiring to bring increased productivity and greater welfare. But there is a very large segment of the population that scarcely seems to be a part of this movement, people who aren't particularly contributing to it nor caught up in it. Of course, there is no way for me to read the minds of such people, nor to know how much they are aware of, or proud of, the accomplishments of the past few years. I wonder if there is a cleft in society, as I think

there was in China before the Communists took over. Anyway, I got no sense of all the people working together vigorously and self-consciously toward a common goal, as one hears is the case in Communist China.

Another thing one feels is how very great is British influence still. The number of persons, at least in cities, speaking English or able to; the number of English-language newspapers and their wide circulation (by Indian standards); the use of English in shop signs; the journals of opinion in English; All-India Radio out-Britishing BBC; the way the British university system dominates higher education in India; generals in the Indian Army more British than the British; the spit and polish of the Indian Army; the adoration of Oxford and Cambridge; parliamentary democracy barreling right along.

Lenin dreamed that communism would conquer the world when Russia and China and India had been joined in the conflict against the West. Now Russia and China are joined by very strong bonds [this was written in early 1955!]. There is no doubt that the Communist world is bidding strongly for India's favor. This is seen in the courting of Indo-Chinese friendship, the courtesy toward India in Russian foreign policy statements, and the approval which the Indian Communist party shows to Nehru's foreign policy. In fact, I was told by Mohan Das in Bombay that there is a school among the Indian Communist leaders who espouse trying to work through Nehru and make him the Indian Mao Tse-tung of an Indian People's Democracy. V.K.R.V. Rao laid heavy stress on the thesis that India must be helped economically so it can match China's economic development. Otherwise, India itself might be irresistibly drawn toward communism, and if India and China were both on that side, the appeal to the rest of Asia and Africa would be irresistible, too.

But is India moving toward communism? That is a big question. Some of the evidence to the contrary is the continued strength of the Congress party and the prestige of many of its older leaders, especially of Nehru. Then there is a record of achievement, or things near achievement, that strengthens the Congress government—e.g., "solving" the food problem, caring for the refugees from Pakistan, getting the Village Development program underway, bringing several multipurpose dam projects near completion. These help Congress. On the other side are some very bad scores. The unemployment problem, especially among intellectuals and professionally trained youth, is still very serious, and perhaps worse than ever as more and more youths pass out of the over-crowded colleges. The talk of corruption among provincial officials sounds sadly like talk of the same among KMT officials. The very slow movement toward land reform, if any.

Another factor I cannot assess is the reflected glory of Chinese communism. The vision of China under communism is so rosy here that it must hold great attraction among intellectuals, at least, for an Indian solution of its problems along Communist lines. Yet I do not remember any persons I interviewed who advocated such a solution.

After a brief stay in Ceylon I took a French freighter bound for Bangkok. Here are my reflections on India in early March:

How to hold onto the atmosphere of a country one has visited and then departed? Taiwan and Burma are fading away. The radiance of India is still with me, but will drift away as new sights and emotions intervene. What were the things about India that were so attractive? Rather, what was so distinctive, which made it India rather than Burma or Ceylon? Why should Bengal be as much India as Delhi State or Bombay, while Burma is something different? Perhaps it isn't separate things but a totality, a "gestalt."

As I came into Calcutta I was struck with the fact that I had left the lands of Mongoloid faces. Now we were in a land of dark-skinned people with a very European cast to their features. That was part of the shock—to see "European" rickshaw pullers and cart haulers. But the racial matter is only a small thing— or is it? There is costume: the women wearing bright sari, the men in dothi. The languages spoken could hardly be part of the impression for they, or Burmese, or Japanese, were equally unintelligible to me. Then is it the looks and gestures of the people? Certainly that is part of it. The Indians have a way of wagging their heads to show they are taking in the conversation or under- standing what is told. It's not assent or dissent, just participation. Furthermore, they use their hands most expressively, in gestures that have an undefined meaning but must be very meaningful to the viewers.

But still, it isn't just physical appearance, dress, and gestures. Any culture is much, much more, and only slowly can you know its richness. For me, talking with people in English, and having them respond in so friendly a way, was important. I had great pleasure in going to dance or music programs, if only half understanding them, and being made so extremely welcome. It was a feeling of being free to go where I wished, and often doing so, and yet every- where finding helpful people, who would explain or guide. It was also sunny skies and warm winter weather, and miles and miles of dry and fallow country- side with only occasional villages. It was cows, buffalo, and oxen everywhere, with an occasional elephant in the south or camels in the north. One made many easy acquaintanceships with Indians, but I never was able to follow them up enough to know whether they could become true friendships.

India is also depressing poverty and pestering beggars, side by side with wealthy people in fine cars and evening clothes. This is what tears me. It is people squatting on their haunches or sleeping on the sidewalks wrapped in shrouds like corpses. But it's people playing cricket, barefoot kids in the coun- try, or young Indian men dressed up in whites just like in England. It is Sikhs with their neat and bright-colored turbans, their black beards, and erect carriage. It is gregariousness: crowds of people in coffee shops talking like mad. Crowds at a football match or at the great Republic Day parade. There is so much color in India, in costume and in the variety of peoples who make it up.

India is also wonderful, monumental architecture, particularly in the Mogul north, from Lucknow to Delhi and down to Aurangabad. It is voluptuous sculpture, but women in real life extremely modest, especially in the north. It is wonderful dance, complex and interesting music, and some painting that is distinctively Indian—but much that's unimaginative copying. I could wish any friend as interesting a time as I have had and as pleasant a one, though a whole year would have been better.

On the freighter I wrote a report for the Ford Foundation about my experi- ences in India. I mentioned that, following the advice of Douglas Ensminger, the head of the Ford Foundation's work in India, I broadened my interest to include learning all I could about economic, social, and intellectual developments, in order not to arouse suspicion of being overly political in my interest in China's influence. I first dealt with what I had learned about the broader topic. I also rhapsodized about my exposure to Indian culture. On the matter of China's efforts and influence, I reported that I had interviewed fifty-nine people, including sixteen Indians who had recently been in China and about whose experiences and attitudes I had been eager to learn.

In searching for information on China's influence in India, I read everything I could find bearing upon it in the Indian press, talked with American officials whose business it is to watch the subject, discussed India's relations with China with officers in the Ministry of External Affairs, other officials, and newsmen, and interviewed every Indian I could meet who had recently been to China, from diplomats to labor union leaders.

I can summarize what I believed to be the situation:

Basic Factors. The general lack of knowledge about China due to limited contact between the two countries during the past several centuries; the deficiency in academic knowledge; limited business and missionary activity of Indians in China; and the lack of Indian press representatives regularly stationed in China. Yet there is a favorable predisposition toward the other country as fellow Asian nations, which have recently shaken loose from colonial or semicolonial domination. Indians are interested in the way China is tackling problems which are similar to those at home. Finally, the policy of the Indian government is firmly set upon friendship with China with public opinion solidly behind it. These factors make a favorable climate for China's attempts to extend its influence in India and to tie the two countries together in the sphere of international politics.

Mechanisms. Three broad fronts on which China operates with respect to India: propaganda, guided tours for Indian leaders in China, and international communism and front groups. I was told that the Chinese embassy and its two consulates conduct themselves with the greatest circumspection, steering strictly clear of the Indian Communist party. There is an Embassy Bulletin and the New China News Agency's daily releases. But there is an extensive publication program out of Peking. Its magazines in English and beautifully illustrated brochures, selections of the works of Mao Tse-tung and Liu Shao-ch'i, are readily available for sale at low prices in larger cities and are found in college libraries and public reading rooms. China has experimented with sending "friendship missions" to tour India and uses every opportunity to send specialists who speak English to conferences in order to make friends and give speeches. Chou En-lai was the most successful missionary to India. There are also handsome exhibits from China on tour, but little exposure of Chinese films, though this is promised.

The guided tour is a form of publicity that China has developed to perfection. Indian groups usually are made up of influential people; only a few in any delegation may be Communists or sympathizers. I described the typical tour and the almost entirely favorable impressions derived, as I found through my interviews or the many accounts I read. There was only one entirely hostile account among them. All the rest convey a decidedly favorable picture of conditions in China.

As to international communism and front groups, all sorts of "All-India" groups push the worldwide common themes: peace, abolish the atomic bomb, Asian solidarity, anticolonialism. Rounds of conferences led by front groups; petitions constantly circulated: the undying friendship of China and India, China's right to Tawian, Communist China's right to the Unite Nations seat, and so on. Yet Nehru has stolen the thunder of the Indian Communists by championing China's cause internationally while emphasizing that conditions of the two countries are different and that India will modernize in its own democratic way.

I devoted a couple of pages to India's policy toward China, mentioning their common frontiers and risk of conflict. As one gentleman remarked, "When you live on the banks of a river, you mustn't annoy the crocodiles." Certainly there is competition between the two countries for influence in southeast Asia. Yet the underlying Indian belief is in peace. As a result of many factors—not the least being the determination of the prime minister—India has been trying to be a worldwide peacemaker, and toward China: determined friendliness and trust, neither trying to impose its will on the other. India is trying to bring China out into the international arena, into the United Nations, in closer contact with non-Communist nations and less tied to Soviet Russia. India has launched a policy of "moral containment." Nehru's toast to Mao Tse-tung at the end of a recent tour of China was cited to me: "I have seen in China a vital people engaged in a tremendous task. I have no doubt they will succeed. I should like to express my deep admiration for the leader of the Chinese nation, Chairman Mao. A man of historic mould, he has been a great warrior, a great revolutionary, a great builder and consolidator. May he now be a great peace-maker also."

Perspective. I kept asking myself how I would regard my propaganda efforts and influence in India if I were on the Chinese or Russian side. From the Chinese side things are going very well, from the Russian side things are just beginning to turn better. But if you make a comparison of influences, the Western democracies are far, far ahead. Cultural influences from the West are built deeply into the educational system, the widespread use of English makes our entire literature as well as our propaganda directly available. Thousands of Indian students are studying in Great Britain or America as compared with almost none in Russia and China. The armed forces are still an offshoot of those of Great Britain in equipment and outlook. The political ideals of India are those of England. As for "propaganda," no other country has anything to compare with USIS libraries. The *American Reporter* has a much larger circulation than any other journal in India. The great advantage that China and Russia have is that they can operate from the inside, as it were, through the Indian Communist party.

On the freighter steaming toward Singapore I also wrote an article on my India findings. An editor trimmed and edited it before it was published in *The Reporter Magazine* two months later. They entitled it "Mao's Paradise as Seen from India."

Who can see seven years ahead? A dispute concerning the Indo-Tibetan border led in 1962 to a brief Sino-Indian military conflict in which the Chinese Army defeated and humiliated the Indian Army. India's misty-eyed view of China, which I had observed in 1954–55, suddenly vanished. India and China were no longer brothers!

In Kobe, Japan. Clarence, Elizabeth, Halsey, and their nurse.

Halsey, Elizabeth, Mary Wilbur, and Clarence, 1916, in Shanghai.

The Wilbur family in Shanghai around 1922.

Clarence Martin Wilbur as a
Boy Scout, age 13.

Oberlin College scenes, 1927–1931.

Clockwise, from top left: Marty and Ed Reischauer as Oberlin freshmen, 1927.
Waiters at Baldwin Cottage, 1929: Fred Ficken, Jack Service, Martin Wilbur, and
Sid Willis. Marty and Kay Edson dating, 1929. Kay in 1932.

Marriage and Peking days, July 17, 1932–April 19, 1934.

Clockwise, from top left: Uncle John and Aunt Ora Fuelling. Kay and Martin married. Kay Edson Wilbur. First home in the Peking Language School, 1933. Father on his 60th birthday in Peking, 1934. A chilly day at the Great Wall.

Family pictures, 1941–1951.

Clockwise, from top left: Mother and Dad, 1941. Kay and the kids, 1946. Trip West, 1949. Parents' Golden Wedding Celebration, August 1951: Kay, Halsey, Beth, Martin, Mother, Dad, Helen, Paul.

Our Japanese house in Tokyo, 1954–1955.

Professor Samuel Chu in 1958 upon receiving his Ph.D. degree from Columbia University.

Bernadette Yu-ning Li on receiving her Ph.D. degree in 1967.

Nollaig MacKenzie and Ann Wilbur upon their marriage, 1968.

Kay and Martin Wilbur, Ann and Nollaig MacKenzie, Shirley Jarmel and John Wilbur on their marriage, 1974.

Kay and Martin celebrating their 50th wedding anniversary, with their daughter, Ann. July 17, 1982.

Caroline and John S. Service in 1980.

Roger and Betsey Wilbur Kodat, around 1986.

Professors Wilbur and Goodrich at the reception celebrating the establishment of the L. Carrington Goodrich Fellowship.

Martin and Kay Wilbur in the Quadrangle garden, summer 1991.

Son, John H. Wilbur, August 1991.

Father and daughter, August 1991, at the Quadrangle.

13

Thailand and Hong Kong

In Madras I arranged to travel to Bangkok by freighter, but I had to catch it in Colombo, the main port for the Island of Ceylon, off the south coast of India. I flew there on a two-engine Viking, which bounced around a lot, and arrived about 4:30 in the afternoon to find Colombo hot and steamy, though it was February 26. Since I learned that I must wait about four days for the sailing of the French freighter *Falaise*, I booked in at an inexpensive hotel and began to learn a little about this former Dutch and then British colony, famous for its tea and rubber, and with a culture different from that of India because the Singhalese are Buddhists of the southern strand, which includes Burma, Thailand, and Bali. I wrote to the family after two days in Colombo:

> This is a funny town. You can hardly step out of the hotel or walk down any street without several men stepping up and in the most ingratiating way offering their services to help you change money, or buy curios, or do other things that men sometimes do in a port city. It's quite annoying and I try to be polite but firm in refusal. However, they are likely to trot along beside you desperately trying to think of things you might be wanting to do so they can edge into the act and make some commission. It sure is a port town with its floating population of transients, who provide a small industry for guides, money changers, curio dealers, etc.

I had a few interviews in Colombo, two with members of the American Consulate and the deputy high commissioner for Great Britain, and one with a junior officer of the Ministry of External Affairs. Ceylon and China did not have diplomatic relations because of a misunderstanding and because the dominant political persons in Ceylon were very anti-Communist. Most were large-scale landowners and had no intention of undergoing "land reform." Many in Ceylon liked to think of the island as a sort of neutral Switzerland. Nehru's influence was very strong. China and Ceylon had a rubber-for-rice trade pact, which favored Ceylon when concluded. This created a favorable attitude toward China. However, because of it, Ceylon was ineligible for U.S. aid, which irked Ceylon greatly. Singhalese knew very little about China, getting their information mostly from British sources. There was no problem of overseas Chinese as economic middlemen as in several other southeast Asian countries.

Mr. Neville Jansz in the Ministry of External Affairs had taken two trips to China and clearly was sympathetic to the new regime. He told me of many incidents that had made a good impression, especially his long talk with Chou En-lai. Everyone was hard at work and there were lots of happy faces. The constitution was passed unanimously at the National People's Political Council meeting he attended, and without debate, he said. It was explained to him that the draft had been circulated to the whole country, had been extensively discussed, and over two thousand amendments had been proposed. So when it came to a final vote there was unanimous approval. However, Mr. Jansz did know of several disturbing circumstances, such as the disappearance of a Chinese woman who worked for the Indian Embassy, the arrest of nuns, the difficulty he had in meeting again a guide from the first trip. He detested Chiang Kai-shek and was much opposed to American support for his regime. He tended to excuse the suppressions in the PRC as characteristic of all revolutionary regimes at the early stage. This talk sounded like many I had had in India with travelers to the "New China."

Sailing by freighter across the Bay of Bengal to Singapore was great fun and very relaxing. The S.S. *Falaise* was a wartime liberty ship, about eight thousand tons. I was the only passenger on this run and had a comfortable cabin where I could do a lot of work, mostly writing up my impressions of India.

It was a six-day run to Singapore. I only had a few hours in that port, and I used every minute, tremendously aided by Dr. S. Y. Liu, a protégé of Dr. Chang Kia-ngao, who had given me a letter of introduction to him. I had written him to say I would be coming on the *Falaise*. He came out to the boat in a launch and did everything possible for me in Singapore. I wrote:

> It's back in the Chinese realm again. Most of the people, 820,000 out of 1,100,000, are Chinese. But it is not completely Chinese in appearance, the parts I saw being a mixture of Western-style shops and Chinese ones, English and Chinese shop signs. The older Chinese are more strongly so in dress (pajamas for women; men working with carrying poles) than the schoolchildren I saw, who were wearing white uniforms or playing cricket or basketball. When we drove into a residential area of lovely gardens, the region was entirely Western looking, though I suppose the residents may as well have been wealthy Chinese as British.
>
> The day in Singapore was rushed. I only had from 9:45 to 4:45 on shore and in that time went to the consulate to get my mail and talk with one of the officers about the situation of the Chinese in Singapore. Then over to the office

of Dr. Liu in some bank where I was introduced to a couple of leaders of the Chinese community, Mr. K. C. Lee, a self-made and very wealthy man of about sixty, and Mr. Tan Chin Tuan, apparently the manager of the bank. Both were friends of Dr. Chang. I also saw a former student, Harrison Royce, but wasn't able to track another, Robert Elegant, and I missed Tillman Durdin. Mr. Liu took me to lunch at about the smartest restaurant in town, after which he helped me mail letters and stuff to Tokyo and then drove me out to call on H.M. Commissioner General for Southeast Asia, Sir Malcolm MacDonald. I had written him from Colombo asking for an interview, and he was able to see me only at 4 P.M., which gave me exactly fifteen minutes before I had to rush off to the boat. He had a lovely home, filled with Chinese porcelains that he had collected over thirty years.

Back on the boat I wrote up four interviews about the situation in Singapore, especially concerning Communist China's efforts to win the battle against the KMT for the loyalty of the overseas Chinese. I was told that neither contestant was winning; mainly the overseas Chinese wanted to be left alone, but both sides were spending a great deal of effort.

From Singapore I sailed to Bangkok, the capital of Thailand. Our vessel entered the river leading to the city a little after daybreak on Sunday, March 13, and I sat on the deck watching the scene, for it took about two hours to go upstream:

We see multitudes of little boats—some sailing, some being sculled by one or two Siamese, maybe a man and his wife, or two children. The river is less than 200 yards wide and runs through close jungle on each side, and along the edge are bamboo and wattle houses right at the waterfront, and built on stilts. With glasses one can see the people at work—washing clothes or lounging about. The houses are amidst the coconut palms and banana trees. Here and there you see great black nets drying. Now you pass a village temple with its sharply peaked roofs, now a school, and now a Catholic church. I see a bright red sign—Coca-cola!

There is a much denser population along the river than on the Irrawaddy on my trip to Maubin. Here we are approaching a big city. I suppose that back from the river edge with its dense growth of trees and its saltwater canals there would be those miles and miles of rice land I saw when we flew over Bangkok airport on Thanksgiving day en route to Burma.

We sailed past some twenty or thirty river gunboats of various sizes—it must be pretty nearly the entire Thai navy—and came in finally to a dock, one edge of the river having been made into a long wharf with godowns, cranes, and everything necessary.

Ken Wells, my old friend from OSS days, was at the dock to meet me, but there was a long wait before he was allowed aboard, and even longer before I was allowed off, with various inspections of passport, luggage, and so on. Ken gave me a briefing about Thailand: They have an efficient government and Thailand

148   CHINA IN MY LIFE

is progressing in many different ways—schools, roads, public health. But it is an autocratic government with an efficient civil service and no nonsense about democracy, as the leadership sets no store by it. They lack the concept of human equality. Officials are also corrupt; they are out to make money for themselves. But that doesn't prevent efficiency.

As regards China, he told me that the Thai have had a long experience with China and were driven out of southern China by Chinese expansion, so there is deep antipathy. The Thai have no intention of being taken over by China and would fight. The Thai are trying to get the Chinese minority integrated. They are not allowed to have their own schools beyond primary.

Ken had spent twenty-seven years in Thailand as a missionary. He was very good in introducing me to people and showing me around. He arranged for me to stay at the Presbyterian Mission Guest House, which made my stay inexpensive. I remember vividly a scene in Ken's home. I saw him working with a Thai scholar on a translation of the Bible into Thai. That sort of collaboration had gone on in China since the first Protestant missionaries worked that way in Macao in the early 1800s.

I began to interview people about my particular interest, seeing Thais, Westerners, the Indian ambassador, and the Chinese Nationalist chargé. I had good connections in Thailand. Walter Zimmerman of the YMCA was an old friend of Dad's. I met the Hamlins, friends of Hal from Oberlin. They had been Oberlin "Reps" in Shansi and then moved to Thailand when China became closed to Americans. Dever Lawton, an old SAS friend, was another I found. From them I got many impressions about Thailand. It soon became clear that Thailand was strongly anti-Communist and fearful of its great neighbor to the north. There was much uncertainty about the so-called Thai Autonomous Region in southern Yunnan, and rumors of a Thai army being trained in China.

I summarize my interview with the Thai foreign minister, Prince Wan Waithayakon:

> I asked him whether there was any evidence of China moderating its attitude toward its southern neighbors. He said he did not think so. Of course, China would like to increase its trade, and so might appear friendly, but he felt that communism by nature was expansive. He thought a test of China's attitude would be what they will do about overseas Chinese. Will China cling to the ideal of dual citizenship? Nehru had been hoping that China would make a clear declaration about overseas Chinese that would allay fears of those countries with large Chinese minorities. But the most Chou has said is that Chinese should obey the laws of the countries in which they live. I mentioned being told in India that Chou would take the position that Chinese must choose the country to which they would give loyalty as a citizen, and those who chose citizenship in, say, Indonesia, should be good citizens and not expect support from China. Prince Wan broke in and said, "No, that was India's own position about overseas Indians, but not the Chinese position." He said he thought the subject of overseas Chinese would be discussed at the Bandung Conference.
>
> He stressed that Thailand's attitude toward China is defensive but not pro-

vocative. China frequently scolds Thailand, and the government information people like to answer back, but he urges restraint.

I mentioned that I believed that India, too, wanted to contain communism, but he disagreed, saying that India's attitude was like an ostrich with its head in the sand. They don't like to talk military matters in hopes that military aggression will not take place. He seemed a bit annoyed.

I asked about the criticism I have heard in Asia about American aid programs. He said he could understand American concerns, and it might appear that Asians were not grateful, but that in Europe feeling toward America was much worse. He said aid programs cause friction. He talked about disagreements between American experts and the Thai trained abroad, who also think of themselves as experts. Also Americans want to do things their way, which is different from the Thai way. They want endless statistics and accounting, and the Thai can't always supply statistical information. Another inconvenience is that money is contingent, that is, Thai think when they sign, the money will be given, but it is sometimes held up until statistics are supplied or the American experts have agreed to its release.

I mentioned the criticism that aid should be given through the United Nations rather than bilaterally, because UN aid would be less dominated by the United States, and the receiving country would be less dependent upon the United States. But he thought the difference an illusion, because the United States gives most of the UN money, and the management is in the West, not in Asia.

As to the argument of dependency of the recipient upon the donor, he said it was true in two senses (neither being political dependency, which is the heart of the India-Burma argument): dependency for training of technicians, which has to be done and takes a long time; and dependency for replacement of parts from the country that provides the initial equipment. But his view was that if you wanted the equipment you should accept that as a fact.

Prince Wan felt that aid programs, military training, and the USIS program might be more adapted to local conditions and traditions. Too much seems straight translation from the United States and not directly applicable to Thailand.

I made another acquaintance in Bangkok that has lasted through the years—with Dr. William Skinner. He was heading a village research project for the Southeast Asia program of Cornell University, and Ken Wells introduced me to him. Bill was an expert on the Chinese in Thailand and later wrote two books on the subject. He told me that the political loyalties of the Chinese in Thailand reflected the position of the government, that is, anti-Communist. There was no scope for open support of Communist China. The Thai police were vigilant and would not allow it. The Chinese community did not feel the power of China in Thailand, and American power was very evident.

He pointed out that the Chinese community in Thailand had a pattern of quick assimilation that went back many decades. This assimilation was set back a little in the 1930s when there was a policy of suppressing the Chinese. Except for that period, the Chinese have been steadily assimilating into Thai society. During the early postwar years, when China was thought to be one of the five powers, some

Chinese who had become Thai began to use their Chinese names again, but with the collapse of the Nationalist Government they soon reverted to being Thai.

Another interesting thing he described was the well-developed collaboration between Chinese businessmen and Thai officials or other elites. Chinese might manage government corporations, or they might get some Thai nobility or high officials onto the boards of their companies; the Thai gave prestige, connections, and protection and were paid in return, but the Chinese ran the businesses and made the profits. The network of interrelations was very close. The Chinese business leaders were also the community leaders, and their relations with the Thai leadership had to be close if they were to serve the interests of the Chinese community by interceding in times of trouble.

This was a part of the process of assimilation; another aspect was in education. Since Chinese schools were not permitted beyond primary, those who wanted to go on to middle school or college must do so in Thai language.

A few years later I was able to arrange for Bill Skinner to come to Columbia to join the East Asian Institute and the sociology department. However, the salary wasn't enough to support his family, and he moved to Cornell, then later to Stanford. He is one of the outstanding China specialists in America.

Since I wanted to get out of Bangkok and see some countryside, I took a train to the old Thai capital, Ayudhya, which was sacked and burned by a Burmese army a couple of centuries ago. I went second class with a Chinese gentleman and two Thai young ladies in the same compartment. After we had left the city, the flat rice land was dry at that time of year, but the farmhouses were built up on stilts. There were rows of yellow straw stacks, each wrapped conically around a central pole, and lines of coconut palms, some with rope ladder tied to them. The houses were of weathered wood, unpainted, the roofs of dark brown thatch, but occasionally of tile or tin. The station platforms had none of the feverish bustle of those in India.

I had a pleasant few hours in Ayudhya because I had a note to a high court judge. This caused a bit of a flurry because Judge Kasem Tipayachan was very rusty in English. After I had been given a ceremonial drink of Green Spot, a car came, driven by another judge, Phot Sunthara, to escort me around. The two judges and the registrar of the court just quit for the day and served as my guides. We went to the ruins of the former capital and to a former temple where a great statue of Buddha stands, very photogenic against the blue sky. We burned our incense and then drove off to see more modern aspects of the city, such as an alcohol distillery and another Buddhist temple, not in ruins.

My last day in Thailand was special. I went out to visit a Thai village, Bang Chan, that was the object of a ten-year study by the Cornell Southeast Asia project to observe social change or "modernization." I was escorted there by Mrs. Skinner and a Thai gentleman. We arrived at the village about 9 A.M., and my first impression was that there was no village, just three stores on either side of the road and a bridge over the canal at that point. After having a coke in one of the stores, we started across the dry fields through narrow paths and came to a few houses along a canal, and a temple compound made up of half a dozen elevated buildings of wood construction. Some were dormitories for monks. We visited the head priest, a talkative man in saffron robes, who sat cross-legged on the floor with a cuspidor in front of him, into which he spat from time to time. His living quarters were rather bare, but there were pictures of the king and queen of Thailand. The king is a symbol of Thai nationalism. After our call on this head priest, we strolled about the temple grounds, and the amazing thing was that no one, no kids and no men or women, crowded around us or stared at us, as would have been the case in China. A few people sitting in a refreshment shop were friendly but unconcerned. The temple complex was the center of the village—the only place where any considerable number of villagers could congregate.

We next went to the home of a village teacher, a bamboo-sided house with a straw roof, elevated about two feet on stilts, and on the bank of the canal. We sat just inside the entrance area and talked with this smiling, mild-mannered teacher who was about forty years old. His wife kept in the background, as did four small children. Since teaching doesn't pay well, the family kept chickens and sold eggs.

Here we boarded a canal boat, about 20 feet long and 3 feet wide, with four cross pieces to sit on. It was shallow-bottomed and was sculled by an oar at the back. It glided through the water even though the canal was quite shallow in places, past water buffalo luxuriating in the water and snorting as we glided by. We stopped to see a family catching fish by diking off a section of a lateral canal, draining that section by means of a pump, and then plunging into the muck up to their hips to feel for fish, which they grabbed and tossed wriggling into a basket. The whole family and some neighbors were doing this work, which we saw going on in several places.

The most delightful interlude was our stop at the house of a man and woman who earn a living by making things out of bamboo and rattan. Their little house was about two feet above the ground, with the front part rather open. The house had a wooden floor, basketry walls, and a thatched roof. They were making fruit pickers, a sort of basket with teeth to pluck off fruit that would then fall into the container. It had a short handle to be attached to a pole. I bought one, and the lady quickly made me a small one as a gift. The couple made about the equivalent U.S. $350 a year from their handiwork.

Our visit was so pleasant because of the absolutely relaxed atmosphere. We were welcomed, but no fuss whatsoever was made over us. We chatted, but they were not very inquisitive. When I asked to take their picture they willingly complied, but not until the man had put on a skirt and the woman some extra garment over her red blouse. After a while I asked if I could look at the rest of the house and they said go ahead, but didn't themselves take me around. Behind the sitting room there was a long but narrow back room, part of which was the area for cooking, which was done on the floor. At the other end was a hammock, which provided extra sleeping space, for there was also a bedroom. The eight-year-old son was fast asleep on a mat, his head upon a hard pillow. Nor did he wake up during the half hour we were there.

The few possessions of the family were hung on the walls or put on the floor near a wall. I saw two saws, a pair of boots, and various pieces of clothing—shirts, pants, skirts—simply stuck on the walls, though there were two boxes that presumably contained important possessions. There was a small altar at one side of the bedroom in which there was a small figure of the Buddha and an urn. I was told by our Thai escort that the urn might contain the ashes of a parent. There were several photographs on the walls. One was of their daughter, who was off helping a neighbor catch fish. Another was a neighbor's daughter, who had participated in a beauty contest in Bangkok. Another showed five girls in evening dress, participants in the same contest, and the neighbor's daughter was one of them. Talk of social change! The picture of a young man in army officer's uniform was of the son of a neighbor, who seemed to be a sort of village head. This neighbor was addressed by the term for doctor, because he was wise and informed about good and bad luck.

When we had stayed there a while, we just left. There was no to-do about farewell, no escorting to the boat landing, no bowing as we glided off. It was one of the most natural, least tense meetings with strangers, and departures, I have ever experienced. A Chinese would have been full of ceremonial and stylized good manners of greeting and parting, rushing to get tea, desperately making polite conversation for fear of a vacuum in the talk, escorting to the front gate, and so on. Our low-key visit was a pleasure.

We stopped at another house to see a new industry, mushroom growing, done between layers of straw and kept shaded and damp. We also were shown a new six-room schoolhouse, with good light and ventilation. Thailand, we were told, was building many new schools.

It was a lovely experience to go to that scattered village and be greeted in so friendly a fashion by the folks at whose homes we stopped. Yet I just wondered, where is everyone? The Thai are reputed to be very easygoing and relaxed. In this village they certainly were. Perhaps it's their form of good manners.

I flew to Hong Kong on Saturday, March 26, and put up at the YMCA guesthouse on Salisbury Road in Kowloon. On this return to Hong Kong I saw Bob Berton, with whom I had stayed on the way out; Allen Whiting, then also on a Ford Foundation study grant; Henry Lieberman, the *New York Times* correspondent; and then a group at the American Consulate General: Arthur Drumright, who had been a language student in Peking when we were there in the 1930s, Larry Lutkins, and Mr. Holdridge, who much later became the head of the State Department's Far East Division. With all these I had exchanges of views about conditions in China and the influence of China among overseas Chinese. But nothing that seemed so notable, except details on a terrible flood in 1954 that had much reduced China's farm output. The contest went on between the KMT and the PRC for the loyalty of overseas Chinese. The PRC was expending great effort and making promises to induce them to remit money to families in China or to invest in government enterprises.

I also had a good talk with John Keswick. He was very knowledgeable about business in the Orient, thought the Chinese would have a difficult time making socialism work, but was optimistic about the future of Western business in areas around China, including Hong Kong, which he knew inside out.

On Tuesday I had a trip out through the New Territory to the colony's border with China. I was a guest of the police, driven in one of their cars through Kowloon and out along a well-laid, winding mountain highway to a village and a police station from which "the Border" is controlled. There Mr. Gordon took me in his charge. He was a polite gentleman with reddish hair and blue eyes, about forty years old, and had lived and worked in Hong Kong for many years.

The border is about twenty-two miles long, and most of it runs along a river or creek. Seven hundred police had fourteen stations along the border, each of which could hold ten men, self-sufficient in food and water, and in constant contact with headquarters by radio or telephone. At night the entire border was covered by search lights and was patrolled by men with Alsatian police dogs. The British side was fenced, except for an ill-defined region in the mountains. The Chinese also had a fence and, according to Mr. Gordon, about five thousand troops on their side. The British kept their troops—English, Gurkha, and Chinese—well back from the border.

We drove in Mr. Gordon's police car to the eastern end of the border where there was a small village. We now had an escort of Chinese police armed with machine guns. Down the street fifty feet away were barbed wire barricades and Chinese soldiers looking fierce. I started to take a picture but a Chinese civilian who had been watching us from across the border shouted that I must not. Mr. Gordon stepped up and said I could take his picture, which gave me the chance to get him and a couple of my police escorts, as well as the Communist side of the border as background.

We then went to Lo Wu, the place where the railway crosses from one side to the other. Now we had another police escort and a British police officer in a jeep. We walked through the railway station on the British side, where a train was standing and receiving passengers who had made it out of China and across a narrow bridge, itself bisected by barbed wire with a narrow passage between. On the far side were four grim-faced Chinese soldiers in khaki uniforms, boots, and round helmets with the red star on the front, all carrying machine guns. Four other men in uniform, but not armed, were checking the papers of passengers who were coming out of China. There were also some farmers driving cattle, presumably for sale in Hong Kong. Along the British side of the bridge there were about twenty Chinese civilians with their baggage waiting to pass into China. One by one the officers checked their papers and let them in. The situation was very tense, the line of people stiff and silent.

There was no greeting from either side when Mr. Gordon and I came up to the transit point. This was the spot where foreigners being ejected from China emerged, or Indians went in to discover Mao's paradise. It was the transit point between two worlds, a length of not over thirty yards.

Walking back a few yards off the British side of the bridge we stepped into a police room. There a Chinese policeman sat inspecting the papers of people coming into the colony. We saw a young woman with a carrying pole and a heavy load on each end, holding the hand of a boy about six. Her face was tense and drawn. She put down her heavy load, sighed, and stepped up to the window with her document, which had her picture and details about her in Chinese. She had used the document several times before, because it had several similar stampings upon it. The police officer stamped the document and handed it back, and she lifted her burden, took her boy by the hand, and staggered on toward the customs station and train. Her baggage wasn't inspected, but she had to stop at the health station. What story was there about this woman?

From upstairs in the police station I was able to take a few pictures of the bridge, and of the Union Jack and Chinese flags flying side by side at the crossing point. Then we went to a third crossing, also with a bridge, but here the traffic was mostly farmers and small merchants passing back and forth. We saw three Hakka women with carrying poles and baskets of produce going into China, and a man driving a water buffalo coming out. Again the grim-faced Chinese troops.

Out in the colony's countryside were farmers tilling their fields, groups of Hakka women dressed in black, wearing the big, flat, round hat with a fringe hanging down or a black kerchief on the head. They carried goods to market in baskets on each end of a carrying pole. They were nice-looking country women who were very shy, I was told. No bound feet among the Hakka. I also saw groups of schoolchildren, out with their teachers on a hike. Very nice looking kids, but then, what school kids aren't nice looking, especially Chinese? I supposed these kids were being battled over by each side, Communist and anti-Communist, as was being done all around the edge of the Chinese realm.

On this second visit to Hong Kong I was struck again by the wonderful vitality of the place. Hong Kong was a going concern. New buildings going up all around, factories being started or humming along, the harbor filled with passenger ships and freighters, as well as ferry boats, tugs, lighters, and tall-sailed junks. The roads were fine, and there was rapid and inexpensive public bus transportation throughout the city and to the towns on the outskirts—big red double deckers, they were, like those in London. The city was clean and the police efficient, and one had a feeling things were really under control. I was told the colony has a very good health service. Not enough schools even at primary level, but there was a program to add facilities for 26,000 new kids a year for the next seven years. There was a rudimentary local government, but Julie How's friend, Francis Pan, told me the elective element of it was very slight.

My last stop on my way back to the family was Taipei. I stayed there only three days, talking with a few people, trying to get a feel for the political situation. I noticed no difference at all after five months away—"which probably shows how superficial my observations are," I wrote. There was no increased tension, nor were there visible signs of sagging morale; just people carrying on their occupations at about the same easygoing pace as before. The Chinese friends I talked with showed the same politeness and restraint, and, I suppose, fortitude. For them—mainlanders—life was grim.

14

Tokyo Again

I wanted to get the feel of Japan after being in southern Asia, and the following is what I wrote in my journal upon my return to Tokyo.

People seem more tense and tired than those I saw in Bangkok, Hong Kong, or Taipei. This is partly the effect of a huge city. You ride on the bus, or train, or subway, and the people around you have the generally sober, unrelaxed look of folk going drudgingly to work. But it isn't just that; it's something deeper. Try to get a smile from kids. Smile at them and they stare back owl-eyed. It isn't that way with kids in China, Thailand, or India. It isn't because people don't know how to laugh or be gay. Here, adults take life very seriously, it seems, and maybe the kids get trained to also.

There is election campaigning afoot. People go about in trucks with loudspeakers addressing the streets day and night. But in this neighborhood crowds don't gather. The loudspeakers bellow, but people go on about their business as though electioneering had no relation to them. Maybe it doesn't. I've been told that it's the most "famous" people who get elected, not those with policies that win them votes.

Japan impresses me by its industry. The hurry and bustle, the long hours of work, the great amount of goods in the shops are all in contrast to India, where the pace is much slower. Perhaps they hide unemployment here. But those who work, work very hard, actively and long. It's true in rural areas, too. In the Izu Peninsula you see agriculture pushed much farther than anything I saw in India. It's in the terraced rice fields, and the little corners of land used for growing vegetables; it's the people working hard in the fields. In southern India they work hard too; and doubtless in northern India after the rains there is great activity. But land there just is not so intensively used. Burma and Thailand don't know the meaning of work in comparison with China and Japan.

156

Since I wrote this part of my journal, Japan has become an industrial and economic giant, and I realize that one part of the explanation is that tremendous work ethic I observed back in 1955.

Another impression of Japan is the extreme crowding and the overflowing child population. Walk down our little Sakura Shin-machi and the street is filled with children, little and big, playing their games. Granted that the street probably is their only playground, but still there are droves of them. Then there are the mothers with one child on the back and a second, and sometimes a third, in hand. You wonder if there is a compulsion to have one child a year. The common statistic is that Japan is adding one million a year to its population. You see crowding on every hand, and it has broad sociological consequences.

One cannot overlook the loveliness of Japan, the beauty of the land and the beauty the Japanese create. You see it in streams bridged with slightly arched wooden bridges and planted alongside with bamboos and pines and Japanese maples. You see lovely seascapes, with villages reaching down to the shore, fishing boats out on the blue waters of coves, islands with gnarled pines growing out of rocks. And then the bits of beauty: the Japanese garden around a house, flower arrangements, a bit of pottery, a little artificial waterfall, the way a meal is served. There is aesthetic delight on every side.

Because it had been warm in Tokyo in late March, Kay had turned off the kerosene stove that warmed our living room, but it got chilly again, so we turned the kerosene flow on again and started the stove up. We didn't know, however, that some kerosene had been dripping into the stove all the time it was turned off, so all of a sudden the stove was bright red and belching flames out of its door. In a house made of wood, straw, and paper that was terribly dangerous! We called the landlord's granddaughter, who rushed in and telephoned the fire department, and then started taking down the shoji partitions so they wouldn't catch fire. Finally we heard a fire engine coming, but when I went to the front gate to welcome the men, I saw way up the street that they were stopping along the way, apparently asking which house had the fire. Finally, twelve men in full regalia arrived at our door, bowed, asked if they might come in, took off their boots, and several of them politely entered our living room while others inspected from the outside. By then the stove had lost its alarming redness and had stopped belching flames—the extra kerosene had burned away and all was well again. The reason the firemen had to stop along the way to inquire was that houses didn't have individual numbers. The whole block had one number. I found a way to thank the firemen for their wasted trip. A friend with PX privileges bought me a carton of American cigarettes, which I took to the firehouse as an expression of appreciation.

Almost immediately I started my interviewing of Japanese journalists, editorial writers, professors, officials, members of the Diet, women as well as men—leftists and rightists, Communists and Socialists and Liberal Democratic party leaders—for their opinions about China. Some had visited China and certainly spoke the Chinese line, but I was glad to get their impressions of what they had seen. Trying to get as wide a range of opinion as possible, still I found the general attitudes were favorable, partly because of the expert propaganda that China was sending toward Japan through several media and that was ardently propagated by leftist organizations; partly because of an old sentimental interest in China—several million Japanese had lived there or been in the army there— that was compounded by a sense of national guilt for Japan's recent aggressions there. Then there was the lure of trade, especially for medium-sized business, which saw a huge consumer market across the sea.

People who had visited China in "friendship groups" or "peace groups" gave glowing accounts of what they had seen on tours. What they told me sounded much like the reports I heard from returned Indians or Burmese but were more perceptive, because Japanese had a much more direct and longer knowledge of China than did those visitors from South Asia. It was quite evident now that many improvements in the material life of Chinese city folk did impress the Japanese who visited there. I must have had some thirty interviews.

An example of skillful propaganda was the repatriation of Japanese prisoners of war and others who had been detained in China for five years after "liberation." The early repatriates were carefully chosen for their favorable attitudes toward the new regime, and their return was played up tremendously in the press. Naturally, individual Japanese getting loved ones back were happy, but there was a national mood of celebration. The first returnees being interviewed gave favorable accounts of the country's progress. Later, however, people began to learn something of the cruelty of the brainwashing and forced labor that the detainees had undergone before being prepared for repatriation.

I arranged to interview a Japanese gentleman, whom I named Mr. Kato, who had just returned. He was of the student class and had attended a college in China after having been thoroughly brainwashed. I believe he gave me a realistic account, during our three extended talks, of conditions as he experienced them, and I wrote up the results under the title "Communist China through Japanese Eyes." I also wrote a shorter, more colorful version, hoping to get it published. Copies of these and other unpublished pieces are among the papers I gave Columbia's Special Collections Manuscript Library.

Whenever I had an interview, I had to go home and type it up immediately from my notes and memory. So, counting travel back and forth and a careful write-up, one interview, if fruitful, could take most of the day.

My interviewing went on till the end of July, and I also followed the English-language press and collected data on attitude polls about America and China. America was the most popular foreign country by far, but China was second. Russia didn't stand high among the European countries with the general public, and Korea was always the pits.

With respect to America there was evidence of much dissatisfaction with our policies that affected Japan. Radicals in Japan were very busy against the United States, and the polls showed hostility to be most frequent among the 20- to 29-year-olds. I wrote an article for *The New York Times Sunday Magazine* entitled "Chinese Doves Flutter over Japan," a summing up of my findings on China's efforts and influences. Shortly after arriving home I also wrote a report for the Ford Foundation. Later I contributed a chapter to *Japan between East and West*, a book issued by the Council on Foreign Relations.

In addition to lots of research through reading and interviews, we had a social life, entertaining Columbia students, of whom there were quite a few in Tokyo, and also a few Japanese with whom we had become acquainted socially. We were entertained quite a lot, too. The Chinese embassy—Nationalist—particularly courted me. We also had some wonderful times with John and Ann, who became quite at home in Tokyo.

Another thing that Kay and I did was to go occasionally to a small liberal Japanese church, vaguely associated with Unitarianism. Kay started a relationship between this church and our own church's Sunday School, through which the children from each side wrote letters to the other. Our Sunday School sent some of their collection money, through Kay, so the Japanese Sunday School could buy some needed supplies.

Kay was preparing to be the director of our Unitarian Sunday School after our return. One thing she did was to visit a Buddhist church with which we had a connection through the young Japanese man I had met in India, who was studying to be a priest, and whose father was the abbot of the church. Kay became acquainted with the mother, who was active in the Buddhist Sunday School, and they swapped information about their respective practices and ideals. Then the young man took Kay to stores that sold religious goods, and she acquired for the White Plains Sunday School a full set of objects for a Buddhist altar.

There is a spring cleaning in a Japanese house, during which all tatami are taken up and beaten, and everything is aired out. We discovered something about the house's construction. Between the two-inch-thick tatami on which we slept on futons there were only newspapers laid across slats, and then the open ground below, because the house was raised from the ground about two feet. Thus all of the cold of winter crept up to those who slept on the floor. Actually, it was Kay and the kids who got the worst of it during the winter while I was away.

But we loved that beautiful house. It had a sense of spaciousness and lack of clutter when the bedding was put away in closets and one low table and cushions on the floor were the only visible furniture. If the shoji were pushed back we were virtually within the lovely garden. And the tokunoma—the beauty spot of the house—would be arranged with flowers, a bit of pottery, and a scroll painting. Such features we later tried to incorporate in our Pleasantville home.

Because dentistry was so cheap in Japan—2,000 yen for my three visits (under $6)—we all had our teeth attended to before departure. Packing, of course, began to intrude into my work, but Kay is very systematic about packing. She started about two weeks before our scheduled sailing date, August 1, 1955. On the last day of July I wrote my parents in Pasadena that we were all packed and that I had taken a truckload of our baggage to the docks—twenty pieces. We were also to take eight small pieces by hand, "but already that has grown, as Johnny has gone out to buy a couple of gifts for friends back home, and someone just gave us a watermelon to take on board." Our boat, the *New York Maru*, was scheduled to arrive in San Francisco about August 14.

As is often the case with freighters, this one started a day late, and we trooped off early in the morning of August 2 to board our ship and say farewell to Japan. Our faithful housekeeper, Kawagiri-san, came all the way on board to say farewell. My journal says, "I think we left nothing behind except a number of friends and the respect, I hope, of our neighbors, the Japanese villagers of Sakura Shin-machi." On board I put down some thoughts:

And what about Japan? I read a wonderful article in the *Nippon Times* today praising the kindliness of the Japanese people and the intense beauty that they create. I agree with it. I can be very sentimental and admiring of this extremely orderly, quiet, and peaceful people, who are hardworking, intelligent, and well educated, too. Living among Japanese is still a wonderful experience. Some visual impressions first:

Young women in clean and demure frocks, or skirts and blouses, riding the buses and streetcars to work—all the conveyances simply jam-packed with people. In the department stores the same clean, fresh-faced girls, their lips carefully made up in thick, heartlike bows. The very formal and polite ones who stand by each landing of the escalator, bowing slightly as you come by and murmuring a thank you for coming to the store.

The endless rows of small shops are another image. Every street or neighborhood has its candy store, senbei shop, flower store, photographer, vegetable store, fish shop, tailor, variety store, hardware dealer, and so on endlessly. They are generally clean and neat. You see the proprietors opening up any time from seven in the morning onward, and closing any time after nine in the evening. Walk into any of them and you will be cordially welcomed. Buy or don't buy, you will be thanked sincerely. There's not much point in bargaining, for the price is fixed. But perhaps you will be given a small gift as you leave if you have bought a lot. In spite of shops filled with goods, there doesn't seem to be blatant commercialism to force sales. The merchants of Sakura Shin-machi had sales on three fixed days, the 8th, 18th, and 28th, and employed musicians to snake dance through the street to amuse and inform the crowd.

Children. So many of them! Healthy. Playing in the streets or trudging off to school in droves with their school bags on their backs. Children on a summer evening wearing their bright little kimonos—yukatas—looking like little fairies. Children in school uniform, from about the age of ten till sometime past twenty, when they finish college. Rather placid kids. I saw no fights, though Johnny and Ann say they saw some. Still, the impression is of happy but subdued children.

How is Japan doing? Will it make it economically? Will it get some form of extreme nationalism? Where will it lodge in the international world? I've asked myself these questions, searched for answers while reading, and made two attempts in writing, without much success.

Economically, I think Japan will make a go of it. The problems are very difficult. And I saw mostly Tokyo and not the impoverished rural areas and cities described in "Undertow." But Japan will find ways to trade and to secure raw materials all over the world, including China, of course.

The Communists are skillful in getting intellectuals to accept and push their worldwide propaganda themes, or in joining with the Socialists in a broad strategy. But they don't seem to get very far as a revolutionary party in Japan. When they are violent they lose followers very fast. Perhaps as a "peaceful, lovable party" they will begin to make headway again. But communism seems to me a poor bet in Japan. The Socialists, leaning far over toward the international Communist position, seem far more viable than the Communists. But in creating front groups and popular movements such as group singing, and pushing propaganda, disguised or seemingly disguised, Communist parties seem devilishly effective.

As to reviving nationalism, of course there are many small signs: Shinto, some nationalistic societies, anti-Americanism (quite understandable). As yet I don't see what it leads to. There is no big objective, such as building an empire, toward which nationalism can be directed. There is no fire in it yet, so far as I can see. Pride in culture, in nation, of course; and this will be stronger and stronger. They have lots to be proud of.

The position of intellectuals interests me. On the whole, professors and students, and many journalists and some social critics, are with the Socialists—left or right. They oppose rearming Japan or greatly fear the effects of it. They are neutralists between Russia and America, seeing much bad and good on both sides. Some are certainly apologists for Russia and China. They are swept along by the campaign opposing the atomic bomb. Or are they? Anyway, a lot of enthusiasm seems to be worked up about peace. PEACE. Is there anything wrong with that? Obviously not, except some of the shouting is an attempt by the world Communist movement to win converts. "The Peace Movemement" and "Peace Fighters" are lingo for Communist front movements and workers. This isn't only in Japan, of course, but here there's great praise for socialism, and a tendency to look on Russia as a socialist country.

This is where my journal ended. We arrived San Francisco on August 14 and joined my parents the next day. We started driving east on August 21. On Thursday, September 1, we arrived back home. We had been away for thirteen months exactly.

15

Teaching and Scholarship

Upon our return from Japan, I was swept into a very busy life. I had my regular courses to teach and, as one recently returned from an interesting year of study in Asia, I found myself in some demand as a speaker. In September 1955 I went to Los Angeles and to Seattle to give talks; and I was asked to give a talk at a regular meeting of our church. In October and November, I spoke to the Americans for Democratic Action, the Japan Society, and an assembly at Wheaton College (arranged by Paul Cressey). In December I gave a talk at Harvard on China's drive to influence Asia. Strange to say, I declined an invitation from Columbia's history department to give a talk at the departmental dinner. That was a silly mistake, for I might have become better known within the department.

I was a member of the Executive Committees of Columbia's department of Chinese and Japanese, the East Asian Institute, and the history department, all of which required meetings. I had work on dissertations to do, and I reviewed books for scholarly journals. In those days, I rode to Columbia by train, getting off at 125th Street in Harlem, taking a bus to Amsterdam Avenue, and then walking about six blocks to my office. This took at least an hour and a half each way. That was taxing. For Kay, who met me with the car at the Pleasantville station, it was a strain because the trains often were quite late, and she had dinner cooking.

In the scholarly arena, I picked up on the book that Julie How and I had worked on, which had been accepted for publication by Columbia University Press. We had to do some revision and to write a conclusion. As soon as that was done, Julie left for Hong Kong, and I had to see the book through the press. It came out in October 1956 as *Documents on Communism, Nationalism, and Soviet Advisers in China, 1918–1927: Papers from the Peking Raid.*

The book was a detailed study of the early history of the Chinese Communist Party, the Nationalists in the 1920s, and the influence of Russian advisers, who worked with both parties in what the Communists called a "united front." The main documentation was a body of papers seized in a raid on the Soviet Embassy compound in Peking on April 6, 1927, many from files of the Chinese Communist leaders in Peking, who were in refuge in the embassy, and others from the files of the Soviet military attaché's office. These were absolutely unique in revealing the inner workings of the Russian mission and the Chinese Communist Party. We used a great variety of other sources to illuminate and explain the documents, of which we reproduced fifty in translation.

Julie had written most of the chapters, though I had been in overall charge of the project. I hired Julie and then accepted supervision of three Chinese intellectuals, refugees supported by funds administered by the State Department. They translated many of the documents—at least in first draft—and Julie and I worked over the book repeatedly, especially the part dealing with the authenticity of the documents, and our conclusions. Columbia University Press requested that my name be given first, as director of the project.

Another activity that took up a great deal of my time, but also earned me much-needed income, was work for the Ford Foundation's Foreign Area Fellowship Program. This was an effort to give young potential foreign area specialists language training and financial assistance in the research for their dissertations. I had scarcely returned to the United States when Abe Weisblatt of the foundation asked me to lunch and suggested that I might become a member of the screening committee for East Asia, which would review the credentials of candidates, interview the most likely ones, and recommend to the board those who should be taken on. I was an appropriate person because I had just completed a tour of East Asia and had some knowledge of academic conditions there. My reports to the Ford Foundation probably had something to do with my selection. Naturally, I indicated interest, and soon I was appointed to the committee—actually, the National Committee, as it was called. Cleon Swayzee in the foundation was in general charge. Work for the FAFP was a three-year relationship. I earned quite a lot, and I traveled to cities such as Los Angeles, San Francisco, Seattle, Chicago, Boston, and Washington, in addition to New York, to interview candidates or attend committee meetings, all expenses paid. It was interesting work and I enjoyed it. However, it did take a toll on my health, as it turned out. For instance, in the first five months of 1956, almost every other weekend was taken up by Foreign Area Fellowship business.

I was invited to write a chapter on Sino-Japanese relations for a book to be published by the Council on Foreign Relations, of which I was a member. I worked on it during the spring of 1956, using materials I had gathered in Japan. The book was published in 1957 by Harpers, with the title *Japan between East and West*. I enjoyed attending afternoon meetings of the council, where important political persons made speeches. Many of the council members were themselves influential in American politics and business; the scholar members added a polish of academia.

My friend Professor John Young asked to come out to our home to see me, and of course I welcomed him. He came to tell me that while he was recently in Japan, he learned that an American agency had warned the Japanese security agencies that I was a "leftist." This probably harked back to McCarthyism and my passport problem. It was good of John to take the trouble to tell me this. Fortunately, I am not aware that the warning in any way hindered the work I did in Japan.

I was sick for a week in late August, 1956. I expected to continue teaching in September, and after registration I met my first class. However, my doctor had me get an x-ray, and this confirmed that I had a serious ulcer and should have an operation to remove part of my stomach, no small matter. I went into the hospital on October 2, stayed there recuperating until October 19, and missed all my teaching till November 18, six weeks. Poor Carrington Goodrich had to find people to substitute for me in several courses. Kay, of course, was just wonderful to her convalescing husband. After that I resumed teaching, gave an occasional outside lecture, and continued with the Ford Foundation work. It seems that the operation did solve my recurring ulcer problem.

In December 1956 I got a bright idea. I saw a list of prominent Chinese living in the New York area—people who had been prominent before the Nationalists were driven from the mainland. Why shouldn't we do an oral history with some of them, on the pattern of the American Oral History Project at Columbia, which Alan Nevins had pioneered? I decided to drive to New Haven to see Professor Franklin Ho, my colleague in the East Asian Institute, to discuss the possibility with him. He was very much in favor of it.

The next thing was to work out a plan and a budget, which Franklin and I did. We agreed that we wanted interviewers who were knowledgeable in recent Chinese history, and we wanted the product to be respectably scholarly autobiographies, potential contributions to the history of the Republican period in China. It took a year before we could arrange funding on an experimental basis. Schuyler Wallace, dean cf the School of International Affairs, was working up a proposal to the Ford Foundation for major support, and I persuaded him to put in an amount for the Chinese Oral History Project, which he did, for a figure of $15,000. But it wasn't till early 1958 that the Ford grant came through and we could actually start.

Franklin, a much respected scholar and wartime official, did most of the negotiation with our subjects, and President Grayson Kirk showed a real interest and always signed an official invitation to a person we wanted to interview. An invitation from the president of Columbia University was an important thing to a Chinese person. In February 1958 we were under way, with Julie How interviewing Dr. H. H. Kung, banker, financier, and wartime prime minister, and T. K. Tong interviewing Dr. Hu Shih, celebrated scholar and leader of the Chinese "cultural renaissance" of the 1917–1923 period at Peking National University, and later China's wartime ambassador in Washington.

The Institute of Pacific Relations was arbitrarily denied its tax-exempt status by the Internal Revenue Service, at the behest of the McCarran Committee on Un-American Activities. The IPR went to court to get the decision reversed, but in the meantime it could not receive gifts from foundations or from private individuals if they wanted the gifts to be tax exempt. The organization meant a great deal to scholars specializing on Asia, and many of us testified on behalf of the IPR at court hearings. I presented an impressive list of books published by the IPR that were on my booklist for students of modern China. Later I was asked to become a member of the board of the American IPR, which I did. Carrington Goodrich also was a member. Although the IPR finally won its court case and had its tax-exempt status restored, by then it was virtually bankrupt and had to fold. I was partly instrumental in getting the files transferred to Columbia's Rare Book and Manuscript Library, where they were much consulted.

Jack and Cary Service came to live in Queens when he was dismissed from the State Department and was offered a job as vice president in SARCO, a company that made steam traps, something he knew nothing about. But he invented an improvement in the steam traps that was very valuable to the company. He was fighting his dismissal through the courts, and eventually the U.S. Supreme Court heard his case and instructed the State Department to reinstate him with back pay. We saw a lot of the Services.

During the spring of 1957, I did a great deal of traveling for the Foreign Area Fellowship Program and interviewed many candidates. Many of those selected later became leaders in the field. Of course, I had to keep up my teaching duties too. Also, I was invited to review books on China for the *New York Times* Sunday book review, a job I did off and on until 1964. I continued reviewing for scholarly journals, such as the *American Historical Review* and *Political Science Quarterly*. Such work got my name around, but in an American university that isn't a substitute for scholarly books or articles of one's own.

I was instrumental in persuading John Everton of the Ford Foundation to make an "officer grant" for a group of scholars to microfilm historically useful archives of Japanese military and police agencies that had been seized after the war and taken to Washington, but which were soon to be returned to Japan. I had the grant go to Yale, rather than to Columbia, to keep our credit good. We had a committee of Jim Morley, John Young, Shitoshi Yanaga, and me to administer the grant, though John Young and Shitoshi Yanaga did the principal selecting of the Japanese documents to be microfilmed in Washington. The master microfilms are kept in the Library of Congress. It was a successful project, done speedily over the summer, and John Young produced a guide to the microfilmed historical materials, published by the East Asian Institute. We distributed it gratis to appropriate libraries and individual scholars.

In May 1957 we had farewell parties for Hugh Borton, who was to become president of Haverford College. I was invited to become director of the East Asian Institute to succeed him. My term began in July 1957. By then I was forty-nine years old and had been teaching for ten years. I had become a full professor, and my annual salary had grown gradually from $6,000 to $9,000 over that ten-year period. It sounds rather scandalous today. I never asked for a raise but just tried to earn more money on the side, for the salary simply was not enough for a growing family.

Being director of the East Asian Institute was fun. We had good students for a program leading to a certificate and a master's degree, and most of them went into careers in government, cultural work, or business connected with East Asia, but not a few went on to the Ph.D. degree and then college teaching. The pattern had been pretty much set by then—Columbia had a good reputation in Chinese and Japanese studies. We were one of the best in the country.

One of the first things I had to do was write a proposal for development of the East Asian Institute to go as part of a larger proposal that Dean Schuyler Wallace planned to submit to the Ford Foundation for development of the School of International Affairs, of which our institute was a part. (It was in this that I asked for funding of the Chinese Oral History Project.) I well remember Dean Wallace calling me up after he had read my write-up and congratulating me on it. He even said—and it is shameless of me to write this—that it was so good that the rest of the proposal would have to be rewritten to come up to it.

I made several innovations as director. One was the development of University Seminars on China and Japan. There were several scholars attached to Columbia in the Chinese Biographical Dictionary Project who were rather isolated, and it occurred to me that we should develop some sort of social and intellectual forum where we could all meet. Columbia had the University Seminars, in which scholars and other persons interested in some important topic of lasting interest met periodically at Columbia to discuss it or listen to a paper: such subjects as slavery, or labor legislation, or Latin America. The core of such groups was usually Columbia faculty members, but members could come from any institution or organization. (I had once given a paper to the Slavery Seminar, back about 1942, after my dissertation had been successfully defended.) Such seminars were democratic, making their own rules and schedules, but the university provided patronage, and there was an office that kept records for historical purposes. Members of recognized University Seminars got free library privileges. Professor Frank Tannenbaum was the original sparkplug for the idea and the system.

I learned from Frank how one went about starting a University Seminar, and then I called together a small group—Searle Bates, Howard Boorman, Morton Fried, Franklin Ho, and Jim Morley—as a convening group, and we decided to call it the University Seminar on Modern East Asia, with separate units on China and Japan, but with an interlocking membership. We sent out invitations to people we thought would be able to contribute, drawn from foundations and cultural organizations, and from other colleges and universities nearby, and were underway by October 1957. Both seminars have continued on their own steam till today, though as separate groups, modern China and modern Japan. By now the Modern China Seminar has met for almost forty years and has a few new members nominated every year. We have a pattern of eight meetings a year, with drinks and then a Chinese dinner held at the institute, with a formal written paper that has been distributed in advance, and which is then discussed by a designated person or persons, after which there is general discussion. We sometimes have an attendance of thirty to forty. Obviously the Modern China Seminar fills a need and is enjoyed. Some members came from New Haven, Princeton, and Philadelphia, and others from most of the colleges in the New York metropolitan area. I think it enhances the reputation of the East Asian Institute. In fact, later, Larry Finkelstein of the Ford Foundation (and a China seminar member) used it as a model in encouraging other regional groups to start up such seminars, with Ford financing, and now there are many, and not only on China.

I invited Professor Ho Ping-ti to be a visiting scholar in the autumn of 1958. He had gotten his Ph.D. degree at Columbia in British history but was teaching Chinese history at the University of British Columbia. The idea was to free him to pursue some research project, using Columbia's rich library resources. Professor Ho studied mobility of the scholar class in China during the Ming and Ch'ing dynasties, and he produced a well-received book on the subject, published in 1962 by Columbia University Press. That book started the East Asian Institute's Studies Series, another innovation. Since then the institute has sponsored and arranged for the publication of more than eighty scholarly books.

I made some mistakes, too. I invited William Skinner to join the institute faculty and the sociology department, a matter that took some negotiation and had budgetary implications. My mistake, and a serious one, was in the salary I offered, which was too little for his family responsibilities. With my own financial problems, I should have known better. Bill was a great addition, but after two years he was lured off to Cornell, his graduate institution.

Kay began teaching in the Pleasantville school system in September. This added about $4,800 to our income, and a good thing, too, since we faced college expenses for John and Ann. Kay took her work very seriously and was a splendid teacher. Each afternoon after school she faithfully read and corrected the kids' homework, so she could return it to them. She did lesson plans and kept excellent records, so that her grading could not be challenged, although her principal, Mr. Clough, advised her, "Set your sights lo-wa, Mrs. Wilba." Of course, she had to give up the directorship of the Sunday School.

Kay taught from 1957 to 1972, with two years off while we were away on sabbatical. It is her savings that now give her an income almost as much as mine, though I taught for twenty-nine years. It was many years before I could stash anything away.

When Kay began teaching, John and Ann were old enough to take care of themselves. They almost always came right home after school, for which we are grateful. No drugs, no experimental sex among the Pleasantville kids in those days, it seems. But parents don't always know. We were fortunate to have such "straight" children. It was that year that Ann bought her Haines flute. It cost $500, secondhand, a lot in those days, and she was able to afford it using money that Nana left her, and her savings from various jobs. Ann won first flute position in the Westchester Youth Orchestra, made up of the best musicians in area high school music programs.

After becoming director of the East Asian Institute, I had more responsibility for the students. We had an annual picnic at our house for all students and faculty of the institute and the department of Chinese and Japanese. Quite a mob. Some of my former students remember and speak of the times we entertained them.

In 1958 we added Dr. V. K. Wellington Koo and General Li Tsung-jen to our list of people being interviewed for their oral autobiographies. Julie How began the interviews with Dr. Koo, dwelling on his life up to and including his study at Columbia and his first positions in the new republican government of Yuan Shih-k'ai in Peking. The Koo interviews went on for seventeen years, though Julie only did the initial part before leaving again for Hong Kong. Eventually it came to 11,000 pages and cost about $250,000. It was so long because Dr. Koo had a career spanning sixty or more years, faithfully kept a diary, and directed that passages from his diaries or minutes of conversation be incorporated at the appropriate places. An extra benefit was that he gave a massive collection of his papers to Columbia University, one of the treasures of its Rare Book and Manuscript Library.

T. K. Tong's work with General Li, an important commander, and eventually vice president and then acting president of the Republic of China, went on for three years. It resulted in an autobiography that was published first in English (as one of the EAI's Studies Series) and then translated and pirated both in Taiwan and in the People's Republic of China. It greatly enhanced Professor Tong's reputation after he went on to teach Chinese history at New York's City College.

Also during 1958, I met Professor Kuo Ting-yee, a historian of modern China and creator of the Institute of Modern History in Academia Sinica, Republic of China. Our lives later became intertwined, so to say. One result of our meeting and of Franklin Ho's persuading was that our Oral History Project began subsidizing a similar one conducted by the Institute of Modern History in Taiwan. We sent Professor Kuo's Institute $1,000 a year for the necessary expenses of entertaining and transporting his subjects, necessary courtesies that were not financed by Academia Sinica. Thereafter our two institutes had a rewarding relationship.

In 1959 our department had Professor Kaizuka Shigeki, a distinguished Sinologist of Kyoto University, as a half-year visitor, and we entertained Professor and Mrs. Kaizuka—an absolutely elegant lady—and their two children at our home on New Year's day. Later, Professor Eto Shinkichi, another China specialist who had grown up in Manchuria, was our guest. In fact, I see quite a few Chinese and Japanese names in our guest book, including Professor and Mrs. Nagai Michio—he, a sociologist from Tokyo University—and, on another occasion, Dr. Hu Shih, who we had together with Professor and Mrs. Franklin Ho. He was to leave soon for Taiwan to take up the presidency of Academia Sinica.

President Grayson Kirk was friendly to me, and Kay and I were invited to a black tie dinner, and also to some musical evenings, in their home. One day I met Grayson in the Faculty Club and on the spur of the moment suggested that Columbia ought to give an honorary degree to John D. Rockefeller III, because of all he had done to cement Japanese-American relations. The exchange program between Japanese and American intellectuals that Mr. Rockefeller financed and the East Asian Institute administered was a great success. It was that situation, and my knowledge of Mr. Rockefeller's efforts to revive the Japan Society, that led me to suggest to President Kirk that Columbia confer an honorary degree on him. Grayson jumped at the idea, and of course had no difficulty in persuading the Columbia trustees that it would be appropriate.

To my surprise, when commencement time approached, Grayson asked me to be Mr. Rockefeller's escort in the degree presentation. Kay and I were invited to the big-shots' luncheon before the ceremonies, and Kay became acquainted with Mrs. Rockefeller, as her companion during the ceremonies. As escort, I marched with Mr. Rockefeller in the academic procession and helped in placing the hood over his head. No big deal, but he got to know who I was, and later I was invited to be a trustee of the Asia Society, another of his efforts in bicultural understanding.

John Fairbank enlisted me as a sponsor for a conference to map out ways to stimulate the study of Communist China, now ten years old as the People's Republic, but not much studied by American academics, though certainly by the intelligence community. I had already made a name of sorts for writing on CCP history. The costs of the Gould House Conference, held from June 19 to 21, 1959, were met by the Ford Foundation, which was much interested in promoting modern China studies. Both John Everton and Doak Barnett, friends of mine in the foundation, were concerned. At this two-day conference we discussed and debated what needed to be done to organize, stimulate, and finance a real program of studies of that mysterious, enemy country, as it was then perceived in the years after the Korean War. We decided there should be an interdisciplinary committee representing the major graduate centers to determine the best use of funds that were anticipated to be available from the Ford Foundation, and to administer them. Though the conference voted to put such a committee under the Association for Asian Studies, in the end Bill Lockwood and John Fairbank, negotiating with John Everton, Doak Barnett, and others at Ford, determined that it would be better if a committee were set up under auspices of the Social Science Research Council, which was experienced in managing such work, as the AAS was not. The auspices were made joint with the American Council of Learned Societies.

Thus was the Joint Committee on Contemporary China established. I was a member during the initial three years, when we mapped out procedures. Bryce Wood, an SSRC staff member, served as staff for the committee. One decision was to set up less formal disciplinary committees to organize conferences or find other ways of stimulating research in economics, politics, sociology, and so forth. We met several times each year. The JCCC became very influential. I should call it a resounding success in doing what it was set up to do. America became the leader in contemporary China studies (sharing the honor with Japan, if one really understood how much Japanese scholars of China were doing). Later many other area committees were established in similar fashion under joint SSRC and ACLS auspices.

Carrington Goodrich retired from Columbia on July 1, 1960, and I found myself acting chairman of the department as well as director of the East Asian Institute. But I was to go on sabbatical in 1961 and didn't want the post of departmental chairman. Carrington had been my mentor from 1934 onward. I held him in great esteem, and Kay and I are very fond of his wife, Anne. He continued to be a presence at Columbia when, after a two-year absence, he became director of the Ming Biographical Dictionary Project, a fifteen-year endeavor and a monument to his scholarship. He passed away in 1986 at the age of ninety-two.

In mid-July 1960, I was at Seattle for a conference arranged by George Taylor and financed by the Asia Foundation, to bring together Chinese scholars from Taiwan and American China specialists to share information about each other's work. It was an effort to help the Taiwan scholars break out of their isolation. Besides meeting many of the men I was to know better the following year in Taiwan—Li Chi, Kuo Ting-yee, Lo Chia-lun, Chiang Fu-tsung, etc.—I got the chance to see Jean and Marvin Durning, now living in Seattle, and also my old friend from Field Museum days, Millard Rogers, who had become a curator at the Seattle Art Museum. Such friendships mean a great deal to me, as I hope these pages show.

I planned to apply for a Fulbright grant for a year in Taiwan because my sabbatical was coming up in 1961. Remembering the cruelty of the 1954 application, when there was every reason to believe I had been accepted and then I was turned down at the last minute, I made a one-day trip to Washington to consult with Dr. Francis Young at the Conference Board, the organization that recommended to the State Department which candidates should be awarded fellowships. Dr. Young was an academic, not a bureaucrat. He listened to me sympathetically. I told him I would not go through the hassle of making an application unless I were assured that I would not be summarily turned down because of lingering McCarthyism or some adverse record in the State Department. He promised to investigate and inform me whether there were any reason why I should not apply. In about two weeks he wrote to tell me that I should go ahead and apply. I did and was given an award, with the Institute of Modern History and Mr. Kuo Ting-yee, its director, as my sponsors in Taiwan.

As I look back over my pocket diaries for the years 1955 to 1961 I see that for most of the weekdays there are notations of some person I was to meet or have lunch with—students, fellow faculty members, deans and directors, persons in the world of foreign area studies and foundations, and visiting foreign academics or Asian political leaders whom I was to hear speak or to entertain. Many of these people I can't even remember. I was rather scrupulous in keeping engagements. This took up a lot of time, and many, many trips into New York, in addition to my Monday, Wednesday, and Thursday teaching days. The little books reveal many trips to other cities, many speaking engagements, and an active social life. I seemed to be making a mark in my field as a promoter of Chinese studies and an "expert." However, there was a price. I made very little progress in any scholarly writing in those six years. It was enough to do the necessary reading to keep up with my field and enrich the courses I taught. Certainly my speaking ability in Chinese declined.

16

A Sabbatical in East Asia,
1961–1962

Kay and I flew off from New York for Japan on August 25, 1961. I wrote in my journal:

> We came in from the airport by limousine through the deserted early Sunday morning streets of Tokyo. So familiar, the gray tile roofs, the wooden store fronts, the police boxes, the laundry hanging from second-story balconies. Kay and I pointed out memory-evoking sights. Smells, too, evoke memory—pickles, and very odorous fish.
>
> We are impressed how extremely courteous everyone is, and also how purposive. In Takashimaya Department Store, the girls bow deeply to welcome you into the elevator, the clerks are unfailingly obliging. In the department store men's room, clearly so marked, a young woman in a pink frock calmly walks in where men are standing at urinals and finds herself a booth toilet, seemingly quite unconscious of any incongruity. It's really a quite refreshing lack of prudery on this matter of nature. Yet conventionally, the women are so socially shy, so artificial. Yet, by contrast with earlier decades they are, of course, very free. There seems a mixture of casualness and purposefulness in the people strolling or working this Sunday. Are the Japanese relaxing a bit? The courtesy is infectious—one finds oneself automatically and unconsciously being a little more polite than before.

Our days in Japan were spent mostly in seeing friends—Professors Eto Shinkichi and Hosoya Chihiro, and Professor and Mrs. Iwanaga—all of whom had been visiting scholars at Columbia and guests in our home; and former students—Bill Morton, Paul Langer, Peter Berton, and Edwin Beal.

One evening, Mr. and Mrs. Matsumoto entertained us at dinner at International House, a new facility set in a beautiful old Japanese garden. He was head of and the inspiration behind International House in Tokyo. John D. Rockefeller III provided much of the financing as part of his effort to help Japan and America build a friendship. It was meant to be a place where Japanese and foreign scholars could meet each other and thus develop good international understanding and relations. Indeed, it was an excellent place. I remember with embarrassment that we forgot oriental manners and stayed much too long after the Matsumoto dinner, thus keeping all the other guests immobile. In China and Japan you visit first, then dine, and almost immediately depart. It is hard for us to remember that. We were also entertained for lunch by the president of International Christian University, who showed us some of his famous collection of Japanese folk art. It is really an admirable art form, in basketry, textile weaving and dyeing, ceramics, and other products of everyday use.

Mr. and Mrs. C. Y. Tung, he a wealthy shipping magnate and friend of Franklin Ho, entertained us at a lovely Chinese meal. He had invited us to use his villa in Hong Kong. He introduced us to several Chinese connected with the Nationalist Embassy in Tokyo. Another occasion was a sukiyaki party on the roof of Tokyo Kaikan, amid Japanese lanterns and popular music, as guests of Mr. Tanabe Sadayoshi and his son, Tatsuo (our friend from International House).

On September 1 we flew to Hong Kong where we were guests of Mr. Tung in his villa, the Island Club, on Deep Water Bay, with a charming view of boats moored in a sheltering cove, green islands, and shimmering water of constantly changing hue, depending upon the ever-shifting weather—now hazy, now showering, now enveloping clouds. His home faced a residence for top staff members of the Bank of China, meaning the "Red" bank. It was interesting to be so close and yet so far from such neighbors.

Julie How was our real hostess. She met us at the airport and took us to see many of her friends. The second day, for example, she took us for lunch with Mrs. Walter Kwok so we could talk with Dr. Wellington Koo, one of our "subjects" in the Chinese Oral History Project. After lunch Dr. Koo entertained us on the balcony, until his friends, who had come to spend the afternoon playing mah-jong, became quite annoyed at us for wasting their time. Julie also took me to see two others of her subjects, Mr. K. P. Chen, the founder of the Shanghai Commercial and Savings Bank, and General Chang Fa-k'uei, an important commander during the Northern Expedition and the war against Japan.

After a delightful week, we flew to Taiwan on September 8 to begin our eight months as "Fulbrighters" under the auspices of the U.S. Educational Foundation in the Republic of China. There was a Sino-American Board, of which the chair was Mrs. Robert Phillips. She soon became Hope Phillips to us, and we have known and liked her ever since. The supervisor of the operation was the U.S. Embassy's cultural officer, Mr. Pardee Lowe, an American of Chinese ancestry, but the real operators of the Foundation were Mr. Y. T. Shen and Jennie Wu—

she a Yenching graduate with a flat midwestern accent in English. She was a wonderful person, a real fixer-upper. Our academic sponsor was Professor T. Y. Kuo and the Institute of Modern History, Academia Sinica, located way out in an eastern suburb of Taipei, a refuge area from feared bombing from the mainland. Dr. Hu Shih was the president of Academia Sinica. The American ambassador was Arthur Drumright, whom we had known thirty years before in Peking as a fellow language student.

We were met at the airport by Dr. Shen, Jennie, and Winston Hsieh, a staff member of Academia Sinica who was soon to leave for Harvard. Also at the airport was Allen Linden, a graduate student of mine, and his wife, Adina. We were taken first to the International Student Hostel, and who should we see there but my colleague Morton Fried, who reported having a wonderful time with his Chinese anthropological friends. Then we were taken to the Grand Hotel—the top spot in town—for a good Western dinner, our hosts being Pardee Lowe and his Peking wife. At a concert we went to afterward, I sat next to the minister of education, Mr. Huang Chi-lu, a fat, jovial man with whom I later became very well acquainted. From my journal:

> This morning Kay and I took a walk along the interesting street that fronts the International House. There is a row of shops and homes that have been built up by "squatters' rights" down the middle of a two-way road—Hsin-yi Lu. They are now fairly substantial and all busy shops—furniture makers, coppersmiths, dress shops, restaurants, tatami makers, dentists, etc. Each shop front is about 10 to 15 feet wide, the houses two stories, but quite low at that. When you come along the other side of the road, you see all the backs, that is, the living quarters, and it is quite interesting. Ducks tied by a foot, browsing on the doorstep, babies in cribs, all kinds of domestic work done on the doorstep—splitting wood, washing clothes, etc. Also peddlers, using tricycle carts, which are three bicycle wheels and a peddling mechanism, and a considerable superstructure. One was a little school bus with room for four children and pedaled by one man. Another was a traveling animal store, with four or five dogs in individual cages in the cart, and pet birds in cages above. Similarly, a small traveling grocery store on three wheels.

Taipei was still a rambling small town, rather sleepy, which had once been the Japanese capital of their colony; but now the Japanese were gone—repatriated. They had left a few impressive government buildings of 1890s style and some areas with Japanese houses that were considered quite desirable by Americans as residences. The streets showed the typical southeastern Chinese architecture— two- or three-story brick buildings, with the ground floor set back for a covered gallery that provides a shaded sidewalk. Traffic consisted of antiquated buses, pedicabs (three-wheeled cycles that transported a passenger in the seat at the back), taxis, some man-drawn carts loaded with goods, and an occasional ox cart with huge, solid wooden wheels. The U.S. Army was in evidence because by then the American government was helping to rebuild a Chinese army, navy, and air force to protect the island from invasion by the People's Republic across the Taiwan Straits.

We were provided a house in a compound for visiting scholars on Chi-lung Lu, near the campus of National Taiwan University, a university that had been built by the Japanese colonial administration but now was the leading university in the Republic of China, that is, Taiwan. Living in a compound was quite familiar to me from my boyhood in Shanghai, yet there was something "colonial" about it, because our newly built house, small but efficient, was better than those of most Chinese faculty members. Also our income, equivalent to an American academic salary, was far more than Chinese professors received. Their pay was just miserable!

We knew some people already, such as Dr. Lo Chia-lun, director of the KMT Archives and of the Palace Museum collections that had been brought to Taiwan and were now hidden in a great cave near the center of the island, safe from possible bombing from the mainland. We knew Professor Li Chi, China's outstanding archaeologist. We met Professor Tung Tso-pin, an expert on Shang dynasty script; Professor Lao Kan, also an archaeologist; Mr. Pao Tsen-peng, director of the Historical Museum; and Professor Hsiao I-shan, historian of the Ch'ing period. We also met senior and junior members of the Institute of Modern History, made good friends among them, and have a departure picture showing us at the center of a group of thirty. Some of these we still see, either there or here, when they come for refresher periods in America—a reflection of the tremendous economic change in Taiwan over the past thirty years, and the improved material life of intellectuals there.

When I was first introduced to the institute I was shown my office in a small building on the campus of Academia Sinica and then taken to the cafeteria for lunch. It was such an awful lunch, both meager and tasteless, that I never tried it again; but it was what the younger staff members had to put up with in those straitened times.

We knew a few American graduate students in Taiwan who had been students at Columbia, such as Donald and Ann Munro (now at University of Michigan) and the Lindens (now at the University of New Hampshire), and we quickly became acquainted with others, such as Lyman Van Slyke and his wife and two young sons. Sam and Lucy Chu were fellow Fulbrighters. Bill White, who had been a student in the East Asian Institute, worked for the U.S. government in Taipei. Later J. Mason Gentzler came on a Ford Foundation grant; we are still good friends, and he married one of my most devoted graduate students, Bernadette Yu-ning Li.

The Lindens introduced us to Wang Yu-tien (Jadefield Wang), who became our housekeeper, a very wonderful find because she was a Manchu, born and raised in Peking, and she knew no English. Her family lived in a town farther south—the husband was part of the air force ground crew, poorly paid. She worked in Taipei to help support the family. To have her in our home was wonderful for rebuilding our Chinese—proper Peking-accent Chinese. Besides, she gave us delightful but simple Chinese meals twice a day. She lived in our house, did the marketing, and was a constant source of information about goings on in Taipei, as well as advice to us about the proper things to do in certain special circumstances, such as New Year's gifts (no pears, a word homonymous with a word for separation).

Wang Yu-tien had worked previously for Jonathan Mirsky and his wife. Jonathan was a Columbia graduate student but had gone on to Cambridge University. We paid Yu-tien the equivalent of U.S. $20 a month, and she had her meals and such profits as she could get doing our marketing. It sounds unfair now, but at that time all her costs were low, and an American dollar brought 40 National Taiwan dollars. There were two disparate economies, the American and the Chinese.

Kay and I resumed formal study of Chinese at an institute set up to train missionaries, not so different from the College of Chinese Studies in Peking, where we had studied nearly thirty years before, though this had no campus. I remember walking there during the hot September days. After about six weeks, I hired a teacher to come once a week to help me with my reading and translation; but Kay kept up her formal studies a little longer, going to the school in a pedicab peddled by O-yang, our other servant. He was a lazy and ignorant man who had grown up in Hunan Province, had been drafted into the Nationalist Army, and then simply been moved with his regiment to Taiwan in the great retreat. After serving in Taiwan for a while he had been demobilized, given a lump sum pension, and bought his pedicab as a source of income.

Some impressions:

One very forceful impression is the large number of children. They are everywhere! Those below school age play by the side of the roads, in the alleys, in the doorsteps, having the best time playing with sticks, making mud patties, almost always in small groups. The kids are dressed in old odds and ends of clothes, their hair not fixed in any particular way. They all seem relaxed and happy. I've seen very little quarreling or bullying, or older ones ordering little ones around. It gives an impression of great freedom and affection.

There are regiments of schoolchildren, all in uniforms. Girls in blouses and dark skirts, boys in scout uniforms or other uniforms and schoolboy hats. This dressing in uniforms goes on through middle school. College students apparently don't wear uniforms, but there are some schools that do use them, perhaps military academies. The kids are produced so fast they are outgrowing the school capacity. It's a real problem to train enough teachers and build enough school buildings. In middle schools they have double shifts and run throughout the week.

Another impression is the fragmentation and irrationality of economic activity as one sees it on the streets. There is a myriad of small shops, probably family enterprises, strewn at random along the streets and alleys and canal fronts. None seems very active. Business seems divided and parceled out between so many of them that few have enough to do. So there is a great deal of sitting around, tending the shop but doing nothing much else. Pedicab drivers loll or sleep in their cabs. This is not to say there are no busy people. There is a great deal of hurried and disorderly traffic downtown, and considerable activity of peddlers hawking their toys, their chestnuts, their shaved ice and soft drinks. But there is a vast amount of apparently aimless wandering and passive sitting. This gives an impression of leisure, of calmness amidst bustle, of time being of no particular concern.

There are sections of the city where more substantial shops are concentrated—bookstores, furniture stores, dress shops, curio shops, and variety stores. But they aren't very big establishments. We haven't yet seen a department store by Japanese standards. Most of the shops in the central business district have a ten- to twenty-foot frontage behind an arcade. Only on Sunday did we see a few stores—dress shops and book stores—comfortably filled with shoppers.

The city has a public bus system, with scores of routes, and many government offices have their own buses. Taxis are cheap, numerous, and small. There are lots of motorcycles, bicycles, trucks, and tricycle carts, but also a few plodding ox carts mixed in. This leads to a thronging street scene.

People's faces seem rather stolid and impassive, but not tense. When friends are together there is much animation. One sees some schoolgirls walking hand in hand, but seldom a man and a woman holding hands. I have seen only one young couple doing so, on a bus. But certainly the married folk here have a sex life of great intensity to judge by the uncontrollable baby boom. The natural rate of increase is 3.5 percent a year, one of the highest in the world. The economy must grow rapidly to create enough jobs for 400,000 more people a year in a population now of just eleven million.

From the briefings we've had on industrial and agricultural growth, the picture is optimistic. Industry is growing rapidly to make use of Taiwan's rich natural resources in agricultural and forest products. Taiwan exports foods and textiles and consumer goods of many kinds and earns valuable foreign exchange. Its pineapples are wonderful. It makes newsprint and plywood, fabricates aluminum, and exports bicycles. It refines all gasoline consumed on this island but as yet has no domestic oil. Irrigation and electric power are constantly being expanded.

Farmers have much higher incomes per capita than the average of the population, and agriculture is being improved all the time. There is a wide 4-H club movement, farmers cooperatives everywhere, and an active agricultural extension service. The Joint Committee on Rural Reconstruction is constantly seeking new methods of crop growing, introducing dairy industry, and doing many things to encourage it, such as planting new grasses for upland grazing, teaching young farmers how to keep cows properly, and lending to graduates of training classes cows to start their herds. It also encourages better use of forest resources and fish cultivation in ponds, coastal areas, and the sea.

Upon reproducing this passage from my journal, I wondered about the disparity between the fragmented commercial and handicraft economy and the growing industrialization. The two were out of sync. Chinese society had not changed much either. But it did over time, as we saw on later trips to the island.

During our early months in Taiwan, I was going some days to Nankang, riding in the Academia Sinica car with other senior scholars and reading in the

Institute of Modern History library. Other days I stayed home, practicing characters and reading Chinese articles. Also, I was taken to interview older men, who had played important parts in the Northern Expedition of 1926–27, which was my special subject of study: such men as generals Pai Ch'ung-hsi (of the Kwangsi Clique, who was chief-of-staff) and Yang Shen (a Szechwanese warlord, reputed to have had many wives).

We entertained Chinese couples in our home, insisting that the wives come too, and always having a simple meal. We made a special point of this, because we disapproved the elaborate feasts that some academic friends seemed to feel they must put on for us; feasts, by the way, at which Kay would find herself the only woman present, to her intense discomfort. We tried to make our modest dinner parties occasions to get acquainted, as we do when entertaining in America. Wang Yu-tien may have lost face at our not serving our distinguished guests with elaborate dinners, and I have no idea how the guests took it. Each culture has it own peculiarities. I guess we had the missionary spirit.

I must describe the trip that we Fulbrighters were treated to on November 4, when we toured Kinmen, the island only a few miles off the coast of Fukien, an island that the Communists and Nationalists had fought over bitterly in 1954 and 1958, and which the Nationalists still held as an impregnable fortress.

We had an early morning flight that went in very low over the Pescadores islands and then west, almost skimming the gray-green ocean to escape detection. Our plane, a box-car, carried provisions and mail for the garrison, a large force, perhaps a quarter of the Nationalists' effective forces. At 8:35 we sighted the mountain that runs like a spine the length of Kinmen, and very soon flew in over a red sandy beach strung with barbed wire. Pill boxes, trenches, and barbed wire entanglements were very evident, as were gun emplacements and entrances to tunnels. We could also see from the air various garden plots and evergreens planted along the roadways.

On landing at an airfield near the beach on the east coast of the island, we were greeted by General Wang and by a colonel, who became our principal escort. We learned later that he was in charge of psychological warfare, and our trip, it turned out, was a form of such effort, practiced on the friendly side. He was also the mayor of Kinmen city. Soon another plane came in, this one, we were told, bringing a group of overseas Chinese. They were to be greeted by a procession of middle-aged Chinese women, all neatly dressed. Schoolchildren carrying red and gold welcoming banners rushed up to the plane to meet the passengers. It turned out to be a party of Buddhists in lovely yellow robes. The welcoming women in their blue gowns, black cloth shoes, and black hair neatly combed all made the Buddhist sign of greeting with palms pressed together.

Soon we were loaded into jeeps, a small bus, and a couple of trucks and sped along perfectly clean roads—the cleanest I have ever seen—closely lined with evergreen trees, which made a good cover, though the bottom two feet of each tree was painted white to help in night-time driving. The roads had no other traffic, but there were smart military police at all crossing points directing us onward. We saw troops everywhere, some on duty, some doing road work, some at leisure. Neat piles of stones lined the roads at about 200-yard intervals, and we were told they were kept there to be used for quick repairs in case of bombing. We saw no sign of bombing.

We went through two tunnels carved in the solid rock, each tunnel having long side chambers filled with boxes of ammunition, and in one spot what looked like a field hospital. There must have been more than fifty of these side chambers running back a hundred feet or so, and there must have been a lot of ammo in these piles and piles of boxes. We climbed to near the top of Mashan (Horse Mountain), the highest point on the spine of the island, something like a thousand feet high. Looking south and east we saw roads and fortifications; looking north and westward toward the mainland we saw many fields and villages on the island. In a chamber in the rock near the top there was a lookout point from which we had a misty view of the mainland. The only moving thing we saw was two sailboats.

Another brief drive took us to the north end of the island, the nearest point to the enemy-held islands. Here we went into another tunnel where broadcasting and direct shouting to the enemy was done. Next we were taken to a small village. It was uncommonly clean for a Chinese village. No trash, little smell, but, of course, swarms of children. The streets were spotless! There was a park for children with two fine cement slides, but no children playing on them. There was also a reading room with magazines in racks and several tables with chairs, but nobody using it. Had they all been ordered out to make room for the guests, or was it only a showplace? The kids we saw seemed well fed, but Kay thought them dirty and their clothes unwashed. Of course, there wasn't too much water to waste on that dry island.

We saw not one shell hole, not one ruined building, not one shattered tree or battered road. It gave a queer feeling of peace and calm amidst vast military preparations. The same note of contradiction was carried by a camouflage net over the entrance to a gun emplacement. Purple morning glories were blossoming on it. Later I heard an explanation that after each shelling, "our side" immediately tore down the damaged buildings and removed traces of bombing for psychological reasons, so the local population would not be too upset.

We had lunch with General Wang in a large chamber carved out of the rock. A party of overseas Chinese from many countries was being entertained too. Kay and I were at the general's table. He made a speech of welcome, and I answered in Chinese—halting and inadequate as it was. It was a tasty meal, and there was much drinking of a very fine *kao-liang*, a kind of clear liquid fire.

General Wang was a self-confident, healthy man, about fifty years old. I asked him for his history, and he told me he was born in Antung, near the

Korean border, and after the September 18 Incident of 1931 (which began the Japanese seizure of Manchuria) had come to Nanking and entered the military academy. "Since then I have never doffed my uniform," he said. He fought the Japanese at Shanghai, then in Hupei, then went to Shensi, and then to Yunnan. He participated in the campaign across the Salween in Burma, and when the war ended he was sent back to Manchuria in the 71st Army. I guess he had been fighting Communists ever since.

After lunch we went to see a psychological warfare exhibit, with examples of "our" propaganda, delivered in bottles, by balloons, and by shells. A cake of soap might carry the Nationalist flag in it. A fake Communist newspaper would have anti-Communist messages in it. Their side also sent over shells containing leaflets. On the walls were many cartoons and posters sent by the Communist side, much of the propaganda being anti-American. Some of our party released propaganda balloons, which sailed high into the sky and then drifted off toward the mainland where, we were told, they would arrive in about twenty-five minutes. The farthest penetration by balloon was Hankow, which must have been a thousand miles away. We weren't told how they knew of this success.

We visited the island's middle school, a new and orderly place. There were deep air-raid shelters for all the children, down about twenty concrete steps that made a couple of turns to bunkers, each said to be big enough for fifty kids. They would all have to stand up, and I fear they would suffocate! In the two I went into there were doubledecker bunks nearly filling up the space, and they were evidently being used at night. The school kids were well dressed in khaki uniforms, and all classes were in session even though it was Saturday afternoon.

The city of Kinmen was also neat and clean. Many of the stores were newly built, probably restored after the 1958 shelling. Some old sections remained, however, and seemed a bit more authentic, with narrow and crooked streets. This was our last stop. Thence through the peaceful, parklike countryside to the airstrip and our waiting plane. Two hours later we were back in Taipei. It had been a wonderfully interesting trip and refreshing after nearly two months in Taipei. One thought I carried away: It would be quite impossible to persuade the Nationalist side to give up this island into which they had put so much work, investment, and emotion. And it would not be an easy place to take, short of an atomic attack. Talk in America about the Republic of China giving up the islands and drawing back behind the Taiwan straits seemed quite academic.

A few weeks later we met a young man from Church World Service, who had just returned from his trip to Kinmen. His mission was to find out whether Church World Service could be of help. He was shown ruined villages! Thus, we were deceived about the perpetual cleanup of destruction. Apparently they kept some of the destruction to show those for whom this sight will be most effective.

One of the most educational experiences we had was a tour put on for us alone by the Joint Commission on Rural Reconstruction, on November 10 and 11. I knew Dr. Chiang Mon-lin, the chairman and one of the five joint commissioners—three Chinese and two Americans. In fact, we had entertained him in our home in Washington. He also had a Ph.D. from Columbia. After the first day, I wrote this in my journal:

> This was one of the most eye-filling days we've had in Taiwan, and it has given us a lift concerning the island and its people that we were beginning to need. Kay and I were greatly impressed by the many signs of rural prosperity—new houses, radios, bustling towns, excellent buses, electrification everywhere, and regiments of schoolchildren in pretty good clothes.

Mr. Shih Pen-su, administrative assistant in the JCRR Secretariat, picked us up in a big Plymouth ranch wagon at 7:45, and we went off southward to Shu-lin Township (28,000 people), where we went first to the office of Mayor Chen, a very courteous man, who told us about his work and some of the problems. The most time-consuming was arbitrating disputes, often family disputes, if they could not be settled at a lower level. Property disputes were most frequent. The township was divided into seventeen administrative districts, each with an elected head. Mr. Chen, too, was elected. A local man, he had taught for seven years in primary schools and two years in the middle school. As he told us, he had been "chosen by the people." It was not a contested election.

Mayor Chen spent much time visiting the villages and talking with the people. His most difficult problem was flood control and dikes, but it was too big a problem to be solved at a local level. Every male from the ages of twenty to forty-five owed the township ten days each year of "compulsory volunteer work" or payment for a hired replacement. That is a very old Chinese system for getting public works, such as diking, done.

We visited a Farmers' Association, met the manager, and heard a lecture, mostly by our Mr. Shih, on how the association was organized. Members were of two categories: those whose income was derived more than 50 percent from farming, and those for whom farming was a subsidiary occupation. The latter were only associate members. The twelve to fifteen board members were chosen exclusively by regular members. The board hired the manager for a two-year term. There were five departments: administration, finance, credit, extension (which tried to acquaint farmers with pesticides, new fertilizers, and new crops and did educational work among women), and purchasing and marketing as a cooperative. The association made some money on commissions from collecting the land tax in grain; from sales of government land; from distribution of monopoly salt and fertilizer; and from profits on rice milling. Later we learned that farmers could get chemical fertilizers (a government monopoly) only in exchange for grain, and the prices of each were governmentally controlled, which meant that the government got its grain, needed to supplement governmental and military salaries, at a price that farmers considered unfair to themselves.

We next called at a rural health station, of which there were 395 on the island.

It was a genuine little clinic with several nurses, mothers with children, a small pharmacy, and inoculations in progress. Twenty years later Kay and I visited a commune clinic outside Hsian. The commune was evidently a showplace, but the clinic could not compare with the one we saw on the JCRR trip. Of course, Taiwan had the advantage of Japanese public health pioneering, and the scale of its public health problems could not be compared with that of the vast mainland.

Next we visited a primary school with 2,300 students! Seven first grades and about 64 kids to a room. They were in recess when we arrived, so the school yard was teeming, but the bell rang and they swarmed into their rooms. The kids looked respectably clean and there were lots of bright-eyed ones among them. The teachers I saw were all women, neatly dressed and with a kindly look and way with the children. The "Dean," Mr. Wang, met us and escorted us around. He showed us the water-purifying plant that put clean drinking water into the faucets. The building wasn't as new as many we saw later, but it certainly was being used.

We were still being escorted by Mayor Chen, and we next visited a farm-house, crossing the cement grain-drying floor and entering the central ceremonial hall, a feature of nearly every farmhouse we saw. Facing the door was a table about five feet high, holding candles, vases, incense, fruit, and some other offerings. Behind the table was a brightly printed poster with pictures of various deities, and wooden ancestor tablets in the center space. We were told there were sixteen members of the household. We saw two old-fashioned bedrooms, each with a large covered bed and clothes and other effects hung on hooks. We also saw two newly built bedrooms, later extensions of the house, and the rooms seemed in Japanese style, with no bed but a raised platform, polished floors, and sliding doors with paper—that is, *shoji*. We also went into a large kitchen, with large but shallow pots nesting into the stove. I also counted twelve cups with toothbrushes and individual towels hung along a rod, all very neat. Near the kitchen was a neat pigsty, with twelve wonderful black pigs.

At this point Mayor Chen left us, riding off on his bicycle, and we proceeded south on a good road through villages and past farmers working in their fields, harvesting grain and threshing it in small, two-man threshing machines operated by a foot pedal. These efficient little threshers were everywhere, and Mr. Shih said the design was introduced by JCRR, or at least that JCRR subsidized the research done by the agricultural college of National Taiwan University, which developed the model. After perfecting the thresher, which had been first developed in Japan, the government gave the design to local manufacturers. The little machines cost about twenty U.S. dollars.

Next stop a dairy farm—more in Kay's department than mine. She got on famously talking cows, milk content, and so on. The cows were Holstein, bred by artificial insemination with frozen semen imported from the United States. There were eighty-five cows on forty-two acres, but all were stall-fed. We were given fresh milk to drink, which was delicious. The point of our visit was to see a new enterprise of JCRR, trying to introduce and encourage a dairy industry for upland areas of Taiwan.

We saw an exhibit in Tao-yuan about land reform that was pushed through by Ch'en Ch'eng when he was governor of the island. JCRR helped with the planning, which was done very carefully, and it also helped to train the administrators to carry it through. Land reform was effected without bloodshed, and with payments to the dispossessed over a ten-year period, with care lest the former landlords suffer loss from inflation (as had been the problem in Japan under the American Occupation).

Land reform was done in three steps: (1) in 1949 rents were cut to 37.5 percent of the annual yield, the basis of this calculation being 25 percent as the cost of production, and the remaining 75 percent being divided between owner and tenant. (2) In 1951 public lands were sold to the tenants on the land at the price of two and one half times the value of the annual crop. Payments in kind were spread over ten years. (3) In 1953 landowners were required to sell to the government all land they were not actually cultivating themselves, except for three hectares (about eight acres). The government paid two and a half times the value of the annual crop, 30 percent immediately and the rest in bonds repayable over ten years, two payments a year. The 30 percent payment was made in shares of stock in four government-owned industries, but the landowner could sell the shares if he wished. He could also elect to take his return on the bonds in either cash or kind. The tenant was given the first right to buy from the government the land he had been cultivating, at a price two and a half times the annual yield, and to be paid for twice a year over ten years. Thus in any year he had to pay only 25 percent of his crop toward the purchase of the land, considerably less than his rent of 50 percent before land reform, or 37.5 percent thereafter.

The government had made very thorough investigations so as to know what the value and the true ownership of the land was. Also, it used committees made up of landlords, self-cultivators, and tenant farmers in order to have inside knowledge. There were not over a hundred landlords owning more then 100 hectares, and only about 300 with land from 50 to 100 hectares. So opposition was not powerful, we were told, and Governor Ch'en Ch'eng used his personal persuasion to quiet such as there was. I wrote: "I think there can be no doubt that it was a very important social revolution, which did much for the prosperity one sees so widespread in rural areas. What a contrast to the violence and fraud of 'land reform' on the mainland!"

There is an irony about both of the land reforms. In Taiwan, as society evolved, with industrialization and urbanization, it became difficult for farmers to keep their sons and daughters-in-law on the farm. There became a shortage of agricultural labor. The obvious solution was to use efficient farm machinery, but this meant that land should be consolidated. The government was bound that any such consolidation of land should not be regarded as collectivization, so, although they encouraged farmers to adjoin their lands and cultivate with machines, the actual individual ownership was jealously maintained.

On the mainland after the bloody, enforced redistribution of land, with thousands of landlords slain after mass mock trials, the farmers were first led into cooperatives, then forced to give up their lands to higher-level co-ops. Finally, under communization, villagers were forced into gang labor as members of teams under brigades, and those under large communes that directed planting and harvesting. The farmers were paid workpoints in proportion to the hours of labor put in. Eventually, this forced labor reached a dead end, limiting national production. The Communist Party then scrapped the communes and allowed farmers to work land by the old family system and to sell most of the product in open markets. Production soared; farmers began to become rich.

I guess one can see where my sympathies lie.

After lunch at the site of a dam under construction, the great Shih-men dam that would irrigate thousands of hectares and provide lots of electricity, we drove on southward through farm country, visiting one farmhouse of a former tenant, who now owned 3.5 hectares. He was building a fine addition to his house, and he had seven sons, of whom four were married, so he had four daughters-in-law to help with the farm. Two of them were slowly turning the unhulled rice that was spread on the cement courtyard, nice-looking young women, lips rouged, hair curled, wearing big hats, leggings, and arm covers to protect their skin from becoming tanned. The central hall had a radio, electric lights, and a sewing machine, in addition to the traditional altar. There was a rice storage room near the large kitchen, where toddlers were being fed, and outside, a pig house with ten pigs, and nearby a fine big police dog. One of the wives was feeding the pigs from two large wooden buckets that contained a terrible-looking mess of steaming mash, which we were told was made of soybeans and sweet potatoes. The pigs were a crossbreed of Berkshire or Yorkshire with the local strain. JCRR had a lot to do with the improvement in the breeds.

Our next to last stop in this wonderfully interesting day was at a tidal lands reclamation project in which a Dutch method of reclaiming land from the sea was used. The project was under a reclamation commission, which owned a lot of heavy equipment, but the labor was done by ex-servicemen, who would have first priority to buy the reclaimed land for their own farms. The sea was moved back stage by stage by means of dikes, and we were shown the old sea line, beyond which we went about half a mile to the new dike. There were still a few pillboxes standing in the reclaimed fields that must once have been beach defenses.

Next day we visited The Taiwan Health Center, where we were given a lecture on child and maternal care by a man whose English was not too good, and in the presence of four very competent women, some of whom spoke much better English than he did. The discussion of midwife training, of births unattended by qualified people, and of gradually improving conditions was quite interesting when the ladies got to talking. There are not enough midwives, though more were being trained. Cost of pre- and postnatal care, if given in one of the 395 local health stations, was less than one U.S. dollar. There was also discussion of family planning and the local women's desire to space births, but their timidity to ask about methods because custom called for a wife to have "a hundred sons!" Taiwan had, at that time, one of the highest rates of natural increase in the world, about thirty-four per thousand, and the population was already the second most dense of any country in the world—the Netherlands being first. If mountainous land was excluded, Taiwan was the densest.

We next visited a very active Farmers' Association and went to several farms. At one we saw women shredding manure to be used for mushroom culture, mushrooms being an important export product. At a very modern farmhouse, the owner offered us Taiwan-grown coffee. Not bad. His thirteen-year-old son was a member of the 4-H Club and showed us his projects. One was a pile of wood on which he was growing lichens for the market. He had to water the pile three times each day. His other projects were cabbages and corn, which he took us to his fields to inspect. This future farmer was already banking about forty dollars a month from his cabbages. We went away from this farm feeling quite good about the state of the union, so to say.

We then went on to a seed testing and experiment station. The good-quality seeds were grown on a seed stock farm, retested, and then given to farmers in exchange for an equal weight of their own seed. The scientists were proud of their American testing equipment and their cold storage facilities, and that they were up to the standards of the International Seed Testing Association.

We came home on a new, reserved-seat train. There were smart young stewardesses in tailored uniforms, like airline stewardesses, who served tea and distributed magazines. The car was bright and clean, with reclining seats, and the piped music was Mozart. The fare was U.S. $1.78.

On the way, Mr. Shih told us a good deal about JCRR. Our friend Dr. Chiang was one of the two men most responsible for the idea of rural reconstruction, and for the work of JCRR. All commissioners keep regular office hours, and all projects must have unanimous approval. The commissioners had directing duties and divided the work on a functional basis. Under the commission was a professional and clerical staff of about 200, divided between administration and research.

But the JCRR was not so much an operating organization as a foundation. It dispersed grants for experimental and promotional work of great variety related to rural reconstructions. Its funds came from the money derived from sale of U.S. surplus farm produce, to which was added an equal amount of National Government funds. Only a small amount of U.S. currency was provided by the Economic Cooperation Administration for purchasing foreign equipment. The program interest was very broad—health, crop improvement, upland use, fish culture, tideland reclamation, forestry, orchards, animal husbandry, and so on. JCRR-sponsored programs were able to convert Kinmen from a seriously deficit area to one that provided food for all the troops on the island and even had some exports of special products to Taiwan.

JCRR had been so successful that many delegations came from other East and Southeast Asian countries to study its methods, and it sent some teams to work in South Vietnam and other countries. As I wrote after our trip, "It is an inspiring example of Chinese initiative and ability and American cooperation."

Here let me quote a passage from my journal that concerns Chinese ideas of politeness:

Interesting and amusing conversation with Mr. Ho of the language school about differences between Chinese and American forms of politeness, which cause misunderstanding. For example, when he first met me at the school and asked me what I do, I replied, "*Wo shih li-hsueh chia*," meaning, "I am an historian," this sounded to him quite impolite and immodest. To say one is *chia*, "specialist," sounds boastful! On my part, I had just learned the term in Talks on Chinese Culture. What I should have said was, "*Wo yen-chiu li-shih*," "I study history." Much more becoming. Also, I shouldn't say I am a professor, *chiao-shou*, but that I teach: "*Wo chiao-shu*. To be a professor is to have a very high station, and one would not announce it.

Also, he tells his students there are two points of view in which Chinese differ much from Westerners. One is in regard to age, or *lao*, old age. Age is much revered. But to us, to be old is not desirable. Example: An elderly, unmarried American woman who knew a few words of Chinese, came to the language school to start studying. The dean said to her, "*Lao t'ai-t'ai chin-lai, wo-men huan-ying nin.* Come in, venerable lady, we welcome you." But she took great offense, left, and never came back. Yet the dean could not possibly address her as *shao-chieh*, "miss," because she was elderly and he must show here respect. If he had addressed her as "*lao shao-chieh*," it would be equivalent as calling her "old spinster," quite impolite to Chinese ears.

The second difference is in regard to *p'ang*, fat or plump. If you want to praise the looks of the wife of a Chinese gentleman, you can say she is *hen p'ang*, "very plump." But, of course, no American woman would enjoy being called fat!

We could counter that to inquire a person's age on first meeting is not done, especially one would not think of asking a woman her age unless one were very close friends. Yet a few days ago Mr. Ho and Wang Yu-tien had discussed my wife's age right in her presence! Another difference is asking the price of something owned by a friend. When we bought a reproduction of one of the palace paintings, our Chinese friends much admired it, and several immediately asked what we had paid for it—from our point of view, not a very tactful question.

Mr. Ho then said there was another form of discourtesy we have, from their point of view. Suppose you want to compliment a woman on her dress. In Chinese you would say it is *hen hao-kan, chen p'iao-liang*, "good looking, really very beautiful." The American answer would be "thank you," or, in Chinese, *hsieh-hsieh*, a direct translation. But this is quite the wrong answer to a Chinese ear. It is much too immodest. One should say, *kuo-chiang, kuo-chiang*, "you flatter me," or, more familiarly, "*na-li, na-li*, "it's nothing." That is, you deprecate that which is your own; you do not accept praise or admiration as though it were merited.

Also, one cannot translate into Chinese the request, "would you please" do so and so, as *Ch'ing ni tso....* In English, the "please" makes it polite, but in Chinese it is an order. The way to convert it into polite request in Chinese is to provide a choice, so you must end the request with *hao pu how?*, or *hsing pu hsing?*, or *ch'eng pu ch'eng?* all of which mean, "would you care to or not?" though not so sharp as that sounds in English. The point is, by offering a choice you convert an order into a request. In fact, even if asking a person whether he would like to do something—say, to go for a walk—you must give a choice: would you like to or not? Which do you prefer? He doesn't have to say "no."

Mr. Ho thinks most Chinese believe Americans to be arrogant and proud, but that much misunderstanding arises simply from different habits of speech, and the dangerous error of Americans converting their form of courtesy directly into Chinese, word for word.

One or two observations of my own. When you offer a person a cigarette, you take one out and hand it to the friend. You do not extend the package for him to struggle with. Our next move is to light his cigarette for him, but he is sure to refuse to let you, or if you insist, he will jump up. He cannot sit while you stand to light his cigarette for him, for this would imply that you are his servant. Chinese will make a great fuss over not letting you help them on with a coat, for the same reason. It is difficult for a Chinese, for courtesy reasons, to decline a cigarette, candy, or other small food, when offered. Even if one does not want to smoke, if you offer a cigarette he is almost compelled to smoke it. The same with candy or small food. He will take a piece over and over again, but I've observed he usually will eat very little of it, as though courtesy demanded that he pile his plate but eat very little. At a dinner, the host is constantly plying the guest with food and the guest constantly tries to decline or to take a very small portion.

The Chinese hate a conversational vacuum. There is nothing more tense or embarrassing as a long pause in the conversation. Someone is sure to jump in with some trivial observation or question. Sometimes it seems one must say whatever polite nothing pops into one's head. Chinese seem to chatter amiably all the time they are together. Many fatuous statements are advanced and solemnly discussed, just to keep the conversational ball rolling. The life of the party is constant small-talk. It all leads to a sense of euphoria, but to us, a feeling of a vacuous time.

Try to get a Chinese through a door before you! Can't be done, or only after a long, polite struggle. This leads to much attempting to get behind the other and push him through first. When you see a person off from your house, you must go out the door right to the side of the car. You will shake hands and say goodbye three or four times, and you will stand by the street side to wave until your guest is out of sight. But it isn't that simple. The guest will insist you mustn't come out because it's too cold, or too hot, or raining, or late, or whatever can be called upon to prevent you actually seeing him off to the limit of your land, knowing full well, however, that you must and will do this last courtesy.

Also, if you give a gift, there must be demurs, even though both you and I know that you are pleased and will accept in the end. Our housekeeper gave our pedicab man a gift at Chinese New Year's time. Kay and I overheard the long wrangle—he declining and she insisting. In the end he took it, of course, as all knew would be the result. After all, if he really had refused and stuck to it, that would have been irredeemably impolite and could have ruptured the household. But much declining and much persuasion had to be gone through for good form's sake before the happy O-yang had his edibles to carry away!

Be very careful how you admire something in a friends house. He is very likely to give it to you, and then how do you get out of that!

Lest one think that our life was all excursions and social life, let me say that we both worked hard at our Chinese, and Kay got lots of practice with Wang Yu-tien, who told her by the hour about life in Peking, where she grew up.

I became well acquainted with two of the young scholars at the Institute of Modern History, Chia Ting-shih and Chang Peng-yuan. Professor Kuo had assigned them to be helpful to me. They were interviewers in the institute's oral history program. We received an invitation to attend Chang Peng-yuan's wedding, which filled us with excitement. I was asked to make a speech about the groom. Wang Yu-tien coached us as to what we should give—it must be a sum divisible by two, and offered in a red envelope. The wedding was held sometime after 5 P.M. in the large hall of the municipal building. We arrived about 5:15 and were greeted by a young man wearing a red ribbon that indicated he was a welcomer of the guests. He asked if we wanted to give a gift, and since we had one, properly wrapped in red paper, we were taken to a long table where five people were counting and recording the gifts. A lot of money was coming in, and crowds of people. We entered a large hall, two stories high, about 120 feet long and 80 feet wide. Seats had been set up on either side of a red carpet leading to a platform, on which was an the altar where the ceremony would be held. There were already several hundred people there, including lots of kids dressed in their brightest clothes, the girls all wearing red.

Red was certainly the dominant color. All around the walls were large red cloths about the size of bed spreads, on which there were gold paper inscriptions wishing good luck to the couple. They simply covered the wall space. A band in red uniforms played popular music to entertain the guests. It was a happy, talkative crowd, with lots of visiting back and forth before the ceremony began. We were given tea, watermelon seeds, and cigarettes from a red package.

Soon it was evident the ceremony would begin. Some dignitaries took their places up front, and then in marched the groom and his best man, both dressed in formal black suits, but the groom, Pengyuan, wearing a red vest. After a long wait the bridal procession began with two little boys in formal dress carrying cushions with two rings, and then tiny flower girls in white dresses scattering petals. Then came the bridesmaid marching in slow, formal step, and behind her the bride in white, on her father's arm. For the bride to wear white, instead of red, shows how Westernized the ceremony had become.

There was a master of ceremonies, who called out on a loudspeaker each stage of the ceremony. He called for the "introducer"—theoretically the matchmaker, who had brought the couple together. The introducer made a speech. Then the "guarantor," or principal witness, made a speech. Then there was a good deal of signing of documents in this civil ceremony. The young couple was called upon to bow on several occasions.

I wasn't sure when the marriage had been effected, but soon selected friends were making speeches. I had prepared mine in Chinese but got cold feet before that huge Chinese crowd and gave it in English with Mr. Chia interpreting for me. After four or more speeches by friends, the father of the bride made a long speech, after which the bride and groom hurried out together arm-in-arm. There was much photographing with floodlights. Also much applauding. The externals were somewhat Western—costume, music, deportment of the guests—but the spirit of joy, the hubbub, the kids, and the ceremony itself were entirely Chinese.

At this point we all adjourned to round tables for the wedding feast, with no particular rhyme or reason to the seating. Each table sat ten persons, and I calculate that there were sixty tables. Quite a party! Quite an uproar! It was a full twelve-course feast, with cold dishes, duck, chicken, fish, and soups. First the bride and groom, then the father and mother of the bride, went to each table and toasted the guests, who arose to return the toast. Obviously the principals didn't toast sixty tables in wine, though at some tables the close friends of the young people insisted they drink real wine.

During the course of the dinner the bride went out to change her clothes two or three times, and she had some lovely dresses to show. At the end, the father, mother, and the bride stood at the door to thank all the departing guests. It was a wonderfully Chinese affair, with everyone having a great time. We were the only non-Chinese persons there, so it was gratifying to have been included. We wouldn't have missed it for anything.

Chang Peng-yuan was an orphan. He was born in Kweichow, had been in the Nationalist youth army, and was then brought to Taiwan as a young man during the great retreat. He must have done well in his graduate education to have been picked by Professor Kuo to be one of the young historians in the institute. His wife, Teresa Wang, had an M.A. in library science from an American university. Her father was a well-to-do businessman, and he must have borne most of the expense for the wedding, for Peng-yuan had nothing. We have remained friends with Peng-yuan and Teresa ever since. Teresa is in charge of book exchanges with foreign institutions for the National Central Library and often attends international library meetings. They have visited in our home several times, and in 1985, when we were on a VIP trip in Taiwan, they joined us on an all-expenses-paid trip to South Island, as the lower end of Taiwan is called. We had a wonderful time together, and Peng-yuan loved spending the host's money.

One day Professor Kuo took me to call on Chiang Ching-kuo, who was minister of the interior, I believe. We went to his office in Intelligence headquarters, where he directed both foreign and internal intelligence, probably his principal job at that time. The place was a beehive of activity, and much of it reputedly quite sinister by our standards. All I remember of the interview, which lasted about twenty minutes, was that Mr. Chiang asked politely what I was studying and offered any help he could give. I suspect the interview helped clear me to see certain closed files, for soon thereafter I was permitted to work in the KMT archives and later in the library of the Ministry of Justice, actually an intelligence agency.

Mr. Lo Chia-lun escorted me to Taichung for an introductory visit to the KMT archives, which were housed in a large farmhouse and a two-story cement building about forty-five minutes by bus from Taichung, in the middle of rice fields. The archives were there for safekeeping against the possibility of bombing. I met some staff members and was shown a bewildering number of boxes that contained materials gathered by the Kuomintang over many years, a great historical trove. The staff apparently spent much of its time cataloguing, though I never was allowed to roam the catalogue itself. I was introduced to two young archivists, Chiang Yung-ching and Li Yun-han, both of whom later became my good friends. Both came to Columbia and so are members of the club that consider themselves my students. Mr. Chiang is now Professor Chiang, teaching Chinese history at Cheng-chi University, and Mr. Li is now director of the archives. Mr. Lo asked Mr. Chiang to help me get materials useful for my study of the Northern Expedition period, the mid-1920s.

For several months thereafter I journeyed to Taichung on Tuesday afternoons and checked in at the Railway Hotel, spent Wednesday through Saturday mornings at the archives, and returned to Taipei Saturday afternoons. I gathered a great deal of information from documents that Mr. Chiang brought me, for both he and Mr. Li had done research on the period and knew what was available. I never was able to use all the notes I took in duplicate, but many I used in two books on the subject, and I gave those notes to Columbia's Rare Book and Manuscript Library. It was really a happy time for me.

At noontime, I would eat a lunch I had brought from hotel and then take a walk in the countryside:

More impressions—I have strolled by fields and through small villages near the archives. Preparing the fields for the next rice planting is all the rage now, late February. Rice fields are first plowed dry by buffalo and plowman, using a deep cutting plow that turns the black earth up in big clods. The plowed field is then flooded and left to stand in water for a week, I should judge. Then it is plowed again through the muck. What would rice culture do without the water buffalo? Next it is harrowed and then the earth is flattened smooth by a man standing astride a sort of sled pulled by the plodding buffalo. It is still flooded several inches deep, and the soil is mucky. Next comes transplanting the seedlings that have been growing, brilliant emerald, in small seed beds. The beds are allowed to dry out a little so it is easy to cut out clumps of growing seedlings and not disturb the roots. Women and children carry baskets of these seedlings to the flooded fields where men and women rapidly plant them in perfect lines and rows about eight inches apart. A newly planted field is like a regiment of small green soldiers, all in perfect order—you can look at the rows lengthwise, crosswise, or at an angle. and the rows are all in order. While this preparing and transplanting was afoot, I noticed other rice already about ten inches high, and also on March 1 I saw rice being harvested near Taichung.

This irrigation system is tricky. Each rice field must be perfectly flat and have a low dike around it, usually no more than a foot wide and a few inches higher than the desired water level. Some fields are flooded just when adjacent fields are dry and with maturing crops. It is quite a trick of native engineering to be able to use land wet or dry in adjoining fields. Ditches sometimes encircle fields with a dike on either side, part of the complex system of channeling the water to wherever it is needed.

I've walked through some quite humble villages and now believe the big, red brick farmhouse with black tile roof and curving eaves is not typical. In these villages—and they are merely clusters of houses along narrow lanes—most of the houses seem to be sun-baked brick with earthen floors and quite small courtyards, which are really barnyards. From the outside, the houses look rather dirty and certainly dark. Yet most have tile roofs, and most, if not all, have electricity. One hears radio music coming from one after another. In Pei-t'ou, a hamlet near the archives, there are two clusters of houses, each with a lane, and they are perhaps half a mile apart. Each has a fine temple, the best-looking buildings in the village, and probably the communal gathering place. In one I saw a large table standing before the altar, probably measuring five feet on a side. It was elaborately carved, painted, and gilded. An inscription carved on it was dated in the Hsien-feng period (1852–1862).

The kids of the village, and the ones seen on the road, are rather dirty and dressed in nondescript clothes, but they seem well enough fed. I walked with a group of them returning home at noon from school. Some were barefoot, some wore sneakers. Their native speech was Taiwanese, from Fukien. The women largely wear trousers and jackets, and large straw hats held on by a bright kerchief tied under the chin. The men wear a miscellany, but mostly shirts and pants. As many adults are barefoot as are shoe-clad. Little children are often dressed in kimono-type very long gowns. They play together industriously in groups of three to seven. Many quite young children, no more than six or seven, carry brother or sister on the back.

In the village I pass through on the way to the archives I have often counted the kids in sight on one block about seventy-five yards long. The lowest number was in the forties, the highest, ninety-three! Almost all are under six years old. Talk about your population problem!

I lay no claim to being a trained observer, but being in this rural setting for several days each week was a lovely experience. Taiwan has been a fruitful field for study by anthropologists, at first mostly Americans, several from Columbia. The scientific literature about rural and urban Taiwan is both extensive and fascinating.

My journal for March 2, 1962, reads:

Hu Shih is dead. He died of a heart attack on February 24, just after presiding at the annual meeting of Academia Sinica. We only saw him a few times during our first month here when paying courtesy calls. He was over seventy, had suffered several heart attacks, and wouldn't take good care of himself. The whole free world press praises him, and Taiwan seems beside itself in doing him homage. Thousands and thousands from the humblest people to high government officials and scholars, up to President Chiang Kai-shek, have gone to the funeral parlor to pay their respects. He stood for rationalism and humanism and gradual progress. He was urbane and humane. He represented fine things in both Chinese and Western liberal tradition. China needs many more such people.

John Orchard also died that week. He was a professor of economic geography at Columbia and one of the founders of the East Asian Institute.

We lost still another friend while we were in Taiwan: Dorothy Hu, the lady who managed Columbia's Chinese Oral History Project. Jim Morley telegraphed the news to us. She was the wife of Dr. C. T. Hu, a professor at Teachers College, also a good friend. They had two young sons.

One result of my regular trips to the KMT archives was that I heard Mr. Chiang Yung-ching give a talk on Borodin and the Wuhan government of 1927, a subject I was much interested in because it came right during the Northern Expedition. The archives had the minutes of the meetings of the Joint Council, which Borodin advised. I told Mr. Chiang he ought to publish his findings, but he replied there was no way he could publish his essay. This set me thinking, and I went to the head of the Asia Foundation office and told Douglas Pike about the situation and suggested he set up a fund to publish promising work in the social sciences and history by younger scholars. He jumped at the idea; it was right up the Asia Foundation's alley. The result was a committee of Chinese scholars, headed by Kuo Ting-yee, who managed a competition among younger scholars, with an award for good papers and the publication of the best of them. My friend's paper was the first published, and he received a prize of U.S. $500, a very big amount. Later a two-volume book by Li Yun-han also won a prize and was published. The Asia Foundation awards went on for ten years, and about fifty volumes of works by younger scholars were published. One might say that idea partially repaid the kindnesses to me of so many scholars in Taiwan. Both Mr. Li and Professor Chiang are now noted historians, and each has published much in Chinese.

Toward the end of my time in Taiwan, I interviewed President Chiang Kai-shek, who was, of course, very important to my subject. I had been trying for the opportunity since October 1961. Professor Chang Chi-yun offered to assist me. I was to prepare a set of questions that would be submitted to the president in advance. I carefully prepared five and went over them with Kuo Ting-yee. Then I gave them to Professor Chang, who was to have them translated and submit them to the president. Nothing happened for months, until on April 9 I received a phone call from the president's appointment secretary to say the president would meet me at 10:00 the next morning, with Professor Chang to accompany me and

Mr. James Shen to act as interpreter. I should report to the Presidential Palace at 8:45 and should boil down the questions, since the interview would have to be short. I arrived on the dot and soon was ushered into a waiting room.

This waiting room had a long center table flanked with chairs, and with sofas around the walls. Already in the room were half a dozen Chinese, including a general and two ambassadors about to be sent to posts abroad, who were waiting for appointments. Already there were Dr. Chang Chi-yun and Colonel Wu, the appointment secretary. Before my time came, several more important persons came in. It made me think of the Ch'ing dynasty when officials awaited their turn for an audience at dawn.

Shortly after ten, someone came in to say that I was to see the president. Dr. Chang remarked, "You are to have the first interview!" This was clearly an honor. Dr. Chang and James Shen accompanied me into a room about thirty feet on a side, near the far end of which was the president's desk.

The president arose and came around the desk to greet me, which he did courteously and with many smiles. The introductions were very Chinese. President Chiang was dressed in a mustard-colored serge uniform with no medals. My impression was of a rather slight man, nearly bald, with gleaming white teeth, which no doubt were artificial. His face seemed small and he was aging, for the skin had a thin quality of elderly people. Yet he was certainly vigorous and in good health. The president asked me to be seated at the end of a sofa near the easy chair in which he sat, while Mr. Shen sat between but behind us.

I opened the conversation by saying that it was a great honor to be received, and I thought there were very few scholars in any country who would have the privilege of meeting the president. I also said that I had been in Taiwan for seven months and had received the greatest assistance from scholars and from participants in the Northern Expedition, in my research on the subject.

The president then asked whether I had any opinions about the Northern Expedition. I replied that I had no opinions but that I had many questions still unanswered. He then said I might ask what I pleased.

It seemed the president hadn't seen the Chinese text of my carefully worked out list of five questions. I decided to bring up only the first two. First, "As the president thinks back over the Northern Expedition, which were the most decisive and important battles?" The answers were interesting, for all three involved political matters and all involved foreign relations. (None was a military battle.) I give his replies in the sequence in which he raised them.

Most important was the Tsinan Incident in May 1928. On this occasion Japan sent two divisions to Shantung to try to stop the progress of the Northern Expedition and to prevent our taking Peiping and Tientsin. But we avoided a head-on clash with the Japanese troops and went around Tsinan. While this was not part of the civil war, it was a turning point in the success of the Northern Expedition.

The second important incident was the Nanking Incident when Communist elements in the Second Army [this is as he stated it] made an uprising and attacked foreigners in Nanking. Their object was to involve the National Revolutionary Army in a clash with foreign powers.

The third important event was before the start of the Northern Expedition. The Soviet advisers and the Chinese Communists were both strongly opposed to the Northern Expedition. There was a long argument in Canton over this issue. Finally, Chiang Kai-shek told them he had made up his mind decisively to go ahead with the Northern Expedition whether they cooperated or not. Only then did they come around and decide to support the campaign. His determination on this matter was decisive for the launching of the Northern Expedition.

My second question concerned the Party Purification Movement. I told the president that I understood, and most Western scholars believed, that he was the principal architect of this movement. "Can the president remember when, at least what month, he decided that the Party Purification would have to be carried out?"

The decision was made in his own mind in Canton before the launching of the Northern Expedition. He then realized that a break would have to be made one of these days. The opposition of the Communists toward the Northern Expedition convinced him; and his decision to launch the Northern Expedition over their opposition was a sign of his decision. The purge that took place after the occupation of Nanking was the second phase of the movement. [Perhaps he meant the first phase was the March 20 Incident of 1926, before the Northern Expedition began.]

I then asked why, if the decision was made in Canton, it was a whole year before the purge was carried out. He replied that when the Northern Expedition began there was need for continued cooperation with the USSR and the Chinese Communists because of the opposition of both Britain and Japan to the Northern Expedition. Had the purge been ordered earlier, he would not have received Russian help in the expedition.

The president seemed to show signs of nervousness in the rapid tapping of his right foot, which may have meant he wanted the interview ended. I then asked the final small question: "As the president thinks back, which persons were most helpful in executing the purge?" His answer was that it was the members of the Central Supervisory Committee, particularly Wu Chih-hui and Chang Ching-chiang.

At this point, after nearly twenty minutes with the president, I said I believed I must go because he was very busy. There was a final exchange of courtesies, and a handshake. His last word were *tsai-hui* (till we meet again).

Wang Yu-tien got a brief vacation on Buddha's birthday and went back to Chiayi to be with her family. After she had been back with us for a while, she told Kay she was pregnant. She was a Catholic and I suppose could not prevent getting with child, although she had three boys already. She was one of four women from Chiayi in similar work with American families, and each Tuesday they got the day off and enjoyed it together. Under Kay's inspiration, the American ladies conspired with the three Chinese friends of Yu-tien to give her a baby shower, which was prepared in great secrecy. One Tuesday, Yu-tien was lured back to our house by one of her friends, only to find the other two and the four American women gathered to shower her. She was overwhelmed and wept. Apparently a baby shower was not among the inventory of Chinese customs. Kay felt very good about doing that for our faithful Yu-tien.

During my last few weeks in Taiwan I worked in the library of the Ministry of Justice, where I was introduced by Professor Kuo. The director of the Fourth Section of the Investigation Bureau of the Ministry of Justice was Mr. Wu Mo-feng; and the Investigation Bureau was descended from the Bureau of Investigation and Statistics, the Communist-hunting outfit started by Chen Kuo-fu and Chen Li-fu. I told the librarian, Mr. Lin, what I was interested in, and he brought me, among other early CCP documents, copies of *Chung-yang t'ung-hsin* (Central newsletter), published secretly, I assume, in Shanghai during the latter part of 1927 and early 1928 by the self-appointed Central Committee of the Chinese Communist Party. To me it was a wonderful source, because I was much interested in what happened to the CCP after its split with the KMT. I found frank, and I believe honest, reports of the failed Nanchang Uprising of August 1, 1927, by the main Communist participants, reporting back to headquarters. I paid to have all these reports copied and checked by a second person for accuracy.

I spent many early mornings during four months on the way back to America translating the accounts, and after having my translation checked by Dr. T. K. Tong, who pronounced them "letter perfect," I submitted an article to *The China Quarterly* entitled "The Ashes of Defeat: Accounts of the Nanchang Revolt and Southern Expedition, August 1–October 1, 1927, by Chinese Communists Who Took Part." It was published in the April-June 1964 issue. It included the verbatim translations of accounts by Li Li-san, Chang Kuo-t'ao, and Chou I-chun, and reprimands by the Central Committee. The article has been much used by other historians.

We started planning our departure from Taiwan on April 1, in consultation with Bob Chang of the U.S. Educational Foundation Office, setting the date for shipping stuff to America by sea, the date for our departure, and an itinerary for the four months till we were to arrive back in Pleasantville on August 25, 1962. Kay took charge of the packing so that I could keep on with my now very productive studies. She is such a good sport!

We wanted to entertain lots of friends but felt we should space out our intimate dinner parties because of Wang Yu-tien's condition. We prepared a farewell letter to our Chinese friends and took it to the foundation to be translated into literary Chinese, then typed and mimeographed. We estimated, without making a list, that we would need about seventy-five. We actually sent seventy-eight, mailed on the last day.

We also gave a feast for the members of the Institute of Modern History, who were our official hosts, and among whom we had made many friends. Jennie Wu, the incomparable aide to the wives of Fulbrighters, arranged it for us in a restaurant that only served private parties. We had a good, but not elaborate dinner for two tables of thirteen each. All but one of those invited came. Kay and Sam Chu hosted one table while Mr. Chia Ting-shih and I hosted the other, and we switched hosts around in the middle of the dinner. It was a little stiff, but a very pleasant affair. It cost us U.S. $55.

The same group then gave a luncheon party for us at Academia Sinica after a lecture I had given. It was a much better party, more lively and more relaxed. After that there was a group picture. In the first row, among all the staff members, are three women, Mrs. Kuo, Kay, and Mrs. Wang Ping, the only female on the research staff and a very fine person. Other friends in that picture, whom I still see on visits to Taipei, are Chang Yu-fa, who later came to Columbia for a year and became director of the Institute of Modern History; Li En-han and Huang Chia-mu, solid scholars; Chang Tsun-wu and Su Yun-feng, who both also came to Columbia; Wang Yu-chun and Lu Shih-ch'iang, who became successively directors of the institute after Professor Kuo came to America; and our dear friend, Chang Peng-yuan.

During the last two weeks we had an engagement every night except the last, which we reserved for ourselves, and also many noon engagements. We hosted Dean Shen and Professor Liu, head of Tai-ta's history department. We invited some Fulbrighters for dinner and after dinner had a talk with Jim Leonard of the U.S. Embassy. We took our Columbia student friends to dinner at a Japanese restaurant. Dr. Chang Chi-yun, commandant of the National War College and my "introducer" for the interview with President Chiang, came together with the Nelsons; and on another night we entertained General Pai Ch'ung-hsi and his literary son, with whom Kay had become well acquainted, together with Professor and Mrs. Kuo. We were entertained by Don and Ann Munro, General Pai, the China Institute, and Y. T. Shen on successive evenings. We called on other friends, and many came bearing gifts of books, scrolls, or other things after our freight had been shipped, requiring us to mail off several more packages. Toward the end, our schedule became very tight indeed. I kept doggedly at my studies, and Kay kept things going smoothly and did all the business details, such as paying the bills. She had saved enough during the second half of our stay to pay her own air fare home via Japan and Korea, and then across India, Iran, and Europe. What a wife!

> Today, our day of departure [April 30], we were called upon by Professor Liu and President Ch'ien Ssu-liang and met at our home by Sam Chu and later by Professor and Mrs. Kuo, and taken to the airport. There we were seen off by about thirty friends, mostly Chinese. Our two servants came for farewell, and we were genuinely sorry to say good by to Yu-tien.

A departure picture shows Wang Yu-tien, a quite small person, holding the hand of one of her sons. It was our last view of her. Two months later she died of encephalitis.

On the airplane winging our way to Tokyo, I wrote my impressions of the land we were leaving:

> We have enjoyed Taiwan enormously. Our Chinese friends have been more kind and generous than we had any right to expect or hope. Courtesy is the most evident behavior pattern where acquaintances are concerned.
>
> The good things about Taiwan that meet the eye are its lush productivity in agriculture, the evident good health of the people, its stable and orderly society. The children are darling and they swarm. Schooling is a terrible problem, for the aim is to supply universal elementary education. The competition becomes stiffer and stiffer the higher they go, and middle school kids are in a very tough grind.
>
> We know mostly intellectuals. Our information comes from them, and we somewhat reflect their mood. I fear their mood is one of deep despair under a bright exterior. This is evident in the flight from Taiwan of young intellectuals. The old guard stays on, gradually growing older and more staid in their ways. The bright young ones mostly go away if they can get away, and it is very hard to lure them back.
>
> Several factors account for this. One is the very low salary scale for intellectual and government workers here. A professor at Taita, the leading university in Free China, receives about U.S. $50 a month. In addition, a rice allowance, oil allowance, and fuel allowance. If he is lucky he gets a rent-free house, but many receive a pitiful "housing allowance" equal to just $1 per month. There are many ways to add to their salary—outside teaching, counseling, writing articles, private business. But it is surely unhealthy to have to earn three-fifths of one's cash outside the teaching job. Professors at Taita are relatively well paid—they stand at the highest level of the bureaucracy. This is one reason for depression.
>
> Another is the curtailment of freedom. The excuse is given, and it has its validity, that China is in a war situation. Nothing can be permitted that will undermine morale or confidence in the government. Seen from the point of view of the KMT and the government, in view of the disaster on the mainland twelve years ago, it is understandable that true freedom of opinion and vigorous dissent are feared and repressed. But there is much more to it than that. The KMT has a basic philosophy of monopoly of political power. It is a large, vested bureaucracy. It doesn't care for challenges to its power. It is not a monolith, and it is very inefficient and stolid. But it has an ideology—the San Min Chu-i—the official ideology of the country [Sun Yat-sen's "Three Principles of the People," delivered as lectures in 1924]. It is quite empty and now rigid and infertile. Revision or enrichment of this ideology is not encouraged, perhaps not even permitted. So, in my understanding of the matter, no intellectual takes San Min Chu-i seriously. It is just a body of mummified creeds. Not only is there no intellectual inspiration in it, but no real pride in it, either. And there isn't much scope for personal development of new ideas in social, political, or humanistic fields.

There is real repression when a challenge arises—witness the case of Lei Chen, who was getting just too provocative and was beginning to get a following. He was put in prison for ten years on charges that went back to ten years before, very unsubstantial charges, and that had nothing to do with the magazine he was publishing. The whole matter was handled by a military court. This taught intellectuals a lesson: don't talk too much; don't criticize too deeply. A sad thing to me is to have heard not a few intellectuals defend the government's handling of Lei Chen, on the basis that he went too far in his criticisms.

Another reason for depression, and now we are getting deeper, is that everyone knows all important decisions are made by Chiang Kai-shek personally, and he has his mind primarily on return to the mainland. Many pressing problems of Taiwan are unattended or are treated arbitrarily or unwisely because of this "dream," if such it be, of returning to the mainland. The very large military force that takes up 90 percent of the government's budget prevents raising salaries, building enough schools, or making adequate long-range investment here on the island.

Politics on Taiwan are a mystery to me, but apparently they go on at the level just below the Generalissimo, with various groups contending for privilege. No intellectual seems to have an interest in politics, realizing, I suppose, that there is no way they could have any influence. Yet academic politics seem to be fiercely contested, but possibly on the mundane level of money for the individual and his group, just to help out on the subsistence budget. This makes efforts to help develop new intellectual enterprises, and to revitalize intellectual life by grants—as done by our Asia Foundation—very discouraging indeed. These may be some of the reasons for the spiritual ill ease one senses here increasingly as one stays. Increasingly, because at first one sees only the bright exterior.

But we must remember that homesickness is another very strong factor. Here the intellectuals are aliens. [I was thinking only of "mainlanders."] Many have relatives on the mainland. To be cut in two cannot but be dispiriting. Almost every person we know from the mainland left children, wives, or parents behind. Not a few of those were executed by the Communists. Yet can they go back? When can they go back? No evidence yet of weakening of the Chinese mainland army. The quarrel between the Russians and the Chinese does not seem to be so deep that the Russians would not help. But will America help the National Government? The whole thrust of our policy is against it. And without our active logistic support, how could Taiwan's army ever get there? Logistics across 100 miles of water is no little undertaking, and only the Seventh Fleet in those waters would be capable of providing it.

When I wrote that I did not know of the terrible famine that had struck the mainland as a result, in part, of the Great Leap Forward, nor of the flood of refugees trying to escape to Hong Kong that year. Nor did I know that Chiang Kai-shek, thinking his time had come to strike, tried to persuade our government to support him. We turned him down, I have been told.

Another thing about Taiwan that puzzles us is the state of relations between the Taiwanese and the mainlanders. The relations seem latently hostile, but is the trend toward better or worse relations? I would guess that they are slowly getting better as more and more young people grow up together, go to school together, can speak a common language, and come to feel a common identity on Taiwan. But I am far from sure of this. There is discontent on both sides, yet the discontent is repressed. I know of very little overt hostility.

I left Taiwan very much in favor of the Republic of China as against the People's Republic of China, where the revolution had been so cruel and policy seemed so irrational, so destructive of all that I admire in Chinese culture. I have been back to Taiwan about ten times.

17

Academic, Cultural, and Social Life, 1962–1967

A few days after our return to Pleasantville, Paul and Beth Cressey came for a brief visit, bringing Dad. Sad to say, Dad was becoming blind, though not completely so. As it turned out, he had only two more years to live. After that visit, we had a week or so with Ann before she had to return to Rochester for her final year of college. Kay went back to teaching at Bedford Road School the day after Labor Day, and I started going to Columbia again for a variety of appointments.

After that most rewarding year abroad, I resumed my position as director of the East Asian Institute, one of the key places in America for graduate study and research on China and Japan. I had a great deal of research material that I must organize and use. Our Chinese Oral History Project was still underway, which took some time, too. I had classes, seminars, M.A. theses, and doctoral dissertations to attend to, and since I took teaching seriously, as my main responsibility, such work took a lot of time. Even though I had been giving a basic lecture course for twelve years, I tried to improve each lecture before giving it. And, let me confess, I usually took a tranquilizer an hour before going to the rostrum.

In addition, I was a member of the Council on Foreign Relations, a trustee of the Asia Society, and at times a member of the board of the Association for Asian Studies. I was still a member of the Joint Committee on Contemporary China, and soon the Ford Foundation enlisted me along with several colleagues to form a committee to encourage and select senior and junior China scholars to spend time familiarizing themselves with, or studying at, the Institute of Modern History in Taipei and the Modern China Seminar of Toyo Bunko, both of which the foundation supported financially. (I had had a consultative role in Ford

Foundation's five year-grant to the institute. Under the influence of John Everton and Doak Barnett, the foundation was pouring money into support of modern China studies.)

In August 1963 I became a member of the board of the Shanghai American School, together with Doak Barnett and Wallace Merwin as the actual core group, though there were members representing some national Protestant church bodies, who seldom came. We met only once a year to stay legally alive, for it was a holding operation to keep claim to the value of the SAS property that had been confiscated by, or in the name of, the People's Republic of China. Before we turned over the school's assets to an interdenominational mission board, I had become chairman of the SAS board, a most unexpected outcome for this 1927 graduate!

Another involvement was to become a member of the founding board of the Inter-University Center for Chinese Language Study in Taiwan, started under the initiative of my friend Professor Lyman Van Slyke at Stanford, but endorsed by eight—later ten—graduate schools with strong China programs. We met once a year but had committees on admission and fellowships that met at other times. "The Stanford Center," as it came to be called, gave excellent language instruction to many American graduate students, to some undergraduates, and eventually to many Europeans and Australians as well. It was housed on the campus of National Taiwan University and was an asset to the beleaguered island in that many future teachers of Chinese subjects in America and Europe had lived there and been influenced, mainly favorably, toward the Republic of China.

Sometime during these early postsabbatical years, I was asked to be a trustee of the C.T. Loo Educational Foundation, which at that time gave grants to young scientists from Taiwan to study in America, and I was on the selection committee, which involved a fair amount of work. Through this relationship I became acquainted with a lovely person, Mrs. Maurice T. Moore, "Beth," a sister of Henry Luce. She is an "old China hand."

I guess one might say that I was involved in a variety of academic promotional work!

In terms of research, I polished up my translations of documents from the Nanchang Uprising for publication in *The China Quarterly*, a prestigious British journal, and I spent one day a week at the British Information Office reading and taking notes from *Further Correspondence Respecting China*. Because the subject interested me so much, I started an analytic study of the phenomenon of warlordism in China, trying to see it in a wider historical perspective, and to outline its fundamental features—a sociological approach. I presented my preliminary findings in a paper for the Modern China Seminar entitled "The Structure of Militarism in China during the 1920s." It formed the basis of a paper I later delivered at the International Congress of Orientalists in New Delhi. During the next two years, I wrote about ten reviews for *The New York Times* Sunday Book Review, *Political Science Quarterly*, *Journal of Asian Studies*, and other journals. And I was called upon occasionally to give talks on China.

My intellectual curiosity, and hence my research, began to center upon Sun Yat-sen, because it was his decision to accept Soviet Russian assistance in 1923 that opened the way for the Chinese Communist Party's initial growth, which was a vital step toward its later triumph in China, a matter of world import. I wanted to know much more than was readily evident about Sun and his circumstances in the 1920s, in order to understand better the basis for his decision. The quick answer, a sort of apologia proposed by Nationalist historians, was that he turned to Soviet Russia because none of the Western powers nor Japan would help him. True enough; but one needed to know much more about international politics and Chinese internal conditions in the 1920s, as well as about Sun himself, to begin to understand the decision. Why, and under what circumstances, did Russia decide to help Dr. Sun? What considerations might have influenced him? One must try not to read back into those times the anti-Stalinist view of communism and the Cold War view of Russia.

John returned from Germany and was mustered out of the army early in 1963. But the best thing was that he applied to go back to Lycoming and was admitted for the autumn term of 1963 and given considerable credit for the work he had done in the University of Maryland overseas college program and for his study of German.

Ann graduated from Rochester in June 1963, having taken a double major in psychology and philosophy, in an honors program. She had been greatly stimulated intellectually by her teachers. We were terribly proud parents at her graduation. The new president of Rochester already knew her, because he heard her perform at her honors oral exam. He congratulated her by name when she arrived on the platform to receive her diploma. Ann was so stimulated at Rochester that she decided to go to graduate school to work for a Ph.D. in philosophy. She won a Woodrow Wilson Fellowship, which just about covered the costs of two years of study and living at Cornell. The school awarded her two more years as a teaching assistant. That fellowship determined her career, and also her marriage.

The day after Christmas in 1963, I started out for New Delhi and the XXVI International Congress of Orientalists. I had only a day in Tokyo, where I saw Ichiro Shirato, our crack Japanese teacher; he had developed ulcers and would have to lighten his teaching load. Then on to Taipei, where I had many friends to see.

Professor Morton Fried, our China anthropologist, was having a wonderful research year, and I persuaded him before he returned to Columbia to go to Korea on an exploration trip, hoping thereby to get some graduate students turned to Korean studies, about which America was deficient, as was our institute. I tried to get some archival material microfilmed but didn't get anything specific settled, though Professor Kuo Ting-yee took me to call upon Chiang

Ching-kuo. I took a sentimental trip to Taichung to see friends at the KMT archives—Chiang Yung-ching and Li Yun-han—and to find out whether I could get some stuff on Borodin in Wuhan copied. I went out to the Institute of Modern History, which was on the verge of a fat grant from the Ford Foundation. Soon I began to get graduate students from there.

I called upon Douglas Pike at the Asia Foundation to learn how the prize for outstanding scholarly essays by younger persons was coming along. He was a bit miffed that the opportunity was not well publicized, and I wondered if it was becoming something of a clique monopoly. I learned that the Joint Committee on Rural Reconstruction seemed to be in trouble: because American financing was winding down, the operation's future was in doubt, and morale was low. However, that wonderful organization was not demobilized and was still going in 1977, when I had a refresher research summer in Taiwan.

After a strenuous four days, I set off for India with two Chinese scholars from Academia Sinica in tow. They also were to attend the International Congress, but they were glad for my assistance in this sudden exposure to the outer world. Good thing I shepherded them through entry procedures at the New Delhi airport, because India had been humiliated by China in the 1962 border war, and now Indians were not shouting about the eternal friendship of the two countries. Quite the contrary. At least I prevented my two Chinese friends (who, after all, came from the Republic of China, not the People's Republic!) from being gypped by their first Indian money changer.

At a briefing at the American Embassy on Friday, January 3, 1964, for the American scholars attending the Congress, we learned that since independence India had received nearly nine billion dollars worth of foreign aid, of which 89 percent came from the free world, and 57 percent from the United States. My notes say that "This ties India into the free world—a political goal." On later reflection, I guess this view had some merit, though nobody "ties" India! Also, the aid is giving a chance for India to continue being viable as a democracy. A little over half of the American contribution was in the form of agricultural surpluses—one 10,000-ton freighter load a day, mostly of wheat. This prevented starvation of part of the population and kept prices stable. India paid for the grain by depositing rupees in an account in the Reserve Bank of India, from which loans were made to India for rupee costs of development projects.

Some 45 percent of U.S. aid went for development projects—dams, irrigation, diesel locomotives, and so forth. A small proportion went to malarial control, and the results were dramatic in reducing the incidence of the disease, which had been a terrible killer. Another small part went for technical training of Indians in America or for sending American experts to do training work in India. Of 3,700 Indians trained in America, all who had completed their training were back in India, except for one woman, who had married an American. On the basis of interviews with returnees, it was believed that almost all were being employed in India in the type of work for which they were trained.

I find it difficult to square all this effort with the apparent anti-American bias of India's foreign policy, as it developed. However, I suppose that in foreign relations, gratitude is not to be expected.

The next week was busy with congress meetings, receptions, special entertainments with Indian music and dance, and a trip to Agra to see the Taj. North India in winter is beautiful, and I was very glad for another visit. The Indian scholars had arranged a fine meeting. India had taken on a compromise role, for at the congress in Moscow three years before, the Russian side and its cohorts tried to block the United States from hosting the next congress. India then offered to hold it in New Delhi. This made it easier for the following one to be held in America.

There were opportunities to become acquainted with Indian scholars and with Sinologists from all over the world. One I met, and whom I have encountered at other international conferences, was the Russian, S. L. Tikhvinsky, reputedly a member of KGB, and clearly an establishment scholar and front man. I doubt that the Wilbur and How book, *Documents on Communism*, would have endeared me to him, but I don't remember any discourtesy such as I later received from him at another conference.

One of the last events was an address by Prime Minister Jawaharlal Nehru. I remember that he seemed weak and unstable while trying to read his speech, drooping over his lectern. Only a few months later, he passed away.

I left New Delhi on Friday early in the morning and arrived home Saturday evening, January 10. It was a strenuous two weeks, but I was full of vigor then. It was our Christmas vacation period, so I could recuperate.

By now I was beginning to get some fine Chinese students from Taiwan, some sent by Kuo Ting-yee from the Institute of Modern History on their Ford Foundation grant, others as visiting scholars on grants from the East Asian Institute or other sources, and some just registered for graduate study because they wanted to work with me. Among the visiting scholars were Chiang Yung-ching and Li Yun-han. From the Institute of Modern History there were Chang Peng-yuan, Su Yun-feng, Li Kuo-chi, and Chang Yu-fa, who later became director of the Institute of Modern History. These former students form a sort of Columbia club in Taiwan, and they always entertain me when I visit Taipei. Sister Madeleine Chi, of the Sacred Heart order, is another member of that group.

Paula Johnson came from Smith College knowing Russian, and at Columbia she learned Chinese and Japanese, as required for the Ph.D. in Chinese history. She wrote a dissertation on "The Years of the Young Radicals," about Chinese students who studied in Japan during the first decade of the twentieth century and later led the revolution to overthrow the Manchus. We have kept in touch with Paula and her husband Ed Harrell, also a graduate of the institute. They have had an interesting career in the foreign aid field, living in Japan, Thailand,

and Jordan, as well as Washington. Paula has gone many times to China for the World Bank to look into Chinese loan requests. Her dissertation, enlarged and refined, was published by Stanford University Press.

I gave up the directorship of the East Asian Institute in July 1964 but continued with my teaching and had more time for research. Learning more about Sun Yat-sen, a quirky person, became quite entrancing. I did not then plan to write a book on Sun.

My father was deteriorating. He had his ninetieth birthday in April 1964. Paul Cressey was retiring from Wheaton College, and Beth and he were going to the Philippines for a year. Kay and I just had to take charge of Dad. It was clear, however, that we couldn't take care of him in our home, as Paul and Beth had managed to do in Norton, because we both had full-time jobs. James Holden, now our attorney as well as good friend, recommended us to a small home in White Plains run by a doctor, and Dad was accepted there. Paul and Beth brought him to us in June and we took him to the nursing home.

Thereafter we called on him nearly every day, but he wasn't always lucid. In preparation for his birthday I had written to his friends asking them to write him, just as I had done when he had his sixtieth. But now when I read the letters to him, he didn't comprehend much. Yet the basic kindliness of his personality continued. Dad died on August 18, 1964. We had a lovely memorial service for him in our beautiful church, attended by such China and Japan Y folk as we could gather together. We bought a living pine tree—a Chinese symbol of longevity—and used it in the focal area of the church auditorium. Our minister, Cliff Vessey, gave a fine service, and Dad's old friends, Jorgy Jorgensen and Dwight Edwards, gave moving tributes. I spoke too. It was nice that several of my Chinese friends and some colleagues came out to White Plains to pay tribute to Dad.

I began writing seriously on Sun Yat-sen during 1964. I tried to learn everything I could about Canton and Dr. Sun's situation there when he returned for the last time and tried to rebuild his party and his political fortunes. What I learned became a long paper, which I entitled "Forging the Weapons: Sun Yat-sen and the Kuomintang in Canton, 1924." Though I didn't publish this, it became one basis for my later writing about Dr. Sun.

Two important things happened in 1965. John graduated from Lycoming college, and I was given a named professorship. For John's graduation, Kay and I drove to Lycoming, and Ann came from Cornell in a car she had rented. It was a fine occasion.

Andrew Cordier, dean of the School of International Affairs, had raised a considerable sum from the Ford Foundation with which to create five endowed chairs. With the concurrence of President Kirk, he chose me to be the recipient of one of them, this one named for Sir George Sansom, the first director of the East Asian Institute and an eminent historian of Japan. Announcement of the newly endowed chairs, and the recipients, appeared in the *New York Times*. I have a sheaf of letters congratulating me on the appointment. It was an honor, indeed, but so far as I can tell, it did not enhance my salary. I was fifty-seven years old and had been teaching for eighteen years.

Americans were cut off from mainland China but had easy access to Taiwan. To enhance scholarly relations, and at the initial suggestion of John Fairbank, the American Council of Learned Societies took the initiative during 1966 to create a committee together with the Social Science Research Council that would meet with counterparts in Taiwan to work out programs of scholarly cooperation. Fred Burkhardt, head of the ACLS, asked me to be a member of the committee. Other original members were George Taylor of the University of Washington (political science), Walter Galenson of Cornell (economics), Jerome Cohen of Harvard (law), and Morton Fried of Columbia (anthropology)—all known to be friendly with Taiwan scholars and having good connections there. Gordon Turner represented SSRC.

After getting organized, and determining what our position should be in negotiation with our counterparts in Taiwan—an eminent group of academic elders— we took off for a meeting with them in Taipei. I have a journal account of a six-week trip, from May 28 to July 9, 1966, that included, after the conference, a journey on to Europe to meet Kay in Denmark.

I was met in Taiwan by Professor Kuo, Jennie Wu, Sam Chu, and Dixie Walker. Chiang Yung-ching had come up from Taichung; we had arranged for him to come to Columbia in September as a visiting scholar.

A development that could have spoiled our conference was a document addressed to the American people and signed by 1,300 Chinese scholars and officials in Taiwan attacking John Fairbank and Doak Barnett for their testimony at a congressional hearing, in which they advocated a policy of working toward opening relations between the United States and the People's Republic of China—the arch enemy of the Republic of China on Taiwan. Wang Shih-chieh, Ch'ien Shih-liang, and Kuo Ting-yee were among the first signers, and all were members of our counterpart committee.

I talked frankly with President Ch'ien of Taida and with professors Kuo, Li Chi, and T'ao Hsi-sheng about our distress with the letter denouncing Fairbank and Barnett. I called on Arthur Hummel, chargé at the U.S. Embassy (and later our ambassador to the People's Republic), a very impressive young Foreign Service officer.

I took a trip down to Taichung to work in the KMT archives. My friends there had made lists of things for me to see, based on weak points in my paper "Forging the Weapons," about Sun Yat-sen in Canton during 1922–24, his last years there. Also, Mrs. Chiang and Mrs. Li each knocked themselves out to make fine Chinese dinners for me. I met Ed Friedman, now a professor of political science at the University of Wisconsin, who was working at the KMT archives, too. I spent a busy week, and it was hard going because I was trying to read fairly cursive Chinese script, which I am not good at. But I took reams of notes that would be valuable for my Northern Expedition study. Professor Kuo arranged for me to stay at the Teachers' Hostel in Taichung, a comfortable place, where I had good Chinese meals. The manager and submanager were former students of Professor Kuo and were most attentive to me. The other guests were some forty Africans, in Taiwan for agricultural studies.

Professor Kuo brought me a long critique of my paper, "Forging the Weapons," correcting and adding details. I felt greatly indebted to him for all that effort. He told me something of great interest: about six years before, he had been able to see materials brought to Taipei from the KMT archives that had much detail about Russian material aid to the Kuomintang in the 1920s. If they were not in the archives (I had been told there was no information on that subject there) it was because they had been removed. I have never seen such materials and had assumed that the Kuomintang had none. Most of what I know about Russian aid comes from Russian sources. One may speculate that KMT leaders removed or concealed the stuff to protect the images of Sun Yat-sen and Chiang Kai-shek when their Russian orientation became an embarrassment.

Professor Wang Chien-min called at my hotel. I had met him in 1962, when studying in the Ministry of Justice Library. He had published on his own a three-volume work on the history of the Chinese Communist Party, based largely upon archives held in Taiwan. The work had been seized by the police as unauthorized, but Professor Wang had succeeded in getting 150 copies to Harvard, so foreign libraries would be able to secure this valuable work. Professor Wang wanted my help and financial assistance in getting an English version made and published. I backed away as gracefully as I could. Before Professor Wang left, General Pai Ch'ung-hsi came to call, and Mr. Wang turned the meeting into an interview, to my surprise. I would have expected one guest to leave when another came.

Our Sino-American Conference had three days of meetings, and lunches and dinners given by Prime Minister Yen Chia-kang (with whom I later became quite friendly), Wang Shih-chieh, Li Chi, and Fred Burkhardt. The American group had three main desires: to have cooperation with Chinese scholars in the broad field of Sinological studies—history and the humanities; that American social scientists should be given opportunities for field studies of Chinese society in Taiwan; and that American scholars should be granted access to intelligence materials on the Chinese Communist Party and mainland conditions that were held in Taiwan. The first two requests were no problem, but the third was. Even our Chinese counterparts had no access to such materials, and the entire subject was taboo for Chinese academics. However, the Chinese side worked on the problem and one result was the series of conferences on mainland China problems conducted alternately by the Institute of International Relations and American institutions. There have been about fifteen of them, and they were of increasingly high quality. Also, selected American scholars have been permitted to study historical materials on the Communist Party and its administration in China, gathered by Taiwan intelligence agencies.

On the third day of the conference we passed resolutions: We decided formally to set up a Sino-American Committee (whose nature was left undefined); to encourage the establishment of Ph.D. programs in certain strong departments in Chinese universities, to start with visiting American professors while Chinese professors were tooling up to take over; to create a service center in Taipei to assist American scholars; to hold conferences on fields of study or topics; to exchange scholars, and so forth. It was only a beginning, and someone was going to have to raise money and do staff work. One thing the Chinese side did quickly was to create a center for American scholars, not as a work space, but as a place where they could get introductions to their opposite numbers among scholars in Taiwan, and also a facility to set up seminars for American and Chinese scholars to discuss some common scholarly issues.

Our meetings ended with an audience with Chiang Kai-shek and Madame Chiang, at the official residence in Yang-ming Shan, though we were kept uncertain till the last minute whether he could fit it into his busy schedule—a device to enhance his majesty. Each of us was assigned to a specific seat, so the president could know whom he was looking at or talking with. Then we lined up in two files, Chinese in one and Americans in the other, just before his arrival was announced. He looked vigorous and healthy, wearing a simple uniform with no medals. After inviting us to have tea and noodles, he inquired about the conference and then asked each for his opinions. George Taylor had the only real discussion: about relations between the Soviet Union and the Chinese Communists. George and I each got in a plug for American scholars to be granted access to mainland intelligence materials, one of our group's main concerns. Our Chinese colleagues may have gotten more from the occasion than we did, for it gave them "face." Or did it just bore them?

I have several pictures taken at the conference—everyone looks so young, particularly those of us in the American delegation. I see my Chinese friends: Herbert Ma, now a justice of the Republic of China's Supreme Court; Li Chi, the pioneering, Harvard-trained archaeologist, now deceased; Hsu Cho-yun, now teaching at the University of Pittsburgh; Wang Shih-chieh, whose early article on Chinese slavery I had used in my dissertation, and who later became foreign minister and then head of Academia Sinica in Taiwan. He, too, is gone.

Perhaps our committee did some good in calling attention to the importance of the scholarly community in Taiwan, whose economic condition was still quite unsatisfactory because academic matters ranked far below military affairs in the government's priorities; or maybe one should say in Chiang Kai-shek's priorities, which determined matters. The committees met annually thereafter, alternating between Washington and Taipei.

On a stopover in Hong Kong, I called with Julie How on General Chang Fa-k'uei, whom she was interviewing for our Chinese Oral History Project. The new development was that he now was beginning to bring out dairies and letters that are so important in enriching and correcting one's memory. Eventually he allowed us to microfilm them, so they are preserved at Columbia for open use by historians.

While in Hong Kong I visited the Universities Service Center, an institution set up by the Western scholarly community—under American initiative but with indispensable British help—to give China scholars a place to work and enable them to use the files on developments in China that had been gathered over the years by the Union Research Institute. In 1966 China was still closed to outsiders, except "fellow travelers." Many scholars conducted systematic interviews with persons who had left China, so as to gain firsthand information on topics of their research. Dissertations and important books came out of work at the center. When I visited it, Chow Hsun-hsin, Stanley Lubman, Carl Riskin, and Don Munro, all one-time Columbia graduate students, were there, as well as my friend Eto Shinkichi, a student from France, and a Norwegian. The center's records showed that in the two years since 1964, about sixty scholars had worked there for shorter or longer periods. "Really a smashing success," I wrote after that visit. Professor Eto explained his presence in Hong Kong: As dean of students at his university, he was under attack by Japanese Marxists for his nonconforming viewpoints, and the Foreign Ministry arranged for him to be in Hong Kong doing research until things quieted down.

I also visited Hong Kong University, escorted by the acting head of the history department, Mr. Len Young, who said he was eager to send some of the best graduates of the department to Columbia for further work. Eventually I did get three good graduate students from Hong Kong University.

Kay and I had a date to meet in Copenhagen, Denmark, on June 26: she to fly there from New York, and I from Athens. We spent five days in Copenhagen, enjoying the beautiful eighteenth-century architecture, squares, and parks with potted flowers and chairs or benches for idling. We flew to Stockholm on July 1. Stockholm was invaded that summer by hippies from all over Europe and America, a very unkempt bunch of young folks who lolled about and littered up the public places. They were part of the drug culture, I suppose, and protesters against all establishments.

We went to the Museum of Far Eastern Antiquities, famous for its outstanding collection of Chinese painted pottery of Neolithic times, and for its collection of Shang and Chou bronzes and weapons. I didn't venture to try to see Dr. Bernard Karlgren, the museum's famous director and one of Europe's greatest Sinologists, for by now I was somewhat out of touch with Chinese antiquities. Later, my colleague at Columbia, Professor Hans Bielenstein—Karlgren's student—scolded me for not doing so. Professor Karlgren knew me from my book on Han slavery, and we had met at Columbia. My not announcing myself may have been characteristic—I was not one to push myself forward (at least, that is my self-image).

Oslo, in Norway, was the most charming of the three Scandinavian capitals we visited. It is smaller and seemed more closely related to the sea. The final part of our lovely vacation was a three-day bus trip across Norway, from Oslo to Bergen. We had a well-educated tour guide, a student of comparative literature, and our traveling companions were congenial. The mountain scenery was spectacular, especially on the day when our bus was put aboard a steamer for a half-day ride through a long fjord with frequent water falls tumbling down the cliff sides. On July 9 we flew home and were met at the airport by our children, after a wonderful thirteen-day vacation with my first-class wife.

I now mention one of the most enriching things in my adult life, a basis for deep friendships and an enlarger of my intellectual horizons:

Hoch Reid, a New York lawyer and civic-minded man, whom we knew slightly at this time, invited Kay and me to join a group of friends in Pleasantville for monthly discussions. Others in the group were Shirley and Cynthia Boden (both ardent pacifists; he in co-op housing, Cynthia a charming idealist); Reverend Paul Wright (American Bible Society) and Gertrude; Dr. George Gammertsfelder (a scientist and skeptic) and his Kay (an auburn-haired, delightful librarian); and Phyllis Jacoby, at that time treasurer of the Pleasantville school system and later of the village—a very intelligent woman. Our first meeting was on Saturday, November 19, 1966, and this core group has met monthly for more than twenty years and still continues, though the Gammertsfelders died of cancer and the Wrights moved to a retirement community in North Carolina. Their places were filled by Werner Klugman and his wife, Bruni Verges (Werner a businessman, and Bruni a management librarian though she also died of cancer) and Tom and Robbin Levy (he a lawyer, and she a certified public accountant). Later additions were Leonard Stokes, who teaches art in a nearby college, and his wife, Anne, a civic-minded lady.

We have read plays, discussed national and ethical issues, talked about what we find good in art, learned about the lives and works of great authors, given our own autobiographies (up to age twenty), taken short trips together, attended plays, and in the process have become fast friends. We are all rather liberal in our middle-class way, though we do not see alike on some questions of foreign policy. We all love to travel. No one will miss a meeting unless off on a trip, or burdened with some overriding conflict. The usual format is desert and coffee, then comes someone's opening presentation, followed by several hours of lively discussion, open and frank. We may disagree on some issues, but there never is any rancor. Those of us in the original group have met and talked together more than 200 times!

Columbia University Press said they wanted to do a reprint of the Wilbur and How book, *Documents on Communism, Nationalism, and Soviet Advisers in China, 1918–1927*, but by then it was out of date. A great deal of new scholarship on the subject had been published, and I had discovered many unpublished documents emanating from the Soviet advisory mission in China. We felt that we must do a thorough revision. This work became a long-time project that only ended in mid-1988, when I delivered the index to Anita O'Brien, my wonderful former student and accomplished editor. Julie had died six years before.

An interesting event was the International Congress of Orientalists, held in August in Ann Arbor, Michigan, under the joint auspices of the American Oriental Society and the Association for Asian Studies. One thing we were determined upon was that scholars from the People's Republic of China must be given visas to attend the congress. This was to underline its academic and nonpolitical nature. The United States did not then recognize the People's Republic, but the State Department agreed to this stipulation. In the end, however, no scholars from mainland China came: it was just at the beginning of the Cultural Revolution. The Congress was efficiently run, without great political controversy of the sort at the earlier Congress when Russians used it to attack the United States. American scholars were not of one mind on the issue of recognition of the People's Republic. Professor Derk Bodde, my old friend from Peking days, got a meeting together to gather support for a petition to our government to change its policy to one of recognition. I did not attend the meeting and hadn't even heard of it, when later, to my astonishment, I read a statement by a scholar from Taiwan, Li Tungfan (Orient Lee), that I was one of five who organized the meeting. It was a smear. I sent off a hot statement to the Taiwan newspapers denying the whole thing, for I was a strong supporter of the Republic of China on Taiwan and had many academic friends there, whom I did not want to leave misled.

With a sabbatical coming up, I applied for a visiting scholar fellowship at the East-West Center in Honolulu. (Though my sabbatical year should be 1968, I had postponed my first sabbatical to accommodate Professor Goodrich, and now won that year back.) Hawaii was ideal because I intended not to do more research but to write up the results of extensive archival studies. A former student, Professor Minoru Shinoda, was in charge of the program at the East-West Center, and he wrote me the happy news that I was accepted for a year. It was a wonderful opportunity: a long trip away to a new environment, and the chance to do just what one ought to do on sabbatical leave.

In Berkeley we had a lovely visit with Jack and Cary Service, who drove us all through Marin County and then to their lovely home in Berkeley that overlooks the Bay with San Francisco beyond. Jack had me signed up to give a talk at the Center for Chinese Studies the next day, and I saw a couple of friends, one being Dick Irwin from Oberlin, who also had been a Shansi "Rep" and a former student of mine.

> In the evening we had a long talk about things that trouble us—the Vietnam War, revolt of negroes in the cities, failure of antipoverty programs, etc. Cary is a deep-down humanitarian liberal. Jack, less led by emotion, but much opposed to the Vietnam War. Me more cautious, and Kay forthrightly against it. Anyway, it was a fine talk.

18

Hawaii, Europe, and a Wedding, 1967–1968

Honolulu was a fine place to spend our sabbatical. If one was not a tourist but a member of the academic world, interested in getting on with research and writing, the East-West Center was ideal. The university had a respectable East Asian library, there were good academic colleagues, and the center was most helpful in providing a research assistant, Mr. Anthony Ma from Hong Kong, and with as much manuscript typing as I could use.

We soon discovered that the social atmosphere was very different from that in New York and other large American cities in which we have lived. There was a delightful informality: people dressed casually and seemed much more relaxed than those in the tense metropolitan mainland. There was a high proportion of people of Oriental extraction in the population—second or third generation—and considerable carryover of Chinese and Japanese culture, especially Japanese. Young folks were courteous to us elders, spontaneously asking us to go first, or rising to give us their seats on a bus. In that respect it seemed we were moving back into the 1930s. On Fridays, as a sort of celebration of Hawaii's distinctive past, many of the women wore mu-mus.

We had dear friends in Hawaii, John and Kay DeFrancis. We had known John since Peking days and had been colleagues in OSS. He had had a rough time during the McCarthy era and for a time couldn't find another teaching job, but he had landed on his feet in Hawaii. Kay and John met us at the airport and took us to their attractive home in a valley that was high enough and humid enough for John's asthmatic condition. Their home was very "Japanesy." One sat on tatami in Japanese style. There were shoji partitions. John was creating a Japanese-style

213

garden on the hillside sloping toward the house. It was wonderful to be taken in by them till we could find our niche.

Friends told us that we really must rent an automobile, but we found we could get on very well using public transportation or taxis, if need be. Our apartment, actually one room with a big closet and bathroom and an open kitchen at the back, had a bit of view of the ocean. It cost us $175 per month and was quite enough for our purposes. We entertained by serving drinks in our apartment, then taking our guest to a restaurant where meals were inexpensive, usually Japanese or Chinese ones. We entertained Jim and Bobby Morley, who were passing through, and former students on their way to Japan or Taiwan, such as Paula and Ed Harrell and their baby, Mathew, and Fox Butterfield, whom we had known as a fellow Fulbrighter in Taiwan six years before.

I began a study of the May 30th incident in Shanghai in 1925, reading what American consular officials reported to the State Department, similar to reports I had read by British consuls and others in *Further Correspondence Respecting China*. I worked first on labor conditions in Shanghai, because strikes in Japanese factories were one element behind the incident, then on the demonstrations of Chinese students supporting the strikers, protesting imperialism generally, and objecting to certain discriminatory regulations in the International Settlement of Shanghai in particular. Unplanned though it may have been, there was a violent confrontation between the Settlement police and students and their Chinese sympathizers, in which a few demonstrators were killed and many wounded. This aroused a tidal wave of nationalistic indignation. Shanghai was tied up for several months by a commercial boycott and strikes. The International Settlement became an armed camp for the first few weeks. The affair mobilized national support for the Kuomintang and the Chinese Communist Party and began the historic retreat of Western imperialism in China. (Our family, less Elizabeth, was in Shanghai at the time. We boys went from the east part of the city to the French Concession and our school in the west by special taxi, though I don't remember anything untoward happening to us.)

Besides reading the court records and the reports of an investigation by an International Commission of Jurists, I also read all I could find in Chinese, in hopes of seeing the events in some perspective. After many weeks of research, I wrote a long chapter on the subject, thus breaking out temporarily from my concentration on Canton. I never published it, but I used it as background for writing about that event in two books. Later, I wrote another long chapter on agrarian conditions in Kwangtung and the Communist-led farmers' movement there, using Chinese sources primarily. I published that chapter in 1988. I also wrote a chapter for a book edited by Professor Searle Bates, and toward the end of our stay I wrote a conference paper (the Ditchley Conference, discussed below) that was published in *The China Quarterly* and later incorporated in a book edited by John Lewis, entitled *Leadership in Communist China*. My chapter dealt with "The Influence of the Past: How the Early Years Helped to Shape the Future of the Chinese Communist Party." During that productive ten months, I guess I turned out about 400 pages of scholarly typescript. All is now in Columbia's Rare Book and Manuscript Library.

We took two very pleasant sightseeing trips to other islands in the Hawaiian chain. On May 13 I wrote the following in my journal:

> This is my sixtieth birthday. It makes me remember a wonderful time thirty-four years ago when my Dad was sixty. We celebrated in proper Chinese style when he came to see me and Kay in Peking. I wonder if Dad then felt no older than I do today. Kay and I look back with deep satisfaction and joy to the honors and affection we gave Dad that day.
>
> And I look back on nearly thirty-six years of a wonderful married life with Kay. No man could desire a more loving wife or more beautiful companion.
>
> I look back on a very happy life, with minor accomplishments, but with wonderful loved ones and a great many warm friends, and on a career full of interesting experiences. The interest of my life—that is, the people of China and their historic past—came to me partly as a result of the happenstance of being born into a "Y family" that served in China. But also I've had to work hard at the frustrating, terribly time-consuming struggle with the Chinese language. Thus, pleasure and frustration have attended the career I chose so long ago.
>
> I was blessed by fine children. Probably the portion of anxiety they have given Kay and me is no more than most parents should expect from the long job of raising infants to maturity. We've had wonderful times with John and Ann and can think of them now as well started upon useful and, we hope, happy adult lives.
>
> At sixty I suppose one can look forward to no more than ten years or so of productive and creative work. I pray that good health and continued enthusiasm will attend the coming years, but the world is so full of turmoil that no one can feel confident of undisturbed years in which to do his jobs. Others have their plans, which could upset all calculations. Yet I don't feel gloomy; only cautious about the future.
>
> The Chinese make a great thing out of sixty years, and indeed I am fortunate to have come this far.

Sometime in the spring, Ann told us that she and Nollaig MacKenzie, a fellow Cornell graduate student whom we had met once, were going to be married. We suggested they come to Hawaii for the wedding, but she preferred to have the wedding be out of our home in Pleasantville, so their friends could attend—a very sensible plan. They set a date of September 14, and that got us mobilized.

I had been invited to present a paper in England in early July, so we planned to spend two months in Europe, for our house wouldn't be available to us until August 28. This meant that all the last hustle and bustle to prepare for the wedding would be crammed into two weeks. But we could prepare wedding invitations while in Hawaii. We had to engage the church and be sure that our minister, Peter Samsom, would be available for that Saturday afternoon. We attended a Chinese wedding, and when, at the appropriate time in the wedding dinner, there was a deafening roar of firecrackers, we determined there and then that we must have firecrackers at Ann's wedding dinner.

I wrote to Jim Holden, our lawyer and close friend, to solicit his assistance:

Dear James:

This will be among the more unusual requests for professional legal assistance. Kay and I have been dreaming about Ann's wedding, and we are considering incorporating certain Chinese features into the occasion. The Chinese are a very civilized people, have had a hundred generations of experience in marrying off young people, and we think there is something to be learned from them. One thing the Chinese have worked out is a way to assure that evil spirits don't hang around and mess up the wedding or make trouble for the couple in the future. The way to assure that is to drive the evil spirits away by scaring them to death; and the way to do that is to fire off a long string of firecrackers. Here in Honolulu they do it all the time among couples of Chinese ancestry giving weddings, and having attended a couple of such weddings we now realize how important it will be to Ann's happiness and domestic tranquility, that her parents should provide her wedding ceremony with a proper blast of firecrackers (after the religious part is over).

The legal advice I need from you, and kindly regard this as a request for professional services, is whether it is legal or illegal to import fireworks to New York, whether a license is needed and if so whether it is difficult or routine to acquire; and whether and how permission would be gotten from White Plains authorities (Police and Fire, I suppose) to shoot off a string of small firecrackers in the woods behind the WP Community Church. (I have written our minister, Peter Samsom, to see whether we may have his permission.) To be entirely aboveboard with you, a string of small firecrackers means 10,000 small firecrackers, and they will make an indescribable uproar for about five minutes. However, just consider the insurance value of this operation for Ann's future! Ann's wedding is going to be well-remembered if we can so arrange it with your valued assistance.

Sincerely, [signed] Martin

Jim's answer was discouraging. After investigation he reported that we must hire an off-duty fireman and an off-duty policeman, and must get written assent from all the nearby neighbors. Hence, we had to leave behind the 10,000 firecrackers that a Chinese friend gave us when I thoughtlessly inquired where one could buy them.

By the end of June our wonderful stay in Hawaii drew to an end, with a round of farewell parties given by some of our new-found friends as well as by Kay and John DeFrancis. I had used my ten months in nearly continuous scholarly work and had to buy a footlocker to ship back the new notes, translations, and carefully crafted manuscripts I had generated. But, of course, I didn't have as nearly a completed book as I had hoped to have when we started out. Kay, too, had an enriching experience with the college courses she took in anthropology, American literature, and Spanish. She wrote several reports to the Pleasantville school superintendent, for she was also on sabbatical leave and was supposed to account for her time. Surely she would be a better teacher for the growth and the knowledge attained while we were away.

After quick visits to my sister and family in Seattle, and a short time with Ann and Nollaig in Toronto, we flew off to Vienna. Kay wanted to go to Vienna because her great Uncle Harvey Wiley had studied there, and of course it is a city to see. I could only stay with Kay in Vienna for three days and then flew to London for the conference for which I had written a paper. Kay stayed a little longer and then flew to Amsterdam, where I was to meet her later. For the first time, she was to be alone in two strange cities.

In London I met up with other conference members—Doak Barnett, Mike Oksenberg, Don Klein, John Lewis, Rod MacFarquhar, and many other old and new friends. We were driven to Ditchley in Oxfordshire.

> Ditchley is a fine country house set in expansive gardens, which merge into open country side. It is now managed by a foundation as a conference center. They maintain the fine traditions, with a head butler, an efficient staff, semiformal dining. I was given the room which Winston Churchill used at times during the war as a security measure so as not to be always at Checkers or Blenheim. [Think of sleeping in the great man's bed!] In all the living rooms and the dining salons there were handsome, over life-size portraits of the ancestors; but I forget who they were! In the morning, promptly at 7:30 came a maid with tea—very strong and needing lots of sugar to go down—but refreshing. Breakfast at 8:30, and at 9:30 began our daily conference sessions.

My paper came on the first afternoon because it was a sort of historic background to the subject of CCP leadership. I tried to show how the experiences of the formative period from 1921 through 1928 shaped the party thereafter: how, in effect, a group of mostly young and patriotic Chinese intellectuals, gathered together in a "party" under a common ideology and a discipline, was transformed from idealistic reformers to toughened revolutionaries. I was able to give quasi-statistical evidence about the age groups, provincial origins, education, and previous occupations (if any) of 121 early leaders about whom some information was available. This group had a rich and rather successful experience in trying to organize labor and farmers, devise and spread propaganda, work in United Front organizations to steer them and recruit from them, or receive Russian military training, and to command troops—in short, to try to apply their Marxian and Leninist theories to the realities of Chinese society. They also had the harsh experience of pressing violence against their class enemies, and undergoing counterrepression from those enemies. The faint-hearted fled the party, and the toughened remaining leaders finally had to flee the cities for the protection of the mountainous countryside. They also had to break away from their dependency upon the Comintern for strategic and tactical guidance, and work out their own ways of surviving and growing. Such a series of events and experiences did, I am sure, have a powerful influence on the next decades of the Chinese Communist Party history.

Everyone was polite, but did my paper fall flat? It seems it was acceptable enough for publication in *The China Quarterly* and as a lead-off piece in the volume edited by John Lewis, *Leadership in Communist China*. I hope it influenced a generation of student readers to think of the CCP both in human terms and in historical ways.

In Amsterdam, Kay and I had a pleasant room in the American Hotel, overlooking a quiet canal, and with Kay's beloved private bath. We had three lovely days in Holland, visiting the wonderful museum of modern art, with its great collection of Van Gogh paintings and drawings. We took a tour to Delft, Leyden, Rotterdam, and The Hague; and we saw a flower auction one early morning. We also took a train on Sunday to Utrecht and walked about that quiet town with its eighteenth-century houses in rather narrow streets. Fine organ music came pealing out of the cathedral.

We had five weeks and two days in London, my favorite city. I spent nearly every working day in the Public Records Office, reading dispatches from China to the Foreign Office and the Colonial Office, and on the development of British policy toward the climactic events in China of 1925. I greatly enriched my knowledge and took a stack of notes. I was immersed in the papers and seemed to be living with the British gentlemen who were writing minutes on incoming dispatches and telegrams, or preparing responses and thinking about policy. That was the main thing I did during those last weeks of my sabbatical, though I did write a few more pages on my book. Kay, too, was writing on a novel, but sad to say, somewhere along the line she abandoned it. About 5:30, when I would get back to our hotel, we still had many hours of summer daylight in which to enjoy London's riches. Saturday afternoons and Sundays we spent in St. Paul's Cathedral, the National Gallery, the Tate, or Kew Gardens.

To end our sabbatical year of 1967–68, we toured Scotland before flying home from Glasgow, arriving exactly a year after our departure. This was the end of a most satisfying and enriching period for us both.

Kay and I returned to Pleasantville on August 28, and we had a little more than two weeks to get everything fixed for Ann's wedding, Saturday, September 14. Our house and grounds were a mess. The downstairs had to be repainted, and weeds were rampant in the grounds. For such sticklers as we, with many guests invited to come from afar, we had plenty to do. Ann came about a week in advance. She had been invited to teach at Glendon College, where Nollaig had been teaching for a year; in fact, each of them got an invitation from the other's school, so they were able to pick the most attractive deal. They decided on Toronto, and Ann had already moved up there. Hence it is that our Ann lives in Canada and is a Canadian, having lived in Toronto for twenty-five years.

By the time Ann arrived we had repainted the downstairs halls and put the gardens back into prime condition. I hadn't given up the idea of fireworks and suddenly thought of having sound effects instead of the real thing. A place in White Plains answered that, yes, they had a tape of firecrackers, so I went down to listen. It was the real thing, but the crackers went off too intermittently: it wasn't the terrific blast I wanted. I asked if they could double the noise and frequency, and they said they could. It was worth $50 to get things right. But when we tried it out on the church's tape recorder it was still too tepid. So I rushed around and rented a loudspeaker to hook up to the recorder.

The ceremony was set for four o'clock, so Ann and her parents and John went to the church early. Nol and his best man were to come separately with some of his other friends. Guests arrived, Mrs. Greitzer began playing wedding music, but the groom didn't appear. He had gotten lost! The music went on and on. Finally, the missing groom and best man arrived, so Ann took her father's arm and we marched up to the high ground behind the garden where the minister, Nol, and the best man were waiting. When Peter Samsom asked, "Who giveth this woman away?" I responded, "Her mother and I do" and descended the stone steps to where Kay, Nol's parents, and our guests were seated—nearly a hundred of them. And so Ann and Nol said the vows that they had written, and Peter pronounced them husband and wife.

For me, the high point of the wedding dinner came when our dear old friend Joe Jordan proposed his toast to the bride. He knew of our frustration at not having firecrackers, but not about our substitute scheme. So he brought a sparkler, which, with an explanation, he lit at the end of his toast. I signaled to our sound engineer, and so our blast of recorded fireworks burst forth, to the great enjoyment of our Chinese guests particularly. I can still see their delighted, laughing faces. Ann and Nol went from table to table to exchange toasts with the guests, and we followed after to thank them all for coming. It was a great occasion.

19

The Last Years of Teaching, 1968–1976

When I returned to Columbia I began to see the aftermath of the student upheaval of the spring of 1968, which had disrupted the campus, riven the faculty, and driven President Kirk from his post. For some reason there was considerable tension between top persons in the department of East Asian Languages and Cultures and the East Asian Institute. Since I had not been involved and was the senior person in both organizations, I thought it up to me to try to reconcile the antagonists. This I attempted to do by trying to find out what the grievances were and to get the men together for frank discussion. We created a Coordinating Committee of the senior members of both organizations that should meet occasionally, which happened for a while. Maybe my peace-making efforts had some effect, for things did quiet down. However, there was still a mood of radicalism on the campus, with the Vietnam War arousing strong discontent among students and some faculty. The trustees decided to invite Andrew Cordier to be president of the university, and he agreed only to an interim appointment. He asked to continue as dean of the School of International Affairs. He was known to be a great conciliator, and he did bring peace to the campus.

I resumed several academic duties outside my teaching. As a member of the board of the Inter-University Center for Chinese Language Study in Taiwan, I attended meetings in Stanford, and I was chosen to be chairman for a year. I was a member of the ACLS-SSRC Joint Committee on Sino-American Scholarly Communications and so attended meetings to plan activities and was frequently host to Chinese dignitaries visiting Columbia. I was also still chairman of the Ford Foundation committee that promoted academic relations with the Institute of Modern History, and a member of the Association for Asian Studies Nominating Committee for a couple of years. These duties did require a lot of domestic travel.

The East Asian Institute was now a very prestigious place, with John Lindbeck as director (drawn away from Harvard), Doak Barnett on contemporary China politics, Morton Fried, by now a senior anthropologist concentrating on China, and myself on the modern Chinese history side. We had a powerhouse on modern Japan, with Jim Morley, Donald Keene, Herb Passin, and several younger persons. We were still quite weak on Korea, to my regret. We had very good students, both in the two-year institute program and among those going on for the Ph.D. This meant lots of oral examinations and defenses of dissertations. Most of the students under my guidance are now teaching, and their dissertations, after more work, have been published. The institute's publications program of scholarly books on modern East Asia had grown substantially.

The Ford Foundation had given Columbia more than a million dollars in a five-year grant for our modern China program. Among its several purposes, the grant made it possible for us to invite visiting scholars to spend a year using Columbia's resources. Among the most happy selections—going back chronologically a little—was David Wilson, a former editor of *The China Quarterly*, who was doing a study of Great Britain and the Kuomintang during the 1920s. Columbia's library holdings and my offer to help him on the Chinese side made our institute a good place for him to finish up his dissertation under the School of Oriental and African Studies, University of London. The institute found an apartment for David and his sweet wife, Natasha, and their two young boys, Peter and Andrew, and of course we had them out to our house on several occasions. We have remained friends ever since. David went on to a brilliant career in the British Foreign Office, then as cabinet secretary, next as political adviser to the governor of Hong Kong, and then as Sir David Wilson, governor of Hong Kong. They are now Lord and Lady Wilson of Tillyorn.

Another of our visiting scholars was Roderick MacFarquhar, also a former editor of *The China Quarterly*, who spent a year working on a study of the origins of China's Cultural Revolution. The result was two books on the subject so far, both published by Columbia University Press as part of the East Asian Institute Studies Series. Much later, Rod ran for and became a member of the British Parliament, and then he was chosen by Harvard University to take their chair in Chinese politics. We made good use of the Ford grant in those cases. Some of the money also went to continue the Chinese Oral History Project.

I had several interesting students, among the many who were working on their Ph.D. programs. One was Lydia Holubnychy, of Ukrainian parentage, who I first met when she was a senior in the Columbia adult college program. She had to write a senior thesis and came to me for a suggestion. When I learned that she knew Russian and wanted to work in modern Chinese history, I suggested she do a study of Borodin—Michael Gruzenberg was his original name—and I outlined his importance in modern political history. Lydia fell to on that subject and did a very good thesis. Then she wanted an M.A. topic, and I suggested she study Comintern policy toward China up to the time Borodin left for China in 1923, as a way of deducing the policy he was trying to carry out. Again she did an excellent job. Later, Julie and I engaged Lydia to translate or abstract for us the growing Russian literature on the first Soviet aid mission, the one to China from 1923 to 1927. In all, she produced some two thousand pages of materials that were extremely valuable for the revision of the *Documents on Communism* volume in which Julie and I were then engaged.

Lydia had a very difficult life. Her husband, an aspiring academic, was a drunk. They were always in debt. When our institute gave Lydia a $2,500 grant, she wept in gratitude. The money we paid her for translating probably put the food on their table.

Li Yu-ning, who calls herself Bernadette, came to the East Asian Institute from Taiwan, where she had gotten her A.B. degree from National Taiwan University, the best of the colleges there. She was, however, of a mainlander family, and she had married the son of Professor Li Fang-kuei, who taught at the University of Washington. It was not a good marriage, and she divorced him. I remember that she took my regular lecture course on the history of modern China, and when we came near the end and I talked about the type of persons who organized, or first joined, the Chinese Communist Party, she was astonished to learn that they were idealistic people, not evil persons, which was the way she had come to think of them when growing up in Taiwan. She decided to study Ch'ü Ch'iu-pai's career for her dissertation. He was one who, almost by chance, went early to Soviet Russia and there was converted to Marxism. He even taught in the University of the Toilers of the East. He also was a journalist, and hence became a publicist for Russia. He was an important figure in the early Chinese Communist leadership, partly because he was bilingual and could interpret for Russian advisers who came to China in the 1920s.

In 1927, when the Comintern dictated that one of the original founders, Ch'en Tu-hsiu, should be blamed for the disaster of that year and expelled from the post of party secretary, Ch'ü was put in his place. He held that position for about a year before he was replaced. He then lived an underground existence, since the Nationalists were repressing fiercely their former collaborators. He was captured in 1935 and executed after a prison term during which he wrote an autobiographical account in which he stated that he felt he was most unsuited by temperament for the political role he had lived.

Bernadette's dissertation brought Ch'ü's life only up to mid-1928 when he went off to Moscow for the Sixth Congress of the CCP—the one at which he was replaced. Her work was so fine a job of historical reconstruction that the China Committee of the institute voted to give her a one-year stipend so she could go farther on the subject. She has become known everywhere as the Ch'ü Ch'iu-pai expert and is respected among scholars in China who specialize on CCP history.

She married Mason Gentzler, who taught Chinese literature at Columbia before he was snatched away by Sarah Lawrence College, and we see them frequently. For over twenty years she has been editor of *Chinese Studies in History*, a quarterly of translations. It is a valuable source for learning what Chinese historians in the People's Republic are writing (permitted to write?) about the past. Bernadette pays great respect to her old teacher, and he is very fond of her.

Another former student is Sister Madeleine Chi, a member of the Convent of the Sacred Heart, who had a Ph.D. from Fordham University and taught at Manhattanville College. One day this tall and slender Chinese lady came to my office and said she would like to enter the East Asian Institute and work for our certificate. Since the certificate program was at the M.A. level and she already had the Ph.D.—in fact, her dissertation had been published by the modern China program at Harvard—I wondered why she would want to take our program. She replied that she wanted the stimulation. So we enrolled her, and she did very well. She was multilingual. She has been a warm friend of Kay and me ever since. At one stage she held a position in the State Department's Historical Policy Research Office and used to write most interesting letters giving a worm's eye view of the bureaucracy. Later still, she went to Taiwan to join her "sisters" there in a Catholic middle school, of which she became dean for a time. She also began teaching European history at the Catholic University, Fu-jen. She has visited in our home, and we always looked for her when we were in Taiwan. Recently she has been teaching in China.

On the home front, we continued to see our dear friend from Chicago days, Edna Mandel, then Mrs. Georges Seligman. On the other side of the ledger, we had lost our dear friend Alice Openhym, who died after several strokes.

Paul Cressey, my brother-in-law, died suddenly in March 1969, though his Parkinson's disease had been gradually debilitating him. I went to Seattle to give a eulogy to Paul at the memorial service.

In mid-1969 I took off for another trip to Taiwan, under ACLS auspices, for our conference on Sino-American cultural relations, routing myself through London and then to Vientiane, Laos, where Hal was stationed under the Agency for International Development. I had a good week in London, spending five days in the Foreign Office archives. However, London without Kay was not the joyous place it had been when we were there together twice before. After visiting my brother and family in Laos, I went on to Taipei, for one of those busy times seeing many academic friends and then sitting through a boring conference in which the Chinese were proposing big plans and the Americans were being cautious, sensing that the Chinese side regarded us as potential pathways to big American money. We had our formal audience with Chiang Kai-shek and Madame Chiang. He was "made up" but seemed still in good health, and she was as beautiful and gracious as ever. After the conference was over, Fred Burkhard was furious at the emptiness of it all, though we did agree to promote small, substantive conferences of the same sort that had been so successful among the American and Chinese scientists.

It may have been about this time that I began to work toward a biography of Sun Yat-sen. Although I had stacks of notes on the period after his death, I didn't really know Sun Yat-sen's career in great detail. I began to read or reread articles and books on him and take notes systematically. I was hooked.

Dr. Sun was a very interesting person, bicultural, in the sense that China and the West had both contributed to the forming of his character, in perhaps roughly equal parts, and he lived as much of his life outside of China as within. After he became famous he produced several short autobiographical accounts, which differ. After his death his disciples began collecting his papers and writing reminiscences about him. Eventually there was an enormous literature from and about Sun Yat-sen in many languages, much more than any biographer could truly master. There is much hagiography, too. But as Harold Schiffrin's seminal 1968 work, *Sun Yat-sen and the Origins of the Chinese Revolution*, showed, there was much material about him in police records and in foreign governmental archives for, as a professed revolutionary, agitating in foreign countries, particularly in Southeast Asian colonies, he was considered a man to watch. And also, because of his self-image as the important leader of a new China, he attempted to influence foreign governments or to win their support: Japan, France, England, America. This means that governmental archives contain material from and about him as he roamed the world seeking money and support.

I asked the institute for a research leave in the second semester of 1970 to be spent at home in writing. It takes a long time to write a book. With all my other activities, and perhaps due to my slowness in composition, it was not till 1974 that I had a full-length book manuscript to submit to Columbia University Press. *Sun Yat-sen: Frustrated Patriot* was published in 1976, the year I retired. In the meantime, however, I had written a long article for *Encyclopedia Britannica*, 15th edition, entitled "China. History of: The Republican Period." As usual, I also wrote quite a few reviews and shorter articles.

I was elected vice president of the Association for Asian Studies in 1970 and automatically became president for 1971–72, and then "immediate past president" and member of the Executive Committee. These positions were not just honorary, they did take up time. I did a lot of traveling—to Ann Arbor, San Francisco, Washington, Philadelphia, San Diego, and other places, either for meetings or to address regional meetings of the association.

In December 1970 I went again to Taiwan via London, to attend the First Sino-American Conference on Mainland China, a result of our ACLS-SSRC Committee's earlier plea for the Chinese side to open up its collections of mainland China materials for use by the scholarly community. Again I spent a few days reading British Foreign Office materials, this time seeing some never-published papers seized in the Peking Raid, which David Wilson had drawn for me. These, and ones I found earlier or had discovered in the U.S. National Archives, would add much to the long-delayed revision of the Wilbur and How volume. There also was a set of photographs of the Chinese who were seized in the raid on the

Soviet Embassy in Peking, where they were in hiding. One was a marvelous picture of Li Ta-chao, the scholar-librarian, a convinced Marxist, founder of the Chinese Communist Party with Ch'en Tu-hsiu, and one of the first to join the KMT on Comintern insistence. He led the CCP and the KMT in Peking and was a humane and patriotic man. I wrote to Kay, "There he stands in Chinese long gown, about 45 years old, quite impassive for his photo. He was strangled about three weeks later. Another photo was not of a Communist, but a well-known KMT and perhaps rather anti-. He was strangled too. A third photo was of a young woman captured [in the embassy]. She could have been any postgraduate girl student. She may have been on the execution list, too." Later, I learned that she was executed, though in fact one of our documents showed that the local Communist Party considered her a "wavering leftist."

From Taipei I wrote Kay on December 16, 1970:

> The great "conference" is going full blast. Every moment taken up, and we are whisked from place to place by bus. You can't spend a cent, nor can you do anything on your own. This is due to excellent planning plus an overly full schedule. I hear the Gimo will receive us at tea tomorrow, maybe, so the schedule must be rearranged. Today there will be a lunch at which I am to respond briefly to a toast proposed by Dr. Ch'ien Ssu-liang, now president of Academia Sinica; then a series of exhibitions we go to in the afternoon; and then to dinner in the evening given by the Bureau of Investigation's "Ministry of Justice." So you get the picture.

Actually, the exhibitions of documentary materials in the KMT archives from the days of the collaboration of the KMT and CCP, before their fatal split in 1927, contained material I had not seen in my several periods of research there. The Bureau of Investigation showed masses of captured material from the CCP over a long span of time, and so did the Intelligence Bureau of the Ministry of Justice. In a way, these exhibits were to show foreign scholars how much more the Chinese side knew about the CCP than we so-called experts. But how easy or difficult access would be is hard to know.

An amusing thing happened even before the conference began. Mike Oksenberg, reading an official Chinese newspaper, found that the writer even described the conclusions we were going to reach, of course in highly anti-Communist terms. This got some of the Americans upset, and I had to go to a meeting with Mr. Wu Chen-ts'ai, head of the conference, to protest such a non-objective start. We wanted the press excluded from our meetings, but he had already told newspeople that they could attend. I'm not exactly sure how we worked through the conflict, but the American exponents of a free press wanted restrictions, and the side with a kept press and very little press freedom wanted the meetings open!

Some of us American professors paid a visit to the Inter-University Center to talk with some twenty of the American students, who wanted to query us why we were there, and why we would be attending such a conference. This was only two years after the student revolts of the late 1960s, and the Left still had a rosy picture of the CCP. The Cultural Revolution was not then seen by the American Left for all its cruelty. Our interlocutors were young folks from Princeton, Harvard, Columbia, Yale, the University of Washington, and so forth. We had what I hope was a free and frank discussion with them: How we hoped to open the way to access of materials, the importance of gradual development of contacts and reciprocity, of the relative freedom of our conference discussions, and so on. Also, I turned the discussion toward their own contacts with Chinese students. Were they making the best of that opportunity?

Our conference was again favored by a tea party given by President Chiang and the Madame, and this time it seems I was the foreign guest of honor, presumably as the senior scholar among us. President Chiang was certainly more feeble than when I had seen him eighteen months before. Mme. Chiang, though still beautiful and charming, was apparently in pain from a car accident about a year before. It was the last time I saw Chiang Kai-shek, for whom I hold no great respect as the leader of his people for two decades, though he may have done a better job after 1949, in his protected island retreat.

The Sino-American Conferences on Mainland China continued in alternate years in Taiwan and the United States, became more international, and got better and better in terms of scholarship. I attended several more of them. This allowed me to see my Taiwan friends every now and then, though I was politely retired a few years ago along with some others of the original participants, such as Franz Michael, which was sensible. Columbia never hosted one of the conferences because the East Asian Institute leadership didn't want it to be seen as tied to the Taiwan side and hence perhaps to limit our scholarly access to the mainland.

Sad to say, John Lindbeck died of a sudden heart attack one wintry morning in January 1971, when he was out shoveling snow. He was a very dynamic promoter of modern China studies worldwide and a fine person, of China missionary parents. His colleagues conducted a fitting memorial service at which John Fairbank, Doak Barnett, Alex Eckstein, Jim Anderson, Mark Mancall, and I spoke about our admiration and love for John. The East Asian Institute published a small but lovely memorial volume taken from the service.

An interesting thing happened at Columbia in the spring of 1971. Some of the students tried to shut down the university again. But this time other students started an opposition movement, "For Columbia." They distributed buttons so people could show their colors. Some faculty and students banded together to prevent the troublemakers from occupying buildings and preventing their use. We took shifts guarding the entrance to the International Affairs building and keeping out any students who didn't have a legitimate reason to be in there. This time the university remained open, for the troublemakers soon realized they had no public backing.

In March 1972 the annual meetings of the Association for Asian Studies were held in New York. As president I had to preside at the annual membership meeting. Because the "Young Turks" had made a lot of trouble the previous year when Cora DuBois was president, we hired a parliamentarian and prepared ourselves in other ways not to let this year's meeting get out of hand. Fortunately, it didn't. The Young Turks apparently had given up on trying to convert the AAS into an advocacy organization and had started a rival organization, the Committee of Concerned Asian Scholars.

I had to address the annual luncheon meeting of the association. I chose as my title "China and the Skeptical Eye." By then, America had taken the first halting steps toward improving relations with the People's Republic, a move I applauded, though I favored continuation of our protection of Taiwan. This was after the worst of the Cultural Revolution, but before it was over. There had been a lot of idealization of Communist China in America; and Mao, especially, was seen by leftists as a great hero. The burden of my talk was that it was up to scholars to search rigorously for the truth about Asian countries, in whatever discipline they pursued: "It is our job to try to understand Asian societies as they actually were in the past and as they really are today; to see them in great depth, in their multifaceted variety; to view them with sympathy but with historical perspective and detachment."

Our Chinese Oral History Project was well along, and I put out a brochure that would describe our work. We had interviewed in depth sixteen eminent Chinese, trying in each case to extract a full and truthful account of their careers, both through research and through cross-questioning done by younger historians, in some cases working with them over several years. Columbia's name and Franklin Ho's prestige had allowed us to work with such persons as generals Chang Fa-k'uei and Li Tsung-jen; eminent bankers Ch'en Kuang-fu and K'ung Hsiang-hsi (H. H. Kung); diplomats Wellington Koo and T. F. Tsiang; intellectual leaders Hu Shih, Li Huang, Li Shu-hua, and Tso Shun-sheng; important officials Ch'en Li-fu and Wu Kuo-chen; Mme. Huang Shen I-yun, widow of Huang Fu and a leader of women; an overseas Chinese leader, Choy Jun-ke; and my dear friend Ho Lien (Franklin Ho). Several of these persons gave to Columbia their papers or permitted us to microfilm them. I asked the interviewers— Julie How, T. K. Tong, and Crystal Seidman, as well as Minta Wong, Lillian Chu Chin, and Alice Kwong (all three former students of mine)—to write brief accounts of the main topics in each autobiography, and then I edited them and provided an introduction. More recently some of the autobiographies have been published and others pirated in Taiwan and on the mainland, but the work we did with Ford Foundation support has, I believe, enriched the sources for modern Chinese history. No one dictated what the subjects could say about their lives, or about Mao Tse-tung or Chiang Kai-shek, and no one censored them.

However, some of the memoirs—those of Dr. Wellington Koo, General Chang Fa-k'uei, and Mr. Ch'en Li-fu—were uncompleted, and our Ford grant for work on China was coming to an end. I prepared a grant proposal to the National Endowment for the Humanities to try to raise more money. This takes a lot of time, and one has to clear such a request through Columbia's Office of Projects and Grants, and get the signature of a higher officer. My effort in 1972 was unsuccessful, but the letter of rejection encouraged me to try again. I did and in 1973 was successful in getting a grant to the East Asian Institute of $75,000, which, after Columbia had taken its overhead, allowed Crystal Seidman two more years with Dr. Koo, though I had to make it clear that there would be no more thereafter. The Wellington Koo memoir turned out to be some 11,000 typewritten pages long, took seventeen years, and in all cost about a quarter of a million dollars. It was so extensive partly because of Dr. Koo's fine memory, and partly because he had saved his public papers and diary, and he directed Crystal to quote from them extensively. He gave his papers to Columbia, his alma mater, and they are a treasure trove for research and are much consulted by scholars, for Dr. Koo knew all important political persons during his years as China's ambassador to France and the League of Nations, to Great Britain during the war, and to the United States from 1945 to 1955.

Kay retired in June 1972 at age sixty-three, after teaching in Bedford Road School for fifteen years. She was greatly beloved by her students and admired by their parents for her effective and kindly teaching. After retirement, she became her own boss in the use of her time, devoting much to homemaking, gardening, reading, writing, and entertaining. She has always made a lovely home, and now she had more time for it.

Kay and I made a trip to Philadelphia to see Ida Pruitt. Ida grew up in China of missionary parents and was more Chinese than most "mishkids" because all of her early acquaintances were Chinese. Then she worked for many years in Peking at the PUMC as head of the social work department. It was then that she wrote the outstanding book *A Daughter of Han*, the life story of a peasant women whom Ida interviewed at length. We did not know about Ida when we were in Peking in the 1930s; our acquaintance really began when she persuaded me after the war to join the American Board of the Chinese Industrial Cooperative Movement, essentially a fundraising and publicity-generating organization in New York. Ida leaned toward the Communist movement, as did many American liberals during the civil war years—mainly from disgust at the corruption and incompetence of the Nationalist Government, and perhaps from the illusion that the party in Yenan was somehow democratic. (It did try to capture that word for itself.) Ida was, I think, trying to divert the last of INDUSCO funds to the work of Rewi Alley in Sandan, Kansu, where he ran a training school for cooperative workers. Later, I persuaded Ida to give the files of the American office to Columbia's manuscript library, where Douglas Reynolds, another of my Ph.D. students, spent a year in getting the papers coherently organized and catalogued, and then wrote a dissertation about the work of INDUSCO in China. They contain valuable reports on conditions in wartime China as sent in by field

THE LAST YEARS OF TEACHING, 1968–1976   229

workers. When Kay and I visited Ida in Philadelphia, she was leading a sheltered life amidst her Chinese things. I know a young historian, Marjory King, who became closely acquainted with Ida, has possession of her letters and other papers, and is working on a biography of her. Ida turns out in Marjory's dissertation to have been an extraordinarily interesting and complex person.

In 1973 the annual meetings of AAS were in Chicago, and Kay and I went back to see our old haunts. I visited Field Museum, but few of my old friends still worked there. George Quinby was now the head of the Anthropology Department. Some of the exhibits I had installed thirty years before were still there; but the spectacular Smith jade collection for which a special room had been made was dismantled, and a more appropriate exhibition showing Chinese jade through the ages, from Neolithic times onward, was on display. I suspect the museum sold most of the Smith collection of more recently carved, and very expensive, jades. They weren't appropriate for a natural history museum, anyway.

I took a trip to Taiwan in December 1973, for another Sino-American Conference on Mainland China. On this trip I was impressed by the growing prosperity and how well dressed the young people were, but also by the great anxiety among my academic friends concerning the dangers to the Republic of China that might result from President Nixon's trip to the mainland. Would the United States abandon Taiwan, after all?

Kay and I had a lovely trip to Spain in May 1974 after another busy end of an academic year. We enjoyed thirteen days of art and architecture in Madrid, Toledo, Granada, and Seville, among other wonderful places. Then on to London, where we again went to our favorite museums and spent part of June 5, Kay's sixty-fifth birthday—though one would think she was only forty-five!—in Kew Gardens.

We had to hurry home because John was to be married on June 14 to Shirley Jarmell. We were delighted that John had found such a nice girl to be his wife and would like to have had the wedding in our church, but she, being Jewish, wasn't ready for that, preferring to have a civil wedding in Newark, which had once been her home. So it was arranged that Ann and Nol from Toronto, and John, Kay, and I would all meet Shirley and her father for breakfast in Newark and then go over to the city office building where a judge would tie the knot. However, we waited from about nine in the morning till about three in the afternoon for a judge to be free. The ceremony was in his courtroom, and Shirley's father and Kay stood up as witnesses. When it was all over, about four, we were all exhausted. The only place to sit while we waited for a judge was in a telephone booth. Poor Mr. Jarmell was in failing health. There was no excuse, only bureaucratic thoughtlessness, for such a sorry procedure of keeping a couple and their relatives waiting six hours for a marriage. Kay wrote an angry piece for the Newark newspaper to describe the situation.

I became involved in fundraising for East Asian studies at Columbia in the autumn of 1974, an involvement that was to go on for years. It began when Dean

Harvey Picker of the School of International Affairs encouraged Gerry Curtis (then the director of the institute), Jim Morley, and me to get organized to raise money for the East Asian Institute, and Peter Buchanan, the university's officer for fundraising, gave us advice. However, the Department of East Asian Languages and Cultures, of which I was a member, also wanted us to raise money for them—or so it seemed. No one in the department, except for me, wanted to be involved, or maybe they were afraid to try. I remember that Hans Bielenstein, departmental chairman at the time, wanted an equal division of everything that was raised, no matter who raised it. This wouldn't work, and the institute group went ahead on its own. It was one of those academic messes! We created an advisory council of persons whom Peter and Harvey thought could be helpful in leading us to contributors, and who might themselves contribute, but except for a few meetings not much came of the advisory committee, though one person, Tristan Beeplat, did try to induce some executives with businesses in Asia to give us company money. However, that didn't have much appeal. Everything was quite discouraging. A couple of years later things brightened up.

I became sort of an adviser to Eugene Loh at the Chinese Cultural Center, attached to the information office in New York of the government of the Republic of China on Taiwan. I joined the board of the Cultural Center and for several years was chairman of a committee giving fellowships to Americans to spend about a year for study in Taiwan. The committee made its final decisions by telephone conference. I became a very good friend of Eugene Loh, who had attended Columbia's School of Journalism, and whose family was growing up American. This friendship went on even though years later, when the U.S. government recognized the People's Republic, he became persona non grata and had to leave the country. For a while he was trade representative in Austria, and we visited him in Vienna. He then became ambassador of the Republic of China in Guatemala, and later ambassador to the Republic of South Africa.

In May 1975 I received a tragic letter. It began, "Lydia is no more. She committed suicide." The letter was from Visvold Holubnychy, her husband. Lydia was one of my favorite students, and I had guided her through her senior thesis, her M.A., and work on her dissertation. I asked her husband to send me the draft of her dissertation, which I had edited, as I wished to publish it posthumously; and I also asked him to save all Lydia's academic papers as I would try to get them preserved in Columbia's Rare Book and Manuscript Library. This was done, and later I oversaw the publication of *Michael Borodin and the Chinese Revolution, 1923–1925*, by Lydia Holubnychy, for which I wrote a prefatory note in November 1978. It was done by University Microfilm as a way to show her draft directly. In book form it came to 512 pages.

We had an invitation to visit Sam and Lucy Chu in Columbus, Ohio. Sam was my first Ph.D., and we had attended their wedding. Lucy, that powerhouse, taught music and Chinese cooking and had scads of students. We went there at the end of June 1975. Elaine and Laura came home from school and immediately went to one of the grand pianos (the house held three!) and began practicing. In the evening Lucy and the girls played for us movements from Mozart's Triple Piano Concerto, which they were to play soon with the Cincinnati Symphony Orchestra in its regular concert series. I think the girls were fifteen and thirteen years old, and they were very talented. One went to Yale and the other to Indiana to continue their music.

In the summer of 1975 we planned a vacation for all our family—John and Shirley, Ann and Nol, and Kay and me—in Cape Cod, where we had taken the kids several times when they were younger. We rented a cottage for a week in North Truro, a bit farther out on the Cape from Wellfleet. We had scarcely returned from Columbus when Ann flew down from Toronto. Five of us, less Nol, were about to start our drive on the morning of Saturday, July 6, when I heard the telephone ring. I went back into the house, and Pauline Ho was on the phone telling me that her father, my dear friend Franklin Ho, had died the day before. He was eighty years old. She asked if I would speak at his funeral service, and of course I would, though it meant flying back from the Cape for a day. I had to compose a eulogy, and could do so with no reservations. The funeral was a Christian one and of Western pattern, very different from one I attended a few weeks later.

After we got home from Cape Cod I spent a lot of time in August and September at the office working with Julie How on the revision of our book. We had agreed to divide our work chronologically, with me writing the first part, up to mid-1926 when the Northern Expedition began, and she writing the part dealing with Russian aid to Feng Yu-hsiang, and the Northern Expedition till about mid-1927. We would each be responsible for editing those documents that related to the periods on which we were writing. This was a fair division in terms of work involved and led from our separate strengths. By now the material translated by Lydia Holubnychy and coming from recent Russian scholarship or reminiscences of participants greatly enriched our materials. We could supplement our Chinese and Western sources with this Russian material. We criticized each other's drafts and called attention to topics overlooked.

My friend Professor Kuo Ting-yee died in September 1975. Professor Ho and I had been instrumental in helping to arrange three years of fellowships for him, first at the East-West Center in Honolulu, then at John Fairbank's shop in Cambridge, then at the East Asian Institute of Columbia. He was to work on his history of modern China. For reasons that I do not understand, he had given up the directorship of the Institute of Modern History in Academia Sinica. Perhaps he was forced out by academic rivalries or quit in disgust because of them.

The funeral was held at a well-known funeral parlor in Manhattan. We were sent up to the third floor to a nice room with many flowers, and in the far corner Professor Kuo was lying on a couch, face toward the room, looking very natural as if in sleep, but wearing his glasses. Grouped at the foot of the couch were two daughters-in-law and five grandchildren, all on their knees. Mrs. Kuo was beside the couch, weeping and caressing Kuo *Hsien-sheng's* hands, and the three sons were standing about her, weeping and also consoling her. This emotional scene was carried on for about ten minutes, with all the guests observing solemnly—about thirty I would say, and at that time I was one of only two or three foreigners. A photographer was snapping this intimate scene and also photographing the audience.

Then the sons escorted Mrs. Kuo to a couch and an older woman in black consoled her. The three sons went among the guests, shaking their hands and thanking them, but themselves sobbing and wiping their tears. Then the guests filed up in groups to stand reverently before Professor Kuo, each after a few moments making three bows in farewell. After that ceremony some left and some stood about chatting quietly. It was not necessary, nor apparently expected, that all would stay until the entire ceremony was over.

The word of Professor Kuo's death had spread rapidly in the Chinese community, but most of the people there were scholars. I saw no one in an official capacity. Chang Peng-yuan had hurried up from Washington with P. K. Yu and Chi Pei-feng. Wu Chang-chuan and Bernadette Li, T. K. Tong and Cynthia Hu were there, among my acquaintances, and many elderly Chinese. Mrs. Ho, who had so recently lost her own husband, was there, seemingly very composed. It was a strange but collegial farewell to an old friend. I departed as the group began to thin out.

Our Oral History work with Dr. Koo came to an end in the autumn. On May 28, 1976, we had a celebration when Dr. Koo made the formal presentation, with Columbia's President McGill receiving the twenty or so volumes. We got good publicity from the event, and the story appeared in the Taiwan press. Dr. Koo gave Columbia his enormous collection of diplomatic papers, diaries, and minutes that he had dictated immediately after a conversation with someone of importance.

The year 1976 was a busy one for me, for I formally retired from teaching. The Association for Asian Studies met in Toronto, and Kay and I went because Ann was there. We were able to introduce Ann to some professors in my field who teach in Toronto.

Kay and John Irwin, Tim and Jane, came from New Zealand to visit us from April 25–30, and Ann and Nol came down, too. The occasion was a dinner that my friends at Columbia gave in my honor on April 29. It was suggested I wear a black tie and tux, which I did. It was a large gathering, including quite a few Chinese friends (Eugene Loh took a table). Speeches and me having to thank everyone for coming; my Kay all dressed up and looking great (we have an album about it).

Ted deBary, the power in the Department of East Asian Languages and Cultures, asked me if I would continue to teach one seminar after retiring, but I declined because I was sixty-eight years old and had twenty-nine years of teaching behind me. But the Development Office wanted me to continue working on fundraising, and by now I had two specific projects, to raise $100,000 each for fellowships in the name of L. Carrington Goodrich and V. K. Wellington Koo. So Peter Buchanan offered to pay me half salary to come in three days a week to help his office and work on those fellowships.

We attended a similar retirement dinner in May for my friend Beth Moore, who was ending her chairpersonship of the American Board for Christian Higher Education in Asia. There was a lot of glitter to that party at Hotel Pierre.

The name S. K. Chow comes into my notebook in May. He had been China's ambassador to the United States. We became friends and have kept in touch ever since. He served for many years as the Republic of China's ambassador to the Vatican, the only ambassadorial post in Europe for the ROC. He finally gave up the post in 1991, and he died July 31, 1992.

I took a trip to Taiwan from June 1 to 16, 1976, for another of those conferences, but this time also in pursuit of money from Columbia alumni, and from friends and admirers of Dr. Wellington Koo. Early on I was entertained by Dr. Koo's son, who was in business, and I met Nancy Huang, publisher of one of the English-language newspapers and head of the Columbia Alumni Association, which was rather dormant. Also I met several former subordinates of Dr. Koo. I worked on several fronts. One was to get the Columbia alumni together and to plant the idea of their help for China studies. Another was to see several Chinese officials, among them the minister of education and the minister of foreign affairs, to plant the idea of the Chinese government giving Columbia half a million dollars toward a Wellington Koo chair. However, I was there too short a time to bring about any concrete results, and half my time was taken up by the Sino-American Conference.

The day after I returned from Taipei, Jack and Caroline Service came for a few days. A lovely visit. By then my book on Sun Yat-sen was in galley proof, and Jack read it through, finding errors I had missed. Columbia University Press published the book in the autumn of 1976. It is not a full biography, though a reader can get from its pages a clear idea of the career of Dr. Sun, and probably of his personality. The book concentrates on two themes, Dr. Sun's constant, and ingenious, search for money—lots of money—for his revolutionary efforts, first to overthrow the Manchu dynasty, then to replace the warlord rulers in Peking by a government of his own; and second, his repeated efforts to involve one or another of the powers or foreign individuals in his causes—Japan, Great Britain, France, the United States, even tsarist Russia. These two themes help to explain, but only in part, his final courting of Soviet Russia and his ready acceptance of its financial aid, advisers, and arms from 1923 till his death in early 1925. The effects of this brief international encounter were far-reaching for China.

The International Congress of Orientalists met in Mexico City from July 31 to August 10, 1976, and Kay and I decided to attend. It was a chance for her to get back to the country, though not the particular region, where she had spent some of her youth.

Because of the smog and crowding, we didn't find Mexico City attractive, and our first impressions were of inefficiency and great rudeness in our hotel, and mix-up in tour arrangements. However, we moved to a different hotel, a quiet old one on the great ancient square with its cathedral on the north, and government buildings on two other sides. Before the conference began we found the National Anthropological Museum, a most magnificent building and a breathtaking exhibition of the antiquities of Mexico. It is one of the great museums of the world. As I wrote, "There are few archaeological museums I have visited which gave me such a thrill, the thrill of discovering a new cultural world—something I experienced in Athens at its great museum of Greek antiquities, and in Denmark at the ethnological museum devoted to man in the circumpolar world."

The International Congress was held in the Medical Center, which we could reach from our hotel conveniently by the new and really wonderful subway. Once there, we received invitations to various receptions and performances. During the next five and a half days, Tuesday through Sunday, we met in plenary or separate regional sessions. I saw many friends, Chinese, Japanese, French, and Americans, but no Russians that I knew. I saw Irene Eber of Israel and Marina Thorberg of Sweden, who had studied with me at Columbia, and Professor Flora Botton, the organizer of the China section of the conference, which probably was the largest. I met Herbert Franke of Hamburg and Professor Makkaris and Dr. Sakuto Matsui of Australia, and a very nice Polish Sinologist, Stanislaw Kuczera, who worked in the Institute of Oriental Studies in Moscow. He told me that my former Polish student, Rene Goldman, had sent him a copy of the slavery book. During the course of the congress more and more facts came to light that Chinese from the Republic of China had been denied visas to enter Mexico even though they had received invitations and even were on the program. This was clearly a political move of the Mexican government to discriminate against the scholars from Taiwan. This aroused the ire of many of the scholars from America and other Western countries as being against the principles of nonpolitical scholarship, and a resolution was drawn up by Professor Hungda Ch'iu and signed by many of us, my name being prominent because I was first signer on one of the sheets, which was then placed first. The resolution was implicitly critical of the Mexican government for discriminating against a group of scholars, and it urged that in future congresses no such discrimination be permitted. (When the congress had been held in the United States nine years earlier, the American organizing committee had insisted that the U.S. State Department give visas to Chinese from both sides.) The resolution was sent to the president of the congress and was debated and then emasculated in the executive and advisory committee on the night before the congress closed. Ted DeBary, who was on the international steering committee, protested to no avail in that meeting, and then I was asked to voice our protest at the final plenary session. The president, a Mexican woman scholar, granted me the floor, and I read our protest. To my surprise a storm of applause greeted my speech. That served as a rebuke to the Mexican Foreign Office's action, though it was too late to remedy the discrimination. Many persons congratulated me after that brief speech. Word of it surely reached Taiwan.

The International Congress of Orientalists had a long tradition. This was its thirtieth triennial meeting. But the notion of Oriental had been stretched under pressure from Soviet Russia, and the name changed to include many Third World countries. Russia had tried, sometime before, to dominate the congress, in fact, to make it a Cold War instrument. As I wrote after the congress closed: "I fear the International Congress of Orientalists, under its new name, will gradually become a Third World conclave and lose its scholarly character."

A few days later I went up to Cambridge to an organizing conference that John Fairbank called in preparation for a volume of the *Cambridge History of China*, which he was editing. This one, volume 12, would be on the Republican period. There I saw many friends who worked on the same period as I did. We all had accepted assignments and were supposed to bring drafts of our chapters, or at least outlines. The conference was devoted to discussing these drafts. My chapter was to be about the period in the mid-1920s, when the Nationalists came to power in China.

20

Beginning Retirement,
1976–1979

Columbia's personnel office informed me of the advantages of being an emeritus professor, a status conferred on me when I retired on July 1, 1976. I would still carry a card allowing me to use the university libraries, and would stay on the university's mailing lists. I could continue membership in the Faculty Club, and so forth. The East Asian Institute made me a Senior Research Associate and continued to provide an office, though I insisted on going into a small one, and secretarial help while I was raising money. Though I didn't conduct any more classes, some students continued to see me about their research, and I still participated in a few Ph.D. examinations. I had been on the faculty for twenty-nine years, though three of them had been sabbaticals and I had had one half-year research leave, so I actually had classes for fifty-one semesters and two summer sessions. That surely was enough.

During that time I had hundreds of students. I kept individual records on students in my classes, in most cases rather cursory records, and there were six loose-leaf notebooks of those personnel pages that I later turned over to Special Collections Library. I also kept a file drawer on students who completed the M.A. under my guidance, and another for students who worked toward, or gained, the Ph.D. With many of those students I maintained a correspondence, either about their scholarly work, or concerning letters of recommendation they wanted from me. Quite a number of the M.A. persons went into government work, and most of the Ph.D.s went into teaching. I will mention some of them and the positions they held at the time of this writing.

I had a few older students, who had broken off their studies during the war and resumed them afterward. One was Edwin Beal Jr., who worked in the Chinese Section, Orientalia Division, Library of Congress. He did a dissertation on the origins of the *likin* tax, one of the major ways the suppression of the Taip'ing Rebellion was financed. We have long been friends. Another was my old friend John DeFrancis, who did a dissertation on language reform in China. He has stayed on the broader subject of Chinese linguistics. After much difficulty because of his association with Owen Lattimore at Johns Hopkins, he found a permanent teaching position at the University of Hawaii. Then there was Olga Lang, who wrote on Pa Chin, the famous Chinese novelist who was so popular with students when she and her husband, Karl August Wittfogel, were in China in 1935–36. She, too, continued to be my friend, though she became afflicted by Alzheimer's disease and died. Harriet Mills returned to Columbia after imprisonment by the People's Republic and completed here Ph.D. on Lu Hsün. I was a member of her doctoral committee. Besides these older students, I also helped on the dissertations of some Catholic fathers who were under Carrington Goodrich's guidance.

Two exceptional students had come through Columbia College and wartime intensive language training and then into the Department of Chinese and Japanese for graduate study—Wm. Theodore DeBary and Donald Keene. As a member of the departmental faculty, I participated in their doctoral examinations. They won faculty appointments and grew in eminence until each became a University Professor, the highest academic rank at Columbia. They brought great prestige to our department.

I have already written about my close relationship with Bernadette Yu-ning Li Gentzler. She teaches at St. John's University. Also I have told about Lydia Holubnychy. Our good friend Rhoda Weidenbaum, one of my first M.A. students, much later went on to the Ph.D. at University of Connecticut. She wangled me onto her dissertation committee. The dissertation was a psychobiography of Chou En-lai in his early years. I have also written of Julie How, who did a classic study on Ch'en Tu-hsiu, the founder of the Chinese Communist Party, as her history M.A.

My first Ph.D. "from scratch," so to speak, was Samuel Chu, now my good friend, who wrote on Chang Ch'ien, a pioneer Chinese modernizer. He teaches at Ohio State University. Jim Harrison wrote a dissertation on Chinese Communist historiography concerning the peasant movement in China, and later wrote a much admired history of the Chinese Communist Party, *The Long March to Power*. He teaches at Hunter College. Richard Howard became a specialist on the Chinese conservative reformer K'ang Yu-wei and is well known for his knowledge of K'ang's career and thought. He succeeded Ed Beal in the Chinese Section of the Library of Congress. Allen Linden did his dissertation on Chinese educational reform under the Nationalist Government and now teaches at the University of New Hampshire. Tom Kennedy, a tall Marine officer who spent seven years in Taiwan in intelligence work, some of it in following the activities of the

Shanghai Arsenal, decided to do a dissertation on the history of that establishment, set up as part of China's self-strengthening effort after the Taiping Rebellion and the Second Anglo-Chinese War. He now teaches at Washington State
University and has been a dean there.

Another early student was Chun-tu Hsueh, now retired from teaching political
science at the University of Maryland, to whom I suggested his dissertation
topic—on the revolutionary Huang Hsing. Professor Hsueh is now the authority
on this man, who should share honors with Sun Yat-sen for sparking the 1911
Revolution. Paula Johnson I have mentioned previously. Recently she has had a
consultantship with the World Bank, going to China to look into the feasibility of
projects for which China seeks loans. She has had many such missions and been
in many parts of China. Robert Lee, an American of Chinese ancestry, did a
pioneering study of the Chinese occupation of the Manchurian frontier during
the Ch'ing dynasty, a splendid job, which John Fairbank published in the Harvard East Asian Monographs series.

Charlotte Behan came from Michigan State and married Robert Hegel, a
student specializing in Chinese literature. I suggested that she study the women's
emancipation movement in China, which she did, but she had difficulty in getting the work published. She teaches at the University of Kentucky. Beautiful
Mrs. Carol Corder Andrews did her dissertation on the Chinese peasant movement in the 1920s under my inspiration, though she did it in the political science
department. Both Carol and Charlotte had broken marriages. Jane Price Lauden
wrote on the Chinese Communists' internal educational system for training cad-
res. However, she moved into the computer business. Larry Shyu, a mainlander
from Taiwan, did his dissertation on the wartime People's Political Council and
then taught at the University of New Brunswick; and Britten Dean studied Amer-
ican-Chinese relations in the 1860s and teaches in one of the state colleges in
California.

Hillel Soloman and Kai-fu Tsao earned the Ph.D. under my encouragement.
Hillel teaches at the University of South Carolina, while Dr. Tsao has retired
from college teaching. Douglas Reynolds, after getting the files of the American
office of the Chinese Industrial Cooperative Movement into shape, wrote a dissertation about that wartime movement in China. It was very critical of the
Nationalist Government for obstructionism and graft, based on what he found in
the files. Doug now teaches at Georgia State University. His wife, Carol, also
completed a dissertation, but after I retired. They became quite immersed in Japanese culture through long stays in Tokyo but maintained their interest in China
and skill in Chinese. Carol won a position in the U.S. Foreign Service and was
posted in Japan and then in Peking.

Several other students went into government work. One of the first was Paul
Kreisberg, who took the institute certificate and the M.A. under my guidance,
went into the Foreign Service as a China specialist, had a long career around the
fringes of China and in Taiwan, and ended as an ambassador somewhere before

retiring. Burton Levin, another certificate holder and China specialist in the Foreign Service, became the American ambassador in Burma, probably his last post, and a difficult one. I read a *New Yorker* article on the current situation in Burma that lauded him. Another institute student, Harvey Feldman, an international relations specialist, remembered me warmly when I met him after his retirement as ambassador in New Guinea, a post he asked for because it was so exotic. Then there was Daniel Kiang, American born, who worked toward the Ph.D., then moved into the Foreign Service. We saw him in London, and later in Taipei, but I have lost touch with him. The same for Jack Froebe, who disappeared into the State Department. This doesn't exhaust the list of my former students in the United States government.

I had three Chinese students from Hong Kong, all of whom earned the Ph.D. and regard me as their permanent mentor in true Chinese fashion. All have become American citizens, I believe. Gilbert Chan (Chen Fu-lin), who taught at Miami University in Oxford, Ohio, undertook at my suggestion to study the career of Liao Chung-k'ai, Dr. Sun Yat-sen's right-hand man during his last years. He has published many articles on Liao, and soon a chronological biography done in collaboration with a mainland scholar will be out. Unfortunately Gilbert had to give up teaching in America. Another is Ka-che Yip, whose dissertation on the Anti-Christian Movement in China of the 1920s was published with some delay, but it won him tenure at the University of Maryland, Baltimore. The third is Odoric Wou, who teaches at Rutgers. He did a dissertation on the Chinese warlord Wu P'ei-fu, published in the institute's Studies Series. He is a fine scholar and has since done basic research in Honan Province, using Chinese Communist archives on the wartime struggles of the party to survive there—truly obscure materials. I read his excellent University Seminar paper on how the Communist revolution of the 1940s was actually carried out in several villages in Honan, quite in contradiction to the theories of generalizers on peasant revolution. Stanford published his book, *Mobilizing the Masses: Building Revolution in Henan* (1994).

Two younger scholars who started with me but finished their dissertations after I had retired are Josh Fogel and Bill Rowe. Josh became good at Japanese and has made a reputation as a translator of Japanese historical work on China. After teaching for a few years at Harvard, he took a position at the University of California, Santa Barbara. Bill Rowe became interested in metropolitan China in my seminar and fastened on Hankow as a great commercial center worthy of study. He now has two great books on Hankow in the late nineteenth century—social histories they are. He won the position on Chinese history at the Johns Hopkins University out of two hundred applicants. Josh and Bill are close friends, and while they were still studying at Columbia they organized a Festschrift in my honor. They got a number of my former students to write chapters, and Anita O'Brien, another M.A. student, was the editor. By then, Anita was the institute's editor and production manager. The book came out in 1979, and other former students and friends contributed toward publication costs. It is entitled *Perspectives on a Changing China: Essays in Honor of Professor C. Martin Wilbur on the Occasion of His Retirement.*

To end this affectionate catalogue I'll mention a few others, none of whom I can claim as "my student" to the end of their graduate work. One is Merle Goldman, whom I taught long ago as an undergraduate at Sarah Lawrence College. Her going into modern China studies was partly due to the interest I sparked in her. She got her doctorate at Harvard and is now the leading authority on modern intellectuals in China and how they have fared under the Communist regime. I read a fine article by her in the *New York Review of Books*, November 9, 1989. Second, David Keightley, who started graduate work with an interest in modern China, and hence with me, but then switched to ancient China under the influence of Hans Bielenstein's teaching. David is a professor at the University of California, Berkeley, and is the leading authority on Shang history, that is, China's first well-documented dynasty. Recently he won a MacArthur award, and I was one of those who wrote an evaluation of him, as did Jack Service. In his book *Sources of Shang History* he mentions the influence of Bielenstein and Wilbur thus: "And my awareness of the importance of historiographical problems, the rigor with which they should be pursued, and the rewards of doing so owes much to Hans Bielenstein and C. Martin Wilbur, my teachers at Columbia University."

Mike Oksenberg says he decided to come to the East Asian Institute after talking with me when I was director. He is a political scientist and took work with me, though his mentor was Doak Barnett, a star on the East Asian Institute faculty. For a while Mike was a key member of our faculty, but then he decided to move to the University of Michigan. Later he was on President Carter's National Security Council as the China expert and was closely involved in the negotiations for American recognition of the People's Republic of China instead of the Republic of China. Then he became president of the East-West Center in Honolulu. Ken Lieberthal came to Columbia to do graduate work in political science and is another disciple of Doak Barnett, but he did take work with me. Recently I heard him give a talk at Swarthmore College, and he said kind things about me as his teacher, but mentioned I was one whose exams he feared. He also teaches at Michigan. Both men appear frequently on TV, interpreting developments in China, and are important promoters of China studies, as was Doak Barnett. Michael Gasster took a summer session course with me, got fired up enough to decide to specialize on China, and went to the University of Washington for his Ph.D. He now lives in New York and teaches at Rutgers. Beatrice Bartlet took a course with me, then went to Yale for the Ph.D. Now she is a professor at Yale and the foremost Western authority on "high Ch'ing" and Ch'ing dynasty documents.

Others who I remember well because of their fine M.A. theses are Alice Kwong Bolocan, Margaret Chan, Lillian Chu Chin, Cheng Hsi-ling (teaching at Iowa State University), Pauline Ho, and Anita O'Brien. One could add that group of scholars from Taiwan who studied with me, probably more to hear English than about modern history: Chiang Yung-ching, Li Yun-han, Chang Peng-yuan, Chang Yu-fa, Hsia Pei-jan, and Su Yun-feng.

Most of the above former students are good friends of mine now, and the Americans call me by my first name, though the Chinese ones—except for Sister Madeleine Chi—all call me Professor Wilbur. Chinese tradition has no room for intimacy across generations.

The idea of trying to raise a fund for a scholarship in honor of L. Carrington Goodrich came to me, and I asked his permission to do so. He had been head of the department of Chinese and Japanese for many years, had supervised my dissertation, helped me get that job at Field Museum, and then offered me my position at Columbia. Mrs. Goodrich helped on the fellowship enthusiastically. The goal was $100,000, and we got good boosts from their more wealthy friends, such as Mrs. Sidney Gamble and her daughter, and Mr. Dodge, who had a foundation. Among them, I think we got some $30,000. Then I was able to persuade the director of the China International Foundation, an Oberlin graduate with whom I had run cross-country, to give $10,000, and the head of the Markle Foundation to chip in $4,000. All the rest came in smaller amounts from individuals—relatives, friends, and academic colleagues. To raise this part took a great deal of writing (I used the Goodrich's Christmas list) and making calls. Five ladies in Riverdale organized themselves to call on friends of the Goodriches there. Fortunately, I had a good secretary, and together we watched the money come in and wrote the letters of thanks. Gradually we approached the goal. Mrs. Goodrich herself was a generous contributor. When we had reached the goal we had a fine party in the Faculty Room of Low Library, and there is a picture of Carrington, wreathed in smiles, cutting the cake as I stood by. Anne Goodrich adds to the fund from time to time. It is the only fellowship the Department of East Asian Languages and Cultures can claim as its own.

Carrington died on August 10, 1986, at the age of ninety-one. I wrote a brief obituary for *The Journal of Asian Studies*. Anne has continued to be our warm friend and writes to us several times a year. In one letter she told me that the fellowship had grown to about $179,000 and provides a stipend of about $9,000. I sent her a picture of Carrington, and the one of us together at the celebration party. In response she wrote:

> PS. In my enthusiasm over the portrait of Carrington I forgot to mention my enthusiasm over the picture of Marty and Carrington cutting the celebration cake. It is a beautiful picture of two unusually beautiful, charming, lovable gentlemen. I shall cherish it both for the event it recalls and the person who made the event possible. If for no other reason, Marty, I'll always love you for what you did.

The effort to raise money for a V. K. Wellington Koo fellowship started with a generous gift from a wealthy classmate, Mr. Manville, who contributed $30,000, and his wife added $5,000. This excellent start was arranged by Peter Buchanan, who always wanted an effort like this to start with some convincing first major contribution. Mrs. Koo had asked two Chinese friends, Mr. Morley Chow and another gentleman, to help with the Chinese world, where Dr. Koo had many well-to-do friends. Strange to say, even though in the end we got many good gifts from Chinese, they were very slow to contribute. Mr. Chow expressed puzzlement one time, saying many of the people he was after would lose thousands of dollars in one evening's mah-jongg. We did get $10,000 from General Ho Shilai, with prodding from General Wedemeyer, whose help Dean Picker and I had solicited, and with the help of Professor C. T. Hu. Mrs. Koo's children contributed $10,000 through a foundation. Another bloc of money came from Dr. Koo's friends and former associates, now retired in Taiwan. I directly planted that idea in my money-raising excursion in 1977. The rest came in gifts ranging from $25 to some thousands. We had another celebration of the establishment of this fellowship, which I lodged in the East Asian Institute. The first recipient was a Chinese young man from Taiwan (of mainland family) who had studied in the Russian Institute, and whose dissertation dealt with Sino-Russian relations. He returned to Taiwan and is a professor in Cheng-chi University. Since then, half a dozen dissertation-writing students have received the fellowship, one being Caroline Tsai, a Taiwanese, writing on the Japanese colonial administration in Taiwan.

Dr. Koo died in 1985, just short of his one hundredth birthday (by Chinese count—ninety-nine years by ours), and his daughter, Mrs. Patricia Tsien, asked me to give a eulogy at his memorial service. I made sure to start my speech with some words of praise for Dr. Koo by Columbia's president, Dr. Michael Sovern (I wrote the passage and then had Peter Buchanan secure the president's approval). The other main memorialist was Dr. Frederick Chien, the Republic of China's representative in Washington.

It gives a lot of satisfaction to have helped students with the heavy expenses of graduate study with income from those two fellowships.

My friendship with Jennie Wu of the U.S. Educational Foundation in China helped me to get a summer in Taiwan in 1977 as a refresher Fulbrighter. It was her idea, and I was invited; that is, I didn't have to apply. I used the time for three main purposes. One was to study documents that Chiang Yung-ching brought up from the KMT archives—tough work for me, as most of it was in fairly cursive script. A second was to learn all I could about contemporary Taiwan in a social and cultural sense, for a chapter I was to contribute to a book on the Republic of China being edited by Ramon Myers, and which I entitled "The Human Dimensions and Its Problems." For this I had another JCRR tour, studied how population control was coming along (very successful), read recent field studies, and interviewed lots of Chinese and a few knowledgeable Westerners. I also got acquainted with Marie-Claire Bergère, who was studying Chinese intensively. She teaches Chinese history in Paris, and we see one another from time to time at conferences.

The third use of my two months on the island was to raise money for Columbia. There was an alumni association, to whom I appealed for the Koo fellowship, but really I was after government money, too. I thought it was time that the government that had received so much help from the United States, both for its defense and for its economic development, and now was secure and becoming wealthy, really ought to reciprocate a bit. I talked this line with several top officials I knew, but the real helper was S. K. Chow, who had a nonportfolio position in the cabinet. He came over to the YMCA where I had a room and explained to me what my problem was with the alumni—jealousy and rivalry between two ladies, and the dislike of one of them for the person who was supposed to do the direct soliciting. S. K. helped by persuading Mr. C. K. Yen, the president of the Republic of China, and later my friend, to call up Vivian Wu—the most wealthy alumna—to ask her to head up the campaign. Somehow the leadership of the alumni association was thus shifted and a new person was persuaded to be the hustler—Wang Chi-wu, whom I knew quite well. With that change, a mysterious process to me, the alumni got going and raised $136,000 (in addition to what was given for the Koo fellowship), and the National Government contributed an additional $100,000 to the alumni fund. S. K. told me that because several universities were now after them, the government had decided to limit its gift to any one university to that amount, and the alumni must take the lead in fund-raising.

One bit of Columbia politics: Ted DeBary was then Columbia's provost. Although I had certainly done most of the work in cultivating and prodding the Chinese alumni, he later visited Taiwan and also met with them. When word of the gift of $236,000 came in to him, he decided how it should be parceled out—the National Government's gift to go to the East Asian Library, his own Oriental Studies Program to take $36,000, and the East Asian Institute to receive $100,000. Naturally, I was miffed that he took on Solomon's role, but it wasn't a bad division, since all of us were dependent on the library, which had no fundraisers.

With this gift, the two fellowships, and other fundraising that I participated in, I think my efforts resulted in about half a million in endowments for East Asian studies at Columbia. Considering that it was raised "retail," that wasn't bad. I worked on that job for two years after retirement. I personally gave about $2,500. My salary during my last year before retirement was only $25,000.

Kay and I had a wonderful trip to New Zealand and Australia in the winter of 1977, where our dear niece, Kay Wilbur Cressey Irwin, lives and has raised her family. After two days in Seattle, during which we saw our old friends Millard and Janet Rogers and learned that Jean's husband Ding was going to run for

Congress, we flew on to Honolulu where we had a couple of very happy days with John DeFrancis. John had arranged a party for us with Doak and Jeanne Barnett, Bill and Ginny Lockwood, and Minora and Mrs. Shinoda. Doak must have been there to write a book; he had already left Columbia, to everyone's regret, and joined the Brookings Institution, which allowed him time, at last, to get out several books on China. My boyhood friend Bill Lockwood, also the son of a China YMCA secretary, must have been retired from Princeton by then; Bill was unwell, and he died only a few years later. Minoru, a former Columbia graduate student, had arranged for my East-West Center grant of ten years before. It was a lovely, warm reunion. We also had a dinner at Danny Kwok's house: he teaches modern Chinese history, and we became friends while I was on sabbatical in Hawaii.

Space does not permit me to go into detail about our visit to New Zealand and Australia. Let me say merely that we spent a week in Aukland with our niece, Kay Irwin, and her family, doing considerable sightseeing. Then we had a week in South Island viewing marvelous alpine scenery. We flew from Christchurch to Sydney and had a most interesting ten days in Australia. One high point was attending "The Magic Flute" in Sydney's famed opera house. One of the nicest things about our Australia tour was going to Canberra, the capital, where I had friends in the faculty of the Australian National University. It was very hot, and Canberra was an unfinished capital city when we were there, but laid out on a grand plan around a large, artificial lake, with very wide streets and long blocks of buildings, but not many people, it seemed.

Professor Wang Gung-wu, the director of the Research School of Pacific Studies, who I had met at conferences and knew as a fine China scholar, took us to his home for dinner where we had a delicious Chinese meal, family style. Next day I brought Professor Wang an inscribed copy of the Sun Yat-sen book, only recently published, and addressed a faculty seminar. There I learned that Dr. Sun's alleged letter offering a treaty to Japan may be a forgery, and I was shown the evidence. I also learned that Professor Lo Hui-min's six-volume work in progress devoted to George Morrison, a China correspondent of nearly a lifetime, contains quite a lot about Sun Yat-sen. Later I was entertained at lunch by professors Lo and Wang Ling and then was taken to see the National Library. The library is to be Australia's main depository library, as is the Library of Congress for the United States. It has rapidly built up its Chinese collection, buying the library of my old friend the scholar Fang Chao-ying, the output of P. K. Yu's cooperative operation in Washington, which reproduces twentieth-century Chinese periodicals in American and other libraries, and virtually everything being republished in Taiwan.

Professor Stephen Fitzgerald, who teaches Chinese history and had recently returned from being Australia's ambassador to the People's Republic of China, entertained us at his home for dinner. I'll quote here from my journal:

He enjoyed being ambassador and was able to travel to most provinces of

China though not to Tibet and Sinkiang, or to Szechwan. He lived through the turmoil of the April 1 Tiananmen demonstrations in honor of Chou En-lai. In fact, he was returning to Peking at the end of March 1976, and in Nanking his train was swarmed over by students who painted slogans on the train (though I'm not clear whether they were anti-Chiang Ch'ing or what). He and Dr. Lo Hui-min observed the Tiananmen demonstrations, but in his position as ambassador he could not be as free as Dr. Lo was. Both conveyed to me the impression that the demonstrations were spontaneous, although Dr. Lo described the later pro-leftist parade as clearly contrived, and the marchers showing their unconcern.

Ambassador Fitzgerald seemed to be telling me that Americans were making too much of the Taiwan issue—Peking would let the whole matter rest in suspension so long as they are not required to put something they do not agree with in principle into writing or public declaration. (For my money that merely means the United States should just trust China's leaders indefinitely, including all changes in leadership.) Mrs. Fitzgerald found life in Peking very confining, with the limited circle of diplomatic personnel, and little or no contact with Chinese. However, she told Kay that she worked for a while in a Chinese factory.

That night Dr. Lo Hui-min took us to his home for a dinner party, with about twenty guests, one of whom was the vice chancellor of the university (which means the president), a scholar specializing on Indian history. Ambassador and Mrs. Fitzgerald were there too, and the son of Dr. Morrison and his wife, and lots of others. One of the most unexpected persons we met was Jennifer Cushing, who knew Ann at Cornell and who is the daughter of my SAS and Oberlin classmate Mary Barlow, who married a professor of Engineering at Cornell.

When we returned to New York, Kay and I resumed our enjoyable life in retirement, so full of reading, writing, gardening, entertaining our many friends and being entertained, music and art museums, and our beloved church in White Plains.

I used my writing time for the chapter that I had promised to John Fairbank for the *Cambridge History of China*, and the text grew longer and longer because I was condensing from the chapters I had written in Honolulu and thereafter and the notes gathered over many years. It became a history of the Chinese Nationalists' rise to power. Volume 12 of the *Cambridge History of China* was published in 1983, with my chapter by far the longest. I suggested to Cambridge University Press that they consider publishing it as a separate book. They agreed, and in 1984 it came out as *The Nationalist Revolution in China, 1923–1928*, with maps and a separate bibliography and index. It has been well reviewed, but is not a best-seller. None of my books are of that sort.

One of the most enriching trips we ever took was to Italy and Austria in 1979. My Sun Yat-sen book had made me pretty well-known to persons interested in his role in modern Chinese history, and in April 1979 I received an invitation from Professor Gottfried-Karl Kindermann of the University of Munich to give a paper on Sun at a symposium to be held in Salzburg, November 22–24. My fare would be paid and I would receive an honorarium. Kay agreed she would like to come, so I accepted, wrote my paper over the summer, and after several month of planning, ticket buying, outfitting, and reading, we started off on October 26.

We had a wonderful time in Italy, visiting a friend, George Weller, and his wife, touring Pompei and Herculaneum, "doing" Rome, Siena, and Florence, and then taking a night train to Vienna where Eugene Loh entertained us. We then drove to Salzburg. Our conference was underwritten by a German foundation, and our host had seen to the best of arrangements. He was a pro-Taiwan scholar, with an American Ph.D., and he invited a number of scholars from Taiwan, including my old friend Mr. Huang Chi-lu (the old Buddha), who had known Dr. Sun and attended the First Kuomintang Congress in January 1924. Among the German scholars were Professor Jurgen Domes, who, it seems, had been influenced by the first Wilbur and How volume to become an authority on the Kuomintang, and Dr. Deiter Heinzig, who had written a book about the Soviet military advisers in China during the 1920s, under the same influence. The symposium began on Thanksgiving day—relieving dear Kay for the first time in years of the responsibility and burden of preparing a feast—and it lasted for three days.

I'll recount one incident that was important to me. Eugene Loh, as though passing on a message from Chow Shu-kai, asked whether I would be willing to write a preface for the biography of Chiang Kai-shek, which I had read and critiqued in manuscript while Eugene was head of the New York office of the Republic of China Information Service. This put me on the spot. I got Kay to explain to Eugene how difficult it would be for me to sponsor a book that explicitly attacked my best friend, Jack Service. Eugene said that the offensive section could be expunged before printing, and then hinted to Kay of a commission of from three to five thousand dollars for a preface. That burned Kay up! After a couple of days, I got a chance to talk with Eugene and asked him first to convey to Chow Shu-kai my great appreciation for the help he had given me in the summer of 1977, when I was stymied in Taiwan on the fundraising business, describing to Eugene how Mr. Chow had guided and helped me. Then I rather casually asked him to tell Mr. Chow that I didn't think I was an appropriate person to write a preface. He immediately replied, "I understand. I understand." That closed the matter and I didn't need to say any more. It was a great relief. The case was handled in a Chinese way: Eugene approached me as though he were only a middleman. I had a middleman (Kay) explain the difficulty. Then I made my reply—a self-deprecating one—in the form of a message for Mr. S. K. Chow.

On Sunday, November 25, we took an early morning plane for Zurich, where we boarded a plane for New York. I summed up our trip while en route:

This was a fine trip and we two oldsters pulled it off on schedule with no sickness, missed connections, or other troubles, spent pleasant nights in decent middle-priced hotels and pensions except in Salzburg, where we really lived in style, mostly at the conference expense, but considerably at our own because meals were so expensive. We charged through many museums and saw innumerable Madonnas, annunciations, and ascensions, but there was a great deal of beauty in those museums in London, Sienna, Florence, and Vienna, and we learned a bit about some new painters—new to us, of course.

The conference on Sun Yat-sen, which provided the reason for our trip, was pleasant and stimulating. Sun emerged about as enigmatic as ever. But we were forced to consider what it was about him, and what he did, that made him so much revered by Chinese everywhere. On this, Kindermann and Schiffrin were both eloquent: his standing for a liberated and modernized China, for greater democracy, and for pride in China's culture. As Schiffrin put it, "his life is his monument." We also considered what Sun knew about Soviet Russia as he went into the alliance. On this, research could probably be done.

21

Our Trip Back to China, 1980

For nearly a year we had looked forward to, and saved for, a trip to China under the auspices of the National Committee on United States-China Relations, of which I had been a member for some ten years. The committee was deeply involved in intercultural exchanges and so had a fine reputation in China and provided excellent auspices. We left New York on October 5 and returned on November 1, 1980, visiting Kay's sister, Miggs, in Albuquerque, and having three days in Berkeley with Jack and Cary Service. After the China tour of sixteen days, we rested up in Hong Kong at the home of David and Natasha Wilson and had a nostalgic three days in Tokyo.

The eighteen members of our tour group made the trip doubly enjoyable, for they were well-educated professionals or businesspeople, seasoned and observant travelers. It was a guided tour and we saw showcased places for the most part. There was a fine variety: cities in North and South China, two delightful overnight train rides, both urban and rural communes, a tractor factory, several elementary schools—oh! those darling kids!—villages, famous historical sites, beautiful architecture, and several fine museums. Our briefings included virtually no politics and no harangues, but we had no chance to ask questions of any authoritative official higher than a factory or a commune manager.

The drive in from the airport was beautiful on that October afternoon, on a fine highway planted with willows and poplars on either side, and beyond, acres of cultivated fields meticulously kept and banks of three- or four-storied flats here and there. The road had little traffic: some other buses, bicycles, mules or horses, and trucks filled mostly with produce or men in the uniform of the

248

People's Liberation Army. Just the sight of this minor traffic set the driver's horn going. All the way to the city we were subject to his unceasing honking. Maybe it gave him "face." He had important guests. Besides tour buses we noted excellent Japanese-made commuter buses picking up passengers along the way. Such good transportation was unheard of in Peking when we lived there nearly fifty years before. Local city buses were always jammed. There is no wall around the city now, and all the memorial arches that were so much a part of old Peking have been taken down to make room for increasing traffic. But Peking's two front gates still stand, even if the others have vanished with the city wall.

Our first hotel, the Ch'ien-men Fan-tien (Front Gate Hotel) was a Charles Adams type—a vast, gloomy, Russian-built place in the southwest part of Peking, miles from the main centers of interest. One advantage, though, was its location in an old residential area with narrow lanes and old brick houses behind walls, of just the sort we used to see long ago. We loved strolling in these alleys.

Someday Peking will rank high as a national capital. It is being modernized but has a long way to go. The city's central axis, laid out six centuries ago, stretches from the great front gate on the south, through many other gates, plazas, and audience halls of the Imperial Palace, and on past Coal Hill and the Drum Tower, and thence to the one-time northern wall, an axis some ten miles long. The vast Tiananmen square, so much viewed around the world in May 1989, lies across this central axis and beneath the red walls of the palace. It is flanked east and west by two enormous, Stalin-style buildings, the Great Hall of the People and the National Museum. In the square, right on the grand axis, as if to rival the greatest of the imperial audience halls, is Mao Tse-tung's mausoleum, again built in Stalinesque style. To me, this is vulgar. The moat on the north and west sides of the palace and the many trees give a parklike quality to parts of the city, but the older residential areas are cramped and rather shabby. Where the city has expanded beyond its old confining walls there are wide streets flanked with modern office and apartment buildings.

The pace of life in Peking struck us as leisurely. We saw many older folk doing their slow-motion exercises in the early morning, then people by the thousands sedately riding to work on their bicycles. We kept looking but saw no one hustling or even walking briskly. Compared with the bustle of Tokyo, Hong Kong, or even Taipei, the people of Peking displayed an outwardly calm demeanor. All the adults we saw were dressed in pants and jackets of dark blue or gray, interspersed here and there with the green outfits of the army men and women, who were nearly indistinguishable by gender or age. This manner of dress was utilitarian where common cloth was rationed and at a season approaching winter. But schoolchildren in sightseeing groups with their teachers were brightly dressed in reds and plaids.

Department stores displayed lots of commercial goods and seemed crowded. We noticed shelves of brightly printed textiles and were told there was an eager market for modern consumer items made in Taiwan, which, because Taiwan is considered a province of China, pay no import duties. We could hardly think of the people we saw in the nation's capital as prosperous, but we saw few signs of poverty either: just rather tidy shabbiness. The restaurants were filled with simply dressed folk. Egalitarianism prevails—or at least that is the ideal.

At the north end of the great square is Wu Men, the Meridian Gate, the entrance to the Forbidden City. A huge picture of Mao Tse-tung gazes down from the gate. Once inside, my memories across forty-six years returned in a flash. The palace grounds were well kept, much better than when we had seen them last, and the tourists were mostly Chinese. Good! It is their national heritage. I saw one old bound-footed lady being helpfully escorted by a younger woman, perhaps her granddaughter. There were parties of schoolchildren, young pioneers, with their teachers pointing out sights to be observed. Over there was an older man seated on a stool sketching one of the buildings.

On to the Great Wall, which we had visited forty-seven years before. The now restored wall snakes over precipitous mountain crests in an unending parade of battlements and lookouts—at this rebuilt stretch. China's monumental effort to keep out the northern barbarians now attracts barbarian tourists. This Sunday afternoon the wall was crowded with Chinese.

We visited a Friendship store, a well-stocked establishment especially for the convenience of foreigners, reserved for them, and a source of much-needed foreign currency. Most of the goods on display were touristy and quite expensive compared with Taiwan prices.

Kay and I spent most enjoyable hours walking the narrow lanes where the common folk live in ancient houses. We saw them hanging laundry, brushing teeth over gutters, walking their toddlers and airing their birds, ambling off to school, and buying their vegetables from carts or streetside markets. The grandeur of the imperial city—its massive gates and awesome palace—contrasts vividly with the humble domestic architecture and parsimony of Peking's residents that we saw. One large change from before was that the *hu-t'ung* (alleyways) were now paved and relatively clean.

A great thrill for me was our flight to Hsian on our fourth day in China. This was the imperial capital during the Ch'in and Western Han dynasties (250 B.C.– A.D. 25), which I had described in my dissertation on slavery, but which I had never seen. We flew in across the great Yellow River and over the meandering Wei River and the broad, fertile plane dotted with towns and villages, the area "within the Pass," which was the economic base for several dynastic capitals. Now I could see the land that I had tried to describe when writing my first book in the 1930s. The region is noted for its ancient monuments and archaeological discoveries.

Hsian isn't so grand as Peking, but it seemed more Chinese. In Peking the pace seemed very leisurely, perhaps the effect of the vast bureaucracy, but Hsian was more peppy. The city has shrunk in area since it was capital of the T'ang dynasty in the eighth and ninth centuries, but the flavor of China prevails, without so much foreign influence. The Bell Tower near the center of the city is now a museum where tourists may purchase art objects. The great bell, which now rests on a terrace, used to be struck to tell citizens the time. Not far off is the Drum Tower, which housed a huge drum that signaled the gatemen to close the city gates and told the people it was time to rest. From these handsome buildings one can see most of the city and its main streets. Much of the city wall still stands, and beyond it lie the suburbs and villages, fields of cotton, corn, and vegetables. Hsian is also a major production centers for military hardware, but we never would have suspected it from the city we were shown.

After settling in, we went to the Big Goose Pagoda outside the city where we got a bird's-eye view of Hsian, and a distant view southward of the Chin-ling Mountains, which divide Shensi from Szechwan and were part of the ancient capital's protective screen.

By now all in our party of eighteen Americans were pretty well acquainted, so that evening we inaugurated a "happy hour" in our room to open our precious duty-free Jack Daniels, asking all to bring their own glasses. The hotel's huge dining room had thirty or forty large round tables, with tour groups talking in Japanese, German, Australian, French, and American—obviously it was *the* hotel in Hsian, though more modern ones have since been built. The Chinese meal was good, as were all we had during our sixteen days, but the service indifferent. In fact, service was poor in all the hotels we stayed in, though it got better as we moved southward. Here and in Peking, toilet seats were broken, flushing mechanisms on the blink, shower heads leaking, dirty floors and rugs— such things seemed the result of hordes of tourists cared for by poorly compensated staff, who (so we were instructed) must not be tipped.

Hsian was the capital of China's first unifier, Ch'in Shih Huang-ti (the First Emperor of Ch'in), who died in 210 B.C., and it was near his great tumulus that the thousands of life-sized pottery warriors were discovered a few years ago, buried in phalanx after phalanx to guard the tomb. We went the next morning to that site where excavation and reconstruction of broken men, horses, and chariots was going on. On the way we stopped to take pictures of the First Emperor's tomb, an artificial mountain some hundreds of feet high, now rising from amidst fields of corn. It has not yet been excavated, though doubtless it was robbed long ago. At the site of the excavation we saw rows and rows of warriors and horses set in place in their trenches. A few exhibition pieces stood in the small museum.

We asked for a chance to take some pictures of a village, and our bus stopped briefly on a spot overlooking a cluster of mud-walled and thatch-roofed houses and cluttered courtyards. With a telephoto lens I got a few interesting shots of farmers' houses, and one of an elderly woman sunning herself, though apparently most of the villagers were off in their fields or on other business. We also observed traffic on the highway, a few buses and trucks, carts drawn by horses and donkeys, bicycles and a tricycle cart, and men and women carrying their loads slung from poles balanced on one shoulder, as of yore.

Located in the northwestern part of China, Hsian has a great many Moslems, some 30,000, we were told, so a visit to a mosque was most interesting. The mosque was entirely Chinese in architecture, with several buildings set in a series of courtyards and Chinese gardens. The minaret was a four-storied Chinese building with a tiled roof and curving eaves. A mosque was first built on the site in A.D. 742—only 120 years after Hegira. There had been a long time for Sinification. The present mosque was reconstructed in Ming and again in Ch'ing times and was refurbished recently with government funds. (China courts the Moslem world.) It was almost deserted during the afternoon we were there, not yet time for evening prayer. Seemingly it is not a tourist attraction for Chinese! Within the main building there was a large area with prayer rugs facing the sacred niche on the west wall so worshipers would properly face Mecca.

In response to our questions we were told that the mosque did not suffer during the Cultural Revolution, "because the occupants shouted the proper slogans and waved red flags." There may have been other reasons, such as the solidarity and militancy of Chinese Moslems, which would have made for difficulties, just like fooling with a hornets' nest. The vicinity of the mosque was occupied solidly by members of the faith. Fear of offending Moslem countries, which the People's Republic assiduously courts, may have been another restraint. The mosque and its gardens were a quiet, even a reverential place, but much in need of repair: scarcely a showplace for visiting Near Easterners.

In the narrow lanes surrounding the mosque we could peep through the gates into little courtyards, see children playing marbles and throwing lots for comic books, while older folk went about their domestic tasks. Moslem kids were just like the other children we saw when visiting schools, except these were not dressed up for the foreigners. Looking down from the drum tower, we saw men sawing planks in an ancient and very laborious fashion. Back and forth, back and forth, the sawing went, lengthwise of a large log, probably hour after hour. I had seen such work in Shanghai as a boy. We heard school kids shouting their lessons and saw mothers taking in laundry, watering their flowers, and setting tables. They were cramped little homes, but homes the people cared about.

We visited the "Great Brilliance" agricultural commune outside Hsian, one accustomed to tourists, it soon became evident. Its well-prepared briefing room had a cloth on the long table, tea, electric fans, cement floor, and a wall map to show by colored lights where the villages, clinics, and new irrigation works of the commune were located. The manager, Mr. Wang, forty-eight years old, dressed in ordinary clothes, and wearing a cap, gave the briefing in a matter-of-fact way. Some 23,000 people lived in the commune, working under his management, and about 700 worked in Hsian. Forty villages were organized in 23 work brigades that cultivated about 4,200 acres, all of it now irrigated, we were told. Formed in 1958—the year of Mao Tse-tung's big communization drive—the commune now owned 36 trucks and 154 "tractors" (which probably meant power-drawn field tools), had sunk 695 wells, and had set up three pumping stations. Mr. Wang stated that farm production had increased fivefold compared with what it was at the time of Liberation (about 1950 in this region) and had increased three times since 1965 (i.e., after recovery from the Great Leap Forward). Private plots made up 10 percent of the land, but not all were owned by families; some were held by work teams or other small units. He led us to believe that households in the commune were now relatively well off.

Mr. Wang told us that some 5,300 kids were in commune schools (23 percent of the stated population), one school being a higher middle school. There was a hospital with twenty-eight doctors and nurses, every work team [brigade?] had a clinic, and there were eighty-one "barefoot doctors" (about two per village). Health care cost one yuan (about sixty-seven cents U.S.) per person, per year. There were factories in the commune, four department stores, and a mobile movie team to give shows. Each village had a TV set.

After this recital, Mr. Wang admitted three weaknesses: (1) shortage of science in agriculture; (2) only 40 percent of the land cultivated by machines, the rest by hand labor; and (3) the need to train more competent managers. Mr. Wang was assisted by six "leaders," each in charge of a function such as agriculture, factories, health, and so on, and each of them had three or four assistants. There were about 1,000 Communist Party members in the commune, we were told. At question time, when someone asked who decided whether a youth would work in field or factory, the answer was that factories called for a certain number of persons and the rest got field work. Why private plots? To increase production. Did the commune get "sent down" city youths, and frankly, how did it work out? Over several years the commune got about 500, and there were still about 50; they were good workers and some joined the party.

We visited a village where we were free to wander on the tree-lined earthen roads enclosed on each side by walls of plastered brick, with doorways leading into courtyards and one-storied brick homes. A young married couple lived together with their baby and the husband's mother in the first home we visited, absolutely spick and span. There was a sparsely furnished living room and two small bedrooms facing the courtyard, with the kitchen and toilet in a separate wing. The rooms had hard mud floors, whitewashed walls, and curtains in the windows. Brightly colored bedding was piled neatly on a chest near the grandmother's bed and stacked at the foot of the sleeping platform in the other bedroom, used by the couple and their child. Extra jackets hung neatly on hooks alongside, and there were some framed pictures on the walls. Mao Tse-tung and Hua Kuo-feng smiled down from the place of honor in the living room opposite the door. Seeing no ancestral tablets, I asked about them. Grandmother told us they were a thing of the past. In the kitchen was a mud-plastered stove with a wok, a cement sink, a work table with various cooking utensils, and water tubs below, since all water was brought into the village by cart. A straw broom and enamel basin were on the floor; two thermos bottles and some ladles and sieves hung on the wall. In the immaculate courtyard grew a persimmon and a catalpa tree, and along the eaves of the house were bundles of corn drying. Kay saw another courtyard with chickens and children, and a penned in pig. A man doled out water from a two-wheeled tank cart pulled by a donkey. This house, too, was in apple pie order.

It was mid-October and we saw corn drying on all the roofs, and great spreads of corn niblets drying on threshing floors. Corn stalks stacked here and there, ready to be used for burning in the kitchen stoves, gave a sort of Thanksgiving Day air. I photographed a mill in action operated by two very dusty women, the electricity-driven machinery grinding out cornmeal. In the village square there was a large two-wheeled rubber-tired cart, a small gasoline-driven engine to pull a wagon or plow, and several bicycles. We saw no draft animals, though chickens were scratching about; nor do we recall any dogs. In fact, we only recall seeing one dog all the time we were in China; this from the bell tower in Hsian.

We next went to see the commune hospital, probably only a clinic. A woman attended by a nurse was having acupuncture in her leg for arthritis, and there was a dispensary for Chinese and Western medicines. An attractive courtyard with a flower garden separated the front offices from what seemed to be a hospital behind—a two-storied building with central hallway and closed doors on either side as though wards for the sick, but the building seemed deserted. Ushered to a toilet by Manager Wang, I found myself in a brick-walled latrine with excrement standing in a trench along the back. It smelled to high heaven. There was, however, a tub of water and a ladle for washing hands. Nothing like toilet paper.

We visited an elementary school. Oral recitation in unison when we arrived: indeed when you hear this droning, you can be sure a school is nearby. The classes were about sixty kids in a room, and perfectly disciplined, at least when foreigners were visiting. When lessons were completed, the kids put their hands behind their backs and sat quietly. We saw four year olds doing this. The classrooms had wooden desks with inkwells and hard wooden chairs. Some rooms had old-fashioned foot organs, which the teacher played for class singing and dancing. The kids sang enthusiastically, and, wonder of wonders, they didn't peek at the intruders who were watching them and snapping pictures. That must have taken training! In one performance, four kids danced and sang, purportedly about China's minorities. On the walls of several rooms were posters illustrating "Everyone Loves China," with children of all different races and colors depicted together; also pictures of Marx and Engels, Lenin and Stalin. We clapped at the end of the performance and the kids clapped back. As we left, the kids crowded around holding out little hands and wishing us well. Out on the playground an older class lined up for exercises directed by their physical education teacher, going through their routine with gusto.

Another feature of the "Great Brilliance" Commune was its bag factory where we saw fifty or so women making black plastic flight bags on a long row of electrically driven sewing machines that once had foot treadles. Other women were putting in zippers and attaching strap handles. In a storeroom I saw hundreds of pasteboard cases of these bags ready for shipment, while in the factory's store there were many brightly colored plastic bags of various colors, shapes, and sizes. One I bought cost a dollar. The factory also had powerful presses to roll out plastic sheets of the required thinness. Men operated them, but all the other work was done by women.

While others were hearing a final speech by Manager Wang, I found one of the commune department stores, which we weren't being shown, and was astonished at the stock of goods for sale—bolts of bright-colored cloth, children's clothes, shoes, toys, medicines, and toilet articles. There were eight clerks and about the same number of shoppers at eleven in the morning when most adults would be at work. Strange to say, in an agricultural commune we weren't given even a glimpse of work in the fields, nor did we have the wits to ask for one.

The provincial museum of Hsian has an excellent collection of bronzes, mortuary figurines, and the "forest of tablets," or stone monuments on which the Chinese Classics and other literary treasures are inscribed. The setting of flower gardens, rockeries, and pavilions was just charming, and it was a lovely sunny day. Kay had a cold by now, so she spent most of the time sitting in the sun outside the museum shop, and soon had a bevy of clerks around her taking an English lesson. They were charming, eager young women, who already knew quite a little English.

Hsian is also noted for the excavation of a neolithic village, Pan-po, a few miles outside the city, and believed to date from about 4000 B.C. The site is covered by a broad, translucent roof, and one walks past the diggings of each house site, labeled and described in Chinese and English. What one sees, however, is mostly post holes and hearths. Outside the enclosure were three reconstructed huts as the archaeologists conceived them, some half underground, round or rectangular, with mud walls and posts to hold up roofs of mud-plastered reeds. A small museum showed painted pottery and other excavated articles, such as stone tools. It was a matriarchal society, according to information provided, but how that could be known is a puzzle. Equally interesting to me was a cluster of farm women, quite short they were, working on a broad paved area meant for parking tour buses. Near those reconstructed neolithic huts they were drying soybeans and winnowing out chaff. The women beat the plants on the pavement, or flayed them, to separate the beans from the plants, then hulled them and spread the beans to dry. One woman was winnowing chaff from some grain by tossing it in the air from a flat basket.

In Hsian we saw a still poor and drab society. Blue was virtually the only color for clothing except for the green of army men and women and the bright clothes of kids on display. We didn't see a skirt on a Chinese woman during our first week in China. The children we saw in classrooms or out sightseeing were marvelously well behaved. We did see one enterprising boy aged about six, outside the commune, who left his playmates to climb a tree the better to see the foreigners. Good for him! Maybe he'll make it to some position of leadership. Later I did see two boys tussling during recess and was much relieved.

From Hsian we traveled eastward by train to Loyang, also a one-time capital city, notably of the Eastern, or Latter, Han dynasty. Loyang has grown greatly from the sleepy town of 80,000 people that it was before Liberation. Now it is an industrial city and its newer sections have broad streets lined with multistoried apartments. Loyang, too, makes munitions.

Though we didn't get to bed till three, I was awakened in our second-story room by six o'clock with the sound of many people running. Some were jogging but many were really running as if in a marathon. As it got lighter I saw a park outside our window, with people practicing T'ai chi ch'uan, the slow-motion exercise of controlled postures, which devotees find relaxing and refreshing. Going into the park, I saw a marvelous display of slow motion, theatrical sword-play performed by two young women in red gym suits, being instructed by two men in blue. Appreciative spectators admired the ballet-like performance.

The Buddhist caves outside Loyang are rightly famous. Here, overlooking a tributary of the Lo River, Buddhist faithful, beginning in A.D. 481, started carving statues of the Buddha and of bodhisattvas out of sheer cliffs that face eastward into the rising sun. The site is called Lung-men, the Dragon Gate. Carving continued for several centuries, and there are thousands of figures, some fifty feet high, some of human size, others only little ones in niches, but all of them testimony to the devotion of generations of the Buddha's Chinese converts. Unhappily, through the ages and during the recent Cultural Revolution, many statues have been defaced, some even removed from their sites for commercial gain. Many museums in Japan, Europe, and America have specimens from Lung-men. But the enormous statues are still intact and remain majestically grand in contemplation of the mundane world from their rocky fastnesses.

The mundane world was all about. It was almost as exciting to see the Chinese visitors below or among the statues as to see the monuments themselves, for Lung-men is a fabulous tourist attraction. Chinese visitors swarmed the rocky paths, sat in Buddha's lap having their pictures taken, and viewed the awe-inspiring scene from rowboats in the river. Entrepreneurs in booths nearby sold noodles, ice cream, candied crabapples, and postcard views of the site. It was at Lung-men that we saw the only ragged boy on our trip, shoes worn through, clothes dirty and wispy; but he was smilingly cheerful and was not begging. We saw no beggars. We did see again an elderly bound-footed woman resting on a rock, attended by a younger woman.

A party of foreigners excited tremendous curiosity. Kay found herself in the midst of such a neck-craning crowd when a Chinese man asked to practice his English with her. In no time they were surrounded by curious spectators. The staring was not rude nor calculating: it was just curiosity, but it was unwavering. Chinese stared just so fifty years ago when we were in Peking as young folk. It was just the same when our bus stopped on a village street. As though at a signal, kids began rushing toward the bus and soon surrounded it. Of course, we were staring too, at the village doorways, at the brick and tile-roofed houses draped with drying corn, and at a farm wagon pulled by a two-wheeled gasoline motor.

The Loyang City Museum had an excellent display of bronzes, ceramics, and other objects, for Loyang is an ancient center of Chinese civilization, very near the cradle, so far as is now known. The museum displays only objects excavated in its vicinity. The biggest surprise was a crude little bronze jar labeled as being of the Hsia dynasty, the first of all the dynasties in Chinese belief, though archaeological evidence that it ever existed seemed lacking heretofore. The intelligent lady curator informed me that the dating had been arrived at through stratigraphy, with a Shang site above. There was also an ox scalpula similar to ones used during the succeeding dynasty, the Shang, for reading the oracle. This one had no characters incised on it but did have many incised circles. This, too, was said to be of the Hsia period. One extraordinary photograph showed a burial field with many skeletons neatly arranged, each with a headstone bearing a name. Our local guide told us in English that the dead had been slaves, but the label in Chinese said they were criminals forced to work on a royal project, who had died on the job. The curator confirmed to me that our guide had misspoken. A small matter, but the issue of slavery causes great heat among Marxists. The burial was of Latter Han date (i.e., after A.D. 25), when China was no longer a "slavery society," according to the official interpretation.

We drove to a park where a long building exhibited replicas of simply wonderful Han dynasty frescoes: spirited dragons, phoenixes, and other miraculous beasts. I went down into an excavated Han tomb, but Kay resisted. I have a book illustrating Han and T'ang murals, copied from just such tombs, which give most absorbing glimpses of the culture of those days from some 200 B.C. to the seventh or eighth centuries.

After our "happy hour" we went out to a fine restaurant specializing in Loyang dishes: delicious, but unfortunately lethal for Kay, who was attacked again by her ancient enemy in China, the amoeba. So she skipped the trip to a tractor factory that we went to the next day. Apparently it is a famous factory, China's first to produce tractors, according to our briefing. It was interesting to see the part-by-part assembly of the little red machines, which at the end of the process rolled out triumphantly to a parking field, at the rate of one every ten or fifteen minutes. It may have been great for China, but it seemed an inefficient production method—much piece-by-piece handwork, and the little twelve-foot tractors were greatly out of date by Western standards. Was this one of those left-behind Russian contributions?

We were told in the briefing that some 27,000 workers and staff, of whom some 7,500 were women, produced 87 percent of the tractor parts right in the plant. Steel and glass came from other factories. In 1979 the plant had turned out 22,800 tractors and bulldozers, all delivered to the government for sale in China or abroad. The workers had recently received a 40 percent increase in wages, according to the new economic policy. Wages ranged from 33 yuan a month (equivalent to U.S. $22) to 104 yuan (about $70). The average monthly wage was 54 yuan, but with bonuses it came to 74 (not quite U.S. $50). If this represented a 40 percent raise, we wondered what a junior worker got before. On retirement (age fifty for women and sixty for men), workers received a life pension of 70 to 85 percent of their (last?) pay and continued to have free medical care, haircuts, baths, and to live in their workers' quarters. We noted that the factory area was filled with three-storied flats. The factory ran a hospital with 400 beds with free care for the workers and half price for their families. The safety measures in the factory were poor by American standards. Our briefer told us of five primary schools and three middle schools for the workers' children, with a total enrollment of 13,500, and in addition five kindergartens with 5,000 kids. Wages may have seemed poor, but the workers seemed well cared for.

We went to a school near the factory and were greeted by adorable kindergarten children and their teachers, lined up in groups ready to clap for the arriving foreign friends. Inside, we saw kids at their desks singing and gesturing in unison, following the teacher who sat at a foot-peddle organ. In another room kindergartners were folding paper into origami birds and rushed to give them to us. In another room, perhaps first grade, four little girls put on a dance for us, holding up bright hoops, bowing and prancing, and keeping very good time to the music. China's secret weapon! And to think that a few years earlier teachers taught the innocents songs of hate for Americans.

Later we visited a primary school. In the first classroom sixty-two children were reciting an English lesson in unison after the teacher, phrase by phrase. It was a conversation between two people going to market. Then, on command, the kids recited the conversation without the teacher, keeping perfect rhythm, as though it were a catechism, and better done than most church congregations in America would do responsive readings. Two girls then took the parts, and then two boys. As a gesture of appreciation, two ladies in our group then read the parts. Wild applause!

Suddenly a loudspeaker in the room gave out a command and all the kids assumed what looked like an attitude of prayer. What? In a Communist country? Not so. All in rhythm the kids began to massage their foreheads, cheeks, and eyes. This went on for five minutes as a form of muscle relaxation, we were told, when suddenly the bell rang and everyone leaped up and bolted for the door for exercises in the courtyard. There we saw several hundred kids, probably up to junior high age, vigorously doing calisthenics.

In the afternoon we went to the White Horse Temple, built during the T'ang dynasty (618–907) and restored several times, most recently by the present government. It is a famous Buddhist temple and has a sequence of halls within a surrounding wall, separated by beautiful courtyards. Each building has a statue of Buddha or of bodhisattvas, and the last houses a statue of Kuan-yin, the goddess of mercy. We saw no worshippers. I found my way clear back to the office of a monk, perhaps the abbot, who was writing at a desk that had many photos under its glass top. He welcomed me and showed me the many pictures of Japanese tour groups together with himself. On the walls of the abbot's room were banners in Chinese proclaiming "China and Japan are friends."

On the way to the temple, I had seen a group of young women pulling a plow through flat, dry fields, although we saw a harrow drawn by horses. We saw no tractors. The fields were about three acres. The men and women we saw worked in separate groups. Perhaps pulling a plow in a group would not be such difficult work. Later, our old friend Anne Goodrich told us that outside Peking fifty years ago she had seen a woman and a donkey hitched together to pull a plow. Yet what an outcome of communalism and women's liberation it is that in North China, field work was still women's work. Of course, they got workpoints for the number of hours per day they did farm labor, and thus contributed to the family income.

On the dot of 6:30 P.M. we boarded our train for the long trip eastward and then south to Shanghai. We shared with a French tour group a fine sleeping car attached to the rear of a splendid train that had started in Chengtu in Szechwan and came through Hsian to Loyang. Our car had clean washrooms and toilets and compartments to sleep four, and we were served boiling water for our teapots. We were told that at the next stop, Chengchow, we would go forward for dinner. There we walked on the platform nearly the length of the train to the dining car. Maybe we could never have made it through the train itself, for the common class cars were simply jammed with passengers. As soon as the train reached Chengchow, people were shoving their baggage in through the windows and trying desperately to squeeze aboard while others were still getting off, a frantic scene, to which we were privileged spectators enjoying an uncrowded car reserved exclusively for visiting foreigners. One wonders how Chinese must feel about hotels, stores, separate dining rooms in restaurants, and train cars they may not enter, luxuries reserved for the "foreign devils." The segregation imposed by the government for the sake of tourist revenues is much stricter than what the "imperialists" imposed before Liberation.

When we awoke next morning we were in Anhwei Province, approaching Nanking. This was east-central China, in the fertile lower Yangtze valley, with a milder climate than that of the northern areas we had been in, a transition zone between wheat and rice culture. We passed by broad stretches of fields, all absolutely manicured. Men and women were laboring in the fields, but we saw no powered farm machinery in use. There were neat villages of brick or earth-walled houses with tile or straw roofs, and ponds with great flocks of geese. After we passed over the famous new bridge spanning the Yangtze and past Nanking, there were many canals with native craft—punts, sailing junks, and rafts, and a few motor-powered boats. We saw water buffalo—the gift of the gods for rice culture, which requires several plowings, some underwater. Some buffalo were tended by young boys sitting astride, exactly as celebrated by Chinese painters. The farther we went into the delta toward Shanghai, the more prosperous the farm villages seemed, and there were more small factories. Thus, we spent the whole morning drinking in this fascinating scene.

We pulled into Shanghai about 1:45 P.M.—late! Our local guide, Mr. Tang, an old hand at escorting foreigners, greeted us in excellent English.

I grew up in Shanghai and had been there again at the end of the war, but Kay had never been there. I looked forward to seeing it under Communist rule, for part of the city had been created under foreign control and management during about a century, and the city is China's most modern. Shanghai had grown enormously in the past thirty years. Driving to our hotel, we passed through the incredibly crowded former Chapei section, across Soochow Creek, and out to the edge of the former International Settlement, with tree-lined streets, where our hotel had been converted from a German-built apartment complex. After a late lunch at the hotel, which was certainly the best we had yet been in, we were taken on a quick bus tour.

All street names in the former French Concession, and many of those in the old International Settlement, have been changed, so it was not easy to orient myself. Suddenly from the bus window I saw the Shanghai American School building, and across the street the Community Church. That was something of a thrill. The church looked rather rundown, but the school, now behind a high wall, was being used as a naval research center and was not accessible. We drove out to Zikawei (Hsu-chia-wei) and the French Cathedral, where it was hard to tell from the outside whether it was being used for religious purposes. Then we drove down the winding former Avenue Edward VII, which once divided the French Concession from the International Settlement, past the south end of the old Race Course, now a people's park. Finally we arrived at the Bund and stopped at the end of Nanking Road for a brief look at the river through the gathering dusk. Then back on crowded Nanking Road past department stores and what used to be the foreign YMCA (now a headquarters for various sports associations), and so out Bubbling Well Road to our hotel.

Shanghai, on that first impression, seemed much more crowded than as remembered in 1946, and now a rather seedy place, many of the old buildings badly rundown. There were plenty of buses, trucks, and bicycles, but few cars or motorcycles by comparison with Taipei. In spite of the population growth there seemed little new building, renovation, or even upkeep in the formerly foreign-controlled parts of the city, though streets were clean and well maintained. The city had spread outward into former farmlands.

Next morning we went to a workers' settlement in the Yangtzepoo district where there is much industry. In the briefing room we were told that "before Liberation" the area had been a slum where workers lived in sheds. This I could believe, because I have read vivid descriptions of just such places and had even seen one such slum as a boy. Now one saw row on row of three-storied flats, neatly kept streets and lanes, laundry hanging on poles, and a little flower garden in front of the briefing room. The fence around the garden was being put to a good purpose—to dry cabbages. A nice young man told the story, with Mr. Tang interpreting.

Since 1952 the Shanghai municipal government had built in this region 1,470 blocks for about 54,000 people in 12,000 families (about 4.35 average). Most of the residents were workers in textile, chemical, or machine-building factories, but there were also teachers, medical personnel, shop clerks, and retired folk. The settlement maintained many facilities such as clinics, shops, neighborhood restaurants, and public dining halls; and there were four nursery schools, two kindergartens, four elementary schools, and one middle school. There was a public library, a craft shop, athletic facilities, and a public park nearby. We were not far from my first home in Shanghai, on then-named Dixwell Road, where I used to see great wheelbarrows bringing women workers to the mills in the Yangtzepoo region. Now there was a hospital and eleven clinics for the workers. Some 6,000 of the residents were retired workers, who received from 70 to 80 percent of their final pay and free medical care. Most lived with their children and were given civic jobs to help manage the community, for example, to supervise the free markets, cooperate with the schools, and control traffic. Since 1968 the settlement had set up nine workshops to make spare parts and locally needed goods, employing 2,000 people, among them some 800 middle school graduates who would otherwise be unemployed. We were told that now the problem of unemployment for middle school graduates was almost solved.

I asked how 54,000 people were organized and governed. The briefer replied that there were thirty paid workers sent by the district-level government. They carried out given policies, but also sent upward the complaints and suggestions of the residents. Below there were eleven residential committees and sixty or seventy residential groups. Presumably these groups, which would number about 800 persons, were the lowest level of control. Someone asked about control of crime. Answer: During the Cultural Revolution there were serious problems with the unemployed, but now there were very few. Those who "made mistakes" were reeducated by teachers, retired workers, and parents. Those under eighteen who committed "crimes" were sent to reformatories for half work and half study. Those who committed "serious crimes" were sent to the people's courts. Did the unemployed receive any payment? Answer: They were given some make-work for which they were paid; or they might be licensed by the city government as peddlers. Some might get work in the neighborhood workshops. Who kept the place so clean? Answer: The residents were responsible for the lanes and alleys within the area, but the city cleaned the streets twice a day. The area had a police substation.

We visited the community hospital which, we were told, had forty doctors and thirty nurses, the proportions being such because most of the sick were treated as outpatients. The hospital was built around a courtyard with a pleasant flower garden. Both Chinese traditional medicine and Western medicine were practiced, with the former preferred by the older folk. The cost of medical attention was minimal. It was a busy hospital with lots of patients and the staff bustling about; not in the least like the sleepy place we were shown at the Great Brilliance commune outside Hsian. A dentist in our group watched a Chinese dentist working on a man's teeth and later remarked on the poor quality of the equipment and sanitary practice. Still, a worker was getting treatment, which was something new.

We visited a kindergarten and then a nursery school. The youngsters put on a dance in costumes to represent China's minorities. In another room, the excellence of the kids' recitations astonished Kay, but she noted that each child, when finished, put hands behind the back, as we had seen in elementary schools elsewhere. The classrooms were clean and fairly cheerful, but without the paraphernalia of toys that our tots would have in their classrooms at that age. Thus it seemed they would have nothing to occupy themselves with when not being instructed.

We also intruded (by prearrangement) into two apartments. Everything was spic-and-span, but small in scale. We observed a simple kitchen with a two-burner propane stove and running water, a primitive bath, bedrooms about eight by ten, and a little living room. There were electric lights, carpets on the cement floors, simple furniture, and on the walls a calendar, printed pictures, and a scroll painting. A man eighty-four years old and his seventy-two-year-old wife occupied one apartment and had a son or grandson living with them. They were nice folks, and we appreciated their letting us look around their home. Did they earn something for the extra work and inconvenience of having their apartment on show? My impression was that the living quarters were adequate by local standards, but wouldn't have been acceptable for a couple in America. Still, they were infinitely better than mat sheds set down in mud and filth, which once existed in working class districts in Shanghai.

That workers' residential area really impressed me. It is an accomplishment to house 54,000 people, a population about that of White Plains, New York, organize them effectively, and provide basic health care and schooling for their kids. And this was one of several similar developments in and around Shanghai.

Telitha Gerlach was an eighty-four-year-old American lady who first went to China as a YWCA worker in 1926 and made China her home most of the time ever since. I had known her in New York about 1948–50 when she was fundraising for Mme. Sun Yat-sen's China Welfare Appeal together with our friend Ida Pruitt. I admired both ladies. She returned to China in the early 1950s and worked for the China Welfare Institute. She came to have lunch with us at the hotel, a tiny person, still attractive, and wearing Chinese clothes and their style of bobbed hair. She even walked like an elderly Chinese—stomach forward, feet pointing outward and shuffling, shoulders rolling a bit from side to side. Charming! She had lived in Shanghai and worked with Chinese colleagues for the past twenty-five or more years, turbulent years, but she seemed content. Apparently the institute was protected by Mme. Sun and Chou Enlai, and her colleagues sheltered her during the Cultural Revolution when most Chinese were fearful of associating with a foreigner. No unfavorable word about events in China passed her lips during our interesting lunch together. She seemed frail, with parchment-like skin, though she continued to work half days at the Welfare Institute, where she was much loved, we felt sure. We walked her to her apartment, provided by the institute, having its own private entrance, a flower garden with gardener, and a housekeeper. She showed us on a map how to find the former YMCA residences where my family had lived so long ago, and then on to the Community Church.

We did find the Y compound on former Route Zayzoong, now called Changshu Road. Behind a high wall there were seven three-storied stucco houses, but some smaller houses had been crowded into the former lawn and tennis court, and a row of shops occupied the street front, so it was not easy to be sure after fifty-three years that it was the same place where I spent my last three years in high school. The houses looked quite rundown after fifty years of existence, and with thirty years of Chinese occupancy, probably by several families in each.

Walking further on we spotted the Community Church behind a wall on which there was a sign in Chinese saying "International Church," with an arrow pointing to its gate. Another sign by the Police Department warned against any acts against the church. Within, we found workmen carting debris from the auditorium, where there was a bamboo scaffolding. The red brick building was overwhelmed by vines. We went around to the Sunday School annex and office where we found an elderly Chinese couple. I explained that I had once been a member of the church. They told us the buildings had been used for a Chinese opera school but now were being cleaned up, the auditorium to be repainted, and then to be used again for Christian services. There evidently had been a high-level decision to allow Chinese to practice Christianity openly, as part of the new tolerance and window to the West. The same was so of Islam and Buddhism. Across the church lawn we saw and heard a young man playing a flute—a bucolic experience. Later, Mr. Li Shou-pao, a YMCA secretary and apparently one of the spokesmen for the regime on Christian matters, called on us at the hotel and told us that Christianity not only had survived but was flourishing, and there was more religious freedom than ever during the past thirty years. Mr. Li confirmed that the Community Church was now to be used for Christian worship, but he also told us its organ had been irreparably destroyed during the Cultural Revolution. We have since learned that the church is used for international Christian services and has more Chinese members than foreign.

Next morning we walked along Nanking Road, the main shopping street, at about eleven o'clock and found it crowded with Chinese on holiday, walking leisurely to enjoy the sights. No one was hurrying. In fact, on our trip through China we saw no Chinese walking briskly, though we kept looking. An explanation for the Thursday morning crowd of strollers was that days of rest are staggered and this was the Thursday contingent on their day off. Department stores were busy, but there were plenty of persons to gather and watch members of our party standing on the steps of the Overseas Chinese Hotel watching them. One member of our group, who spoke Chinese rather well, attracted a crowd by taking Polaroid instant pictures. He asked whether there was any fear of gathering and talking with foreigners. Someone replied that it was all right now, October 1980, but they weren't sure how long this would last. Asked what would have happened previously if such a crowd had gathered around a foreigner, he was told that the police would have taken them away for questioning.

This curiosity in a city which must see thousands of foreigners on tour every week surprised us. Taipei citizens are blasé about foreigners in their midst. But then, we had seen thousands of Chinese so far on our tour, and yet we enjoyed gazing at them!

Kay and I visited Shanghai's city museum in a converted municipal building and saw a fine collection of bronzes, ceramics, and paintings; and also observed noisy groups of schoolchildren on tour. There were spectacular displays of Han and Tang murals recovered from tombs, and several rooms of beautiful scroll paintings by artists from the tenth century onward. I took down the names of some artists we particularly liked, hoping to buy some reproductions, as we could in Taipei at the Palace Museum. Alas, there was only a poor collection of reproductions in the museum shop, so we bought only one.

In the afternoon we had an exciting ride on the Whangpoo River on an excursion boat, with the cabin that had been reserved for our group amply stocked with beer, soft drinks, tea, and snacks. We sailed past the Bund with the Customs House, the British Consulate, and the Garden Bridge and gazed on a fascinating mix of modern shipping and old fashioned junks, some under sail and others speeding along under power, and a medley of tugs and lighters much in need of paint. There were long lines of freighters hitched to buoys near the middle of the stream, mostly Chinese, but we noted one Japanese and one Polish ship. Yet there was no sign of loading or unloading, and we guessed the vessels were waiting a turn at the docks. One almost unbelievably odd sight was of a freighter with several barges at its side far below, each with cone-shaped piles of coal. We saw one man shoveling coal over the side of the freighter onto a pile on one of the barges. No mechanical lifts or cranes were working, just that solitary man! Maybe he was only cleaning up the spilled coal on the deck. I can think of no other explanation.

We sailed down past factories, shipyards, refineries and storage tanks, docks and warehouses, on both sides of the river to the juncture of the Whangpoo and the Yangtze rivers, a trip that I had taken several times as a boy because ocean liners had to anchor out there and transport their passengers to or from the Bund by launch. It was a most enjoyable three-hour trip.

We had to be up by 5:30 the next morning with bags outside the door, breakfast at 6, and then off to Shanghai's airport for a flight to Kweilin in southwest China. We thought the airport for Shanghai, a city of ten million and an important point of foreign contact, was unimpressive. There were perhaps six planes on the runways to which passengers were taken by little buses, but the posted schedule showed domestic flights throughout the day to many cities. Our party was split and Kay and I drew the second plane, an uncomfortable, noisy,

Russian-built turbo jet, which we shared with a French tour group. The plane was delayed about two hours and had to stop at Hangchow and Nanchang to refuel. This gave us a chance to see the wonderful Chinese farm scenery around these provincial capitals. Coming into Nanchang we had a good view of the Kan River and Poyang Lake with their interesting sailing craft.

When we landed in Nanchang, I gave our group a short briefing about the Nanchang uprising on August 1, 1927, which is celebrated in the People's Republic as the founding day of the Red Army. Chu Teh, Chou Enlai, and many other Communist notables participated in the uprising, and I had published an extended article in *The China Quarterly* about it. I also explained how the province of Kiangsi, where we were, had been the scene of a seven-year war between Nationalist and Communist troops, until the latter were driven out and began what is now·called the Long March. We then flew over Hunan Province—the birthplace of Mao Tse-tung and many other rebel notables—in a southwesterly direction to Kweilin, arriving several hours late.

Kweilin is a fairyland. The area is famous for its karst formation. Millions of years ago it was part of the ocean floor, and as the ocean retreated it left behind jagged peaks of limestone pierced by weird caves. Archaeological findings indicate that humans existed in this vicinity about ten thousand years ago, at least. The Li River winds in and out among the peaks like a giant dragon. The town was about 200,000 in population when we visited. Poets and painters have memorialized the scenery. Li Po and Tu Fu, among China's greatest, wrote verses about it, and we have a treasured reproduction of a painting from the imperial collections by Mi Fei (1051–1107), who evoked in an ethereal way the exquisite scenery.

As soon as our plane was over Kweilin we could see the weird peaks and other strange formations, like nothing we had ever seen before, as if we were on a different planet. Once landed, we were whisked off to our hotel, where we joined the rest of our party and then we hurried off to climb a nearby peak from which we commanded a glorious view of the Fu Bo Hill, the Elephant Hill, and the Single Beauty Hill, rising abruptly out of the city or nearby lakes. Below us, boats on the Li River looked like tiny slivers hardly moving in the water. They were being punted or rowed. The city has a lovely promenade along the Li, and this makes a charming and uncluttered walk, quite different from crowded Shanghai or Peking. Around the city were lush rice fields and abundant cane fields, for this was southern China. The reflections of the peaks in the water in the rice fields made an ethereal effect. During the Sino-Japanese War, however, Kweilin was a place of retreat for many thousands of Chinese and was bombed repeatedly by the Japanese. Toward the end it was a training base for America's effort to beef up the Chinese Army, was briefly lost to the Japanese, and then was regained by our side. Kweilin was particularly interesting to me because in 1922 Dr. Sun Yat-sen attempted to mount an invasion of Hunan from there, but it was aborted and he had to return to Canton. He, like innumerable people before us, had seen this lovely scenery.

Next morning we took a day-long boat ride down the Li River. Our boat had open decks and a cabin below. It was towed downstream by a motor boat attached by a long cable. Our boat had a kitchen on the rear deck with coal stoves capable of heating huge caldrons of rice and pans of delicious vegetable and meat combinations, so dearly loved by the Chinese.

On either side of the river rose gigantic peaks of every imaginable shape. It seemed impossible to have such a variety in natural formations. Some were covered with greenery, bamboos or pines; others rose, sheer and naked rocks, piercing the sky. One could see caverns on the sides of some, and twisting paths along their ledges. Between the mountains and all along the river banks, Chinese farmers raised sugar cane or vegetables. We passed by their poor houses along the river banks, with steep steps leading to the water, where we saw women washing clothes and spreading them on rocks to dry. We passed groups of water buffalo grazing near the shore. Lovely clumps of bamboos shaded some villages. Native craft abounded. In paintings they look romantic; close up, they are dilapidated, dirty, seemingly made of any wood available, and patched together in magical fashion. Some were mere rafts of six bamboo poles lashed together, and with a basket in the middle. Some were rowed, most were punted, for the river is shallow, and some were being towed upstream from the land. We saw two women bent double trying to drag a large houseboat along, inch by inch. They were attached to the boat's mast by a long rope, while a man in the stern was poling as well as steering. Then there were sailboats, gliding majestically. We also saw several chains of large boats, or of rafts, being towed up stream by tugs. It was a photographers' paradise. Those five hours on the river were the high point of our China tour.

But not all was paradise. After our lunch we observed the staff washing our dishes in the river water. It seems our party suffered no ill effects from the practice, unless that was what downed Kay next day in Canton.

We had to push on to Canton that very evening, flying there in an hour and a half. Our good master guide had secured us rooms in a hotel in spite of the Canton Trade Fair that was said to be taking up all hotel space.

Canton is a city that I have studied and written much about but had never seen. Unfortunately, we had only one day there, Sunday, and Kay was ill most of that day. We arrived at Canton at night and were taken by bus through quiet boulevards to the White Cloud Hotel, a twenty-storied structure in the northern suburbs. I had asked, while in Peking, to meet a professor from Chung-shan University, Chen Xiqi (Ch'en Hsi-ch'i), who heads the Sun Yat-sen Research Institute, and to whom a mutual friend had sent a copy of my book on Dr. Sun. Although it was Sunday, it was arranged for Professor Chen to call on me in the hotel in the morning.

Professor Chen arrived promptly at nine, bringing a younger man, Professor Lin Jiayou, who had been his student. Professor Chen was in his mid-sixties and seemed frail. We exchanged courtesies in Chinese, inquiring after each other's health, children, and so on. Then he invited me to come to their university in the afternoon to meet colleagues and give a talk. The university is named after Sun Yat-sen (or Sun Chung-shan), and it is across the Pearl River on the campus of the former Canton Christian College, or Ling-nan. Professor Chen had arranged to send the university car for me.

I was interested to find that Professor Chen knew by reputation a number of my scholar friends in Taiwan and commented on some of their works. He also knew about the International Sinological Conference that I had attended in Taipei in August, two months before. He admitted that his institute did not have the funds to buy the many documentary volumes published by the Kuomintang archives. He also knew the work of several China scholars in America, and of Harold Schiffrin in Israel, though not of his latest biography of Dr. Sun, which I later sent to him.

I was eager to explore a bit between my two appointments. After my guests had left I hired a taxi and had the driver take me to historic Shameen, the sand bar in the Pearl River that the British and French had converted into a green island and had held as their concession area for eighty years till 1941. Once on Shameen, I saw a fine promenade facing the city, beautiful old trees, and rather grand buildings in European style, but now deteriorated, since all were more than fifty years old. In what had been a beautiful tree-lined mall, perhaps a mile long, there were now one-storied brick houses and even a few shanties crowded in. A building that had once been the Anglican Church under arching trees, its exterior now in disrepair, contained a printing establishment going full blast on this Sunday morning. Across a narrow canal that separates the island from the Canton waterfront was Shakee, a bund that in June 1925 was the scene of a massacre of parading Chinese, including schoolchildren, college students, workers, and cadets of the Whampoa Military Academy, then headed by the youthful Chiang Kai-shek. The paraders were shouting patriotic and anti-imperialist slogans when someone started firing across that narrow canal. On the Shameen side were British and French troops sent there to guard the concessions. Testimony as to which side fired first is in absolute conflict, but the carnage on the Chinese side was awful.

Today sanpans, small rowboats, tie up at the Shakee wall to sell vegetables at the side of that important thoroughfare, lined with colonnaded shops and office buildings. Leading off from the Shakee is a street market that was jammed with Sunday shoppers. This part of Canton where foreigners lived so independently is now completely Chinese, while foreigners come as tourists, or for trade fairs, as in the days of the imperial tribute system two centuries before.

In the afternoon Mr. Lin came in the university car, driven by a lady chauffeur with white gloves on, and we went by an interesting route across the Pearl River by a new bridge with lots of pedestrians and bicyclists to Chungshan University. The old Ling-nan campus had been out in the country when Sun

Yat-sen spoke there in 1923, and one reached it from Canton by launch. Now the city had engulfed it. Professor Chen and some colleagues awaited us at a guest house, and of course I had to take the center seat facing the door, with Professor Chen at my right and on my left Professor S. T. Jiang, a Ph.D. from the University of Washington, whose dissertation I knew in published form. About ten members of the Sun Yat-sen Institute scattered themselves about the room and tea was served. The conversation was partly in Chinese and partly in English, translated by Dr. Jiang, when I was asked to discuss recent trends in American scholarship on the Chinese Revolution of 1911–12. The topic may have been chosen in anticipation of a planned celebration of the revolution's seventieth anniversary, a year hence. A similar celebration was being planned in Taiwan, each side, of course, looking back on the revolution as their own. After an hour, we all went over to a small museum that contains photographic displays of Sun Yat-sen and mementos of his career, including a very worn suit of his clothes (the display in Taiwan has a pair of his shoes). Professor Chen was familiar with *Sun Yat-sen: Frustrated Patriot* and discussed some issues raised in it. His greatest flattery was to say that the author "had the eye of a dragon"—that is, that he could pierce right to the core of a matter! While walking on the campus he pointed out the building where Dr. Sun gave a lecture to the students and faculty of Ling-nan in December 1923, in circumstances described in the book. The campus, incidentally, could very well have been for a small Ohio college, except that the students I saw were all Chinese.

The university had been closed for seven years during the Cultural Revolution, and the library had been roughly treated by the Red Guards; it was far from having recovered its losses. On the ride back to my hotel Professor Lin confided to me that Professor Chen had been sent to work as a farmer for three years, and that his health still suffered. We have remained friends ever since.

On our way back, I saw one motorized bicycle—in Taipei there would be thousands—and three young Chinese women in skirts, the first seen in sixteen days in China. Were they from Hong Kong? Or was it an indication of Canton's greater Westernization? The contrast between the clothes worn in a regimented society and those worn by Chinese in Hong Kong and Taiwan was striking. The time was just at the beginning of China's reopening to the world, as encouraged by Deng Xiaoping.

Our final night in China we had a banquet scheduled, but Kay didn't feel up to it. Everyone was solicitous for her. After seeing her get a light supper, I went off with the group of fellow travelers to a fancy restaurant with room after room connected by winding bridges set above a great pond with willows and goldfish. We were told the restaurant could feed several thousand guests at one time. We shared a room with another tour party, but our own two tables were a world to themselves, with a great deal of affectionate toasting between courses of exotic food, and several toasts to the missing Kay. As always she had won everyone's heart. We paid for this meal ourselves, about U.S. $19 per person, including wine and *mao-t'ai* (as the Chinese call this particular firewater). There were speeches of tribute to our most efficient escort, Mrs. Qi, and for the local guide, Mr. Chu, who had met us at the airport twenty-four hours before with a "Hi, folks."

We were up early next morning, October 27, for a seven o'clock departure by train for Hong Kong. Everything on the Chinese side went like clockwork, with Mr. Chu leading our "gang of eighteen" to reserved seats in a first-class coach. We rode through beautiful countryside, past manicured rice fields in the delta lands, across East River at Sheklung, and then into more mountainous territory as we approached the border of Hong Kong's New Territories, acquired in 1898. At the border we detrained and Mr. Chu led us through exit procedures—customs declaration, money changing, and passport stamping. That took about an hour because of the crowds of overseas Chinese and foreigners—literally, some thousands of tourists—departing via our train. Without Mr. Chu's guidance the procedure would have been quite bewildering. We then walked with our hand baggage to the famous Lowu Bridge, where Mr. Chu delivered his charges to a man from the Hong Kong office of the China Travel Service. In making our departure we saw several large parties, mostly Americans, excitedly starting inward. I do believe we had exceptionally fine treatment on our tour because of our auspices, the National Committee on U.S.–China Relations, which had done much for amicable cultural relations and, more specifically, to assist many official groups coming from China.

Kay and I were to have three wonderful days as guests of David and Natasha Wilson at their home on the Peak. He was then the political adviser to the governor. We didn't suspect that eight years later he would be Sir David, and himself be the governor.

The following is what I wrote after our trip:

> On leaving China, I characterized it as "the struggling giant; the self-wounded giant." In 1950 the vast country had almost half a billion people and had just come out of thirteen years of war. Now the Chinese People's Republic had passed thirty years without civil war, rebellion, or invasion. The nation had made great material progress during three decades in which most private land and business was nationalized, new forms of social organization and systems of production were created, and great capital investments were made for industrialization. Yet our outstanding image is of an underdeveloped nation in material terms compared with Taiwan, Hong Kong, and, of course, Japan, a crushed and devastated country only thirty-five years ago.
>
> One sees a stolid and seemingly docile people, masking their individuality, compared with the brisk and confident Japanese or the assertive Chinese in Hong Kong. Does this air of placidity result from caution in the face of an all-powerful but quixotic political regime? As far as we could see, the people were healthy and enjoying enough food: open-air markets were filled with vegetables and buyers, restaurants crowded. Shops in Loyang and Shanghai were full of people, but many goods for sale were shoddy.

What struck us most vividly was the incredible amount of hand labor still used, and the scarcity of power-driven equipment. We saw tractors being produced but none in use. We saw small motors pulling wagons now and then, fine Japanese-made buses, and trucks more common than motor cars. In Taipei the motorcycle has nearly driven the bicycle off the streets, but we saw very few in China's cities. There were striking sights of three men in Shanghai pushing a great two-wheeled cart loaded with bamboo poles, as of old; and those men in Hsian sawing planks from a huge log by hand. Outside Loyang we saw several score of women and men plowing, hoeing, and raking a few acres manually, fields that an American farmer would plow and harrow with a tractor in a few hours.

We vividly remember people bent double to pole their boats or rafts upstream, and especially those two women in harness inching a junk up the Li River. In Canton we passed a team of men leveling a hillside to make the foundation of a building, doing with hoe and shovel what a bulldozer could level in an hour. En route to Hong Kong we saw a great stretch of coal beside the tracks, half a mile long on estimate, and swarms of men and women attacking it with shovels and handcarts. These are memories of human muscle expanded on tasks that in Taiwan or Hong Kong would be done routinely by machine.

However, there are signs that motor power is moving in—pumps driven by gasoline or electric power, drawing water into fields, lorries carrying farm produce, and motorized junks on the Whangpoo River, as examples. The railways we rode for perhaps a thousand miles were great. There is much building of residential flats, some fine new railway stations and airports, a few modern hotels, and broad boulevards in newer sections of several cities we visited. No one showed us a labor camp, a prison, or a state farm, nor did we see any of China's heavy industries. We saw no military displays and only one soldier on guard, armed with a submachine gun and carrying two pistols, though we kept looking. The streets everywhere would shame the filthy ones of New York or even the littered streets of Pleasantville. There are many pluses as well as minuses. The great intangible is popular attitudes.

The Communist Party is doubtless proud of its accomplishments in guiding the Chinese nation for thirty years in its boot-strap operation, but the regime inflicted terrible blows as well: its cruel elimination of "class enemies" and harsh discrimination against the survivors; its oscillations in policy; and its costly mistakes such as the Great Leap Forward followed by famine, and the Cultural Revolution's "ten wasted years." There were millions of blighted lives. A less violent and less repressive regime might have moved the country farther ahead, more steadily, in thirty years. Yet, to its credit, the regime has persistently tried to bring a more abundant, more egalitarian life to China's common people, while at the same time seeking to remold them to fit Mao's vision of the true socialist proletarians.

22

More Retirement Years, 1980–1983

The chairman of the board of the Mount Pleasant Public Library, located in Pleasantville, asked if she might propose my name for appointment as a trustee. Perhaps this was because Kay and I had gone to a village board hearing where salaries for the librarians was being discussed. We were indignant that an experienced person with an M.A. in Library Science would join the staff at a salary less than that of a beginning garbage collector! Did we make a fuss over that!

I enjoyed those years of public service and think my main contribution was to insist, year by year, that we upgrade the salary scale. This meant battles over budgets each year with the village and town boards, for it was a public library, supported by tax funds. My first year on the board I was made chairman of the Budget Committee, a way to educate me. One had to debate Charlotte, the director, over details of her proposals, for we knew we would have to defend the budget before those other two boards.

In February 1980 I had a most interesting experience. I was invited to join an academic committee that would visit the University of California, Berkeley, as part of the process of its reaccreditation. I was to look into its international affairs and foreign area studies program. Our team of academics had many illustrious people in their several fields. We had about five days in Berkeley, being welcomed by the provost and then going separately on our specific assignments to appraise as best we could how a department or school was doing in its field. I interviewed my old friend Bob Scalapino about the East Asian studies programs, also members of the Slavic Department, hearing complaints as well as boasting of accomplishments. Of course, the University of California at Berkeley is one of the very top American universities, rivaling Harvard, and I already knew something of its eminence in the East Asian field. However, I didn't think it any better than our East Asian program at Columbia in those days. My report got a couple of sentences in the overall appraisal, which was favorable—should the reader be anxious. The university did win its reaccreditation. Naturally, I worked in an evening with Jack and Cary Service and saw a few other academic friends in Berkeley.

Kay and I had a trip to Taiwan in August 1981, her first visit since May 1962, when we left from our Fulbright year. I had been invited to give a paper so my way was paid, and we shared Kay's expenses. I did research on the Second Kuomintang Congress in January 1926 and wrote a pretty good paper because I had the published minutes of the Congress. Later it was published in the Kuomintang historical journal, *China Forum*, in both English and Chinese, and it started a series by Chinese scholars on other KMT congresses.

In Taipei we got the royal treatment and had our best times with old academic friends. To enjoy some scenery we decided to take a cross-island tour. It was easy: just pay and go. So different from travel on the mainland.

We started Thursday morning, August 20, and went by cab to the travel office for a bus ride on the new super-highway to Taichung. That trip sped through lush farm country with rice fields emeralded with foot-high plants, prosperous farmhouses, bamboo clumps swaying, and grave mounds here and there on the hillsides. We noted a great deal of new building in the towns along the highway—rows of apartments, factories, and other buildings, all looking rather forlorn in their raw state. Cement and red brick seem to be the staple building materials.

Taichung, where we arrived in about two and a half hours, is greatly changed from twenty years ago, a little Taipei, in fact. We saw a great plethora of shops piled high with all sorts of goods, many office buildings, and rushing traffic. Ladies driving motorcycles were quite evident; but there were touches of the past, too—the old railway station of red stone built under the Japanese administration facing a big square, and a few old Japanese-style wooden buildings, unpainted and behind unpainted wooden fences, the color of weathered gray.

After lunch we took a walk in the very hot sun. The contrast in appearance with cities we saw on the mainland seemed incredible. People were smartly dressed in a variety of outfits, and the clothing stores had racks and racks of bright dresses, piles of handbags; many ladies wore heels. In a word: individuality, wear what you like, frocks, short skirts, slacks, even a few young girls in shorts. Men seemed mostly to wear business suits or open collar shirts. There were plenty of cabs, buses, and private automobiles; motorcycles outnumbered bicycles.

On the cross-island trip, the descent to Hwalien was more spectacular than the ascent, because the surrounding mountains are higher and the road more curvy, if that is possible. Hwalien, which was a sleepy town up against the Pacific Ocean when we had seen it twenty years before, was now fairly bustling. On the way to the railway station we counted in a few blocks more than twenty women driving motorcycles. They were fewer than men, but just as much at home on their vehicles. There were more motorcycles than bikes.

Our visit to Taiwan gave an opportunity to compare the two Chinas. Partly because of my anti-Communist bias, but mostly because the realities face you immediately, the advantage in material terms is all on Taiwan's side. But I believe it also is somewhat favorable for the Republic of China in ethical and other nonmaterial aspects, too.

Here one is immediately struck with the autonomy of the individual, everyone bustling about doing jobs with energy, be it so humble as selling wares on the sidewalk before the gate of New Park, operating a noodle shop, charging along on a motorcycle to some appointment or occupation, or managing a small bookstore. Everything seems to depend on individual decision and effort. The work ethic is strong in Chinese society wherever one experiences it, in Hong Kong, Singapore, Chinatowns, or Taiwan, except in cities on the mainland. How could this individualism and enterprise have been suppressed there? Years and years of "brainwashing," persecution of intellectuals and entrepreneurs, and indoctrination of the entire population with the virtues of socialism and noncompetition, and years of nonincentive through nonreward of individual enterprise as a factory worker, or builder, or clerk, probably even as a bureaucrat—these are part of the explanation for the drabness, the uniformity, the leisureness, the masked emotions that one senses in the street population. In a Chinese restaurant in Taiwan there is boisterous conviviality; over there, in our brief opportunity to observe restaurant publics, there was considerable reserve, a subdued atmosphere. There the folks going to work either mount a bus from a queue or pedal sedately along among phalanxes of bicycles; here there are few bikes but thousands of motorcycles, taxis, cars, and buses weaving in and out. People waiting for a bus are orderly, but they certainly don't look in the least regimented, either in dress or behavior. At least this is so for adults. Kids below college age wear uniforms, fixed lengths of bobbed hair for girls and virtually shaven scalps for boys. Ironically, on the mainland it's the kids who are most colorfully and individually clad, at least those on excursion.

Chinese mainland society is regimented. In Taiwan not only does society seem unregimented, it seems free and easy. That is superficial. In fact, there is quite tight control through education, censorship of press and television. One sees more police and military here than on the mainland. There you see members or retired members of the People's Liberation Army in their baggy uniforms, but off-duty, touring. We saw almost no armed police or soldiers.

Goods in Taiwan are superabundant. Food, food, food; shops of every sort overflowing with books, radios, clothing, textiles, tea, or whatever you could want to buy. There was no such evidence of prosperity on the mainland. On the contrary, scanty displays in store windows, and what was for sale was quite expensive by local purchasing power.

I guess there is much greater equality of income and of lifestyle there than here in Taiwan. Salary scales are pretty uniform there, but here they are quite variegated. Factory labor is well paid, I was told by a respected person, because of labor shortage and competition between factories to keep skilled workers, who are free to move to better paying jobs. Is this situation limited to certain industries? Certainly there can't be much mobility for clerks, waitresses, lower-level bureaucrats, and all those humble occupations that people hurry off to each morning. And here there are many very wealthy persons.

The difference in dress! Here young ladies are fashion-conscious. Many wear heels and attractive frocks. But the main thing is that young women can go to the beauty parlor, they can have a wardrobe full of frocks, they can carry a bright parasol, they wear sheer stockings and attractive shoes. This doesn't apply to most middle-aged and older Taiwanese women—the skirt, blouse, and slippers make up their daily dress. Men wear Western business suits or open collar and patch-pocketed shirts of grey, blue, or tan, the color representing the institution where they work, a well-starched quasi-uniform, but fashionable. Our male academic friends looked smart and quite pleased with themselves in their outfits, which permit a bit of strutting.

How could our friends Chang Yu-fa, a teacher and staff member of the Institute of Modern History, and his wife, Li Tung-wen, a teacher of accounting in a commercial school, afford to shell out U.S. $10,000 for a thirty-day tour in Europe with over forty others from here, almost all academics? It was a pleasure tour and I doubt it was subsidized. How fine compared with the deep poverty of our academic friends nineteen years ago! But again, what a lot they spend on entertaining their "old teacher" and his wife. It must be a relief when the foreign friends are gone and they can be back at work and recuperate.

After the conference was over there was a breakfast for the foreign participants, hosted by Mr. Chiang Yen-shih, secretary general of the Kuomintang, an old friend from the days when he held the same position in the Joint Commission on Rural Reconstruction. The gathering turned out to be the occasion to have the official version of the death of Professor Ch'en of Carnegie-Mellon University explained. Apparently he was active in the pro-independence movement for Taiwan, which is a frightful sin in the KMT's eyes. The last person to see him alive (so far as is acknowledged) was his friend Professor Teng. He attended the breakfast as a sort of exhibit, but he didn't say much. We were all given abstracted versions of the conclusions of the official investigation commission and of the Control Yuan's two-member reinvestigating group. The cause of the death was obviously due to a fall from the top of a high building, but the reason for the fall itself remains uncertain. The meeting was an attempt to clear the Republic of China's name among us academics, but it was not convincing, instead embarrassing. At the American Institute in Taiwan—the quasi-embassy—we heard much grimmer accounts: torture and probable murder, and speculation that the murderers and all evidence were quickly done away with.

There were two sad events for me in 1982, the deaths of Kay Gammertsfelder and Julie How. We had a beautiful memorial service for Kay. As usual Peter Samsom gave a wonderful talk and read poetry that she loved. I was privileged to be one of the speakers. The church was quite full, because Kay had many, many friends and admirers. Nearly all the library staff was there.

Julie How (Mrs. William Hwa) was one of my first graduate students, and we had labored together, off and on since 1967, on the revision of our joint book.

However, during the past few years we hadn't seen each other, and my letters to her remained unanswered. I should have suspected she had some fatal disease. She did: cancer. Julie died on April 27, 1982. Her husband asked me to speak at the memorial service, which was held on the 29th, with a mostly Chinese attendance of her friends. I gave a tribute, which was not difficult, since Julie was an accomplished scholar.

Now the responsibility for getting out our revision would fall on me. I had lots to go on, for we had accumulated a great deal more information, most of it already written up. What was needed was patching together, editing, and retyping. At least that's what I thought. In fact, I spent about six years of work before the book finally came out in 1989.

The big event for Kay and me during 1982 was our golden wedding celebration on memorable July 17. We had planned long in advance for a celebration. In July 1981 we reserved the dining room of the Pleasantville Country Club just one block west of our home. At Christmas time we talked over plans with our kids and it was agreed that invitations would go under their names, that John would be official photographer and Ann would be mistress of ceremonies. We made up lists of relatives and friends, and finding too many of the latter we had to boil the list down. We arranged in January for Hope Phillips in Taipei to have our invitations printed in gold on red paper. The wording was cleared with the kids. We gave Hope a date for delivery because we wanted to mail the invitations on June 1, six weeks before the event.

In addition to the big party on the 17th, Kay wanted to entertain relatives at home on Friday night, so our invitations had a special insert from Kay and Martin, asking relatives to be with us for dinner on the 16th. We also alerted our closest friends ahead of time to save the July 17 date, and six of them offered to put up our out-of-town guests, and to help Kay with her dinner by providing special food.

Some of the fun, after we knew who was coming, was to organize the seating by affinity groups—church friends, relatives, academic colleagues, village friends. We did arrange congenial table groupings.

Ann came down on July 5 to help, and she was a wonderful helper. Also we had the longest visit with her since she was married nearly fifteen years before. One amusing thing sticks in our memory: Kay and I had planned to split the cost of the bash, but Ann became furious at that, for she had the idea of paying for it herself. I remember her pacing around and accusing us of treating her like a child! We calmed her down and persuaded her to split the cost three ways, and that we did.

Kay's party for relatives drew twenty-four. Everyone was soon on congenial terms. A most successful party!

Next day, Saturday the 17th, was sure to be hot. The more removed relatives took care of themselves or went to see friends, but the direct descendants of Hollis and Mary Wilbur, that is, Beth and Jean, Hal and Betsey, John, Ann, and

I, together with Kay and Nol went for lunch at a nearby Japanese restaurant, which got Kay out of the kitchen and was a pleasant diversion. Then we all went to take a nap. At 2:30 Ann and I went over to the club to take flowers and seating lists, the guest book and picture albums, and had a shock to find the dining room not air conditioned, as it had seemed to be in the mornings when we had been there to discuss, and the parking lot was filled with cars—naturally, on a Saturday afternoon at a golf club. Murphy's law!

We went back home to dress, Kay in her beautiful plum-colored and brocaded Chinese long gown (she is a knockout!) and I in my white and blue corded suit with a red tie, naturally! When we got over to the club we immediately abandoned the idea of a receiving line, invited the men to put their jackets at their tables, and everyone went to the bar for cool drinks. In the end ninety-seven people came. Everyone knew some other folks there, and the terrace was the best place for socializing.

Ann, as mistress of ceremonies, was charming. Many friends later commented on her beauty and presence. John was busy taking pictures, and the fine pictures he took still remind us of a lovely occasion. Ann wove a theme of our life together, inviting Hal to talk about us as brother, Sam Chu as a former student, Jim Morley as an academic colleague, Thelma Carter as a church friend, and Hoch Reid as a fellow villager. Spencer Brown read a humorous poem he had written for the occasion. I said some word in appreciation of my dear wife. After the speeches, Kay and I went from table to table toasting our guests in Chinese style. A waitress preceded us to fill the guests' glasses. We then cut the first slice of cake.

Finally everyone repaired to the terrace again, which had gotten much cooler by 7:30, and there was much picture taking, both formally and quite informally. We have many mementos. After much more visiting the party began to break up, and we gathered our stuff and went home to relax.

Sunday was sort of sad. Ann and Nol, John and Shirley, Hal and Betsey all took off in the morning. The Edsons and the Meeches stopped in to say goodbye. Beth moved back to our house for a couple more days, and Jean left in the later afternoon. So our long-anticipated golden wedding celebration was behind us, with fond memories of many kindnesses, affection, help from John and Ann, and a generally great good time.

I had to face up to the completion of the manuscript that Julie How and I had been working upon since Columbia University Press asked us in 1966 to prepare a revised edition of *Documents on Communism, Nationalism and Soviet Advisers in China, 1918–1927*. In taking up this task alone, I first had to determine how long the manuscript would be and find a way to finance its retyping. Anita O'Brien, who was the publications manager for the East Asian Institute, and who also did freelance work, estimated her typing time after I had calculated how long the manuscript now was. There were chapters Julie and I had completed, but some of hers in draft form only. Then there were the documents in various formats, and necessary introductions and conclusions still to be written. My estimate turned out to be too low, and hers was also. I then made an application to the American Council of Learned Societies for a grant of $7,700. The council had a Ford Foundation-financed China Committee to support research. After the usual several months wait, I was informed that the committee was giving me a grant of $8,000. I wrote IRS to get a ruling whether the grant was taxable and was told it would not be. I kept meticulous accounts of all expenses, most of which were to pay Anita for work on her computer. I also kept a log of the hours and days that I worked on the book. It took up most of my mornings for five or six years.

I decided to begin with the documents, of which we now had about fifty new ones never published, as well as the fifty in the earlier edition, but now needing improvements. I rearranged them in chronological sequence—previously there was a topical arrangement—but clustered them into nine groups. All had to be carefully edited and provided with explanatory introductions before I sent them in batches to Anita. It soon became evident that the documents alone would run to some six hundred pages, so I decided to take out those dealing with the Soviet effort with Feng Yu-hsiang in North China, and Julie's completed chapter about them, and publish these separately under her name. Bernadette Li, editor of *Chinese Studies in History*, accepted that part for an issue of her journal, Anita typed up the manuscript, and it was published as *Soviet Advisers with the Kuominchun, 1925–1926: A Documentary Study*, by Julie Lien-ying How, *Chinese Studies in History*, vol. 19, nos, 1–2, 1985–86. That gave Julie the prominence she deserved and removed fourteen documents from our volume. I decided to leave out a few Soviet reports on the condition of the National Revolutionary Army in March 1926 that were well covered in an overall report. This reduced our total to eighty-one documents, and the page length for the documentary section to a bit under 400 pages as finally published.

I kept feeding batches of documents to Anita, and she would send back the typescript for my proofreading. Also, I employed a proofreader because two are better than one in this aspect of publishing. I took out insurance against the loss of a unique manuscript, and Anita kept backup discs. This work went on and on until the documentary part was done. I then had to confront the incomplete manuscript of our historical accounts of the events with which we were dealing. Here I could do some cutting, sharpening, and also provide a few topical sections that neither Julie nor I had covered. Some of these supplements were based upon the two thousand pages of translations from Russian that Lydia Holubnychy had done for us before her untimely death. These were either reminiscences of participants in the Soviet effort in China, a diary and a few dated letters from the period itself, or more modern Russian scholarly accounts based on Soviet archives.

I became more and more interested in those Russians working in China for the revolution and decided I must present them as real people plunged into a strange but exciting environment, just as all foreigners are who go to China. So I combed the reminiscent accounts for information on recruitment and motivation, on first experiences, on sicknesses or deaths among the missionaries, on their group life and conflicts and romances among them, and how they reacted to the Chinese people with whom they associated. There was enough documentary and reminiscent material to write quite an interesting introduction. Previously most of the persons in the drama had been mere shadows, in fact, sinister shadows, as viewed by other Westerners in China and by many Chinese. But not by all. There was evidence that Chinese supporting Sun Yat-sen and the revolutionary Kuomintang adored the Soviet advisers, particularly "Galen."

By now I had assembled a long list of pseudonyms and corresponding real names of these Russians. "Galen" was the assumed name of Vasilii Konstantinovich Bliukher, one of Russia's brilliant civil war commanders, who later became the commander-in-chief of the Russian Far Eastern Army.

In June 1983 I received a signal honor: I was awarded a citation by the government of the Republic of China. Dr. Frederick Chien, the chief representative of the Republic of China in Washington, invited me to come to his home for the presentation. Dr. Chien was an old acquaintance. He was not China's ambassador, for the United States had switched diplomatic relations to the People's Republic of China. We stayed with Joyce Edson, and of course she was invited to the presentation dinner. I had suggested a few other guests—Ed Beal, the Ray Clines, and Ed and Paula Harrell. The Chiens added Franz Michael and Dave Rowe, whom I knew well. They, like me, were firm supporters of the Republic of China. And, of course, there were a number of Chinese officials.

The presentation ceremony was very nicely done, with enough solemnity to seem official. I was given a framed plaque about eighteen inches on a side, signed by the Chinese foreign minister and written in the name of President Chiang Ching-kuo, and stamped in red with a large official seal. The plaque, which I now have over my desk, is dated August 21, 1982, though the presentation was on June 6, 1983. I also received a ribbon and an emblem for the buttonhole. Dr. Chien pinned a similar emblem on Kay. Pictures were taken and I made a little speech of appreciation. Then we all sat down to dinner, a splendid Chinese meal. Dr. and Mrs. Chien are gracious hosts. This time Kay and I had our wits about us and gave the signal for arising, and then for departure, at the appropriate times, à la Chinois.

Much later Dr. Chien told Roger Kodat in Taipei that the award was the highest one the Republic of China gives to a foreign person. I had not realized that I was receiving that distinction.

We spent a couple more days in Washington so I could do some interviewing in connection with a paper I was writing for a conference to be held at St. John's University on Sino-American relations, my assignment being relations in scholarship as seen from the American side. Professor Chang Peng-yuan was to do a paper on the same subject as seen from the Taiwan side. I had suggested these subjects and assignments and had asked the conference organizer to bring Professor Chang to America at the conference's expense, which was done. In Washington I saw David Dean, head of the American Institute in Taiwan—that is, the part of the State Department setup outside the District of Columbia to conduct relations with the Republic of China as part of the deal whereby the U.S. government "recognized" the People's Republic but still maintained quasi-diplomatic relations with the Republic. He brought me up to date on current relationships. I also talked with John Hughes at the National Academy of Sciences, Bert O'Connell at the National Science Foundation, and Howard Gleysteen, who had been in the Taipei Embassy but was now retired and heading Asia Society in Washington. Each gave me good insights into how various cooperative enterprises, particularly joint scientific programs, had worked out. I knew quite a bit about the humanities and social sciences side, having been involved in promoting such cooperation.

In August 1983 we went to London on an Interhostel at the University of London. We stayed in a dormitory of the School of Oriental and African Studies in Bloomsbury, a fine location near the British Museum and the Courtold Galleries, both of which we visited when on our own. The program was about two weeks and included good lectures by faculty members on such subjects as the British social security system, historic English gardens and gardening, contemporary British literature, Shaw, and other engaging topics. The Interhostel also included two plays, a trip to Cambridge, and another to Dover and Canterbury, and we had some free time to visit the National Gallery and the Tate—very worthwhile. After the Interhostel, Kay and I had a one-week cruise on a narrow boat on the British canal system. A delightful way to see rural England.

23

Rich Years, 1984–1986

The Community Unitarian Church at White Plains was an important part of our lives. We joined it in 1948 so our kids would have a place to learn something of our Christian heritage, and many years later our daughter was married there. Many of our closest friends were members of the church, including all those, now dead, who took us into their social circle when we were newcomers in Westchester. It is a nontheological church; each member finds his or her own truth. There is no creed. Over the forty years of membership, we listened to three ministers, Cliff Vessey, Peter Samsom, and more recently, Shannon Bernard. Cliff was the most poetic, and listening to only a few of his sermons persuaded us to join the church, then in its old location on Maple Avenue. Peter always gave carefully prepared sermons, sometimes quite inspiring, though he wasn't an outstanding church leader. Shannon did a lot to revitalize the church after Peter left, though her sermons became somewhat tiresome. We also heard many other stimulating speakers, such as Norman Thomas, Michael Harrington, Whitney Young, and John Fisher, editor of *Harpers*.

A wonderful feature of our church life was the fine classical music played by accomplished soloists. Year after year, we heard Lillian Goodman on the cello and Harold Bogin on our magnificent Steinway play selections from the repertoire of cello and piano, and we still have a recording of some of their favorite pieces. About one in four Sundays some other performer would play in their stead. The service usually began with a short concert, and there would be another concert at collection time. This music set a reverential tone for the services. The beauty of the setting, the lovely music, and the interesting speeches made for an enriched Sunday.

Services during the summer were informal, organized by members of the congregation, using our own talent, of which there was plenty. During three of the summers, Kay and I gave talks, for each of which we did a lot of research. One was "On the Prophets Isaiah," so entitled because the book was written over a period of more than two hundred years. In addition to its inspiring teachings, it is interesting to note how the concept of God developed during those centuries. Another talk was on "The Gnostics," a fascinating early Christian sect that eventually died out—or was repressed by the Catholic Church. The Gnostics had some scriptures that are not included in the New Testament, but which were discovered recently in upper Egypt and have been translated. Their alternative concepts of Jesus make them most interesting. The present New Testament version is not necessarily the only one. The third talk we gave was "On Ecclesiastes," the latest book included in the Old Testament (it barely made it!) and different in its outlook from any other. The philosophy seems permeated by fatalism, epicureanism, and stoicism. The date, ca. 250 B.C., may explain the writer's outlook, for this was Alexandrian times in the eastern Mediterranean. We learned a lot from these three talks, and I became much interested in the historic Jesus, whoever he may have been.

Betsey Wilbur enriched our lives. She spent some vacations with us when in college and later when she was a volunteer worker in Haiti. Her visit in August 1984 was especially memorable. It was the time when she met Roger Kodat, with whom, at the insistence of a mutual friend, she had begun a correspondence. During three visits from Betsey, we saw a romance grow until it became an engagement, and on the third the young folks planned their wedding in our downstairs guest room. It was a lovely time for us. In mid-July 1985 there was a great gathering of the clan in Wooster to attend the wedding.

The day after the wedding, Kay and Ann and I drove to Haverford, Pennsylvania, to inspect the site of a planned retirement community called "The Quadrangle." We had visited an old Pleasantville friend at her Quaker-managed retirement community called Kendall, near Philadelphia. This got us thinking of our own future plans, and we had taken a trip southward in September 1984 to Raleigh, North Carolina, to visit Paul and Gertrude Wright, and to inspect the place where they were going to retire, as well as another place near Chapel Hill. On our way back north we had visited several retirement communities near Washington and Baltimore, and still others, Quaker-run communities, around Philadelphia. We had learned that all of those already established had long waiting lists, seven to ten years. Could we wait that long? When visiting Pennswood, we had learned of the Quadrangle, a Quaker community still in the planning stage. We had put down our $200 registration fee and made a date to see the person in charge of applications in July 1985. Ann had to be persuaded that her parents were not immortal and might someday really need to go into such a place. Since we did land in the Quadrangle four years later, I'd like to set down our first impressions:

Mrs. Harrison showed us a scale model of the planned buildings. Our first surprise was to learn that the date of entry is postponed till September 1987 because more financing must be acquired. The facility will cost about $50 million to build. However, the rates for purchase of a unit and the monthly fee will not go up, she said, before the end of 1987. And if we sign a contract and then become ill, we still will be admitted, she told us. We may be asked to choose our quarters and sign a contract in September. If so, we must then mount some $14,000 as a 10 percent returnable payment.

The 67-acre grounds are really beautiful, rolling and heavily wooded. There is a stream running through. Much will be left natural, and the living facilities will be sited like arms off from the manor house. I suspect it will be difficult to make a decision, balancing southern exposure, ground floor, distance from dining room and recreation rooms, etc.

If I look at the little engagement books for these years, I see a great similarity year after year: visits from John and Shirley on most holidays that came on weekends, but infrequent visits from Ann—perhaps once a year, she living so far away. Concerts in Chappaqua or Ossining, plays in New York theaters, "Mostly Mozart" concerts at Lincoln Center during summers. I see an occasional summer trip to Boston to visit the Museum of Fine Arts (four hours door-to-door to drive there, four hours to see a beautiful exhibit and eat a sandwich lunch, and four hours to drive back). I also see meetings of the Library Board, "Brown Bag" luncheons at the East Asian Institute, Modern China seminars, monthly conclaves of our talking group, and many dinners with our friends the Bodens, Reids, Holdens, Greenbaums, and Dakins, and, of course, reciprocating dinners at our home. This rich cultural life went on simultaneously with editorial and research work on *Missionaries of Revolution* (as it came to be named), gardening, and reading. Kay and I were both in good health, but I did have to have operations for hernia and, later, for prostate.

My friend Dr. Shaw Yu-ming had become head of the Institute of International Relations, a research and think tank with which I had long had relations through my work in promoting academic relations between American and Chinese scholars. He invited Kay and me to come to Taiwan as guests of the institute, all expenses paid, and first-class travel on China Airlines. I was asked to give one public address on a topic of my choosing.

The subject I chose was "Modern America's Cultural Debts to China"—to point out the reverse of what is so obvious, modern China's debts to the West. I pursued that topic for several months and divided the subject into four headings: contributions of individual Chinese, who chose the United States as their home, stressing the work of Chinese scientists, architects, doctors, engineers, performing musicians, even philanthropists and politicians; Chinese art in American museums; China in American popular culture—Chinese restaurants, for example; and China studies in America, about which I knew something. To gather materials, I studied *American Men and Women of Science*, a six-volume who's who, and found the names of some 1,333 Chinese, a much higher proportion than the number of Chinese in the American population.

I also studied the work of such outstanding persons as I. M. Pei, the architect who designed the East Wing of the National Gallery in Washington and many other cultural centers; and of young Maya Ying Lin, daughter of Chinese parents teaching at Ohio University in Athens, Ohio, where she grew up, and winner of the contest for the Vietnam War Memorial in Washington while she was still a senior in architecture at Yale. Maya had to overcome much opposition to her stark but beautiful abstract design, which now is fully accepted and visited by hundreds of thousands each year. Of course I wrote of the three Chinese Nobel Prize winners in physics—Li Cheng Dao, Yang Chen Ning, and Ting Chao-chung—and of An Wang, inventor of a computer business system that made him a millionaire; and of the superb cellist Yo-Yo Ma and the violinist Lin Cho-liang. In biology, Dr. Chang Ming-chueh was the codiscoverer of a birth control hormone that is now the contraceptive pill that millions of women use, and which brought about a worldwide change in sexual mores. And there are many more. It's really astonishing. I would guess that only Jews, among ethnic groups in America, have contributed more. I interviewed a number of noted Chinese to get their opinions. In fact, I accumulated a large file and considered someday writing a monograph on the subject, but I gave up the idea when we began preparing to move to the Quadrangle.

About forty American museums have respectable collections of Chinese art—bronzes, ceramics, paintings, and minor arts, and I discussed a few of them to explain how this happened. *Books in Print* lists some 2,700 books on China or things Chinese that one can purchase in America. Chinese cookbooks are particularly popular—I found 96 listed in the catalogues of the Library of Congress and the New York Public Library. There are probably 10,000 Chinese restaurants in America, or is that just a number like "myriad," meaning a lot? This is just a sampling of some of the topics I tried to research.

I didn't just enumerate but tried to explain why China and Chinese had contributed so much to America. The basic explanation was the richness and fertility of Chinese culture, the drive for success through education that its society emphasizes; but also the golden opportunities—and rewards—for accomplishment that the open society in America offers to motivated and talented individuals. Nor did I gloss over the harsh discrimination that our society has imposed on Asian minorities in the past and still imposes upon newly arriving immigrants.

I'm rather proud of that essay and the research that went into it. I wrote two drafts and then the final version. It was a good topic for a lecture to a Chinese audience in Taipei, and later the paper was published in the January 1986 number of *Issues & Studies* (the monthly journal of the Institute of International Relations) and copied by another Taiwan publication, *China and America*. With the research done and the paper written, Kay and I were ready to head off on our deluxe journey to the Far East.

We started on the night of September 13–14, 1985. After thirty-six hours of sitting (about twenty in the air), we arrived at Taipei airport at 6:30 Sunday morning. Our escort, Mr. Fan Li-ming, arrived a little later and we waited for friends, who we understood were coming to meet us. We soon were engaged in a loving reunion with Chang Peng-yuan and Teresa, Li Yun-han, and Chang Yu-fa. We were taken to the Ambassador Hotel, which I knew well from previous stays, and had the morning to rest. Then Peng-yuan and Teresa came to take us to lunch at a family-style seafood restaurant. Delicious! After that we went to a tailor and picked out dark blue cloth for a suit, bargained for by Teresa. With two pairs of trousers, it cost U.S. $212.50 and probably will last my lifetime. Also Kay bought tea, not cheap, three packages for equivalent of U.S. $22.50. In the evening Chang Yu-fa came to take us to his house for a dinner with friends from the Institute of Modern History, an enormous meal prepared by his vivacious wife. Dinner was served by the children—dish after dish appearing like magic. It probably took several days to prepare, but such is the way our Chinese friends wanted to honor us.

Beginning the next day, Monday, I was scheduled for a round of calls on important officials. First was Mr. Ma Shu-li, secretary- general of the KMT Central Committee, an apparently amiable gentleman, who told me about press freedom in Taiwan, including the statement that Seagrave's book, *The Soong Dynasty*, had been translated into Chinese and was for sale in Taipei. The book is unbelievably hostile to Chiang Kai-shek and all the Soongs, except for Mme. Sun Yat-sen, who then lived in Beijing. If it is for sale in Taipei, that, alone, doesn't prove press freedom. Mr. Ma gave me a catalogue of Palace Museum treasures and a small box, which, when we opened it at our hotel, contained a beautiful white and blue porcelain teacup with saucer and cover.

Next I went to see the foreign minister, Mr. Chu Fu-sung, who had signed the large citation awarded me in Washington by Dr. Frederick Chien. His message was that American scholars who had advocated American recognition of the PRC would still be welcome in Taipei, such as my friends Ed Friedman, Mike Oksenberg, and Doak Barnett. Minister Chu insisted that his government needed all-weather fighter planes to defend the island against attack from the mainland, a message that I was sure he also conveyed to visiting members of congress. From Minister Chu I received a big box containing a modern replica of a Tang horse, about 6 inches high.

I also called on my friend Wei Yung, now an important bureaucrat, head of the Commission for Research, Evaluation, and Development of the Executive Yuan, which provides bright social scientists the opportunity to do research on opinion trends and approaching societal problems, and to make policy recommendations to the government. I called upon Dr. Chang King-yu, Ph.D. Columbia, now director general of the Government Information Office. I gave him a copy of my book on the Northern Expedition and then was taken off for an on-camera interview in which I was supposed to pontificate, and from which the GIO could select clips for television showing. I scarcely remembered what I discussed, but I probably said a few things from the lecture I was scheduled to give. Of course they asked my impression of the mainland as compared to Taiwan, which is easy to be glib about, since material conditions in Taiwan are so very much better.

After those calls, back to the hotel to rest before a dinner hosted by Dr. Shaw Yu-ming, who had put together our VIP trip. Among the guests was Sister Madeleine Chi, our dear friend of long ago. Mrs. Shaw, an engaging hostess, was trained in library science and teaches at Taita in the island's only School of Library Science.

One pleasant occasion on Tuesday was a luncheon at Cheng-ta National University, hosted by President O-yang, and with some members of his faculty. I also saw a briefing about the university, which has some 7,000 students, many colleges, and even more graduate institutes that give higher degrees. Then to the Institute of International Relations, where I had been asked to give a talk and decided to give a précis of my hostile review of *The Soong Dynasty*, really a travesty of a book from a historical viewpoint.

In the late afternoon, Kay and I were taken to a place near the Palace Museum where the eminent painter the late Chang Ta-chien had lived in considerable style. He made a fortune from selling his paintings and lavished a lot of it in creating this house in Brazilian style (he had lived there for many years), but placed in a Chinese garden setting with rockeries, ponds, falling water, and so forth. He willed the house and garden to the Palace Museum. There we were received by Mr. Chin Hsiao-yi, director of the Palace Museum, whom I had met several times before. He had been a secretary to Chiang Kai-shek and was said to be a protégé of Mme. Chiang.

I was immediately drawn into a conference to discuss Mr. Chin's proposal that my historian friends Lu Shih-chiang and Li Kuo-chi and I should coproduce a book on Sun Yat-sen and Chiang Kai-shek. Apparently the idea was to counter Seagrave's book, and the two luckless Chinese scholars were supposed to complete the book, with its 100-year coverage, in eighteen months. I discouraged the possibility of doing it so quickly but agreed for courtesy sake that it was my intention after two years (which I explained must be devoted to my own book on the Soviet advisers)—and if my health permitted—to read a translation and make suggestions; also to write a preface. Actually, I doubted we would see any results of their efforts; but if a manuscript emerged, I expected it would simply be a rehash of the glorification of Sun and Chiang. In fact, nothing did come of Mr. Chin's apple-polishing scheme. However, the discussion, in the presence of a number of scholar friends, was embarrassing to me, because I could not, even for courtesy sake, agree to Mr. Chin's insistence that I become a coauthor, and that right away. Incidentally, I thought afterward that a Chinese way to get out of such a situation would be to agree to the request but then later do nothing about it.

Wednesday we went to the Institute of Modern History, where I improvised a talk about the new documents in the Wilbur and How book. When we were to depart, I was asked to sign a receipt for an envelope, which I gave to Kay immediately, and later found it contained 2,000 yuan (U.S. $50). Quite unnecessary, and I protested, but Chang Yu-fa, now the director of the institute, said it was their custom, and I should accept it. After admiring the new library building and seeing how the archive preservation was going on, we were taken to lunch downtown. Mrs. Wang Ping was particularly companionable to Kay.

After that Dr. Shaw took me to call on former President C. K. Yen, a dear old gentleman who seemed to appreciate our coming. He had been quite helpful eight years before in my effort to raise money for Columbia. We know one of his daughters, Nora, married to Professor Tony Leng of the University of Virginia. We then went to the National Science Council to call on Dr. Chiang Yen-ssu, former executive director of the Joint Commission on Rural Reconstruction, whom I had last seen when he gave that breakfast for visiting scholars to try to convince us of the innocence of the government in the slaying of the Chinese professor from Carnegie Mellon University. When he heard that Kay and I were going south to see other parts to the island, he urged us to visit Nan-yuan and to go to Chang-hua to see the growing of flowers for sale abroad. He even made arrangements for our visits. In the evening our closer Columbia friends gave us a Chinese dinner with a warm and informal atmosphere and much picture taking.

Our first call on Thursday was upon an old friend, Dr. Chiang Fu-tsung, formerly director of the Palace Museum. Dr. Chiang was eighty year old—we were then seventy-eight and seventy-seven ourselves—and after our visit, he insisted on escorting us in the hot sun to the museum, his home being only a little ways away. It was a courteous gesture, but surely unnecessary. There we saw some of the exhibits, especially a newly installed one of choice paintings arranged in chronological order from Tang through Five Dynasties, Sung, Yuan, Ming, into mid-Ch'ing—a spectacular display.

Then off to *United Daily News* (*Lien-ho pao*) for our luncheon with the president, Mr. Liu, and some of his staff. I drew Alice Ho as a dinner companion; she had been a Nieman Fellow at Harvard the previous year and was quite outspoken. I raised the question why their newspaper was so successful. Because, we were told, of the broad coverage and in-depth reporting, just like the *New York Times*. The *Lien-ho pao* publishes numerous magazines and thirty-eight editions of its daily, each having a page of local news, as well as editions in New York and Paris, and it has half a dozen news bureaus abroad. They also publish an economics paper, a daily for amusements, and a home interests paper. Quite a business.

After a brief rest period I was taken to a hall seating about 300 for my talk. There was a welcoming banner with my name in both English and Chinese. After too much introduction, I was allotted forty minutes to talk, and since Chang Peng-yuan was to interpret, I had to cut my twenty-two-page paper drastically as I went along, but the main theme—America is indebted to China culturally—came through and seemed much appreciated by the Chinese audience. Later I received an honorarium of a thousand dollars. Unusual for me!

That evening Dr. Chang King-yu hosted a dinner at the Ambassador Hotel, the other guests nearly all being Columbia graduates of long ago, now big-shots, and most of them contributors to the Wellington Koo Fellowship or the fund for China studies at Columbia. A pleasant occasion until our host made a speech about me that was inordinately flattering, to which I had to give a deprecating reply.

As I write this, I am impressed that we were able to carry out the schedule that had been planned for us at the pace that was required. This was the fourth official day, I had given three talks, we had seen many friends, eaten much great Chinese food, and I had called on a lot of most courteous officials. Columbia University is an important name in China because of the many eminent Chinese who graduated from there in the early years of this century.

I had asked for a few days outside of Taipei to see some of Taiwan's lovely scenery, and Peng-yuan had offered himself and Teresa as our escorts. Together we toured for three wonderful days in the southern part of the island in a car with driver. On our return to Taipei we gave a buffet dinner for our closer friends—a party of thirteen in a private dining room in the hotel. We had flowers on the table, and the friends knew we cared for them. The next morning we departed for Japan. Our visit to Taiwan, arranged by Shaw Yu-ming, was one of the happiest weeks Kay and I have had—or so it seems to me in memory.

We had one idyllic week in Japan, staying at International House for a few days and then going by bullet train to Kyoto for two days of sentimental sightseeing. A high point of the week was the half day that Professor and Mrs. Iwanaga gave us. We had become friends back in 1954–55. Now both of us professors were retired, he as professor of international relations at Tokyo University. They took us first to the National Museum of Art, a rather musty place but showing some fine Japanese and Chinese paintings. Then they took us to the Mitsukoshi Department Store, where we were gorged with the beauty of contemporary Japanese decorative work. It was a juried show of the outstanding productions of the nation's renowned master craftsmen. There were incredibly beautiful ceramics, lovely lacquer boxes and trays, small furniture, basketry, and the most gorgeous kimonos—one more lovely than the next. After taking us to dinner, Mrs. Iwanaga presented us with a covered dish in black lacquer, with design of iris painted in gold from the base up and across the cover. We always display this beautiful work of Japanese craftsmanship in a central spot in our living room.

The librarian at International House, Mrs. Kami Togasaki, who had worked in Columbia's East Asian Library, found us and persuaded us to go with her to an ancient and famous soba shop, dating back to the Edo period (before 1860). Our kids would have been jealous, for the soba was very good.

On the plane into San Francisco, I wrote the following reflections:

The two nations are very well managed, it seems. Prosperous and consumer-oriented, too. In both Taiwan and Japan, farming is small scale and marvelously well done. The villages we saw were fairly tidy, and for China this says something. The cities, however, are all abustle, with vast numbers of autos in Tokyo and motorcycles in Taipei. One is astonished at the number of restaurants and the amount spent on eating out in both cultures. There are hordes of schoolchildren in both countries—all in uniform and seemingly very well behaved, or even regimented. But Western pop culture has hit both urban cultures, and television can make it instantaneous. Compared with 1954–55 Japan and 1961–62 Taiwan, the change in material culture is impressive, but it seems to me that the personal behavior of each people—the manners and mannerisms—is much the same as before. Behavior patterns are taught early and definitely by parents, older siblings, and teachers, perpetuating national character traits, to use a now somewhat passé phrase.

I guess I like Chinese better than Japanese—the one more open, the other more introverted. Chinese women seem more "liberated" than Japanese women, who act very differently from men. Also, most Japanese women still seem squat-legged and not nearly so sexy as Chinese girls when they want to be. But many Japanese women and men are handsome, and many are taller than a generation ago.

It is so good to know that life is much easier now for our Chinese academic friends. Both husbands and wives have careers, children are mostly grown up, some married or in the States. They own their own homes or apartments, but none owns a car, though two have the use of the office car. They were very cordial to Kay and me. Several have visited in our home, and we encouraged them to come again.

An interesting item in the Tokyo English-language press—an opinion survey of the prime minister's office—found America and China the two countries most liked (America a little ahead) and Soviet Russia much disliked. This is just as it was thirty years ago. But Korea, which used to be at the bottom of the list, is moderately well liked, or, better to say, liked by about 20 percent.

In October/November 1986 I had a most interesting trip to Taiwan, Hong Kong, and China for three conferences in rapid succession. The first was in celebration of the one hundredth anniversary of the birth of Chiang Kai-shek, arranged by Mr. Chin Hsiao-yi, the head of the KMT archives and director of the Palace Museum, the one who tried to persuade me to join with two Chinese historians in writing a joint biography of Sun and Chiang. At that conference, which had many foreign members, I was a guest of honor, and all I had to do was comment on one paper—it was rather weak—and make a couple of brief speeches. Everything about the conference was lavish.

Toward the end of the conference I asked Mr. Chin if it would be appropriate for me to say a few words of thanks. He agreed and asked me to write out something that could be given to the press. I spent a couple of hours on my brief talk and then gave it to his secretary as a draft. She corrected a couple of points and then had the talk translated into Chinese.

The Hong Kong conference was hosted by Chu Hai College and its president,

Mr. Leung Wing-sun. The college must be financed by the KMT; at least it is not a Communist front. We were put up at the YMCA International House, a six-teen-story building, very modern, comfortable, clean rooms and private bath, a far cry from old-fashioned Y buildings. It seemed to be very much patronized.

At the end of the conference, which dealt with the "Kuomintang Decade," as the years between 1927 and 1937—the beginning of the Sino-Japanese War—are called, I wrote:

> Our two-day conference is over. To me it was a strain trying to understand papers being rapidly delivered, trying to be cordial to people I hardly know, and being excessively flattered, which, given my temperament, makes me recoil. Just as in Taipei, I am pressed into the seat of honor at the feasts, and anyway there is too much food. A drink at night—when offered—helps.
>
> Last night we had a farewell party like none I've ever experienced. It was at Aberdeen on a floating restaurant, although I doubt that it actually floated. It is a huge place with three floors of restaurant rooms, and our party of about ten tables took up only a small space. It is the most garish restaurant I've ever seen. Real South China vulgarity! The meal was good but what made it so delightful was the joy and festivity. Various guests were pressed into singing Chinese opera arias, done in a mike and wildly applauded. Everyone seeming to get a little drunk, going about toasting one another in brandy or scotch. Young folks from the college, who had helped with the baggage, served at coffee breaks, etc., were having a particularly uproarious time. When the president came over to their table they all gave a great shout of greeting. It was as lively, relaxed, and joyous a Chinese party as I have ever been to.

My coming was appreciated by my Chinese academic friends from Taiwan, Chiang Yung-ching, Li Yun-han, and Chang Yu-fa, as well as by Pichon Loh and Gilbert Chan, for only a few Americans did come. It was only a weekend visit to Hong Kong, but it is an exciting city, with its mixture of British effi-ciency in administration and Chinese drive.

The trip to Canton on an air-conditioned train, leaving at 10:45 in the morn-ing, in a second-class car with a reserved seat, was a striking contrast to the trip the other way six years before. On this through train everything was spic-and-span, nearly as smooth as a good train in Taiwan. It took us just forty-five minutes to reach the bridge, where last time going out we had to detrain, go through customs and change our money, then lug our bags across the bridge to board the British train. This time there was no stop at all: we just flashed across the small river that divides Hong Kong's New Territories from China.

Marie-Claire Bergère was my fellow passenger, and we sat together some of the time. I enjoyed enormously seeing the sights of rural South China and jotted notes as we passed along:

> I see a lot of building going on on the Chinese side, also earth-moving equip-ment. But the acres of bicycles at a railway crossing! (Be careful not to be

overly impressed by signs of material change. Still, it seems as though Hong Kong has spread across the border.) They are double- or triple-tracking the railway, at least near the stations.

South China architecture mixed with lots of apartment houses of cement. The bright red clay one observes along the way. Some real make-shift squatter shacks, too, tin, wood, and cellophane. Also thatch huts. Now a charming village with houses facing southeast. A man leading a water buffalo along the road beside the railway; three women with umbrellas against the hot sun. Now rice fields and soldierlike rows of vegetables growing in little patches cut out of the low hills. Lots of scraggly pines and what looks like forestation. An orange grove, bamboos, and still a lot of uncultivated land. It must be infertile. Some graves facing south in horseshoe shape. [I had read that graves were abolished.] Fishponds but no little paddle-wheels as observed in southern Taiwan. Some small tractor-drawn carts and a man with two buckets at either end of his carrying pole, transporting—guess what!

It's getting to look more and more Chinese. Perfectly rectangular rice fields, ponds with wallowing buffalo, farmers diligently weeding, but so far no duck farms.

We have just crossed the East River at Shih-lung [locally, Shek lung] so we must be about forty miles from Canton. Lots of old-style buildings. They are building a new steel bridge, perhaps for truck traffic. A road seems to be under construction parallel to the railway. I've seen perhaps ten bulldozers, but every one of them standing idle. Is it the lunch hour? What explains this lack of industry? I should expect to see swarms of workers, but nary a one!

The rice fields are simply fine—lush, exactly ordered, and in some recently transplanted fields I have seen something mysterious—what seems like rows of ceramic pots or chimneys about a foot high. What is this? Banana, sugar cane now in greater evidence. Some activity now along the railway but very little, and recently I have seen no one working in the fields. Very strange. Is it the wrong time of year or the wrong time of day, a little before 2 P.M.? It is as though the farms were deserted, though there are a few people on bicycles or attending buffalo. [It was *hsiu-hsi* (rest-hour), when almost every Chinese in the People's Republic, I'm told, knocks off for two hours between 12 and 2.]

As we approach Canton, I see a petrochemical complex, and many new apartments of six to ten stories side by side with traditional one-story houses. It is now past 2 P.M., and I see labor crews cracking stone or digging into a hillside with mattocks. I also see the classic Chinese system of squatting on one's heels watching others work. Lovely!

We were met at the station, passed through whatever formalities there may have been, and driven in a little bus to a retreat that was heavily guarded. It turned out to be a hostel for CCP big-shots, and we guests were housed there for one night. After I had settled in, Mr. Liu Tanian, an important person in the PRC historical profession, and Mr. Chin Zhongji, who was the manager of the conference, called upon me. It was a Chinese mark of courtesy. At dinner, I found Professor S. L. Tikhvinsky, who particularly dislikes my work because it does not follow his line on Soviet motives in aiding Sun Yat-sen. He had in tow two younger Russian scholars, with one of whom, Konstantine Shevelyov, I became somewhat acquainted. Later he sent me clippings from *Far Eastern Affairs*, an English-language journal published by the Oriental Department of the Soviet Academy of Sciences, that were translations of articles on the subject I was working upon—the Soviet advisers in China during the 1920s. Also at dinner were Harold and Ruth Schiffrin, Jerome Chen, and a French lady I knew by reputation, Madam Marianne Bastid-Bruguiere. This was to be an international conference, and there were a number of other European and Japanese scholars. When I got my stack of papers, I discovered that I was on the opening panel, along with several other foreign guests—another mark of courtesy.

Next morning we were conducted to the Huang Hwa Kang memorial for the seventy-two martyrs who lost their lives in a failed anti-Manchu uprising in April 1911. It was a Western-style memorial with a statue of liberty on top, broken columns, and wreathes in stone, but also two Chinese lion-dogs. On big stone blocks were lists of overseas Chinese communities that had contributed to the memorial, literally from all over the world. Behind the monument was a tablet with many names of revolutionaries, but during the Cultural Revolution the names of prominent Kuomintang men had been chiseled off. Now the names had been restored. We then went to the Sun Chungshan (Sun Yat-sen) memorial hall, the fine Chinese palace-style building with a blue tile roof.

Most interesting to me was a visit to the building where the first Kuomintang Congress was held, in January 1924, with Dr. Sun presiding and Borodin behind the scenes. It was a school building, and the auditorium was now set up as if for a meeting, with benches and tables, and at each place was the name of the attending delegate (165 of them). A stage up front had a table for the Presidium and a speaker's stand, while behind them was a large picture of Sun Yat-sen in his marshall's uniform, set between the National Government flag and the Kuomintang flag. Around the walls were cases showing materials from the conference period. All this certainly had political significance. I speculated that the great attention to Dr. Sun (including our conference) and his Kuomintang associates was to encourage Kuomintang leaders in Taiwan to believe that the People's Republic still honors the Kuomintang, and to claim Dr. Sun and the Congress as antecedents of the CCP's revolution. (Sun is referred to in the brochure as the "revolutionary forerunner.") In addition, the monument to the martyrs, the memorial hall for Dr. Sun, and the setup of the KMT Congress meeting place would be important symbols for overseas Chinese visitors.

After lunch, we were taken to Chungshan University (on the campus of the former Christian missionary university, Ling-nan) for a reception and picture taking. Each delegate received a packet of books and papers, including a translation into Chinese of my biography of Dr. Sun, *Sun Yat-sen: Frustrated Patriot*. I became aware of this when people started coming up to have me autograph their copies. It was a very nice gesture arranged by Professor Chen Xiqi (Ch'en Hsi-ch'i), whom I had met in 1980. I knew that a translation was under way because I had been asked to write a new preface, but I had almost forgotten that, and I certainly was not aware that the work had actually been done. Next, we were all lined up for our group picture, with seats designated by name. For Chinese, it is mandatory that important people be seated front center. I was on the front row but off from center. After all that we went in for a banquet, where I was asked to say a few words of appreciation on behalf of the foreign guests.

Next morning we were off by 8:30 by bus for a trip to Cui Heng (Ts'ui-heng), Sun Yat-sen's birthplace and now a tourist attraction—sort of a Mount Vernon for the "Father of the Country"—in Chung-shan County, about sixty miles south of Canton, and across the bay from Hong Kong. There we went into a tourist hotel, especially built for pilgrims to the home of Sun Yat-sen, but also a fine place for our conference. After lunch and a rest period, the conference had its official opening ceremony, and after that a banquet given by the county Communist Party chief and the county government. I was placed on the right of the party chief, "a very lively, cocky, self-assured man of forty-nine, who would be a successful Chinese business man—and I bet he is." At this banquet Professor Tikhvinsky made the speech of appreciation, a sort of balancing between the United States and the Soviet Union, for my speech the previous evening.

At the first session, which was for all of us, both Tikhvinsky and I were scheduled to give our papers, as well as Jerome Chen from Canada and Professor Chen Xiqi. At another panel, Tikhvinsky and I had an amusing clash. He accused me of always looking for hidden motives behind Soviet China policy, and he gave a lecture in English on the pristine virtues of such. My English-speaking friends did not swallow it, and the Chinese maintained an impassive position. I still remember how red in the face he got. He is said to be a KGB colonel and is fluent in both Chinese and English.

One afternoon we were taken to see Dr. Sun's boyhood home, or perhaps it was a home maintained for him after he became famous, for it was a fairly imposing place—as befits the patriot he was—but rather simply equipped with old-fashioned furniture. There was a visitors' reception room within the wall, then gardens, then the old mansion through which one walked from room to room. The house may have been expanded because Sun's older brother was a successful businessman in Hawaii. There was also a very well done museum showing stages in Sun's career.

On another day, after two days of conference, we had time to see the sights of Chung-shan County, including the harbor. Then to the Sun Yat-sen memorial hall, a fine building with a central hall, two side buildings, and a surrounding wall which, as seen from an airplane, form the characters Chung-shan, Central Mountain, or Nakayama, the name Sun adopted in Japan. The auditorium would seat 1,050 people and had a large stage. There were four exhibition rooms, three devoted to Sun's career, with memorabilia, and one devoted to overseas Chinese, for which the county is famous, and also is much indebted.

From there we went to lunch in a revolving restaurant atop a twenty-story building in Chung-shan city, where we had a fine view of the large amount of building going on—office and apartment buildings. I sat with Professor Chang Kai-yuan, a friend of Chang Peng-yuan, and thus had a chance to become acquainted. I offered to be a middleman for correspondence, if he wished. Since then, direct mail between the two sides has been instituted.

We were taken to an amusement park with roller coasters, bump cars, and boats floating through a tunnel of love and then down a shoot that made spray. Many of our companions tried various stunts, but not I. I preferred to sun myself. There is a big hotel, which obviously is supposed to attract overseas Chinese.

Saturday, November 8. I must write up a beautiful example of *kuan-hsi*, or Chinese relationships. Knowing I would be needing to mail all my books and papers this afternoon [our final day] and that banks would be closed that afternoon, I wanted to change some money to pay for the shipping. I happened to spot Gilbert Chan, with whom I have lots of *kuan-hsi* as his teacher and one who has done favors for him. He was pleased to help me. But we ran into a snag right away. The hotel doesn't change money, nor does the local commercial bank in front of the hotel. We were in the lobby discussing what to do when Gilbert spotted a friend who happens to come from the same ancestral village as does Gilbert. They had long-established *kuan-hsi* on that basis. This chap is a big-shot in Chung-shan academic circles. He solved the problem by calling the local Bank of China office, vouching for me as a member of the conference. Then the hotel sent a steward over to escort Gilbert and me (again, I suppose to vouch for me). So, without my passport, which I had left in Canton in my other briefcase, I was able to change a U.S. $50 traveler's check. Lucky I did because the mailing of three packages of books and papers cost me $26. Without *kuan-hsi* I wonder how I could have done it.

On Sunday morning we went on a bus trip to the Special Economic Zone of Chu-hai, up next to Macao. The Economic Zone is very well laid out, with wide boulevards, wide bikeways, planting of trees along the roads, circles at crossings, and multitudes of new apartment buildings, mostly unoccupied. It all seems overbuilt, but maybe will fill up soon. We saw very little industry, which must be developed to employ the residents, if the place is to thrive. Then we had a boat ride along the shore line of Macao, which is greatly built up since I was there about twenty-five years ago. I couldn't even see the facade of the nineteenth-century Catholic church which had burned down, for it is now over-towered by tall buildings. Macao gives the appearance of a modest-scale Hong Kong.

Some friendly Chinese scholars here have asked me about Chang Peng-yuan and Chang Yu-fa, and they know the work of other friends. The arrangements aren't as smooth as those in Taiwan were. As to substance, I missed a good deal, of course. One panel had several papers on the so-called Three Great Policies of Sun Yat-sen—alliance with Soviet Russia, alliance with the CCP, and support for labor and peasants. A paper by a Japanese scholar correctly pointed out that the term wasn't used till 1926, a year after Dr. Sun's death, and that it was coined by the Communist side, and that "alliance" between KMT and CCP was incorrect. There seemed to be no protest at this challenge to the much repeated "Sun Chung-shan's Three Great Policies." [We had already pointed that out in the 1956 Wilbur and How Documents volume.]

On Sunday afternoon we had a closing ceremony at which, of course, I was asked to say a few words, as were a good many other Chinese and foreign scholars. All very friendly. Tikhvinsky got in a political speech about Sun's warm friendship for Russia and the friendship of the Russian and Chinese people, but most of what he said was appropriate in expressing thanks.

Reflecting on the mood and manner of this conference, I did not observe much difference from the ones in Taiwan and Hong Kong. Serious, some humor, diligent note taking, and not the undertone of hostility toward the other side of the Straits, as in the Taiwan conference. There was one reference in a welcoming speech that it was a pity that the scholars from Taiwan were unable to attend.

It was a good chance to meet Chinese scholars, many of whom know me by name. I learned that my book on the Nationalist Revolution was being translated in Chekiang and perhaps also in Peking, and would be published.

One most pleasant incident was when my friend Professor Pichon Loh introduced me to Mr. Yang Tianshi of the Modern History Institute of the Chinese Academy of Social Sciences (Peking), who introduced me to a researcher in the institute, Miss Xi Wuyi. She told me that she had interviewed the aged gentleman who had been in charge of the translation and publication work of the documents seized in the raid on the Soviet Embassy in Peking on April 6, 1927, to which, much later, Julie How and I devoted so much scholarly work. She promised to give me a transcript of the interview. Her big point was that the gentleman had confessed to her that one of the documents—the first published—was a forgery, but the only one. That was the document that we had refused to use because we were persuaded by Mr. David J. Dallin, our expert consultant, that it was probably forged. To have that confirmation so many years later—though sadly after Julie's death—was quite a triumph!

24

Last Years in Pleasantville, 1987–1989

This period of our lives centered on three important matters: we had committed ourselves to move to a retirement community; thus, we had to sell our beloved house, with all that those two decisions meant in preparatory work; and before we moved I had to complete *Missionaries of Revolution*. Between the time we chose our apartment in the Quadrangle (October 1985) and the time we actually moved in (August 1989), there was a long period of uncertainty because the Quaker Board of the Quadrangle found it impossible to raise the required $50 million building loan. Eventually they sold all their work and assets to the Marriott Corporation, experts in hotel building and management, and Marriott had to draw more refined architectural plans and specs, get bids, chose contractors, and then build the facility. All this delayed entry for two years.

We had to submit financial statements, showing that our income would enable us to meet expected costs of living in the Quadrangle; send doctors' medical reports; and send our check for $10,625 to nail down the apartment we had chosen. On May 12, 1987, we went to Haverford for the ground-breaking ceremony. Still, completion of the first buildings was two years off.

In Pleasantville, we continued our busy intellectual, cultural, and social life— we may even have lived it more intensely, knowing that soon it would be over. We began attending a foreign films program at the Westchester Community College on ten successive Friday nights in each semester, which we found very stimulating. We attended the Sunday afternoon programs of the New Symphony Orchestra of Westchester, subscribed to the Ossining Chorale for two lovely oratorios a year, worked for and heard our church's Casa Verde Trio about five times a year, attended Mostly Mozart concerts in the summer, and subscribed to the Lincoln Center theater series, where we saw previews at a very low price. I continued attending the Modern China Seminar, and I went to my office on Thursdays, mainly to arrange my academic and research stuff that might have some historical interest to be transferred to Columbia's Rare Book and Manuscript Library. The librarian had asked me to do that, and it turned out to be a very big job.

On December 17, 1986, Anita O'Brien and I took the long manuscript on the Soviet advisers (nearly 900 pages) to Columbia University Press, which back in 1967 had asked Julie and me to prepare the revised edition of the documents volume. It had taken that long for us to integrate our new documents and extensive new research material, to rewrite all the chapters, and to get the entire manuscript typed and proofread.

There was now a new organization. The documents making up the second half of the book were arranged chronologically in seven coherent groups, and our essay chapters, also chronologically arranged, made up the book's first half. We now had six pages of photographs of leading personalities—Chinese and Russian—dividing the two parts. We no longer had an introductory chapter to discuss the authenticity of the documents; that was now proven. Besides our rewriting of the historical and explanatory chapters, I had written two new chapters. One was a general description of the Soviet aid mission, the main personalities involved, their motivation in coming, conditions of their life and military work in China, and the sojourners' impressions of that strange land—all based upon reminiscences of participants or recent scholarly articles by Russians that Lydia Holubnychy had translated for Julie and me. The other new chapter described the Russians' homeward journeys in defeat after Chiang Kai-shek and other conservatives in the Kuomintang turned against their Russian tutors. With a great deal of research, I was able to describe the fate that befell many of them during the Stalin purges and the war with Germany. Many, perhaps most, lost their lives in those bitter Russian days.

Sad to say, the persons in charge at Columbia University Press decided that the press could not afford to publish our now very large work. The book probably never would pay for itself. They wrote me a polite but regretful letter—something of a shock, I must say. So I was back on square one. However, I immediately wrote to several other university presses describing the book and telling straight off of its length. It would not need to be edited and set in type, since Anita's computer already had set it up camera-ready. Harvard replied asking to see the manuscript. After they had sent it to a reader, whose very favorable report they sent me, the editor-in-chief wrote that they would like to publish the work. It would, of course, first have to be submitted for approval to the faculty committee. The very favorable reader was my friend Steven Levine. He it was who suggested the title, *Missionaries of Revolution*.

Now most of the responsibility lay with Anita O'Brien and Ms. Elizabeth

Suttell, the senior editor assigned by Harvard to see the publication through. They already knew each other, for our Anita was now well known in the Asian studies publishing field. I dedicated the book to the memory of my coauthor, Julie Lien-ying How, and to Lydia Holubnychy. The remaining jobs of any consequence were the bibliography and the index. The bibliography was not difficult, though long, because I had systematically kept reference slips. I began work on the index on February 18, 1988, and it took about five months. Doing an index means that one finds typos that had escaped notice before, requiring corrections. But one never finds all errors. The index runs to thirty-three pages in two columns, and Anita shortened it! What a lot of work a scholarly book entails.

Our friends Harold and Ruth Schiffrin invited us to visit them in Israel. Harold was director of the Truman Institute, which would pay our living expenses while there. We left in great anticipation on October 15, 1987, going via London and Zurich. We arrived at Tel Aviv in late evening, and after a very simple entry procedure we came into a tropical waiting area where we found Ruth and Harold. As the reader knows, we have been together at several Sun Yat-sen conferences. After getting our baggage, they drove us through the night to our hotel in Jerusalem, a drive nearly across the width of Israel that took less than two hours.

We learned a lot about Israel, its triumphs, its perils, and its troubling internal problems. We became fans. I wrote the following "thoughts and memories of Israel" the day after our return.

The barren, rock-strewn Judean hills, and the forbidding dry hills just to the east in the Jordan valley, in a completely different climate zone.

The view of Jerusalem with the shining Dome of the Rock and the old city wall as seen from the Faculty Club of Hebrew University, with a few high buildings in the area outside the wall—it makes a sand-colored panorama, sometimes under cloud, sometimes gleaming under a brilliant blue sky.

The narrow, covered, and active streets of the Muslim quarter in old Jerusalem, with shops on each side, some intruding into the pavements. The people: women, some in shrouds, shouting Arab schoolchildren, and many wary tourists in Western dress. This contrasts with the quiet and clean Armenian quarter.

The "wailing wall," a long stretch of large blocks of sand-colored stone, at least thirty feet high, divided two-thirds for men and one-third for women. Most of the men I saw were of the conservative sects, wearing black hats and long coats, some reading scripture, as if to the wall, some leaning their heads against the wall in prayer. There was a large plaza in front of the wall decked with flags for a particular occasion having to do with initiating new army recruits, or the dedication of a newly formed unit.

The fine Hadassah Hospital, supported about 20 percent by Jewish women abroad, but treating Muslims, Christians, and Jews alike. Its gift shop, attended by two ladies speaking American, where I bought an Israeli Defense Force cap.

The quiet church of the Franciscan order, celebrating Mary, Mother of Jesus, and Elizabeth, Mother of John the Baptizer, and the view over a beautiful valley with an Arab village beyond, with stone terraces below to form narrow fields on the hillside.

The ingenious agriculture in the desert where water is pumped in, but plastic is used over the ground—with plants peeking through—to conserve the moisture. Elsewhere along the Jordan Valley, and on the Western Plain, the orchards, bananas, and date palms.

The blue, blue Mediterranean Sea with tall palm trees along the shore, a really tropical scene. And the theater of Caesarea up against the Sea.

The beautiful garden with roses blooming and impatiens on a rocky slope, which we saw from our window in the Faculty Club in the campus on Mt. Scopus.

The vivacity of the people. No lethargy here. Jews and Arabs are active, on-the-go people. And Israel has been built as a modern state in only a few decades. Remarkable!

The helpfulness of persons from whom we inquired directions.

And the overwhelming kindness of Ruth and Harold Schiffrin, who had us in their home three times for meals, and the three days of touring in the city on which they took us; and the trip to Haifa and down to Tel Aviv, giving us a whole day. They were most generous with their time and their concern for us during these last days of their vacation. I think we will never forget our visit to Israel in October 1987.

Notes on Becoming Eighty (written May 15, 1988)

On Friday, I turned eighty. It's almost unimaginable, except that one doesn't feel a bit older than, say, seventy! Our grounds are beautiful in mid-May and we have often given porch parties. We gave one on Saturday, May 7, for about twenty-five church friends, and had one planned for May 14 for village friends. The number that we must invite grew so that in the end we had about thirty-five coming. Kay turned it into a birthday party. One thought at eighty is how many lovely friends we have right here in Pleasantville. But several of the men are visibly aging. It seems I am in better shape than they.

I was asked by a former student and dear friend, Bernadette Li Gentzler, if I would give a brief speech at a Chinese dinner for participants in a conference discussion of the democracy movement in China. She persuaded me, so I reluctantly consented, and then spent a lot of time working on the talk. When Kay and I were driven to the restaurant on 40th Street near Park Avenue and came in, Bernadette insisted I sit in the place of honor at a table of notables who had contributed to the costs of the conference. She is a good organizer and was our host so I had to comply. When it came time for my talk, I tried to lighten it with a few humorous stories. I thought that was it, and my part (thank the Lord) was over. But then my friends turned the occasion into a celebration of my eightieth birthday, with speeches, a scroll brought from Taiwan by Chang Peng-yuan and signed by a group of "students," and a Chinese plaque to express wishes for a very long life. Also an ice-cream birthday cake. It was a lovely, affectionate occasion, and I returned home exhausted.

In March 1989 *Missionaries of Revolution: Soviet Advisers and Nationalist China, 1920–1927* was published by Harvard University Press. It was a big and handsome volume, weighing three and a half pounds, and 904 pages long. On the jacket was the picture of the Kuomintang leaders, mostly left-wing and including some Communists, as they assembled for a Central Executive Committee plenum in Wu-han in March 1927. The picture was given me by Professor Searle Bates, who got it when he was a young teacher at the University of Nanking.

The book was to be on display at the exhibits of books on Asian subjects from various university presses at the annual convention of the Association of Asian Studies, so Kay and I decided, in celebration, to go to Washington, where the meetings were held. There we saw many academic friends and took Anita O'Brien and Betty Suttell (my editors) to dinner.

That spring, China had its Democracy Movement, led by students from other colleges in Beijing. It was a very dramatic six weeks of demonstrations and demands for more popular participation in government, but it ended on the night of June 3–4, when the students and other demonstrators were driven from Tiananmen Square by tanks of the People's Liberation Army, with terrible carnage. American relations with China went into a swift decline, the Chinese government became an international pariah, and Chinese dissenters were cowed.

We had our mid-May porch parties and, since we were certainly leaving, were entertained in turn by most of our friends. The East Asian Institute gave a party for us at a Chinese restaurant, and our church, where we had been members for forty years, had a farewell for us on June 4 after service.

I continued going to my office on Thursdays until all my academic papers of any potential interest had been sent to Special Collections Library and my office had been cleaned out. We disposed of most of our books by giving them to the Pleasantville Library for their book sale. I sold some of my professional books to an Oriental book dealer. Most books and journals on East Asia I gave to Pace College in Pleasantville or to the Orientalia Division of the New York Public Library, where I knew the Chinese librarian. A few rarer Chinese or Japanese items went to Columbia's East Asian Library. We gave many of our paintings and some bric-a-brac to a nearby chapter of Amnesty International for their auction. All were sold. We got tax credits for such charitable gifts.

We had bought the overgrown, south-facing piece of land in 1951, and Aaron Resnick had planned a house of contemporary design, which was built in the summer of 1952. With our own strength, Kay and I cleared the half-acre of brambles, shrubs, small trees, and vines and then gradually landscaped it to a place of beauty. The house was our home for thirty-seven years, during which time we doubled its size and gradually furnished it. There our kids grew up, and there we prepared our teaching, wrote our books, and entertained our friends. We dearly loved that house. On August 1, 1989, we moved into the Quadrangle.

25

Our New Life in
the Quadrangle

We have enjoyed our retirement community for six years now. The Quadrangle is owned and operated by the Marriott Corporation yet is somewhat infused with the original Quaker spirit.

Our apartment faces south with eastern and western exposures, is sunny and very comfortable. We display Chinese rugs and paintings and our collection of ceramics and small sculptures. Our windows look out on woods and a pond, and farther away on several three-story apartment buildings among the seven that house some 470 retirees.

Among them we have made almost too many friends. Our community includes academics, professional people, former corporate executives, career women, artists, musicians, and writers. Most are well educated, traveled, and remember interesting careers. Some could be lifelong friends except that the median age here is over eighty: each year death demands its toll.

We residents do a great deal of entertaining among ourselves, and we have created a rich cultural life of study groups, art exhibits, concerts, and lectures. We enjoy group trips to Philadelphia to the several fine museums, to "The Orchestra," and to theater and dance. Some trips take us to New York or Washington for special exhibits. We created a self-governing mechanism with committees to care for hospitality, to advise management on food and housekeeping, to manage our fine library, to minister to those in our health center, and to help care for our beautiful grounds.

Kay and I have taken trips to Pleasantville to see our friends and to care for our empty house until it was sold. We joined three art and archaeological museums, subscribed to the Philadelphia Orchestra's Friday Afternoon Series, and have joined the nearby Unitarian Church, a vital congregation. We helped to organize the Quadrangle Classics Group, which so far has read and discussed Greek and Roman masterpieces, Gilgamesh, Old Testament literature, Dante, Boccaccio, Machiavelli, Chaucer, Montaigne, and then deep into Shakespeare. We are now into nineteenth-century novels and plays.

We walk a mile each morning and take a short nap most afternoons. We visit the sick in the Health Center one afternoon a week, and have a very productive vegetable garden. For two years I took painting lessons, which I had long dreamed of doing. And I write feature articles for the *Quadrangle Times*, our monthly journal.

A common complaint among the residents here is that "we are too busy to enjoy retirement." Kay and I are fully occupied, too, but that is as it should be, except that we spend so much time writing that there is little left for reading.

I find little time to keep up with the field of modern Chinese history. I still receive *The China Quarterly*, *The Journal of Asian Studies*, *Asian Survey*, *Republican China*, and various newsletters in my field, but I don't read them too carefully. I have been called upon occasionally to review books and manuscripts, but I'm not buying many new books. One subject that interests me is the way Chinese culture has reasserted itself in the People's Republic of China, in spite of the Communist Party's effort to mold a new culture and encourage the emergence of a new socialist man. Now even these ideals seem abandoned.

In May 1990 we finally sold our house, a rather stressful business. No use describing a closing. Our lawyer, Jim Holden, Jr., guided us through swearing and signing, and after about two hours we had our check in hand. We immediately invested the money in bonds and equities.

In September 1990 my friend Professor Edwin Reischauer died of complications from the hepatitis he contracted in Tokyo from infected blood given him in the hospital after an assassination attempt by a demented Japanese when Eddie was the American ambassador. Obituaries in the *New York Times* and the *Washington Post* were excellent, for he was a most accomplished scholar with a distinguished career.

My good friend Professor John Fairbank died in Cambridge in September a year later. I had known him since 1934 in Peking, and many were the projects and conferences we worked on together. He was an outstanding teacher, guide, and promoter of the China studies field.

During our years in the Quadrangle we attended two interesting Elderhostels at Oberlin and Washington, and we took two grand trips. In August 1991 we went to Honolulu via Seattle. I had received a letter from Tu Weiming, director of the Institute of Culture and Communication of the East-West Center, telling me of an international conference on Sun Yat-sen and the 1911 Revolution (this being its eightieth anniversary), and inviting me to come and present a paper. Of course, I was delighted that Kay immediately agreed to go too, and so I replied that we would come. However, this meant that I must spend most of the summer preparing a paper on Dr. Sun.

I decided on an attempt to assess the influences that led Sun to the career of anti-Manchu revolutionary. This meant that I must review the literature on Sun's early life. Fortunately I have the use of Haverford College Library. I got out armloads of books and started reading systematically. I fixed upon four factors leading toward Sun's career: his environment (both proximate and general), his emerging character, chance, and the choices he made. I took lots of pertinent notes, organized them, and went to work on the word processor, doing several drafts. By mid-August I was able to send off the twenty-page paper and the following abstract of "Environment, Character, Chance and Choice: Their Interplay in Making a Revolutionary":

This paper attempts to trace the main environmental factors as well as chance occurrences during Dr. Sun Yat-sen's life to age thirty, which prepared him to be a revolutionary.

Examples of environmental influences were his growing up in a southern Kwangtung farm village, where he "learned to be Chinese" and acquired his basic personality structure; his immersion in a totally different life in Hawaii, where he studied in missionary schools, learning English and being indoctrinated with Christian beliefs; his higher schooling in Hong Kong, where he studied science, medicine, and classical Chinese, where he was greatly influenced by China's humiliating defeats in two foreign wars, by anti-Manchuism, and by reformist literature; and finally his nine months in London, where he experienced the might of the greatest imperial power.

Examples of the play of chance are his being taken at age twelve to Hawaii where, in addition to the beginnings of a Western education, he experienced his first overseas Chinese community; his chance escape from Canton in 1895 with the help of Christian friends; and the chance meeting with his former teacher, who was on a one-day stopover in Honolulu and who encouraged Sun to go to England.

Chance also means opportunity. Sun often seized opportunities, as, for example, his decision to be baptized as a Christian; his choice of profession; his frustrated decision to appeal to Li Hung-chang; the resulting decision to create a revolutionary secret society and to lead a revolt against the hated Manchu dynasty. When this failed, Sun later decided to go to London, where his appeal to the servant Cole in the Chinese legation on the basis of fellow Christianity led to the saving of his life and his temporary world fame. There he chose to cultivate a reputation as a patriotic leader of China's reform movement and to enhance his education.

The intertwining of unique environmental influences, chance opportunities, and the choices that Sun made over and over again—about many of which we will never know—created the personality that was fitted for a career as a reform-minded revolutionary.

We had left Honolulu in August 1968, before Ann's wedding. We immediately recognized the balmy climate and leisurely pace that we remembered, especially when we got out to the university campus for the opening of the conference. The best thing about that was seeing old friends from my academic world: people like Eto Shinkichi, now president of Asia College in Tokyo, and Yamada Tatsuo, a fine scholar whom I had met at a conference in China and who later visited in our home. There were a number of other Japanese scholars, and my friends from Taiwan, Chiang Yung-ching, Lee Kuo-chi, Chang Peng-yuan, and others, and a few acquaintances from the People's Republic. In addition to Harold Schiffrin from Israel, Marianne Bastid-Bruguiere from Paris, and John Wong from Australia, there was a contingent of scholars in the United States whom I was glad to see again, especially Danny Kwok of the University of Hawaii.

This was the first conference I had been to where scholars from both Chinas met, and the East-West Center was appropriately neutral ground. Kay attended all sessions, for there were simultaneous translations from and to all three languages represented—Chinese, Japanese, and English. I do not know what went on between the rival Chinese groups outside the formal conference sessions. There were some pointed differences in interpretation of the 1911 Revolution, depending on ideology, because the PRC interprets it as a "bourgeois revolution," antecedent to the real revolution, the proletarian one that established the People's Republic of China. To the scholars from Taiwan, 1911 was the real revolution—theirs. Sun Yat-sen is the revered Father of the Country to the Kuomintang folks, while to the Communists he is the "revolutionary forebear." However, the only serious heat I observed during the conference sessions occurred when a Japanese scholar who had used the Mitsui archives reported seeing the text of an agreement between Sun, then provisional president of the Republic of China, and Mitsui Company for a ten-million-yen loan to Sun's government, desperately in need of money, in return for the lease of Manchuria to Japan. The document was not signed, and that requested loan was never made. Some Chinese scholars were indignant and disputed the author of the paper, but eventually things were quieted down, partly by Harold Schiffrin's calming intervention.

We returned home via Oakland, where Jack and Caroline Service met us. We had three days with them, mostly visiting, but also going with Jack to the Golden Gate Museum and with them both to the Oakland Museum. We saw fine exhibits of American painters at both. David Keightly—Ph.D. Columbia, now professor of Chinese history at U.C. Berkeley and a MacArthur fellow—came with his Vanney for dinner, and we had a lively discussion of Chinese antiquity, for that is his specialization.

In celebration of our sixtieth wedding anniversary we visited England, Scotland, Holland, and Czechoslovakia in July 1992—a joyous spree. In London we did sentimental things: revisiting the National Gallery, the Courtauld, and the Tate; attending a service in St. Paul's Cathedral followed by a walk through Kew Gardens. We admired the new Sainsbury Wing of the National Gallery, which displayed its Gothic and Renaissance paintings, beautifully hung. I was greatly inspired in St. Paul's by the architectural beauty, the music, and the solemn service. We also saw a stunning play, *The Madness of George III* by Alan Bennet, at the Royal National Theatre across the Thames, beautifully staged and acted. London in summer is delight.

We enjoyed our few days in Edinburgh, especially walking the "Royal Mile," the old part of the city with Georgian architecture. At the end of the mile there is the Palace of Holyroodhouse, where the Queen of England spends a few ceremonial days each year. A palace is a palace, and we've seen too many of them. Just outside is a ruined abbey where one wanders among broken arches and gravestones in the flooring. One stone still standing in a partial wall struck us by the beauty of its inscription, which I copied for Kay, who has ancestors named Maxwell. It read "Here also were interred the remains of his descent, William, Earl of Sutherland and his consort Mary Maxwell, who both died at Bath, she on the 1st and he on the 16th of June 1776. Lovely in their lives, in death not divided."

From Edinburgh we flew to Amsterdam, where we attended a Concertgebouw concert. On Sunday we went to a nearby Catholic church to attend a mass, but whereas thousands attended the service in St. Paul's Cathedral, there were only about two hundred communicants attending this service, mostly elderly, scattered here and there in the large church. The mass was in Dutch and Latin. Kay understood the Latin better than the Dutch, and I had little idea what was going on. I had never been to a Catholic mass. But there was a lovely soprano voice singing from the back balcony, and the solemnity of the service and the stained glass windows made the time there worthwhile. After the service we went to the Van Gogh museum. We gazed on an extensive collection of his paintings, arranged chronologically. Nearly as rich in Van Goghs was the Rijksmuseum Kröller-Müller, on a great estate about two hours from Amsterdam, which we also visited. This is part of an astonishing collection gathered by one wealthy couple and willed to the Netherlands. On our last day in the Netherlands we went to The Hague to see the Dutch paintings in the Mauritshuis, a great collection.

Our last stop was Prague, a fine old city, where we visited Betsey and her family. The older part of the city is quite run down from neglect during the four decades of Communist Party control. Most of the streets there are narrow and cobblestoned, not good for walking.

I have enjoyed my late retirement years in writing a biography of my mother and in working on one of my father. Both parents had interesting lives, centered in the Orient. Mother began at age fourteen to keep a journal, and she wrote fairly regularly till she was eighty-four years old, on the eve of her death. There are also many letters to her mother and her husband. I selected passages that most reveal her personality, her hopes, enthusiasms, and prejudices. Thirty years she spent with my father in Japan, China, and Korea.

Mary M. Wilbur was a talented woman who sang well, painted, wrote fiction, directed choirs, studied the arts of the Orient, and had an active religious, social, and club life. She raised three children and mourned two who died in infancy.

In writing the book I was helped by my sister, my brother, and my niece,

Jean. My daughter, Ann, produced the work on her printer. The completed book came to 273 pages, privately printed in a limited edition. I entitled it In *Her Own Words: Mary Matteson Wilbur in Byegone America, Japan, China, and Korea, 1872–1955.* I spent two and a half years on this book.

My father, Hollis Adelbert Wilbur, wrote his reminiscences during retirement from life-long service to the Young Men's Christian Association, which began in his college years. He had not finished the writing when blindness overtook him. His work in Japan and China required a great deal of travel and sometimes long separation from the family. My mother kept many of his letters, and he inhabits her journals. From these sources, I could amplify his reminiscences of Christian work in the Orient, 1910–1940. I entitled the book *My Life in Christian Service.*

My parents were devoted to each other and to their family, but they had very different interests and dissimilar personalities. This adds a certain pungency to their biographies. In studying their lives, I learned much about myself through their eyes.

Here may be a convenient place for a little reflection.

First off, I must say that the pivot of my life is Kay. We have been inordinately happy in our married life, and we agree that the previous years of courtship were a time of supreme elation for us both—*kao-hsing* (high spirit), as the Chinese say. We dread the probability that one of us will depart first, leaving the other in desolation. Yet this happens around us in the Quadrangle, and among our other friends.

Kay and I enjoy doing things together, virtually anything, be it grocery shopping or taking our morning walks, entertaining friends at an intimate luncheon in our apartment, attending a concert or play, touring familiar rooms of favorite art museums, reading at night, and particularly snuggling in bed together. The fires of passion may have cooled with age, but we do kiss passionately. We have our intimate language, as probably most loving couples do. I call Kay "my fun wife."

We sometimes disagree, but almost never have we quarreled. For example, I am suspicious about food getting spoiled, due to my China background. Kay thinks I am too finicky. I think Kay worries excessively about her children, making up scenarios of what might happen. She has put in many sleepless hours worrying over them. Her disposition is pessimistic; mine optimistic. She fears going to some strange place alone; I love to explore new places. I plan trips; she sometimes fearfully goes along. Yet they all turn out right.

Kay is really a lovely person. She is compassionate and tactful, creatively thoughtful of others, always careful not to hurt people's feelings. She makes friends easily and cultivates them, is a delightful hostess and a fine conversationalist. The Chinese have a word for one of her traits—she is inclined to "give way" (*jang*) to others in a disagreement. She simply dislikes contentious situations. She also sizes up people quickly and, I would say, accurately. She supports causes she believes just, such as Amnesty International, the American Civil Liberties Union, the League of Women Voters, Planned Parenthood, and Unitarian good works. She wants to help, yet also wants to stay detached.

Our friends quickly discover that Kay has an excellent memory for the books she has read—and she had read widely in literature. She will read all available books of some author whom she has learned is good. I've often seen her come from the library with five or more novels or collections of short stories by a single author she is tracking. She remembers plots and characters, the plots of plays we have seen long ago, and the names of the actors, when I have forgotten even having seen them.

My wife is a beautiful lady, but of course she disclaims that. I love to go with her to pick out dresses. We usually find handsome colors and patterns. Kay is about 5 feet, 3 inches tall. She dresses smartly when we go to someone's apartment for dinner. Kay has been remarkably healthy, although arthritis does bother her.

Her children love their Ma very much, and she and Ann are truly companions. Her friends, too, love her. My parents quickly came to admire their son's wife, and my sister named her second daughter after her. Kay is most proud that Kay Wilbur Cressey Irwin is her namesake. She is meticulous about thank-you notes or letters of condolence. She quickly became popular in the Quadrangle and was asked early on to head a temporary nominating committee because she knew so many of the residents. We have an almost too busy social life, mostly because of her popularity, but partly because I, too, love to cultivate friends.

Of course, Kay would disclaim all this praise. Modesty and self-deprecation are among her dominant traits. I often need to enjoin her, "Don't kick yourself." For some reason deep within her psyche, she needs to justify herself: to explain or apologize. On occasions when she seems defensive, I tell her that Aunt Ora is looking over her shoulder. Whatever the reason, Kay is overly conscientious. Duties come first, even housework or ironing, when she would much prefer to be writing or reading some novel.

I feel uneasy about Kay only when she exaggerates or, unconsciously, makes what seem to me quite inaccurate statements. I want to correct her but try to restrain myself. We have had our periods of anxiety—about our children, about finances, sometimes about the wisest course to take—but we have sailed through life together in great harmony. We liven things by gentle kidding. How fortunate I have been in my wonderful companion! Our major regret is that we have no grandchildren.

In sum, as Shakespeare wrote of Cleopatra, "Age cannot wither her, nor custom stale her infinite variety."

So, what about me?

I have had a happy life, as these reminiscences show. I've been sick more than Kay, but on the whole I have been in pretty good shape, except perhaps for that stomach ulcer against which I must take drugs. Our doctor here gives us both a good report. My stooped shoulders have become a bit more stooped, though I regularly try to straighten up. My hearing has declined a lot. My eyes are still better than Kay's. My white hair is receding from my forehead, but I'm not bald, anyway. In August 1994 I had a heart problem and spent a week in intensive care, but the situation has stabilized now.

My career has brought many gratifications and pleasures. Ancient and modern China are fascinating. I worked hard at my jobs, never shirked, and have tried to be creative. I enjoyed my colleagues at Field Museum, OSS, and Columbia, and I believe I gained a respectable reputation.

Among other deficiencies, there is one deep flaw. I'm very bad at learning languages. The years I spent on language study could have been used much better in getting a broader education. Could I have done better as a journalist or in some other academic field? As a result of this faulty memory the focus of my career has been narrow. Not that I didn't learn some varieties of Chinese. When writing my dissertation, I translated from historical texts of the first centuries B.C. and A.D., and I read Chinese scholarly articles. Yet I never became a fluent speaker of Chinese. If I made something of my profession, it was due to fortunate circumstance, hard work, and a narrow concentration.

When I joined the Columbia faculty, Professor Schuyler Wallace, dean of the School of International Affairs, advised me to make my contributions to my field in theory. However, this is not my forte at all. I've never been much interested in philosophy and am suspicious of academic theories that are not substantiated by clear evidence. I am an empiricist. It seems my professional contributions have been in three areas: teaching graduate students with emphasis on evidence; helping to organize the field of China studies in the United States; and the books I have published. They show one characteristic: good documentation. I start with that and only then comes the writing based on what my research has shown.

One's contribution to one's profession rapidly fades away. The newer generation of China scholars in the United States is better trained than I was and has new approaches to the history of China. I am proud, however, to have systematically developed the oral history approach to China studies. Columbia's Chinese Oral History Project produced about fifteen career histories of eminent twentieth-century Chinese. Some of these autobiographical works have now been translated and published in Chinese, so that Chinese readers can enjoy and learn from them.

One other small contribution: the idea of a University Seminar on Modern China. Ours so impressed a Ford Foundation executive that he put up money for other universities to organize foreign-country-centered seminars to bring scattered scholars together periodically. Now there are many such groups in the United States, and others abroad.

I am not religious, though I was baptized at age fourteen at my mother's behest. When in college, I parted company from my parents on Christian beliefs, to their deep regret. When Kay wanted our children to be confirmed and I read the creed to which I was supposed to announce belief, I simply would not consent. She considered it just a formality, but for me to say "I believe in God, the Father, Jesus Christ, his son" would have been most improper. Yet I enjoyed the inspiration of good preaching and fine music at the Unitarian Church in White Plains for forty years. I owe to my parents, both virtuous people, my wish to live an ethical life. I honor and love them.

Friendships are very important to me. Everywhere we have lived, Kay and I have made warm friends, though many have dropped away. I find it easy to make friends, for I am interested in others. Also, I like to be helpful—probably a trait I got from my father, who was noted for his helpfulness. I am inclined to be demonstrative. I am attracted to women, particularly those who are comely and vivacious, but not to the domineering type. Some of my dearest friends are women. Kay understands this and knows she has no rival. Perhaps my appreciation of attractive women is part of my deep love of beauty, a trait that I derived from my mother.

We deeply love our children, my sister and brother, our foster daughter Betsey, and our other nieces and nephew. I have to conclude that the emotional side of my makeup is stronger than the abstract and conceptual.

Index

Academia Sinica. *See* Institute of Modern History

Additional Notes on Tea (Wilbur), 52

Ahmed, Leila, 126

Ahmed, R. A., 126, 128–29, 130

Ahmed, Zohra, 126

Alley, Rewi, 228

Allman, Norwood, 77

Amerasia, 58, 59

American Council of Learned Societies, 169, 206, 220, 224, 227

American Embassy, Chungking, 73

American Historical Review, 165

American Institute in Taiwan, 274, 279

American League for Peace and Democracy, 101

American Oriental Society, 211

American Plant Migration, The (Laufer), 41–42

American School in Japan, 106

American Women's Club of Shanghai, 6

American Women's Party, 39

Anderson, James, 226

Anderson, Otto, 69

Andrews, Carol Corder, 238

antiquities, 82

Armstrong, Margaret, 6

Army-McCarthy hearings, 101

Arnold, Mr., 110

Arts and Crafts of Ancient China (Mary Wilbur), 6

Ashes of Defeat, The (Wilbur), 195

Asia Foundation, 170, 192, 198, 203

Asia Society, 169, 200

Association for Asian Studies, 56, 169, 200, 211, 221, 224, 227

Australia, 244

Ayscough, Florence, 46

Ayudhya, Thailand, 150

Bachoffer, Ludwig, 46

Banerjee, D. N., 127

Bang Chan, Thailand, 150–52

Barlow, Mary, 17, 245

Barnett, DeWitt, 12

Barnett, Doak, 12, 57, 169, 201, 206, 217, 226, 240, 244, 284

Barnett, Genie May, 12

Barnett, Jeanne, 244

Barnett, Robert, 12

Bartlet, Beatrice, 240

Bastid-Bruguiere, Marianne, 291, 303

Bates, Searle, 166, 214, 299

Beal, Edwin, Jr., 172, 237

Beaver, Mrs., 37

Bedford Road School, 95

Beeplat, Tristan, 230

Behan, Charlotte, 238

Benedict, Ruth, 38, 94

Bergère, Marie-Claire, 243, 289

Bernard, Shannon, 280

Berton, Bob, 115, 152

Berton, Peter, 107–8, 172

Bhargawa, J. L., 137

Bielenstein, Hans, 200, 230, 240

Biggerstaff, Camilla, 77

Biggerstaff, Knight, 66, 77–78, 79

Bingham, Woodbridge, 96

Bishop, Carl Whiting, 30, 34–35, 38, 52

309

Blake, Bob, 49
Bliukher, V. K. ("Galen"), 178
Bloomfield, Lincoln, 77, 78
Boas, Franz, 37
Bodde, Derk, 34, 56, 211
Boden, Cynthia, 210
Boden, Shirley, 210
Bogin, Harold, 280
Bolocan, Alice Kwong, 240
Bombay, 137–39
Boorman, Howard, 166
Borodin, Michael, 12–13, 192, 221–22
Borton, Hugh, 91, 92, 94, 102, 166
Botton, Flora, 234
Boynton, Charles, 21, 72
Brockman, Fletcher, 23, 38
Brookport, Illinois, 40
Brown, Norman, 56
Brown, Spencer, 276
Browne, Lewis, 31
Buchanan, Peter, 230, 233, 242
Bureau of Intelligence and Research, 89
Bureau of Investigation (Taiwan), 225
Burkhardt, Fred, 207, 223
Burkhardt, Herman, 20, 24
Burma, 117–24, 131

C. T. Loo Educational Foundation, 201
Cady, John, 56
Cairo, 62
Calcutta, 63, 64, 125–29
Cambridge History of China, 235, 245
Camp Pinecliffe for Girls, 40
Canton, 266–69, 289–93
Carmen, Harry, 97
Carter, Thelma, 276
Casablanca, 61–62
Central Intelligence Agency, 89
Ceylon, 145–46
Chakravarty, Sri Tripurari, 127–28
Chan, Gilbert (Chen Fu-lin), 239, 293
Chan, Margaret, 240
Chang Chi-yun, 192, 196
Chang Ching-chiang, 194
Chang Fa-k'uei, 173, 209, 227
Chang Han-fu, 85, 86
Chang Hsi-jou, 68, 69

Chang Kai-yuan, 293
Chang Kia-ngao, 103, 146
Chang King-yu, 284, 287
Chang Kuo-t'ao, 115–16
Chang Ming-chueh, 283
Chang Peng-yuan, 188–89, 196, 204, 232,
    241, 278–79, 284, 286, 287, 293,
    298, 303
Chang, Robert, 195
Chang Ta-chien, 285
Chang, Teresa, 284, 297
Chang Tso-lin, 99
Chang Yu-fa, 196, 204, 241, 274, 284,
    286, 289, 293
Changsha, 44
Chaterjee, S. K., 128
Chen, Jerome, 291, 292
Chen, K. P., 114, 173
Chen, Mayor, 181
Chen Xiqi (Chen Hsi-ch'i), 266–67, 268,
    291, 292
Chen Cheng, 183
Chen Kuang-fu, 227
Chen Tu-hsiu, 94
Cheng Hsi-ling, 240
Cheng-ta National University, 285
Chi, Madeleine, 204, 223, 285
Chi Pei-feng, 232
Chia Ting-shih, 188
Chiang Ching-kuo, 189–90, 202–3
Chiang Fu-tsung, 170, 286
Chiang Kai-shek, 14, 66–67, 68, 100, 198;
    audience with, 208, 223, 226; Chinas
    Destiny, 55, 56; interviewed, 192–94;
    proposed book on, 246, 285
Chiang Kai-shek, Madame, 53, 208, 223,
    226
Chiang Mon-lin, 69–70, 111, 181–82, 185
Chiang Yen-shih, 274
Chiang Yen-ssu, 286
Chiang Yung-ching, 190, 192, 203, 204,
    206, 241, 242, 289, 303
Chien, Frederick, 242, 278, 284
Chien Han shu, 45
Chien Shih-liang, 206
Chien Ssu-liang, 196, 225
Chien Tuan-sheng, 68, 69, 70

Chin Hsiao-yi, 285, 288

Chin Zhongji, 290

Chin, Bob, 71, 74, 76, 78, 81

Chin, Lillian Chu, 227, 240

Chinas Destiny (Chiang), 55, 56

China Aid Council, 101

China, History of: The Republican Period (Wilbur), 224

China International Foundation, 241

China: and Burma, 119, 121–22; civil war, 68; Democracy Movement, 299; impressions of (1980), 269–70; impressions of (1986), 289–90; and India, 140, 142–43; and Japan, 107, 108, 158; land reform, 184; postwar trip to, 64–87; and Taiwan, 127; trip to (1980), 248–70; war conditions in, 53

Chinese Biographical Dictionary Project, 166

Chinese Communist Party, 85, 86, 96–97, 99–100, 140, 163, 202

Chinese Cultural Center, 230

Chinese Doves Flutter over Japan (Wilbur), 159

Chinese Industrial Cooperation Movement, 228

Chinese Oral History Project, 27–28, 164–65, 166, 192, 200, 209, 221, 232

Chinese Studies in History, 223, 277

Chinthe Bookstore (Rangoon), 119–20

Chiu, Hungda, 234

Chou Fu-hai, 72

Chow Hsun-hsin, 209

Chow Shu-kai, 246

Chow Tso-min, 33, 46

Chow, Minta, 81

Chow, Morley, 242

Chow, S. K., 233, 243

Choy Jun-ke, 227

Christian Student Volunteer Movement, 3–4

Chu Fu-sung, 284

Chu Hai College, 288–89

Chu, Elaine, 230–31

Chu, Laura, 230–31

Chu, Lucy, 175, 230–31

Chu, Samuel, 99, 175, 196, 206, 230–31, 276, 237

Chü Chiu-pai, 222

Chuan, Mrs. James, 74

Chuan, Jimmy, 33

Chungking, 66, 70, 73, 77, 84

Chungshan University, 266, 267–68, 291

Chung-yang t'ung-hsin, 195

Church World Service, 180

Cline, Ray, 278

Clubb, Edmund, 81–82

Clubb, Marian, 82

Cohen, Jerome, 206

Colbert, Evelyn, 56

Cole, Peter, 18

College of Chinese Studies (Peking), 23, 26–27

Columbia University Press, 163, 211, 224, 233, 276, 296

Columbia University, 227; Department of Chinese and Japanese, 92, 162; Department of East Asian Languages and Cultures, 220, 230; East Asian Library, 243; fundraising for, 232–33, 242–43; graduate studies at, 21–22, 36–38; History Department, 94, 162; politics at, 243; Rare Book and Manuscript Library, 165, 168, 190, 215, 230, 296; School of International Affairs, 92–93, 166, 230; student unrest at, 226; teaching career at, 89, 91–94, 162, 220–21. *See also* East Asian Institute

Committee for a Democratic Far Eastern Policy, 101

Committee of Concerned Asian Scholars, 227

Community Church (White Plains), 95, 280–81

Community Church (Shanghai), 7, 12, 13, 73, 260, 263

Community Projects Office, New Delhi, 133–34

conferences, 170, 217–18, 206–7, 211, 214, 223–26, 229, 233, 246–47, 267–69, 278–79, 288, 301–3

Contract for a Slave (Wang Pao), 52

Coons, Arthur, 34, 36, 46, 88

Coons, Edna, 34, 36, 46, 88

Cordier, Andrew, 205, 220

Council on Foreign Relations, 159, 163–64, 200
Creel, Herrlee, 30, 46, 57, 78
Creel, Lorraine, 46
Creel, Wilhelmina, 30
Cressey, Beth, 200, 205
Cressey, George, 56
Cressey, Paul, 20, 200, 205, 223
crossbows, 39
Cui Heng (Ts'ui-heng), 292
Cultural Revolution, 268, 270
Curtis, Gerald, 230
Cushing, Jennifer, 245

Dallin, David J., 100, 294
Damodar Valley Project (India), 130–31
Danton, Prof. 20
Daughters of the American Revolution, 6, 19
Davies, John P., Jr., 6, 22, 33, 35–36, 57
Day, Horace, 22
Dayton, Ohio, 12
Dean, Britten, 238
DeBary, Wm. Theodore, 99, 232, 234, 237, 243
DeFrancis, John, 33, 56, 86, 87, 213, 216, 237, 244
DeFrancis, Kay, 213, 216
Democracy Movement, 299
Deuel, Thorne, 40
Dictionary of Ming Biography, 39
Ditchley Conference, 214, 217–18
Documents on Communism, Nationalism, and Soviet Advisers in China, 1918–1927 (Wilbur and How), 99–101, 162–63, 211, 222, 224–25, 231, 274, 276–78
Dodge, Mr., 241
Domes, Jurgen, 246
Donovan, William, 55, 58
Douglas, Paul, 49
Doust, Howard, 19, 22
Doust, Rosalie, 22
Drumright, Arthur, 152, 174
Dubbs, Homer, 45
DuBois, Cora, 56, 227
Durdin, Tilman, 6

Durning, Jean, 170
Durning, Marvin, 170
Duyvendak, J. J. L., 38, 49

East Asian Institute, 89, 162, 166–68, 204, 226, 228, 236, 282; creation of, 92–93; fundraising for, 230–31, 242, 243; grant from, 102; Korean studies at, 202; publications, 97, 221; research projects at, 99; Wilbur as director of, 166, 200, 205
East-West Center (Honolulu), 211, 213, 303
Eber, Irene, 234
Eckstein, Alexander, 226
Edinburgh, 304
Edip Bey, 34
Edson, Joyce, 278
Edson, Kathryn. See Wilbur, Kathryn
Edson, Mary, 18
Edson, Peter, 18, 58, 102
Edwards, Dwight, 205
Elegant, Robert, 99
Eminent Chinese of the Ch'ing Period (Hummel), 40, 92
Encyclopedia Britannica, 224
Ensminger, Douglas, 141–42
Environment, Character, Chance and Choice (Wilbur), 302
Eto Shinkichi, 168–69, 172, 209, 303
Everton, John Scott, 117, 165, 169, 201

Fahs, Charles, 55
Fairbank, John, 30, 70, 169, 206, 226, 235, 245, 301
Fairbank, Wilma, 30
Fang Chao-ying, 39, 92, 244
Far Eastern Survey, 101
Farmers' Association (Kinmen), 181, 185
Fei Hsiao-tung, 56, 68
Feldman, Harvey, 239
Feng Yü-hsiang, 29–30
Ficken, Fred, 19–20, 46
Field Museum (Chicago), 37, 40, 41–45, 47, 51, 52–54, 71, 78, 80, 90, 229
Field Museum News, 42, 45
Field, Stanley, 40, 41, 43
Finkelstein, Larry, 167

Fisher, John, 280
Fitch, Kempton, 114
Fitzgerald, Stephen, 244–45
Fogel, Joshua, 239
Forbes, Frances, 17
Ford Foundation, 101, 102, 125, 126, 133, 141, 164, 167, 169, 200–201, 203, 205, 220–21, 227, 277; Foreign Area Fellowship Program, 163, 165
Foreign Service, 77, 84–85
Frame, Rosamund, 66
Franke, Herbert, 234
Fried, Morton, 166, 174, 202, 206, 221
Friedman, Edward, 206–7, 284
Friends of China, 43
Froebe, Jack, 239
Fuelling, John, 19, 24
Fuelling, Ora, 19, 24
Fulbright grant, 101, 102, 170, 173

Gailey, Robert, 29–30, 34
Galenson, Walter, 206
Gamble, Mrs. Sidney, 241
Gamewell, Mary, 22
Gammertsfelder, George, 210
Gammertsfelder, Kay, 210, 274
Gasster, Michael, 240
Geiger, Virginia, 120
Gentzler, J. Mason, 175, 223
Gerlach, Telitha, 262–63
Gleysteen, Howard, 279
Goldman, Merle, 97, 240
Goldman, Rene, 234
Goodman, Lillian, 280
Goodpasture, Ann, 78, 80
Goodrich, Anne, 38, 170, 129, 241
Goodrich, Carrington, 21, 32, 38, 46, 50–52, 74, 82, 89, 101, 129, 164, 170; at Columbia, 91, 92
Goodrich: fellowship, 233, 241
Gould House Conference, 169 (conferences)
Government and Politics of China, The (Chien), 70
Graves, Mortimer, 51, 82, 89
Gray, Jack, 7, 12, 21
Gray, Marion, 12

Gray, Maude, 12, 13
Great Brilliance Commune, 252–55
Great Wall, 249
Greene, Agnes, 66
Greene, George, 66, 75, 76, 80
Gregg, Clifford C., 41, 42, 46, 51
Grimball, Elizabeth, 22, 37
Gruzenberg, Fanny, 12–13
Gruzenberg, Fred, 12
Gruzenberg, Michael. See Borodin, Michael
Gruzenberg, Norman, 12

Hanson, Mr. (teacher), 13
Harrell, Ed, 204, 214, 278
Harrell, Paula (Johnson), , 104–5, 214, 238, 278
Harrington, Michael, 280
Harrison, James, 237
Harvard University, 93
Harvard University Press, 296–97, 299
Harvey, Hazel, 21–22, 34, 38
Harvey, Paul, 7, 21–22, 34, 38
Haverford College Library, 302
Hegel, Robert, 238
Heinzig, Deiter, 246
Her Own Words (Wilbur), 304–5
Hersey, Arthur, 56
History of the Crossbow . . . (Wilbur), 39
Ho, Alice, 286
Ho, Franklin, 69, 93, 103, 164, 166, 168, 227, 231
Ho, Pauline, 240
Ho Ping-ti, 167
Ho Shilai, 242
Hoffsomer, Abby, 14, 15
Hogan, Mr., 77
Holden, James, 205, 216, 301
Holdridge, Richard, 152
Holland, William, 66, 70, 107
Holubnychy, Lydia, 221–23, 230, 231, 277, 297
Hong Kong, 115–17, 152–54, 173, 209, 269, 288–89
Honolulu, 213–14
Hoover Institute, 99
Hoover, Helen, 30

Hoover, Lyman, 30, 66, 71–72
Hosoya Chihiro, 172
Housain, Azim, 133
How, Julie: as coauthor, 162, 263, 222, 231, 297; death of, 274–75; hosts Wilburs in Hong Kong, 173; introductions from, 114, 116; and Oral History Project, 164, 168, 209, 227; research project of, 99–101; as student, 94
Howard, Richard, 135, 237
Howes, John, 105, 107–8
Hsi Wu-i, 100
Hsia Pei-jan, 241
Hsian, 251–56
Hsiao I-shan, 175
Hsieh, Winston, 174
Hsu Cho-yun, 208
Hsu, S. C., 111, 112
Hsueh, Chun-tu, 99, 238
Hu, C. T., 192, 242
Hu, Charles, 45
Hu, Cynthia, 232
Hu, Dorothy, 192
Hu, Mr., 51
Hu Shih, 164–65, 169, 174, 191–92, 227
Hua Wen Hsueh-hsiao, 26–27
Huang Chia-mu, 196
Huang Chi-lu, 174, 246
Huang Fu, 227
Huang Hwa Kang memorial, 291
Huang, Nancy, 233
Hughes, John, 279
Human Dimensions and Its Problems, The (Myers), 242
Hummel, Arthur, 21, 40, 92, 206
Hurwitz, Leon, 107–8
Hutson, Helen, 16, 17
Hwalien, 272

India, 63, 125–44, 203–4
Industrial Slavery in China . . . (Wilbur), 52
Institute of International Relations, 282, 285
Institute of Modern History, Academia Sinica, 168, 170, 174, 175, 188, 196, 204, 221, 231, 285–86, 200, 203

Institute of Pacific Relations, 101, 102, 107, 165
Inter-University Center for Chinese Language Study in Taiwan, 201, 225, 220
International Conference on Sun Yat-sen and the 1911 Revolution, 301–3
International Congress of Orientalists, 201, 202–4, 211, 233–35
International House (Tokyo), 173
International Sinological Conference, 267–68
Irwin, John, 232
Irwin, Kay, 232, 243, 306
Irwin, Richard, 99, 212
Israel, 297–98
Issues & Studies, 283
Ito, T., 44
Iwanaga, Prof. and Mrs., 172, 287

Jacoby, Phyllis, 210
Jaffe, Philip, 58–59
James, Colonel, 75
Jansz, Neville, 146
Japan and the Korean Farmer (Wilbur), 36
Japan between East and West, 159, 163
Japan, 104–10, 159–61, 287, 288
Jarmell, Shirley. See Wilbur, Shirley
Jeffrey, Prof., 50
Jelliffe, Archibald, 16, 18, 19
Jiang, S. T., 268
Johnston, Anna Marie, 38
Joint Commission on Rural Reconstruction, 70, 111–12, 181–86, 203
Joint Committee on Contemporary China, 169–70, 200
Joint Committee on Sino-American Scholarly Communications, 220
Jordan, Joe, 219
Jorgensen, Jorgy, 205
Judd, Dr., 39

K'ung Hsiang-hsi (H. H. Kung), 227
Kaizuka Shigeki, 168
Kaohsiung, 113
Karlgren, Bernard, 209
Karnath, Mr., 138

Karuizawa, Japan, 14
Kasem Tipayachan, Judge, 150
Kates, George, 34
Kawagiri-san, 106–7
Keene, Donald, 99, 107–8, 221, 237
Keightley, David, 240, 303
Kennedy, George, 39, 51
Kennedy, Thomas, 237–38
Keswick, John, 116, 153
Khatau, Abhay, 138
Khedgihar, R. A., 138
Kiang, Daniel, 239
Kindermann, Gottfired-Karl, 246, 247
King, Marjory, 229
Kinmen Island, 178–80, 185
Kirk, Grayson, 164, 169, 205, 220
Klein, Don, 217
Klugman, Werner, 210
KMT archives, 190, 203, 206–7, 225, 242
Kobe, Japan, 3, 4
Kodat, Roger, 281
Koo, T. Z., 58
Koo, V. K. Wellington, 168, 173, 227,
    228, 232, 233
Koo fellowship, 241–42
Korea, 25–26, 203
Kracke, Ed, Jr., 56, 60, 81
Kreisberg, Paul, 137, 138, 238
Krout, John, 89
Kuczera, Dr., 234
Kung Peng (Mrs. Chiao Mu), 85
Kung, H. H., 164
Kunming, 64–65, 67–69
Kuo Ting-yee, 168, 170, 174, 189, 192,
    203–4, 206, 207, 231–32
Kweilin, 265–66
Kwok, Daniel, 244, 303
Kwok, Mrs. Walter, 173
Kwong, Alice, 227
Kyoto, 104–5, 287

Laird, Loomie, 17–20
land reform (Taiwan), 183–84
Lang, Olga, 99, 237
Langer, Paul, 107–8, 172
Langer, William L., 55, 58, 59, 66, 67, 73,
    78

Lao Kan, 175
Lattimore, Owen, 30, 31, 237
Lauden, Jane Price, 238
Laufer, Berthold, 37, 41, 43, 45
Lawton, Dever, 148
Lawton, Olive, 113
Leadership in Communist China (Lewis),
    214–15, 218
Lee Kuo-chi, 303
Lee, K. C., 147
Lee, Robert, 238
Lei Chen, 198
Leng, Tony, 286
Leonard, Jim, 196
Lerrigo, Mr. and Mrs. George, 29
Leung Wing-sun, 289
Levin, Burton, 239
Levine, Steven, 296
Levy, Robbin, 210
Levy, Tom, 210
Lewis, Dr., 44
Lewis, John, 214, 217, 218
Li, Bernadette Yu-ning, 175, 222–23, 232,
    237, 277, 298
Li Chi, 170, 175, 206, 207, 208
Li En-han, 196
Li Fang-kuei, 222
Li Huang, 227
Li Kuo-chi, 204, 285
Li Li-san, 195
Li Shou-pao, 263
Li Shu-hua, 227
Li Ta-chao, 225
Li Tsung-jen, 168, 227
Li Tung-fan (Orient Lee), 211
Li Tung-wen, 274
Li Yu-ning. See Li, Bernadette Yu-ning
Li Yun-han, 190, 192, 203, 204, 241, 284,
    289
Liao Chi-tsing, 111
Library of Congress, 39
Lieberman, Henry, 116, 152
Lieberthal, Kenneth, 240
Lien-ho pao, 286
Lien-ta, 68
Lin Cho-liang, 283
Lin Jiayou, 266–67

Lin Lieh, 111
Lindbeck, John, 221, 226
Linden, Allen, 174, 237
Ling, Maya Ying, 283
Liu, S. Y., 146
Liu Tanian, 290
Lo Chia-lun, 170, 175, 190
Lo Hui-min, 244, 245
Lockhard, Mary, 46
Lockhard, Norton, 46
Lockwood, Virginia, 244
Lockwood, William, 7, 169, 244
Loh, Eugene, 230, 232, 246
Loh, K. Z., 72
Loh, Pichon P. Y., 72, 289, 294
Lohman, Karen, 34
London, 218, 279
Lowe, Pardee, 173, 174
Loyang, 256–59
Lu Shih-ch'iang, 196, 285
Lu Ting-i, 85
Lubman, Stanley, 209
Lucknow, India, 132–33
Lung Yun, 67, 68
Lutkins, Larry, 152
Lyons, Grace, 7
Lyons, Jean, 7
Lyons, Willard, 7

Ma Shu-li, 284
Ma, Anthony, 213
Ma, Herbert, 208
Ma, Yo-yo, 283
MacDonald, Sir Malcolm, 147
MacFarquhar, Roderick, 217, 221
MacKenzie, Nollaig, 215,
    218–19
MacNair, Harley F., 46
Madras, India, 139–40
Magruder, General John, 100
Mahabalipuram, India, 139
Makkaris, Prof., 234
Mancall, Mark, 226
Mandel, Edna, 42, 43, 53, 223
Manville, Mr., 242
Mao Tse-tung, 143
Mao, General, 73

Mao's 'Paradise' as Seen from India
    (Wilbur), 125, 144
Markle Foundation, 241
Marriott Corporation, 295, 300
Martin, Paul, 40, 41, 42, 44, 46, 47,
    51
Masud, S. A., 126–27
Matsui, Sakuto, 234
Matsumoto, Mr., 72, 197
Matteson, Horace E., 4
Matteson, Mary Irene. See Wilbur, Mary
Maubin, Burma, 122–23
May 30 Incident, 12, 214
McCarthy, Joseph, 101–2, 120, 213
McCarthyism, 164, 170
McCloy, Emma, 7, 17
McCune, Evelyn, 88
McCune, George, 56, 88
Meeker, Len, 74, 77, 78, 79
Mehta, Ashoka, 138
Menzies, Rev. James M., 45
Merwin, Wallace, 201
Meskill, Jack, 105, 107–8
Mexico City, 233–35
Michael Borodin and the Chinese
    Revolution (Holubnychy), 230
Michael, Franz, 226, 278
Miles, Mary, 73
Mills, Harriet, 237
Ming Biographical Dictionary Project, 170
Ministry of Justice (Taiwan), 195, 225
Mirsky, Jonathan, 176
Miss Jewel's School, 6
missionaries, 14
Missionaries of Revolution (Wilbur), 295,
    299
Mizoguchi, Sachiko, 104
Modern America's Cultural Debts to
    China (Wilbur), 282–83
Modern China Seminar, Toyo Bunko, 200
Mokan Shan, Chekiang, 8–9
Moore, Beth, 233
Moraes, Frank, 138
Morley, Bobby, 214
Morley, James, 99, 165, 166, 192, 214,
    221, 230, 276
Morton, Bill, 172

Mott, John R., 3
Mount Pleasant Public Library, 271
Mukerjee, Sri S. K., 129
Munro, Ann, 175, 196
Munro, Donald, 175, 196, 209
Myers, Ramon, 242

Nagai Michio, 169
Nanchang, 265
Nanking Incident, 14
Nara, 105
National Anthropological Museum
    (Mexico), 234
National Committee on United
    States-China Relations, 248
National Endowment for the Humanities,
    228
Nationalist Party, 163
*Nationalist Revolution in China,
    1923–1928, The* (Wilbur), 245
Nehru, Jawaharlal, 128–29, 140, 143, 204
New Delhi, 133–37, 201, 202
New York School of the Theater, 37
New York Times, 165
Nikko Maru, 103, 104, 105
Niyogi, J. P., 127
Northern Expedition, 14, 193–94

O'Brien, Anita, 239, 240, 276, 296–97,
    299
O'Connell, Bret, 279
O-yang, President, 176, 285
Oberlin College, 13, 15, 16–21
Oberlin Review, 17
Office of Research and Intelligence, 89
Office of Strategic Services, 54, 55–60,
    65–66, 71, 73, 76, 77, 88–89
Office of War Information, 66
Oksenberg, Michel, 217, 225, 240, 284
Oliver, Jay, 14
Oliver, Lucile, 14
Olympian, The, 19, 20
Openhym, Alice, 223
Orchard, John, 93, 192
overseas Chinese, 149–50, 153

Pan Tzu-nien, 85–86

Pacific Affairs, 101
Pai Ch'ung-hsi, 178, 196, 207
Pai, Lily, 33
Palace Museum (Taipei), 285, 286
Panchayet, 134–35
Pao Tsen-peng, 175
Park Fairfax, 57
Party Purification Movement, 194
Passin, Herbert, 221
Passport Office, 102
Payne, Betty, 36, 38
Payne, William, 36, 37–38
Peake, Cyrus, 21, 32, 35, 38, 46, 50, 51
Peake, Marie, 32, 38
Peffer, Nathaniel, 93
Pei, I. M., 283
Peking Union Church, 30
Peking, 23, 26–32, 74–75, 249
Pelliot, Paul, 31
Perspectives on a Changing China (Fogel
    and Rowe), 239–40
Pettus, Dr., 23, 30, 34, 37, 35
Pettus, Sarah, 27, 29, 31
Phillips, Hope, 173
Phot Sunthara, Judge, 150
Picker, Harvey, 230
Pike, Douglas, 203
Pleasantville, 95, 98
Pleasantville discussion group, 210
Pochacher, Gopal S., 137
politeness, Chinese, 186–88
Political Science Quarterly, 165
Pontius, Mr., 17
Porter, Lucius, 30
Pott, Jim, 58
Price, Don, 135
Protestant Theological Seminary, 74
Pruitt, Ida, 228–29, 262

Quadrangle, The, 281–82, 299–301
Quinby, George, 229

Radakrishnan, Dr., 135
Rangoon, 117–21
Rangoon University, 120–21
Rankin, Ambassador, 111
Rao, V.K.R.V., 140

Reed, Dudley, 20
Reid, Hoch, 210, 276
Reischauer, Edwin O., 14, 15, 17–20, 22, 57, 301
Remer, Carl F., 55
Resnick, Aaron, 98
reverse course, Japanese, 107
Reynolds, Carol, 238
Reynolds, Douglas, 228, 238
Riskin, Carl, 209
Robertson, Walter, 77
Robinson, Peggy, 12
Robison, Geroid T., 92
Rockefeller Foundation, 93
Rockefeller, John D., III, 97, 169, 173
Rogers, Janet, 243
Rogers, Millard, 53, 170, 243
Roots, Logan, 32
Rosen, Leo, 101–2
Ross, Lillian, 51
Rowe, David, 278
Rowe, William, 239
Royal Asiatic Society museum, 7
Russia, 81–82
Russian advisers, 163
Russian Institute, 92
Rymers, Howard, 38

sabbaticals, 101–62, 173–99, 211–14
Sakanishi, Shio, 107
Samsom, Peter, 215, 219, 274, 280
Sansom, Sir George, 92, 93, 97, 101, 205
Santineketan, India, 129–30
Sarah Lawrence College, 97
Sargent, Betty, 29
Sargent, Clyde, 29, 50, 67
SAS Nooze, 13
Scalapino, Robert, 271
Schaffner, Franklin, 77, 78
Schiffrin, Harold, 224, 247, 291, 297, 303
Schiffrin, Ruth, 291, 297
Schulz, Caroline. See Service, Caroline
Seidman, Crystal, 227, 228
Seligman, Mrs. Georges. See Mandel, Edna
Seoul, Korea, 25–26
Service, Caroline, 33, 165, 46, 58, 211–12, 233, 303

Service, John (Jack), 211–12, 233, 246, 303; in China as youth, 7; at Oberlin, 15, 16–19; dismissed from State Department, 101–2, 165; in Foreign Service, 33, 58–59; views on China, 53
Service, Philip Martin, 68
Service, Richard, 83
Sewell, Janet Fitch, 29
Shanghai, 3, 4–6, 12–13, 70–76, 79–80, 83–84, 214, 260–64; French Concession, 13, 260
Shanghai American School (SAS), 6, 12, 13–14, 201, 260
Shaw Yu-ming, 282, 285, 286, 287
Shen, Y. T., 106, 173
Shevelyov, Konstantine, 291
Shih chi, 34, 45
Shih Pen-su, 181
Shih-men dam, 184
Shinoda, Minora, 24
Shipley, Mrs., 102
Shirato, Ichiro, 92, 97, 202
Shively, Alice, 14
Shyu, Larry, 238
Sickman, Laurence, 34, 92
Siderani, Mr., 134–35
Sinclair, Gregg, 89
Singapore, 146–47
Singh, Karlash, 132–33
Sino-American Committee, 207
Sino-American Conference on Mainland China, 206–7, 224–26, 229, 233
Sixth World Congress of Buddhists, 118
Skinner, William, 149–50, 167
slavery, 37, 45–46, 53
Slavery in China (Wilbur), 53
Smith, Mrs. George T., 43
Smithsonian Institution, 38, 39
Sneed, Stanley, 14, 20
Snow, Edgar, 33
Snow, Peggy, 33
Social Science Research Council, 38, 169–70, 206, 220, 224
Soloman, Hillel, 238
Soong Dynasty, The (Seagrave), 284, 285
Sovern, Michael, 242

Soviet Advisers with the Kuominchun, 1925–1926 (How), 277
Soviet Embassy, Peking, 99
Soviet Union, 108
Special Economic Zone, 293
Spencer, Joe, 65, 66
Sprouse, Phil, 68, 69
St. Faith's School (Peking), 27
St. John's University, 278–79
State Department, 67, 73, 77, 85, 89, 102
Stelle, Charles, 29, 31, 34, 35, 46, 52, 55, 58, 64, 89
Stelle, Margaret, 34, 46, 64
Sterling, Dr., 38
Stewart, Maxwell, 13
Stewart, Peggy, 13
Stokes, Anne, 210
Stokes, Leonard, 210
students, 94, 97–99, 221–23, 236–41
Su Yun-feng, 204, 241
Sun Yat-sen, 13, 202, 205, 246–47, 265, 285, 290
Sun Yat-sen and the Origins of the Chinese Revolution (Schiffrin), 224
Sun Yat-sen: Frustrated Patriot (Wilbur), 224, 233, 244, 268, 291–92
Sun Yat-sen memorial, 291, 292
Sun Yat-sen Research Institute, 266, 268
Suttell, Elizabeth, 296–97, 299
Swayzee, Cleon, 102, 163
Sweet, Helen, 30
Sweet, Lennig, 30
Swisher, Earl, 39

T'ao Hsi-sheng, 206
Tai Li, 71, 73
Taichung, 272
Taipei, 174
Taiwan Health Center, 184–85
Taiwan: and Burma, 121–22; discrimination against scholars from, 234; and People's Republic, 127; and Japan, compared, 288; 1954 trip to, 110–15; 1961 sabbatical in, 173–99; 1969 trip to, 223; 1973 trip to, 229; 1976 trip to, 233; 1977 trip to, 242–43; 1981 trip to, 272–74;

Taiwan: and Burma *(continued)* 1985 trip to, 284–87; and United States, 229
Taj Mahal, 63
Takeuchi, Stirling, 107
Tan Chin Tuan, 147
Tanabe Sadayoshi, 173
Tanabe Tatsuo, 173
Tannenbaum, Frank, 166
Taylor, George, 170, 206, 208
Temple of Heaven, 28
Thailand, 147–52
Thomas, Norman, 280
Thompson, John Seabury, 117
Thorberg, Marina, 234
Tibet, 132
Tikhvinsky, S. L., 204, 290, 292, 294
Ting, Rev. K. H., 73–74
Togasaki, Mrs. Kami, 287
Tokyo, 105–7, 156–57, 172–73
Tong, T. K., 99, 164, 168, 195, 227, 232
Trezise, Phil, 56, 65
Tsai, Caroline, 242
Tsiang, T. F., 227
Tsien, Patricia, 242
Tsao, Kai-fu, 238
Tso Shun-sheng, 227
Tsou, Tang, 43
Tsunoda, Mr., 37, 38, 92
Tu Lien-che, 39, 92
Tu Weiming, 301
Tucker, William, 46, 48
Tung, Mr. and Mrs. C. Y., 173
Tung Pi-wu, 58
Tung Tso-pin, 175
Turner, Eugene, Jr., 117, 118
Turner, Gordon, 206

Unitarian church, 95, 159
United Nations, 58
United States Army, 76, 77
United States Educational Foundation, 173–74
United States National Museum, 38, 39
Universities Service Center, 209
University of Calcutta, 127–28

University of California, Berkeley, 93, 96, 271–72
University of Chicago, 40
University of Lucknow, 132–33
University of Washington, 93
University Seminars on China and Japan, 166–67, 201, 307
USIS Library (Rangoon), 120

Valhalla, New York, 90
Van Slyke, Lyman, 175, 201
Venerable Amritananda of Nepal, 131
Verges, Bruni, 210
Vessey, Cliff, 95, 205, 280

Wager, Charles, 18
Walker, Richard, 112–13, 206
Wallace, Schuyler, 89, 93, 102, 164, 166, 307
Walman, Gil, 95
Walman, Milton, 95
Wan Waithayakon, Prince, 148–49
Wang, An, 283
Wang, C. C., 21., 38, 51, 91, 92
Wang Chien-min, 207
Wang Ching-wei, 72
Wang Chi-wu, 243
Wang, Ernest, 96
Wang, General, 178–80
Wang Gung-wu, 244
Wang Ling, 244
Wang, Minta, 96
Wang, Mr., 252–55
Wang Ping, Mrs., 196, 286
Wang Shih-chieh, 206, 207, 208
Wang, Teresa, 189
Wang Yu-chun, 196
Wang Yu-tien, 175–76, 178, 188, 194–95, 197
warlordism, 201
Warner, Langdon, 21, 45
Washington, D.C., 38–49, 54
Webb, Herschel, 107–8
Wedemeyer, General, 75, 242
Wei Yung, 284
Weidenbaum, Rhoda, 94, 237
Weinberg, Francis, 107–8

Weisblatt, Abe, 163
Weller, George, 246
Wells, Ken, 56, 58, 59, 147–48
Westermann, W. L., 37, 38, 50, 89, 94
Whipple, Ms., 110
White Horse Temple (Loyang), 258–59
White, Bill, 175
Whiting, Allen, 116, 152
Wilbur, Ann (later Ann MacKenzie), 52, 78, 95, 106, 168, 202, 215–16, 218–19, 275–76
Wilbur, Elizabeth (later Elizabeth Cressey), 3, 12, 14, 20
Wilbur, Betsey (laater Betsey Kodat), 281
Wilbur, C. Martin: as AAS president, 227; attends conferences, 170, 217–18, 206–7, 211, 214, 223–26, 229, 233, 246–47, 267–69, 278–79, 288, 301–3; book reviews by, 201; childhood of, 3–10; homes of; 90, 98, 301; children's weddings, 215–16, 229; citation from ROC, 278; as director of EAI, 200, 205; dissertation of, 37, 38, 45–46, 49–51, 89; engagement of, 19, 21–23; as emeritus professor, 236; festschrift for, 239–40; at Field Museum, 41–45, 47, 51–54; fundraising by, 229–30, 232–33, 241–43; golden wedding anniversary of, 275–76; graduate studies by, 21–22, 36–38; introduction to Kay, 17–18; leaves Pleasantville, 299; Master's degree of, 32; at Oberlin, 13, 15, 16–21; publications of, 34, 36, 39, 42, 45, 47, 52–53, 125, 144, 159, 162–63, 165, 195, 201–2, 211, 214, 224–25, 233, 235, 242, 245, 272, 276–78, 281, 282–83, 295, 302; retirement of, 232–33; runs cross-country, 17; sabbaticals of, 101–62, 172–99; self-synopsis of, 306–8; sixtieth wedding anniversary, 303- 4; studies Chinese, 176; teaching career of, 89, 91–94, 162, 205–6, 220–21
Wilbur, Kathryn Edson (Kay), 61, 169, 196; assistant at New York School of the Theater, 37; childbirth, 48- 49; dances in Peking, 35; described, 305–6; director of Unitarian Sunday

Wilbur, Kathryn Edson *(continued)*
School, 159; engagement of, 19, 21-23; family life, 94–96; introduction to Martin, 12, 17–18; in Japan, 107; learns Chinese, 176, 188; Martins feelings for, 215; as a mother, 64; retires, 228; as a teacher, 33, 167; travels of, 268–69, 272, 279, 283–87, 297- 98, 304; wedding of, 24–25; writings by, 39–40, 216–18

Wilbur, Halsey, 4, 12, 14, 52, 60, 223, 276

Wilbur, Hollis A., 3–4, 5, 13–14, 26, 35, 36, 59–60, 72, 81, 88, 107, 205, 305

Wilbur, John, 48–49, 51, 57, 78, 95, 104, 106, 168, 202, 205, 229, 282

Wilbur, Leonidas F., 3

Wilbur, Mary M., 3–4, 5, 6, 13, 26, 36, 81, 304–5

Wilbur, Rosemary, 5

Wilbur, Shirley Jarmell, 229, 282

Wiley, Nan, 39

Williams, Mrs. Marvin, 27

Willis, Sid, 7, 14, 15, 57

Wilson, Sir David, 221, 224, 269

Wilson, John, 46, 57

Wilson, Mary, 46

Wilson, Natasha, 221, 269

Winfield, Gerry, 29

Winfield, Louise, 29

Wittfogel, Karl, 50, 237

Wong, John, 303

Wong, Minta, 227

Wood, Bryce, 170

World War I, 5–6

World War II, 49, 51–60

Wou, Odoric, 239

Wright, Gertrude, 210, 281

Wright, Paul, 210, 281

Wu, Ben, 96

Wu Chang-chuan, 232

Wu Chen-ts'ai, 225

Wu Chih-hui, 194

Wu, Dorothy (Li Ya-shu), 96

Wu I-fang, 58

Wu, Jennie, 173–74, 196, 206, 242

Wu Wen-tsao, Dr. and Mrs., 77

Wu, Vivian, 243

Xi Wuyi, 294

Yacht Club, 16

Yager, Joe, 56

Yamada Tatsuo, 303

Yanaga, Shitoshi, 165

Yang Shen, 178

Yang Tianshi, 294

Yen Chia-kang, 207, 243, 286

Yen, Florette, 46–47

Yen, W. W. (Yen Hui-ching), 47

Yip, Ka-che, 239

Young, C. Walter, 30

Young, Francis, 170

Young, John, 164, 165

Young, Len, 209

Young, Whitney, 280

Young Men's Christian Association (YMCA), 3, 4, 11, 25, 107, 263

Yu, P. K., 232, 244

Yuan, Connie, 86

Yunnan, 148

Zimmerman, Walter, 148

Studies of the East Asian Institute

Selected Titles

Tokugawa Confucian Education: The Kangien Academy of Hirose Tansō (1782–1856), by Marleen Kassel. Albany, NY: State University of New York Press, 1996.

The Dilemma of the Modern in Japanese Fiction, by Dennis C. Washburn. New Haven: Yale University Press, 1995.

Landownership under Colonial Rule: Korea's Japan Experience, 1900–1935, by Edwin H. Gragert. Honolulu: University of Hawaii Press, 1994.

The Final Confrontation: Japan's Negotiations with the United States, 1941, edited by James W. Morley, New York: Columbia University Press, 1994.

Japan's Foreign Policy after the Cold War: Coping with Change, Gerald L. Curtis, ed. Armonk, NY: M.E. Sharpe, 1993.

China's Transition from Socialism: Statist Legacies and Market Reforms, 1980–1990, by Dorothy Solinger. Armonk, NY: M.E. Sharpe, 1993.

The Poetry and Poetics of Nishiwaki Junzaburō: Modernism in Translation, by Hosea Hirata. Princeton: Princeton University Press, 1993.

Pollution, Politics, and Foreign Investment in Taiwan: The Lukang Rebellion, by James Reardon-Anderson. Armonk, NY: M.E. Sharpe, 1993.

Driven by Growth: Political Change in the Asia-Pacific Region, edited by James W. Morley. Armonk, NY: M.E. Sharpe, 1993.

Schoolhouse Politicians: Locality and State during the Chinese Republic, by Helen Chauncey. Honolulu: University of Hawaii Press, 1992.

Constitutional Reform and the Future of the Republic of China, edited by Harvey J. Feldman. Armonk, NY: M.E. Sharpe, 1991.

Sowing the Seeds of Change: Chinese Students, Japanese Teachers, 1895-1905, by Paula S. Harrell. Stanford: Stanford University Press, 1992.

The Study of Change: Chemistry in China, 1840–1949, by James Reardon-Anderson. New York: Cambridge University Press, 1991.

Anarchism and Chinese Political Culture, by Peter Zarrow. New York: Columbia University Press, 1991.

China's Crisis: Dilemmas of Reform and Prospects for Democracy, by Andrew J. Nathan. New York: Columbia University Press, 1990.

Missionaries of the Revolution: Soviet Advisers and Chinese Nationalism, by C. Martin Wilbur and Julie Lien-ying How. Cambridge, MA: Harvard University Press, 1989.

Single Sparks: China's Rural Revolutions, edited by Kathleen Hartford and Steven M. Goldstein, Armonk, NY: M.E. Sharpe, 1989.